The State of Freedom

What is the state? *The State of Freedom* offers an important new take on this classic question by exploring what exactly the state did and how it worked. Patrick Joyce asks us to re-examine the ordinary *things* of the British state from dusty government files and post offices to well-thumbed primers in ancient Greek and Latin and the classrooms and dormitories of the public schools and Oxbridge colleges. This is also a history of the "who" and the "where" of the state, of the people who ran the state, the government offices they sat in and the college halls they dined in. Patrick Joyce argues that only by considering these things, people and places can we really understand the nature of the modern state. This is both a pioneering new approach to political history in which social and material factors are centre stage and a highly original history of modern Britain.

PATRICK JOYCE is Professorial Fellow in History, University of Edinburgh and Emeritus Professor of History, University of Manchester. He is a leading British historian and has written and edited numerous books of social and political history, including *Visions of the People* (Cambridge, 1991), *The Oxford Reader on Class* (1995), *The Rule of Freedom* (2003) and *Material Powers* (2010).

The State of Freedom: A Social History of the British State since 1800

Patrick Joyce

CAMBRIDGE
UNIVERSITY PRESS

CAMBRIDGE UNIVERSITY PRESS
Cambridge, New York, Melbourne, Madrid, Cape Town,
Singapore, São Paulo, Delhi, Mexico City

Cambridge University Press
The Edinburgh Building, Cambridge CB2 8RU, UK

Published in the United States of America by
Cambridge University Press, New York

www.cambridge.org
Information on this title: www.cambridge.org/9781107694552

First published 2013

Printed and bound in the United Kingdom by the MPG Books Group

A catalogue record for this publication is available from the British Library

Library of Congress Cataloguing in Publication data
Joyce, Patrick, author.
The state of freedom : a social history of the British state since 1800 / Patrick Joyce.
    pages cm
ISBN 978-1-107-69455-2 (pbk.)
1. Great Britain – Politics and government.   2. Great Britain – Social
conditions.   3. State, The – Social aspects – Great Britain – History.
4. Liberty – Social aspects – Great Britain – History.
5. Liberalism – Social aspects – Great Britain – History.
6. Political culture – Great Britain – History.   7. Politics and culture – Great
Britain – History.   8. Public administration – Social aspects – Great Britain –
History.   9. Postal service – Great Britain – History.   I. Title.
DA44.J69   2013
941.08–dc23
                                                                    2012030949

ISBN 978-1-107-00710-9 Hardback
ISBN 978-1-107-69455-2 Paperback

For Simon Gunn and James Vernon, friends, teachers, students

Contents

Figures

Acknowledgements

My greatest debt in writing the book is to two former students of mine who worked for me as archival research assistants, Gavin Rand on the India Office and Francis Dodsworth on the Post Office. Both supplied me models of research assistance that combined intellectual rigour and inventiveness to an unusual degree. My enduring debt to all my students is enormous, and in particular I thank Chris Otter and Tom Crook for their help, also Simon Gunn and James Vernon to whom the book is dedicated. It took enormously long to complete, so there are many to thank: David Vincent, as always, was a rock of support in his reading of various stages of the manuscript, and my editor at Cambridge University Press, Michael Watson, made many useful suggestions. My intellectual debt to the following will also be apparent in the book: Chandra Mukerji, Timothy Mitchell, Nikolas Rose, Paul Ginsborg, Tony Bennett and Mary Poovey. Luckily, this debt was often a personal one too, particularly regarding Nik and Tony who I worked with collaboratively. Chandra was another rock in the often lonely seas of book writing. Among those I talked to about the book were Penny Harvey, Mike Savage, Frank Trentmann, Richard Sennett, Paul Gilroy and the late David Frisby, the latter three when I was a Visiting Professor at the London School of Economics. I also wish to thank my former colleagues in the History, Anthropology and Sociology Departments at Manchester University.

Taking so long, versions of the book were given as academic presentations in many places, and I thank all those in the institutions involved who offered me hospitality and gave me intellectual help. In particular I thank the Institute for Advanced Studies, New York University (now sadly defunct), where I was a visiting fellow and able to work with Timothy Mitchell; the Sociology Department, LSE; the Department of History, University of California, Berkeley, who awarded me a Visiting Professorship; and the Department of History and Civilisation, the European University Institute, Florence (especially Steve Smith), where I was a Fernand Braudel Fellow. During the final stages of writing the book, Lars Edgren and Ulrika Holgerson welcomed me at the University of

Lund. My thanks to Li Hongtu of Fudan University in Shanghai, who welcomed me in that city. I gave academic papers arising from the book in many more institutions, and I hope that this collective "thank you" is acceptable to them, along with the knowledge that I could not have written it without the aid of the many people involved. Thanks also to Tom Devine and Alvin Jackson for giving the book an Edinburgh welcome.

I acknowledge with gratitude research grants for the writing of the book from the Economic and Social Research Council, GB, the Leverhulme Trust, who awarded me an Emeritus Fellowship, and the Centre for Research on Socio-Cultural Change (CRESC), Manchester/Open Universities. CRESC also provided me with a congenial intellectual environment during the period of the book's development, and in particular I thank all the participants, most of all those in our section of the Centre's many activities, "Liberalisms, Culture, Government".

Many people gave me often detailed advice about particular chapters, which was invaluable, and my warm thanks to them: E. Joanna Guldi, Susan Whyman, David Henkin, and David Vincent, again, regarding the Post Office; Miles Ogburn, Ilana Feldman, Peter Becker, David Laven, Mariana Valverde, and Antonia Moon of the British Library regarding writing and bureaucracy. In terms of classics I thank Chris Stray. I benefited from discussing the public schools (and families and states) with Paul Ginsborg, and I talked about the Oxbridge college with Lyndal Roper, then of Balliol College, and with Brian Harrison, also about Oxford and Cambridge. For help on Irish history my thanks to Enda Delaney, Niall O' Ciosain and Patrick Carroll. Mick Moran talked over the final chapter with me as did Simon Gunn and Pedro Ramos Pinto.

I thank Mrs Penny Hatfield, the Eton College Archivist, Gary Savage, then History Master at Eton, and Mike Morrough, the Archivist of Shrewsbury School, who was very hospitable on my visits to the school. I doubt however if these kind people will very much like my picture of the public school. As always, one has a huge debt to professional archivists and librarians, and I thank the unnamed many who helped along the way, in particular the knowledgeable and helpful staff of the British Postal Museum and Archives and the British Library Asia, Pacific and Africa Collections, especially those in the India Office Records division. My thanks to all who supplied the illustrations.

Finally, thanks to my wife Rosaleen for her constant love and support, and for helping me with the preparation of the manuscript. My children, Sean and Roisin, and daughter-in-law Laura, like most rightly amazed non-academic friends who could not understand that one book could take so long, helped put things into perspective, as did my grandchild, Isaac John Patrick Joyce. Amongst the amazed non-academic friends, thanks to Alan White and Tom Cleary in London, and Mike and Joan Abrams, John Roberts and Brian Goodall of the village of Broadbottom. Thanks also to "bro-in-law" Brian Malone for always asking how "the book" was going.

PATRICK JOYCE,
Broadbottom and Manchester

1   Introduction: the powers of the state

I   The social history of the state

What is the state? In the half-millennium or so since "the state" began to assume its modern form this question has been asked time and time again. On the surface it is a simple question, but below the surface a difficult and a troubling one. Hence the multitude of conflicting answers. This book approaches this question again but it does so in a relatively unusual way. It is concerned with what the state did, how it worked, its mundane operations – often the last things students of the state are concerned with. It is interested in the ordinary *things* of the state. This is a history of the state in terms of what on the face of it seem some pretty unlikely candidates: postage stamps, letterboxes and post offices; dusty government office files and office rooms; well-thumbed primers in ancient Greek and Latin; and the classrooms and sleeping quarters of the schools and colleges in which the ancient languages were taught. It is also a history of the *who* and the *where* of the state, of the kind of people who ran it and of the government offices they sat in and the college halls they dined in. It is by considering these things, people and places that I think we can understand the state better, and this is my justification for adding to the many answers given to the question, "What is the state?"

Imaginative literature is where one will find one version of this history of the mundane state, and it was writers who lived through the rise and fall of great states that knew best that the history of the state was to be revealed in the chronicle of its ordinary things. The great Viennese master Stefan Zweig chose as the emblem of the very ordinariness of life in the Austro-Hungarian Empire the figure of "the post office girl".[1] The ordinariness of the everyday state apparent in the post office was how he chose to render most effectively the ordinariness of life in the empire. What follows in my

---

[1] Stefan Zweig, *The Post Office Girl* (Pushkin Press, 2008), published posthumously in German 1982, the author having committed suicide in Brazil in 1942 during exile from Nazi Germany and Austria.

book includes an account of the very ordinary life of the British postal system, and it is with a quotation from Zweig that I open Chapter 4, where I deal with files and "filing technologies" in another kind of government office, the India Office. The quotation runs as follows: "From the millions and millions of such forms piled up in government offices it may one day be possible to glean the only reliable account of the history of the misfortunes of the Habsburg monarchy." To Zweig it was indeed the ordinary form rather than the content of the document that mattered, for it was the form that made government possible in the first place. He meant the literal "form", the standardised document in all its plainness and physical reality, in the shape of what he called "The so-called 'chancery double', a folded sheet of paper of prescribed dimensions and format." This for Zweig was "the most indispensable requisite of the Austrian civil and military administration",[2] and it was in *administration* that the true life of the state was to be found.

This life was also to be found in the real lives of the people of the state, above all in this state the military-bureaucratic class that was its backbone. In his "Author's Note" to the book, in which Zweig mentions the "chancery double", he remarks: "A short explanation may perhaps be necessary for the English reader. The Austro-Hungarian Army constituted a uniform, homogenous body in an empire composed of a very large number of nations and races. Unlike his English, French, and even German *confrere*, the Austrian officer was not allowed to wear mufti when off-duty, and military regulations prescribed that in his private life he should always act *Standesgemaess*, that is, in accordance with the special etiquette and code of honour of the Austrian military caste ... The final criterion of an officer's behaviour was invariably not the moral code of society in general, but the special moral code of his caste".[3] Zweig, in his novel *Beware of Pity*, is a great chronicler of that caste, but there is none greater than Joseph Roth. His unsurpassed account of the trajectory of a state's history, in this case of the greatness and the tragedy of the Austro-Hungarian Empire, is *The Radetzky March*.[4] This, like the work of Zweig, is centred upon the military-bureaucratic caste, for it was this group of governors that was at the heart of that state's tragedy.

My book concerns the governors of the British state, who were very different from those of Austria-Hungary, but no less a caste, that of the

---

[2] *The Post Office Girl*, pp. 257–8.

[3] "Author Note", *Beware of Pity*, after the title page. Stefan Zweig, *Beware of Pity* (Pushkin Press, 2008).

[4] Published originally in German as the *Radetzkymarsch*, 1932. Joseph Roth, *The Radetzky March* (Granta, 2003).

public school- and Oxbridge-educated high bureaucracy. From this caste the high political class was also drawn. While the book is a history of the British state, I am aware of the value of looking beyond Britain. This I do, chiefly to Europe and the USA, and so I am concerned only with "Western" forms of the state. However, I make no claim to write anything like an adequate comparative history. Nor do I draw much on literary representations of the British state. This is because unlike the history of the Austro-Hungarian Empire and its great German-language writers, the relative stability of the British state seems to have produced a far less penetrating literature on the subject. My avenue into the mundane is the social history one, social history being about the mundane anyway; however, unlike older versions of social history this is not history with the power and politics left out, but with these centre stage. It is also a social history that questions what the "social" is in the first place.

More particularly this is a book about the mundane state in its liberal forms, of which the British example, because it was so early and so complete, was of enormous historical significance. I take the long view in considering this history, not hesitating at times to go beyond my already rather long period of detailed examination. This extends from around 1800 and the beginnings of the rise of the liberal state to a situation by about the 1920s when, particularly after 1880, this form had been consolidated. By the term "liberal state" I mean the sort of state that systematically deploys political freedom as a means of governance. This is not the only means it employs but it is the principal one. And I employ 'freedom' in two senses, the mainstream one of political liberty as used in academic and everyday discourse alike, but also to denote governmental techniques that allowed, and still allow, designated governed entities (persons, places, things) to operate ostensibly on their own, without outside interference. Technique is the operative word here, for I am concerned with the micro-technologies and the micro-operations of power. How do these set up zones of ostensible self-regulation, in individuals, families, "publics", markets and so on?

This takes investigation into, on the surface, such unlikely areas as city streets and country roads, public libraries and parks, and particularly in this book, the economic and social use of postal systems. This second sense of freedom, what I call "organised freedom", cuts across established use because it cuts across the established political categories – Liberal, Conservative, Labour and so on. All political parties deployed organised freedom, and in most essential respects (and there were of course important political differences which I recognise) they also deployed freedom as political liberty in the usual sense of freedom. Because this was so, because there was so much overlap between these two senses of freedom in Britain, I use the above-mentioned term "liberal state". I make no apology for doing so, even though this usage may seem undiscriminating to some, as the state in this period went through many different manifestations and was marked by real differences within the governing classes. For example differences in political thought, especially between what have been called "organic" and "inorganic individualism",[5] a collectivist against an anti-statist tradition, positions that also correspond with positive and negative freedom.

However, without labouring the obvious, these are all versions of individualism, taking as their common ground "the individual". This "individual" only makes sense in terms of the freedom which is its raison d'être to practice. The Conservative Party has of course been in power for long periods in British history, yet for most of this time it was no less liberal than its various oppositions, no less concerned to practice freedom. Of course, there was a Conservative philosophy of a more organic sort less favourable to individualism, but what is striking is what little practical effect this has had historically, economic protectionism aside, something which itself has been only of intermittent importance. And if we look more closely at actual politics, we find that the supposedly organic Conservatives were very often the most market-driven "inorganic" individualists, and the supposedly individualist liberals the exponents of a more collectivist state. Thatcherite Conservatism, for example, was ironically more to do with a rather paranoiac, late-nineteenth-century Tory aristocratic anti-statist individualism than with civically conscious, liberal "Victorian values" (to the extent that Thatcher herself was not, as a child of the Cold War, a product of an equally paranoiac age).[6] Therefore, on balance, the underlying similarities mean more than the differences. The liberal state as I describe it here has been the basic, the most fundamentally significant, form of the British state from 1800 to the present. The term begs to be used therefore. It is this basic continuity of the state that I aim to establish and explore, characterisations of the state as laissez-faire, welfare, social and market aside. When I employ the term liberal state I therefore mean freedom in both senses of the word. However, the intricacies of this argument are explained in much more detail in the second section of this chapter, but it is as well to make the matter plain from the start.

---

[5] Michael Bentley, "'Boundaries' in Theoretical Language about the British State" in S. J. G. Green and R. C. Whiting (eds.), *The Boundaries of the State in Modern Britain* (Cambridge University Press, 1996); and Jose Harris, "Political Thought about the State in Britain" in the same volume.

[6] Bentley, "Boundaries", ibid., pp. 43–5.

The book was completed at a time when the liberal state in Britain appeared to be in trouble. The dissolution of social bonds and disaffection with polities that have everywhere resulted from economic and political neoliberalism have taken a particularly acute form in a Britain where neoliberalism was endemic. There the financial crises of 2008 and 2011 framed a series of events that have discredited the political classes, the police and the media, and provoked the urban rioting of the summer of 2011. There has been considerable discussion about the causes and origins of these phenomena, but relatively little informed, long-term historical consideration. There is thus limited appreciation that if one is to understand the present neoliberal state better then it would be no bad idea to know more about the history of the liberal one. For, as I indicate in the book, the former is but an extension of the latter, and "neo" only on the surface.

Comparatively speaking British history has been marked by extraordinary continuity and considerable social stability, and this combination, at times paradoxically, has been highly conducive to the successful management of change. This is evident above all in the capacity of old-established elites and institutions to harbour the growth of capitalism and what has recently been called "liberal modernity".[7] This capacity is very much a theme of the book, though I approach it in a new way. Living in an old country has resulted in other consequences too, one of which is a certain public complacency – not a lack of interest – about British history, for unlike other historical experiences the British one has been less disrupted and less tragic so that history in Britain does not touch the quick of the present to the degree it does elsewhere. This has also meant that there is a fair degree not only of consensus but of approval about what are held to be the core values of British history and British society, namely those that can be said to be "liberal" – chiefly freedom, tolerance and individual self-determination.

My interrogation of "freedom" and of the liberal state it gave rise to will show that both were rather less benign than is sometimes thought. Contrary to many views, both have, historically, always been more about governing people than releasing them from government. The seemingly distant and remote liberal state has over time constantly intervened in people's daily lives, public and private, so that citizens might lead lives that actively practice freedom – freedom, that is, as those in political authority view it. As will be seen, the state actively helps make the spheres of the public and the private in the first place, rather than just being the neutral

---

[7] Simon Gunn and James Vernon (eds.), *The Peculiarities of Liberal Modernity in Imperial Britain* (University of California Press, 2011).

guardian of these things. It also helps *make* freedom, so that freedom as well as being a value is always a political *practice* and a way of governing, involving making us self-governing and "responsible" citizens. The state of Britain has therefore historically been in essence a state of freedom.

Freedom is not only a mode of government, however, for its sources also come from a civil society the state only partly controls and comprehends. Once politically deployed, civil society has its own momentum, serving to criticise the very political institutions that gave it shape. No one should doubt the strength of British civil society historically, and in the present, but while this strength has served to shape the liberal state it has failed to fashion a truly democratic and egalitarian version of the state. Historically, it is the absence of any meaningful challenge to the fundamentals of the liberal state that is striking, something reflected in the lack of any true participatory democracy in the British system, and something compounded by the warped nature of its representative system of democracy, with for example its unelected second chamber and head of state, single-member voting system and (mostly) two-party system. So, in the end, it is the liberal state that fashions civil society, setting its parameters if not controlling it. Therefore civil society does not stand "outside" the state, again contrary to many views on the subject. Often beyond our immediate public and private lives, but nonetheless deeply involved with them, the state not only fashions persons but also structures markets, whole economies indeed. It also configures "society" itself, so that economies and societies are "free" because the liberal state has made them so. Political freedom and power are different sides of the same coin. Thus it is often the case that when we think we are most free it is then we are most governed.

Other nations and states see the relationship between state and society differently of course, and these differences are always the outcome of the social history of the state. In Scandinavia for example, while the state decidedly configures society, because of the different cultural and historical circumstances involved state and society are in a different relationship than is the case in the UK, and elsewhere. Culturally, state and society are far closer than in the UK, something echoed in language itself, for in Swedish for example there is much less difference in meaning between the words "state" and "society" than there is in English.

Because freedom and authority are complements of one another and not opposites, liberalism, whether political liberalism or organised freedom, is in no sense a stranger to order and especially so in the British context, where social hierarchy has been marked. Some have to govern, others have to be governed. Therefore, the kinds of human relations that go with the exercise of authority and the act of governing have historically been central to the liberal state. This is why none of the supposed bastions of hierarchy and "tradition" · the monarchy, the Established Church, the Armed Forces, the Conservative Party, the House of Lords, the public schools (the list in Britain is very long) – is inimical to the liberal state for the simple fact that they are an integral part of it. They are the other side of the same liberal coin, that of authority, order and control. Again, I do not wish to downplay the reality of political differences, and the force of tensions within different versions of the state, but the reality of underlying similarities demands to be recognised. When this recognition is given it is apparent, especially in the British case, that the supposed dualities of "tradition" and "modernity", reaction and progress, and political irrationality and rationality in fact make little sense.

One essential point about the modern state is that it has tended to rely more and more on everyday life as the ground upon which it operates and creates legitimation and "consent", in this case the consent of citizens who will practice freedom. The antique state aim of security increasingly but not exclusively comes to be located in the soul of the citizen. All of life comes within the remit of the state, and is thereby ordered and reproduced under the sway of what can be regarded as "normal" or "proper" thought and behaviour. Another way of looking at this is with the idea of the "habitus", and this is used at several times throughout the book. "Habitus" is a complex concept and its ramifications need not detain us, but the term is useful in denoting the force of habituation, which is akin to "normalisation" and another term I use much more frequently than both, "naturalisation", which involves making what is anything but natural seem perfectly so. The term "habitus" itself essentially means the set of socially acquired dispositions, skills and schemes of behaviour which are acquired by people in the activities of everyday life.[8] It highlights the non-discursive, taken-for-granted aspects of social life that often operate outside conscious awareness.

This "normalisation" enables the ordering and the sanctioning of what would otherwise be regarded as abnormal. This eventually extends to the abnormal in extreme forms, so that the state has been enabled through the routines it has established in its mundane operation to order and

---

[8] Pierre Bourdieu is the great exponent of the concept. See for example his *Distinction: A Social Critique of the Judgement of Taste* (Routledge and Kegan Paul, 1984). The connections of the term with other ones in Bourdieu's conceptual arsenal link it to a social reading of power at variance with the one employed in this book as a whole. However, when reworked the concept can be complementary. See Tony Bennett, Mike Savage et al., *Culture, Class, Distinction* (Routledge, 2009). On *habitus* see also Richard Shusterman (ed.), *Bourdieu: A Critical Reader* (Blackwell, 1999).

incorporate not only injustice and inequality as "normal" but famine, social conflict, and eventually if with some difficulty, mass war and the mass extermination of human beings. In this the liberal state was no exception, for in the period of the book the British state incorporated mass starvation in Ireland and India into its administrative routines. Whether in the form of the secular or the Christian political economy that informed the detail of state policy, famine was either an act of nature or one of God[9]. Thus distanced from the state in liberal fashion, millions were fated to die.

The great architect of the liberal state Charles Trevelyan, whom we shall meet again in the book, was the chief "administrator" of famine. In fact, Trevelyan was perhaps the principal British inventor of "administration" itself, and administration was the science of making the business of the state routine, of making it "normal". Like other, non-liberal as well as liberal, states the state in Britain therefore practised what has been called the violence of order, even as, in the main, it left the order of violence behind. There is little of state violence and social disorder in mainland Britain in this book, though across the Irish Sea the matter was different, as will be demonstrated, especially at the end of Chapter 7. In large part this is simply because in mainland Britain, comparatively speaking, after 1815 and before 1914 there was not a great deal of either state violence or social disorder. However, the essential point is that the violence of the state was only made effective by the routinisation of the mundane seen in the everyday life of the state, so it is to this life that I pay attention. The banality of government explains the banality of state violence, the violence of the state itself becoming mundane.

Of course Britain did not leave the violence of war behind, but after 1815 for almost a century war occurred "elsewhere", in the empire. This served to reinforce the fact that unlike other European states the British one was not dominated by military values or a military class. Prussia, for example, has been called an army with a land, not a land with an army. In 1870 the regular British Army numbered only 135,000, the Prussian army over a million, and this imbalance continued up to the Great War. Also, there was nothing like the tradition of European state service, as in the aristocratic-military Prussian tradition, where public administration emerged out of aristocratic landed estate administration very early on,

---

[9] Christine Kinealy, *This Great Calamity: The Irish Famine 1845–52* (Gill and Macmillan, 1994), and for another view, Robin F. Haines, *Charles Trevelyan and the Great Irish Famine* (Four Courts Press, 2004); Mike Davis, *Late Victorian Holocausts: El Niño Famines and the Making of the Third World* (Verso, 2002); James Vernon, *Hunger: A Modern History* (Harvard University Press, 2007).

in the shape of the so-called cameralist tradition.[10] Unlike in continental Europe the British Army was not a closed organisation, with its own laws and its own technological systems. Nor did it have a system of values specific to army life, like the bureaucratic and professional European armies, so marked as these were by versions of honour such as the Austrian *Standesgemaess*.

Rather, it drew its values from the same sources as the prosperous middle classes more widely, above all those enshrined in the public schools and Oxbridge, as did the higher bureaucracy and the political class.[11] Alone among the well-to-do middle classes in Europe the British sent their children away from home to be educated (something seen in liberal America too). They did this en masse, and this too little remarked and remarkable fact has been fundamental to the particular historical path British society and the British state have followed. Where European children were sent away it was in much smaller numbers and to military school. The educational elite in Britain, those who did the educating that is, was as a consequence more broadly influential across the ranks of the well-to-do than was usually the case in Europe (in Germany the pedagogues were more directly part of the state-service tradition than in Britain). However, all this does not mean that the ruthless creation of systems of order by means of organised coercion was foreign to the British state. This was at home in Britain, but even more so in the empire and in Ireland. What it does mean however is that unlike in other states, where the bureaucracy did not have a culture in common with the rest of the elites, in Britain governance in society and in the state drew strength from this cultural unity, a strength that made it all the better at the practice of ordering others.

However, if these remarks may serve to check complacency and consensus, they can easily give the wrong impression of the state. First of all, the state itself is in question in this book: what this means is that when we begin to interrogate its actual operations it turns out to be something rather less organised, sentient and strong than it is often taken to be. Indeed the very use of the definite article in "the state" begins to look questionable as we go further into the book. If the state is a distinct entity, a "thing", its 'thingness' turns out to be decidedly more indeterminate and problematic than is usually imagined. By the same token, if the powers of "the state" should not be exaggerated, nor should its negative,

---

[10] E. N. Gladden, *A History of Public Administration* (Cass, 1972), vol. II, Ch. 5 on Europe, and Ch. 6 comparing the UK and USA. See also G. K. Fry, *Statesman in Disguise: the Changing Role of the Administrative Class of the British Home Civil Service 1853–1966* (Macmillan, 1969).

[11] Gwynn Harries-Jenkins, *The Army in Victorian Society* (Routledge, 1977).

disciplinary and repressive aspects be the only part of the picture. Like power itself the state is productive. It confers on us identities, rights and values, enabling us as citizens to criticise and refashion it.[12] It should be plain that this book is not a critique of the state as somehow inherently repressive, though it is a book that is very critical of the liberal form of the state and of how it has got off the historical hook. The state, on the contrary, is the greatest and most necessary of all human inventions; and one likely to be with us for some time yet, for neoliberal attempts to "roll it back" paradoxically make state regulation and oversight of the "privatised state" ever more necessary, not less so. Despite these attempts it is also the case that the size of the state has stubbornly refused to decrease in line with neoliberal expectations.

In considering both the powers of the state and of freedom, as alike their limitations, we usually think about them in terms of people and what they think, do and say. However, the powers and limits of the state also owe a very great deal to the importance of the inanimate, material world. Until recently this has hardly been recognised. In fact, most historians, not just political historians, write as if things themselves do not exist and do not have agency in the world, indeed when harnessed to human designs do not have their own "material powers".[13] "Things" here are human things, human bodies as well as non-human, especially inanimate, things. However, it is the importance of non-human things and their place in history that needs to be most urgently recognised, for it is through these that power and social relations, and hence the state, are made *real*.

Above all perhaps this interest in the material world is important for political history and the history of the state in pointing to the significance of *technique* and technology. Technology is perhaps the overarching theme that gives shape to the book. My concern is with technology in the usual sense of the term, but also in a much broader sense, that of the techniques of governing oneself and governing others. Political techniques in fact, although it quickly becomes apparent that the seemingly neutral world of science and technology is eminently political, just as the political world partakes of science and technology. Therefore, I am concerned with the making of the state, with its production and its assembling. For this reason I from time to time employ the term "technostate". If the term "modern state" has any significance it needs to encompass this deepening reach of the technical and techniques of power into all of life. However contrary to many present-centred understandings of technique and the technical the

---

[12] See below, pp. 30, 84, 171–4.
[13] Tony Bennett and Patrick Joyce (eds.), *Material Powers: History, Cultural Studies and the Material Turn* (Routledge, 2010).

account that follows is as much concerned with low and slow tech as with fast and high tech, and with old technology as with new. Not so much railways and the telegraph as letters and filing systems; also at a fundamental level with writing, the techniques and technology of which were decidedly low and slow as well as of ancient pedigree.

In terms of the method of the book therefore, this recognition of the importance of the material world is one of two chief lessons that I take from recent scholarship. The other is the rethinking of power that has gone on in recent decades. Rethinking the state and freedom in terms of power and materiality is apparent throughout the book, in its every detail, but finds more concentrated conceptual expression in the next section. This new thinking is evident in recent social theory, especially in the field of "science studies", and has also been manifest in various sorts of history, including the history of science and technology. The high degree of theoretical and historiographical interest in my book is perhaps unusual in histories of the state, and in political history more widely, at least in Britain. Not all my readers will, I imagine, share this theoretical bent, and so acting on this assumption I leave most of the discussion of theory and method to the next section of this chapter, and readers if they so choose can skip this part and go on with the discussion of the coming of the "technostate" that concludes the chapter. The remaining chapters are very decidedly historical, not theoretical. However, my interest in social theory is inherently historical anyway, concerned with how we might write more searching histories, in this case the history of the state, and particularly how we might write a *social* history of the state in which not only the state but also society and "the social" are put in question.

There are two parts to the book: the first concerns what I call "the state of things", the second "the state of men". The latter means what it says, men not women: until the twentieth century women had almost no role in the state, at least not at the higher end of it with which I am concerned. However, this does not mean that gender was not important in the formation of the state. Quite the contrary in fact, as the second part of the book shows. The creation of a ruling-class mentality depended upon the masculinisation of power and the subordination of women, something evident in the new nineteenth-century division between domestic (feminine) and public, political life (masculine). This was apparent in the formation of governance in the public schools and the Oxbridge colleges, where in the masculine world of the reconstituted home that was the public school and the college the relationship between the original home and the new one was played out to peculiar effect. This (very) peculiar effect will be seen to account for the extraordinary power of these institutions over British life and over the governing classes. Thus because power

in Britain was masculinised the entire edifice of the state was too, so that the state can itself be seen as a kind of home for those who governed, a home in which men ruled, even though a woman, Queen Victoria, reigned for much of the nineteenth century. The institution of monarchy and the growing cult of the royal family only reflected, and reinforced, this state of affairs. Because the rule of men took as its pinnacle of power and status the male head of the house, and because the father most completely represented this head, the figure of the father and the fortunes of the state were deeply intertwined. The state was at once a kind of home and a kind of father, even if the sovereign might be a mother.

All this seems far away from the rationality we usually associate with technology, liberalism and freedom, also from the rationality which is usually assigned to "modern" bureaucracy. Of course it is, but it is not far away from what the state is actually all about, which is irrationality as well as rationality. As well as calculations and calculability it is about emotions and passions, above all about the governing passion, the one inculcated by the actual business of governing but also, above all in Britain, by the educational apparatus. The "magical" qualities of the state have been recognised by anthropologists but less so by historians, certainly historians of the British state.[14] However, even anthropologists tend to ascribe these characteristics to the colonial state and not to the metropolitan one,[15] in which after all they originated.

In terms of a social history of the state, from the point of view adopted here one can say that liberalism and freedom never exist, in the sense that they are never pure but always embedded in the social world, and there-fore in traditions of authority in which passions, emotions and unreason are deeply ingrained. However, emotions and reason are not opposites. In looking at the state we shall come across fantasies of government rooted in the belief that calculation, standardisation and abstraction provide rational answers to rationally conceived "problems". But the point to understand here is not simply that they do not provide rational answers, but that these "irrational" answers are very often just what government needs in order to function in the first place. For example, a fictitious and fantastical unitary "India" had both to be imagined and materially con-structed by the British in order to be governed at all. Above all, at home and in the colonies, without the in truth profoundly irrational model of the liberal virtues and passions that made up Britain's *homo libertas* the gov-ernance of the British state would have been impossible. All government

---

[14] Michael Taussig, *The Magic of the State* (Routledge, 1997).
[15] Laura Ann Stoler, *Along the Archival Grain: Epistemic Anxieties and Colonial Common Sense* (Princeton University Press, 2010). See for example, relating to government offices, pp. 62–3, 134–5, 142, 173–4, 311, also 54.

in this sense is irrational, therefore. This includes the state of things as well as the state of men, for invariably things perform to their own script and not just the "rational" one of their would-be masters. Things go their own way, as we shall see, including again in the case of India the bloated "paper empire" and "monster" of correspondence of the Raj. All of which is not to say that technopolitical power has not been profoundly effective and has not been a defining element of the modern state.

While readers need not consider the theory explored in the next section there is nonetheless an advantage to be had by a brief consideration here of the reasons why the state has come to be thought about in new ways. These reasons include its rapidly changing nature in recent times. Received views of the state have been seen as simply unable to do justice to how the rapidly developing "globalisation" of the 1980s and 90s not only set limits to the power of the nation state, but (especially in the Anglophone world) revealed the dispersal of governmental practices into society itself, on the model of the decentralised market and in the shape of what has become known as "neoliberalism". In Europe as well as in Britain the European Union also posed the most urgent questions about the sovereignty of the nation state. Alongside these changes, and related to them in complex fashion, went the profound changes in communications evident in the "information revolution", and the consequent acceleration of what came to be called "connectivity". Everyone was connected but everyone seemed more dispersed than ever so that new conundrums for the exercise and the analysis of political power presented themselves. While this book is not a history of "connectivity" and the origins of the information "revolution" it does serve the purpose of helping to get this revolution into perspective, so making it appear less revolutionary than is sometimes thought. The central importance of communications and hence "connectivity" to state power long before the recent past becomes apparent. This early history of communications is of a centrality that has not been generally recognised in political history and histories of the state. The state is but one facet of this history of connectivity which awaits its historian, but it was and is probably the most important one, for the state seems to have been the most profoundly important cause and consequence of "social connectivity".

In the face of contemporary social and economic change from the 1980s the key assumptions of political thought seemed inadequate in order to understand the state. As an important contribution of the early 1990s put it:

The language of political philosophy: state and civil society, freedom and constraint, sovereignty and democracy, public and private plays a key role in the organisation of modern political power. However, it cannot provide intellectual tools for analysing the problematics of government in the present. Unless we adopt different ways of thinking about the exercise of political power, we will find contemporary forms of rule hard to understand. It will thus be difficult to make proper judgment of the alternatives on offer.[16]

This is quite so. These "different ways of thinking about political power" inform my book. However, their value is as great in thinking about the past as well as the present, the liberal as well as the neoliberal state, and the old form of the technostate as well as the new.

Dominant understandings of the state have been shaped by the legacy of the nation state, in which the state is the expression of the nation. In these the state is understood as a unitary actor in which sovereignty and the monopoly of violence is concentrated. This concentration takes territorial form. The state is a centre from which power radiates, and state power is expressed in state institutions which have particular functions. The state is also seen as a bounded entity, separate from society. In short, the state is pretty much conceived of as a thing. However, the state is not a thing; at least it is not a single active subject, and if we are to continue to think of it as a thing there needs to be a very different understanding of how it could have been christened "the state". Being made up of the active agencies of many and often conflicting people and things we have come to think of it as a single thing. Why we have come to do so is a principal concern of this book. As the historical sociologist Oleg Kharkhordin has recently put it:

What made possible such a radical reversal from the early modern concept of the vulnerable state, on which everybody feeds, to the active and overpowering entity that we now imagine? What made it possible to think of an almost mystical entity – "the state" – that nobody sees but that everybody presumes to exist and to act, frequently in an overwhelming manner, on our lives?[17]

This understanding of the state, in scholarly discourse called its "naturalisation", is as much evident in everyday life as in academic analysis. This quasi-mystical state has been confused over historical time with its real nature, so that the *explanandum* has become the *explanans*. That which needs to be explained, the "mystification" of the state, has become the explanation. Conceiving of the state as a distinct entity is apparent in different ways in most of the chief conceptual approaches to the state. The great variety of contemporary (post-1950s) views evident in "state theory"

---

[16] Peter Miller and Nikolas Rose, "Political Power Beyond the State: Problematics of Government", *British Journal of Sociology*, 42:2 (June 1992); and see the discussion of this in Patrick Joyce, "Power, the State and the Political", *British Journal of Sociology*, Centenary Number Special Issue, 2010. See also Mitchell's work on the "state effect" for an account of some aspects of the relationship between political and intellectual change: Timothy Mitchell, *The Rule of Experts: Egypt, Techno-Politics and Modernity* (University of California Press, 2002).

[17] Oleg Kharkhordin, "What is the State? The Russian Concept of *Gosudarstvo* in the European Context", *History and Theory*, 40 (May 2001), 209.

can be briefly indicated: there is the distinction between the established and the newer views of the last quarter-century or so. The former were dominated by social and political science, and its theoretical parameters were established by classical social and political thought, particularly that of Karl Marx and Max Weber. These parameters broadly fall into three categories, reflecting various understandings of the relationship between the state and society. They can be described as the pluralist, the elite and the class interpretations of the state.

In the first, the state is regarded as something like a mosaic of different agencies, jurisdictions and organisations, each of which is an institutional response to a series of demands made upon power and resources. Political and economic competition ensures that these demands are filtered so that mediation and compromise at the level of the state result in the more or less adequate reflection of what, in this view, is taken to be an underlying balance of consensus in society. Bureaucratic groups are seen as responsive to a representative controlling agency or to the democratic political process. Social classes are only one of many clusters of interests in society.[18] The political arena is a legitimate expression of society. Such a worldview obviously fits snugly and reassuringly into that of democratic liberal states.

Secondly, elite understandings view large-scale and complex organisation as intrinsic to developed states so that a premium is put on the knowledge and expertise needed by elites to run states. The state is a competition between different such elites, and the political arena itself is seen as relatively powerless. Social classes may be at the base of particular elites, but because elite knowledge is functionally necessary for the existence of the state power lies with the elites not with classes. Such views posit various degrees of separation from society, and included in this category are arguments that the roles of decision-making and purposive political action effectively make the state autonomous from society.[19]

On the other hand, the class view understands the deliberative processes of pluralism and the competition of elites as always working in a framework of economic appropriation and cultural domination or "hegemony" which does not allow or greatly limits challenges to the basic principles of society. These principles ensure the inevitable reproduction of the power of the dominant classes. Pluralistic diversity may be evident but is ultimately of

---

[18] For this account I draw upon the still exemplary exposition of Robert D. Aldford, "Paradigms of Relations between State and Society", reprinted in John A. Hall (ed.), *The State: Critical Concepts* (Routledge, 1994), 2 vols., vol. I, pp. 63–79. See also in the same volume J. P. Nettl, "The State as a Conceptual Variable".

[19] The most well-known example of the so-called "autonomy" of the state is Theda Skocpol, *States and Social Revolutions: A Comparative Analysis of France, Russia, and China* (Cambridge University Press, 1979).

little consequence; elites are necessary but do not challenge underlying class power.[20] Each of the three paradigms I describe tends to explain away phenomena central to the other ones, so that in practice different elements from all of them are often blended together in each.

Following these earlier developments, recent theoretical approaches to the state have become much more eclectic and interdisciplinary than previously. These days geographers, literary theorists, anthropologists, Greens, feminists and of course historians have their say. Many of these take their theoretical stiffening from what can broadly be described as poststructuralism, the present approach included. They commonly identify as deeply problematic what previous approaches have all had in common, namely subscription to the distinction between state and society. Each of the old paradigms seeks to trace the line between state and society differently, but of the existence of the boundary there is no doubt. However, what has come to the fore recently is that the very distinction between state and society is itself politically produced. It is not a distinction between two discrete entities but is, as the influential work of Timothy Mitchell suggests,

a line drawn internally within the network of institutional mechanisms through which the social and political order is maintained. The ability to have an internal distinction appear as though it were the external boundary between separate objects is the distinctive technique of the modern political order . . . This approach can account for the salience of the state phenomenon, but avoids attributing to it the coherence, unity and absolute autonomy that result from existing theoretical approaches.[21]

What Mitchell means is that the state should be addressed as an effect of the detailed operations of power, of its spatial and temporal organisation, and its techniques, functions and symbols. Seen in this way power works not from the outside (the power of state over society) but from within, internally in social life. It does this not by constraining individual actions but by producing them. As he says, power works by "entering into

---

[20] For a roughly parallel account of state theory to this categorisation see also Michael Marinetto, *Social Theory, The State and Modern Society: The State in Contemporary Social Thought* (Open University Press, 2007). See also Colin Hay, Michael Lister and David Marsh, *The State: Theories and Issues* (Palgrave, 2006); Christopher Pearson, *The Modern State* (Routledge, 1996); Joel Migdal, *State in Society: Studying How States and Societies Transform and Constitute One Another* (Cambridge University Press, 2001); George Steinmetz, *State/Culture: State Formation after the Cultural Turn* (Cornell University Press, 1999); Bob Jessop, *State Theory: Putting the Capitalist State in its Place* (Polity Press, 1990); and on Weber, Randall Collins, *Weberian Sociological Theory* (Cambridge University Press, 1986).

[21] Timothy Mitchell, "The Limits of the State: Beyond Statist Approaches and Their Critics", *American Political Science Review*, 85:1 (March 1991), 78.

particular social processes, breaking them down into separate functions, rearranging the parts, increasing their efficiency and precision, and reassembling them into more productive and powerful combinations. These methods produce the organised power of armies, schools and factories, and other distinctive institutions of modern nation states."[22] This view of power, the "disciplinary" power of Michel Foucault, will be considered in more detail later. Key to Mitchell's account is the idea that methods of organisation and control that are in reality internal to the social processes they govern create the effect of a state structure external to these processes. This in turn depends upon the creation and maintenance of a false distinction between the conceptual and material. This ontological distinction between the empirical and the conceptual thus takes on a political role in Mitchell's argument, for it is seen as central to state and political power, especially in the colonial situations Mitchell concentrates on.[23]

It is, for instance, apparent in the case of law, where the details of the legal process, which are in fact the outcome of particular social processes, are so arranged as to produce the effect that "law" exists as a sort of abstract, formal network superimposed on social practice. Or we can take the example of present-day banking: it is in practice extraordinarily difficult to trace any clear line between state and society, public and private, in the vast array of different financial, political and administrative institutions that represent contemporary financial power and regulation. Yet banks are presented as private institutions separate from the state. The appearance that state and society are separate things is therefore part of the way any particular financial and economic order is maintained, as Mitchell writes. In Britain the neoliberal state seeks to maintain the distinction while in practice its attempts to "marketise" the state result in the blurring of the boundary even more, something which can be dysfunctional for the state: the proliferation in the 1990s of what were called "Quasi-autonomous non-governmental institutions" (known as "quangos") is an example of this. Where did "the state" stop and start? Therefore it is the case that "the capacity to regulate and control is not simply a capacity stored within the state, from which it extends out into society. The apparent boundary of the state does not mark the limit of the processes of regulation. It is itself a product of these processes."[24]

The state in this view is the sum of the different ways in which power is produced as external, ways which are evident in the law, the economy and all the other sectors of social life. However, while the work of Mitchell is

[22] Ibid., 93.
[23] Timothy Mitchell, *Colonising Egypt* (University of California Press, 1992).
[24] Mitchell, "The Limits of the State", 90, 94.

important, and while my account is indebted to this recognition that the creation of state power rests upon the production of the state as a distinct social and historical actor, in practice it has the unforeseen and unfortunate effect of drawing attention away from the institutions and personnel of the state itself, as these are commonly understood. Of course states in this novel sense are not the only forces at work in drawing the boundary between state and society (lawyers, business-people and quango appointees obviously matter, and are only part of a multitude of factors, including the multitude itself, the citizens), and the question of where and how the line is drawn is entirely an empirical one. Mine is not an account of how all these many forces interact and so shape the state: this would be next to impossible in one volume covering such a long period as the one studied here. Therefore, it is not my concern to delineate in detail each instance of where and how the line between state and society is drawn.

Rather, I am interested in the role of the state itself in doing this, one role among many, but perhaps the most important of all, which when one comes to think about it is perhaps not surprising. For in the liberal state drawing the line between the state and society was a particularly urgent task, unlike in other state forms which seek to merge the two (which is also an urgent task). As a matter of imminent necessity it was a highly political issue, and as the state itself was where politics was mostly shaped, the state mattered. As I argue in the study of the Post Office, the role of the state was critical in establishing the fundamentals of the state/society divide in the first place. In this way, the state created the parameters of the liberal political game, and so those of the state of freedom. It is in this sense, in so doing – in separating itself from society – that it created itself. This does not mean that the state was autonomous of course, for it was always in the first place the outcome of the balance of powers in the social, as I shall explain in a moment. Certainly, as Mitchell puts it, "the capacity to regulate and control is not simply a capacity stored within the state, from which it extends out into society", but the state appears to have been a particularly privileged site where this capacity was stored and directed. Because the state is palpably "out there" in the social it is also "in here" in its apparatuses.

However, while we should not neglect states as commonly understood we need to bring to them something other than the understandings of earlier paradigms. How do state institutions and personnel *themselves* draw the line between the state and social, but also how does the state *itself* actually cohere into a recognisable and effective force given the inherently dispersed nature of power and of the social? Drawing state/society bounda-ries is only one part of *these* complex processes, just as it is only part of how more broadly the state governs the social. Mitchell's emphasis upon this aspect and upon the politico-conceptual distinctions that underpin it therefore tells us only part of the story. For, as we shall see, in aspects as diverse and as critically important as infrastructural power, legalised coercion, power through and over writing, education and gender, and power as expressed in its actual physical places – most of all in the elemental form of the house – there was vastly more going on in embedding the power of the state than simply drawing the line between it and society. The pen and the house loom larger in my account. At the same time, the separation of state and society seen in the naturalisation of the state, while highly conducive to liberalism, also carries other political potentials. When the state is naturalised its populations may come to feel a sense of their own involvement in, indeed their own "ownership" of, the state, so that the gap between state and society lessens, and more socialised versions of the state may emerge. While liberalism has often successfully contained, indeed itself initiated, such versions, they can and have worked against it too.

In contradistinction to established views, new approaches are particularly helpful because a number of them allow us to think in the more creative vein of processes rather than of structures, and so of the state in "network" terms, as something like an "assemblage", which is held together (sometimes very uncertainly) at particular key sites or nodes and through the actions of key actors and processes, human and non-human. There is an emphasis on the state as heterogeneous and multiplex, so that where once the state and its characteristics were seen in *a priori* terms they are now seen as outcomes or achievements, often insecure ones, and as the product of specific historical, social and material forces. If state and society can no longer be adequately grasped in the old dualistic way then the "network" approach to the state applies equally to understanding "society", or as it should more appropriately be called, "the social". Understanding the social in this fashion informs my social history of the state. The crucial intellectual move in reinterpreting the social has paralleled the analysis of the state in turning away from notions of society as a coherent totality.[25] It also involves looking beyond the familiar division of the world into elements that are permanently and essentially on one or the other side of a line dividing the natural and the social, the human and the non-human, the material and the cultural – divisions that are all predicated on the misleading divide between the immaterial and the material. The social, on the contrary, is performed – or from another angle assembled – by non-human things

---

[25] For amplification and more references see Patrick Joyce, "What is the Social in Social History?", *Past and Present*, 206 (February 2010).

as well as by humans, so that labelling one thing material and one thing immaterial is not a given in the order of things but is itself a product of the very ordering of people and things that make up "the social" in the first place. The general idea therefore is that the social does not lie outside the actors and networks in which it is located (say in "society" or "nature"), but is the outcome of these. The accent is upon the social as a highly contingent matter of process: of flows, connections – something network-like in its operation.[26] In turn this poses new questions about the state.

These I try to answer by exploring just how "the state" is held together in the first place, and if we talk of the centralised state just what do we mean by a "centre" and a "periphery"? Thinking about the state in these ways is essentially to think of it in terms of how thought, conduct and the things of the world were connected together in more or less stable and unified forms. This is why communications is such a central theme of the book, particularly in the form of the postal system, for communications gives us a particularly acute insight into the nature of the state during the particular historical period studied in this book. If at all times the state crucially depends upon securing its lines of communication, it was in the middle of the nineteenth century that there developed a remarkable extension of its communicative powers and an equally remarkable deepening of human and non-human connectedness. Rather than solely territorial, the state was also becoming rapidly extra-territorial, Britain so in the shape of the unified kingdom and the British Empire. Externally and internally, as the state blanketed mainland British life in dense, new systems of communication, the relationship of the state and communications took on a new importance. The liberal character of much of this is striking, for there seems to have been a very intimate relation between securing communication and the development of this sort of state. For both turned on the idea and the practical implementation of communication as free. When it was necessary the liberal state had no hesitation in taking direct control or ownership of all sorts of infrastructure, whether in conditions of war, of economic and political necessity or crisis, or when the very core of the state was at issue, as in the provision of communications infrastructure in the form of the Post Office. However all sorts of regime, liberal or not, saw state ownership of postal systems, and this quite remarkable world uniformity is unsurprising for these were amongst the most sensitive and strategically important infrastructure systems for the state.

---

[26] Bruno Latour, *Reassembling the Social: An Introduction to Actor-Network Theory* (Oxford University Press, 2007). On the literature on webs and networks see Marinetto, *Social Theory*, and the works of the major theorist of "network society", Manuel Castells.

The "network"- and "system"- oriented conceptual approaches to the state and to social life that I shall outline, in which connectivity is emphasised, have a decidedly historical appropriateness therefore: they help us understand the state as it actually was, and not simply as it is. What, however, do these new ways of looking at the state and at society mean for the older understandings that I have described (older only in a relative sense it needs to be said, as these models of the state/society relationship are perhaps still the dominant ones)? While the answer to this becomes apparent as the book unfolds some remarks may be briefly made here. It is not that "older" views are irrelevant, more that they have to be recast in new ways. Each of the three paradigms that have been outlined quite obviously provides important perspectives for understanding the state, although at bottom all are flawed. One obvious example is Max Weber's emphasis upon "rational legal" authority, something explored at length in the following chapters in terms of the micro-technologies of power. When this is done, rather than being the outcome of general social or developmental processes (in which state and society are held apart in the usual conceptual way) this form of authority, central to Weber's account of modern bureaucracy, will be seen to be a consequence of the historically specific creation of paperwork technologies and their micro-management, and therefore fundamentally of inscriptions and the devices of these inscriptions.[27] It is the outcome of what has been called "logistical power".[28] It is also the outcome of elaborate operations upon the bureaucratic self which are highly specific to historical context and circumstances. In fact Weber and Foucault are to some degree bedfellows here:[29] in practice both have relatively little to say about the state, but a great deal to say about rationality and authority, and both say it in unsatisfactory macro-historical ways.

Similarly, there is considerable distance between class interpretations of the state and recent approaches, at least as the former are commonly understood. If in the latter the state is seen as the outcome of the balance of powers in the social this is very far from it being simply the reproduction of class interests. Power, the state and social relations, once their detailed workings are known, appear to be too multiform and complex for this, and consequently the state in class accounts is too little seen as a dearly bought achievement. Not only, as I have suggested, do the institutions and personnel of the state have their own powers and their own historical

---

[27] Chandra Mukerji, "Jurisdiction, Inscription, and State Formation: Administrative Modernism and Knowledge Regimes", *Theory and Society* (February 2011).
[28] See below, pp. 31–2.
[29] Arpad Szakoltzai, *Max Weber and Michel Foucault: Parallel Life-Works* (Routledge, 1998).

dynamic, so too do the pedagogic institutions that were essential for the creation of state governance, and governance more widely than the state alone. The latter helped forge the ruling passion itself, and without this the whole edifice of the state would have collapsed. It is not however that class is absent from my account. Far from it, but what seems to have been the case is that rather than class producing the state it was the other way around, the state producing and reproducing class relationships. The same can be said for the contemporary forms of capitalism. In short, the business of rule has to be understood in its own right and not simply as an expression of particular economic or social groups and interests.

Similarly, when we come to the operations of material power these are seen to eventuate according to their own logics, by which I simply mean their own historical rhythms and priorities, not some overarching "social" or historical logic. The outcome of these, and of the business of rule, was as will be seen often a myopic and indeed "unintended" state, one which constantly outgrew and eluded those who ran it. However, all of this does not mean that the state is "autonomous", for the point of view taken in the book as to whether the state is autonomous or not is that the distinction is a meaningless one: it is both and neither. It is both detached from and embedded in the social, so that the term "relative autonomy" has been used in the literature, sometimes helpfully and sometimes not. Being at once detached and embedded in this way, the state, inevitably only a part of society but aspiring to be all, is forever caught in the bind of its own contradiction: as Bob Jessop puts this, "It is this complex mix of political fiction and political reality which continually reproduces both the hubris and the tragedy of the state."[30]

Instead of the idea of a "class hegemony" therefore, the importance of ideological and corporeal habituation to the state is emphasised in what follows, and its naturalisation through material as well as cultural means. These may undoubtedly amount to a sort of hegemony, as is witnessed particularly by the rule of freedom in Britain, but if so this is something that is much more fluid and diverse than in most class interpretations. Still, the term "hegemony" is appropriate, especially if we are to avoid buying into the self-interested liberal version of the pluralist state, for it indicates the reality of *domination* and not simply of representation. However, instead of a social, economic or cultural hegemony what seems to have been at work might more properly be called a power hegemony, by which I mean both the state's concentration and reordering of different technologies of power *and* of the different power blocs or interests present in the social, whether

---

[30] Jessop, *State Theory*, p. 231. Jessop's account of "relative autonomy" is a sophisticated and credible defence of class/capitalist readings of the state.

these be economic or political. This power hegemony, basically a liberal power hegemony, *reflects* economic and social interests and classes but it does not just represent or reproduce them. However, the devil is in the detail here, and we shall see plenty of the detail as the book goes forward.

As for historical writing on the state in Britain I shall also deal with this in the detail of the book rather than here. In this writing the influence of the older and more established approaches is still uppermost, and so their characteristic assumptions. One illustration can however be briefly given here so as to get my meanings clear, that of what is in fact a fine collection of essays on the twentieth-century British state.[31] The collection is totally characteristic in buying into the idea of the state as a thing, an active, coherent subject, so that the totally familiar state/society and state/individual dualisms are what once again guide thinking. Seeing the state in the way these twentieth-century historians do is to see it in the familiar zero-sum terms, as a quantity, so that most of this particular collection is concerned with the important but in the end limited terms of what quantity there is of it and whether we have had more or less of it in recent times.[32] In general as regards the state in British history it is also apparent that it has by and large not been given the central role in that history it deserves, for while there are many accounts of British history (economic, social and political), because these very divisions remain so real for historians the idea of a social history of the state is still relatively unusual. Putting the state back at the centre of British history merely registers the long-term realities of power in Britain, where the great historical continuity of the state, and the way it has become embedded in society, especially in elite society, have meant that its essential forms have been so little challenged over the long term. Because of this its seminal role in *itself* forming British society has gone largely unrecognised.[33]

While the book is a theoretically informed one, and is long and detailed, it is essentially straightforward and can be summarised relatively briefly. As well as expressing the distinction between non-humans and humans the two parts of the book, "The state of things" and "The state of men", are each taken up with an overriding theme, respectively *connecting* and *governing*. Part I considers the role of state infrastructure in the shape of communications. More particularly the interest here is in connecting

---

[31] Green and Whiting (eds.), *The Boundaries of the State*.

[32] The exception to prevailing writing on the British state is the prescient Philip Corrigan and Derek Sayer, *The Great Arch: English State Formation as Cultural Revolution* (Basil Blackwell, 1985). This work in turn owns a considerable debt to the pioneering work of the British sociologist Philip Abrams.

[33] Ross McKibbin, *Parties and People: England 1914–1951* (Oxford University Press, 2009), Ch. 6. See the discussion in my Conclusion, Ch. 8 below, pp. 321–7.

things, with the things that did the connecting, but also with the things that were connected. Chapters 2 and 3 look at connectedness in terms of the Post Office, and Chapter 4 provides another perspective in terms of government information systems in the operation of the India Office. This theme also finds expression in Part II on the connections of people – the governing classes – as these connections became apparent in new ways through the means of elite education.

The second theme is governing, in the sense of the inculcation of the governing virtues among those who would govern the state, but also those who would govern British society at large. These two parts and themes break down into the three subjects of communication, bureaucracy and education. Behind each of these subjects is a particular question raised in rethinking the state. Briefly, with communication there is the question of the creation of *networks* and *systems* in the state, then in relation to bureaucracy the question of how we might think about what the *"centres"* of the state are, particularly the centres of networks and systems, and finally with education, the question of how *human agency* has been con-figured in relation to the state. Putting the matter in another way, namely that of power and how it becomes organised in the state, communication, bureaucracy and education involve respectively the communication of power, the control of power and the reproduction of power. Running through the book is an exploration of the major figures of the state associ-ated with these recurrent themes, subjects and questions, namely the bureaucrat, the expert (in this case the expert in the education of those who would govern), and, less so here, the politician. There was in practice so much overlap in terms of educational formation and the experience of power between the high bureaucrat and politician that separate treatment of the politician is less necessary than in later times, although a full account of the politician remains to be written.

The inculcation of the governing passions and virtues among those who ran the state and British society at large is, then, the theme of Part II. This is treated in Chapter 5 in terms of the making of state knowledge – in relation to what bureaucrats *did*, their formation in actually doing what I call the "work of the state". Chapters 6 and 7 involve the wider inculca-tion of governance outside the state apparatus and beyond the figure of the bureaucrat alone, for it was in elite education generally that the most basic lessons of all about governing the self and others were taught. Chapter 6 opens with an account of the long-term evolution of ideas about governing, and then, in its second part, considers the curriculum of the public schools and Oxbridge colleges. Chapter 7 looks beyond the matter of the content and practice of what was taught to the daily regime of the school and the college, treating the human person as also a thing, a body to be actively formed in pedagogic practice. In particular, attention is given to the extraordinary significance of the spatial and symbolic forms of the house and the home in shaping the governing classes.

The state in the guise of infrastructure and communications begins, in the argument of Chapters 2 and 3, to appear as very similar to the large-scale technological systems emerging at this time, so that the state, at least in this technological guise, can be considered in terms of the aggregate effect of the infrastructure systems it came variously to own, control, regulate, delegate and so on. This is what in terms of infrastructure and of its daily experience the "technostate" can be said to be (something rather far removed from the state being a unified actor on the historical stage). It is important to recognise that my chosen example of postal communications was probably the leading edge of the state over this long period. Other sectors were not as developed. However, it was the edge that counted most at the time, a period when communications came of age.

Though precocious, the postal system was nonetheless not alone, other only slightly less highly-wrought technological infrastructures, especially in the provision of household utilities (gas, water, sewerage and, later in the nineteenth century, electric light), beating a similar path. Transport was also important – railways of course – but also to a surprising degree roads and canals. After the 1870s central state involvement in education became progressively important, as had, earlier on, involvement in public health, policing and workplace regulation. However much of this, especially with the provision of city and household infrastructure, was, in contradistinction to the Post Office and the India Office, the concern of the local, not the central state. The "local" state was, however, no less "the state" than the "central state", and my aim in this book being to interrogate terms like centre and local, this is the case here too: the much-vaunted British "local state" was the expression of the power of the central state in its liberal form. The (delegated) governance of the everyday conduct of the subject at the local state level of the towns and the cities was of central significance for what I have in an earlier work called the "rule of freedom".[34] That work can therefore usefully be read in conjunction with this one. Delegating authority to the locality was a calculated act of liberal governance, which if sometimes leading to unwelcome consequences rested more and more on central state supervision as time went on. Above all it was marked by central control over information and "intelligence".[35]

---

[34] Patrick Joyce, *The Rule of Freedom: Liberalism and the Modern City* (Verso, 2003). See also the brilliant work of Christopher Otter, *The Victorian Eye: A Political History of Light and Vision in Britain, 1800–1910* (Chicago University Press, 2008).

[35] Joyce, *The Rule of Freedom*, Ch. 1 on central state initiatives in cartography and statistics.

Nevertheless, there *were* limitations to central state infrastructural power before the critical period of 1880–1920, whether the absence of infrastructure altogether or, as for a long time in elementary education, even after 1870, its presence in forms that were still of limited effectiveness. The early twenty-first century state is in several orders of magnitude greater in its remit than the state of 1850 or 1900. However it remains the case that if the British Leviathan of 1900 was by comparison with that of 2000 still a limited one, compared to the state of 1800 it was a titan. By 1914 the die of what was to follow had been cast.

In the second part of the book the social relations in which power was embedded are seen to have involved gender and the family. Historians on the whole are not used to thinking about families and states together (less so gender), unless that is they are historians of countries where family and kin have been structuring principles of the state, as in southern Europe in general, and Italy in particular.[36] The period of which I write in this book saw the transition from patronage to merit-based state organisation, in which there was a decisive move away from the family. However, simply because the family was not the privileged site it had been, and continued to be elsewhere, does not mean it was not important, as the rise of the "royal family" from this time also suggests. The family continued in practice to be very important, as will be seen, for patronage was slow to depart and in the era of ostensible merit and representative democracy family influence in public life continued to be great (it was not harmed by the fact that cousin marriage was widespread among British elites). The Hill clan from which the founder of the Post Office, Rowland Hill, came is a case in point.

At a deeper level, however, the family dynamics of the propertied household, and the material and spatial structures of the bourgeois house and home, were transmuted in the organisation of the state and of governance. This was apparent in the government office and the public school "house", treated in Chapters 5 and 7. The dynamics of gender and family were also apparent in the meanings given "freedom" as well as "the state" in Britain, as will be apparent in Chapter 6. As anthropologists have seen, in traditional accounts the state is taken to be an altogether separate thing from

---

[36] Quentin Skinner (ed.), *Families and States in Western Europe* (Cambridge University Press, 2011). This is a series of essays ostensibly inspired by the brilliant work of Paul Ginsborg on the Italian state and Italian society, in which he advocates bringing the family, civil society and the state together in such a way that we think of their relationship as a circular one, rather than in the compartmentalised, "linear" way that is usually the case. David Runciman's introduction, "A Theoretical Overview", advocates the same opinion, although to a large extent in fairly narrow history of ideas terms. However, the collection is in general a striking illustration of how difficult it is for historians to actually think beyond compartments, most of the contributions being accounts of state policy concerning families, rather than the rethinking of family and state that is the stated aim of the book.

"cultural" things like families, whereas the contrary is the case, for the state is the product of culture.[37] This recognition brings us back to Stefan Zweig's post office girl and his "chancery double", to the things and people, the families and genders, of the state, and how the state works; to the state in terms of action and doing, for the state is created by the repetitive re-enactment of everyday practices, by culture in this sense. It is in truth "performed" by people and with things. It is these, in all their social and cultural differences, that create the state by establishing regularities, precedents, expectations – "normality" in short. These are what make up the social history of the state.

II Power, things and the coming of the technostate

i. Power and things

The intellectual directions taken in history and the social sciences that enable us to see the state in new ways may be approached under two headings, power and materiality. I turn to power first. The real nature of the state begins to reveal itself better when we think less about power as an entity, or a quantity, with some people having more and some less, and begin to think more about it as something enmeshed in our daily lives, as well as in the state. Power does not stand outside us, for we are born into it, as it were. It makes "us" us in the first place. Seeing power in this way is to conceive of it as part of the condition of our actions, making these actions possible in the first place, in short as something which, in order for us to be in the world at all, must be present. Power is thus productive and not merely repressive, as has already been suggested. Assuredly, some people have more power than others, and some less, but the point however is that these inequalities cannot be understood without a view of power that gets away from this zero-sum sense. The question can be put like this: what are the powers of power itself? By what thoughts, practices and technologies are the powers that some possess and others do not assembled in the first place? The figure who has perhaps done most to develop this understanding of power is Michel Foucault.[38]

---

[37] See Aradhana Sharma and Akhil Gupta (eds.), *The Anthropology of the State: A Reader* (Blackwell, 2006), "Introduction: Rethinking the State in an Age of Globalisation", for an excellent overview.

[38] James D. Faubion (ed.), *Michel Foucault: The Essential Work*, vol. iii, *Power* (Allen Lane/ Penguin, 2001). See also Michel Foucault in Mauro Bertani et al. (eds.), *Society must be Defended: Lectures at the Collège de France, 1975–76* (Penguin, 2003), "Lecture Two, 14 January 1976" on power and its "social" origins, esp. p. 32.

This view of power has been evident in the study of what has been called "governmentality". In this perspective, since the sixteenth century there has been a gradual accretion of everyday powers around the state itself. This, following Foucault, has come to be termed the state's "governmentalisation".[39] This term describes the slow process whereby political thought and practice as represented in the state strove to manage the conduct of persons but also the actions of things in new ways, ways now detached from the old monarchical and religious foundations of the state. New state ends were therefore served by these new state means. However, in this view far from being the origin of the various forms of managing conduct the state is more the consequence, for such powers usually originate outside the state which may have limited or no control over them, or be dependent or parasitic upon them, as in the case of bureaucratic power.[40] In terms of liberalism understood in this sense of the "governmentalisation" of the state, a governable "economy" and "society" are seen to emerge chiefly in the eighteenth century, but these were not yet understood to be fully autonomous, as they were to be in so-called "liberal governmentality", until the nineteenth century. Liberalism in this sense confronted itself with realities – markets, civil society, families, the individual – in which these subjects could be identified and operated upon. These realities were held to have their own internal logics and mechanisms of self-regulation which had to be respected. Liberalism therefore depended on cultivating a certain sort of self, one that was reflexive, self-watching and critical of too much governance.

Liberalism in this wider sense than the mainstream usage of the word, the usage concerning liberal political thought, liberal values and party politics, was as I have indicated practiced as fervently by Conservatives as by Liberals and Labourites in Britain. It was also evident in ostensibly non-liberal or partly-liberal political regimes, for instance in the economic

---

[39] Michel Foucault, "Governmentality" in James D. Faubion (ed.), *Power*, esp. pp. 219–20; Nikolas Rose, "Governing 'Advanced' Liberal Societies" in Thomas Osborne, Andrew Barry and Nikolas Rose (eds.), *Foucault and Political Reason: Liberalism, Neoliberalism and Rationalities of Government* (UCL Press, 1996), pp. 42–3, and 43–7; see also Rose on "Advanced Liberalism" in his *Powers of Freedom: Reframing Political Thought* (Cambridge University Press, 1999), Ch. 4, and his *The Politics of Life Itself: Biomedicine, Power and Subjectivity in the Twenty-First Century* (Princeton University Press, 2007). See also Patrick Joyce, *The Rule of Freedom*, "Introduction"; and Mitchell Dean, *Governmentality* (Sage, 1999).

[40] James Ferguson, *The Anti-Politics Machine: "Development", Depoliticisation, and Bureaucratic Power in Lesotho* (University of Minnesota Press, 1994); also excerpted in Sharma and Gupta (eds.), *The Anthropology of the State*. See the deployment there as in this book of Mitchell, Rose, Scott, Foucault and Ferguson as modern exemplars for understanding the state anew. On familial and patrimonial power and the state see Paul Ginsborg, *Italy and its Discontents: Family, Civil Society, State, 1980–2001* (Penguin, 2001).

if not so much the political life of an empire like the Austro-Hungarian one, or a state like Wilhelmine Germany. One distinguishes therefore between the normal (political) and the "governmentality" (practical, technical, conduct-shaping) senses of the term, although in Britain so much was political and intellectual liberalism a central part of British history it is difficult to tease these different senses apart. However, use of the same word for two different if related things can be confusing, so that to avoid confusion with actual liberalism it is perhaps better not to use the term "liberalism" at all when conceiving of governmentality. I therefore employ instead the term "organised freedom", for the reason that it allows us to conceive of "freedom" as a political rationale and technology not necessarily tied to any political regime as conventionally described (liberal, authoritarian, fascist and so on), yet through the term "freedom" retains a link to the kind of political regime where it is most fully realised, namely political liberalism.

In this governmentality view of the state it has no "essential necessity" or "functionality". With this one can agree. However, the governmentality literature, in emphasising power beyond the state, has tended to throw out the baby of the state with the governmental bathwater. It has surprisingly little to say about the state at all. These Foucauldian approaches put the emphasis on the diffusion of certain sorts of power, which may or may not be articulated by the state, notably disciplinary power, bio-power and pastoral power. Useful as they have been, these categorisations of power are too generalised for my purposes, at once too grand and too crude for historical work. Instead, I shall consider aspects that render power down to the details of its operation so as to understand its functioning better. Broadly speaking, there are four aspects to this. Firstly, what I term the *tools* of power, big and little.[41] Secondly, *practices* of power, for example the daily office routines of bureaucrats and the practices of the teaching of classics through which bureaucrats were formed. Thirdly, *rationales* of governance including the ethics of the academic, the politician and the bureaucrat, and more especially the fabrication of the institutional *personae* of these three figures, what Weber called *Lebensführungen*, styles of life that embodied these ethics of office. Finally, I consider the *places* and *spaces* of power in which the former three aspects were expressed: government administrative offices, post offices, the upper-class house, school "houses" and so on. To understand power better one needs in this fashion to start with these or similar constituents, from the bottom up as it were. Not so much the grand *epistemes* of knowledge, Foucault style, important

---

[41] Peter Becker and William Clark (eds.), *Little Tools of Knowledge: Historical Essays on Academic and Bureaucratic Practices* (University of Michigan Press, 2001).

as these are, but what I later call "common knowledge", derived from mundane life, including the working life of the state.

Now, work in the Foucault vein is subject to the routine critique that it emphasises discipline too much, and that it works with a model of power so all pervasive as to leave no space for its negotiation and resistance.[42] This however is to misread Foucault, for in his thinking freedom and recalcitrance are necessary preconditions for the exercise of power.[43] No freedom, no power. Nonetheless, the disciplinary side of the state can be overplayed. Therefore, one of my main arguments is that far from being the source of all power, there were and are many "authors" of the state. This, what has been called the "co-production" of the state, extended to those within and without the state proper: the humble "engineer" of vitally important filing systems, say, but also the citizen him or herself, who as will be seen in the study of the daily operation of the postal system reproduced the state in daily life. Produced and reproduced in this way the state was returned to those in authority in new and often critical forms.

However that said, this sort of critique of the Foucault-influenced liter-ature, that it emphasises discipline too much, runs the risk of losing sight of the force and the subtlety of state power, not least in the supposedly limited liberal state, in that the fact of resistance to and popular negotiation of the state is nonetheless framed by the rules of the liberal game. Outcomes are given a definite shape by these rules, and the parameters of the thinkable and of action are given a decided form. It is advisable not to forget what we have already considered, namely the state's power to normalise, especially to normalise the abnormal in the forms of violence, war and famine.

Turning now to materiality, once we think of power as irradiating every-day life it also becomes apparent that the design and functioning of our basic and taken-for-granted material worlds shape our conduct in powerful and often unacknowledged ways. The word "infrastructure" itself recalls us to a sense of what is "below" and "within", and precisely because of this what is also often below the level of our conscious awareness. Capacities for action, including action upon humans, are built into objects so to speak, and outcomes shaped by them. Because different sorts of knowledge, competency and agency are "engineered" into material objects and pro-cesses this means that meanings and practices are reproduced at the level of the performance of everyday life, and so consequently these frequently

[42] Michael Marinetto, *Social Theory, The State and Modern Society*, pp. 48–9. See the discussion of "resistance" in Joyce, *The Rule of Freedom*, pp. 183–9. Frank Trentmann, "Materiality in the Future of History: Things, Practices and Politics", *Journal of British Studies*, 48 (April 2009).

[43] Michael Hardt and Antonio Negri, *Commonwealth* (Harvard University Press, 2009), p. 59.

operate outside discourse.[44] However, what this also brings into view is how agency is not only given to things by humans but inheres in things and material processes themselves. This question of agency is highlighted by the work of contemporary scholars, where interest in the material world across a wide range of disciplines amounts to what can now properly be termed a "material turn".[45] This in part represents a critique of the limitations of the language- and "discourse"-based approaches which have been so central to the cultural turn, and which have been apparent in cultural history. In a recent article I have criticised the cultural turn not only for its neglect of materiality and non-human agency but also for its almost complete neglect of the state, both aspects being in large measure due to its obsession with "representation" and "identity".[46] However, on the other hand, the impact of the material turn on the history of power and the political has also been a somewhat limited one, especially among mainstream political historians. Indeed, a good many historians of whatever stripe continue to write as if things do not exist. In cultural history, when things are brought in it still tends to be discourse about things, "cultures of" things, rather than an understanding of what things do and how they are active agents in the making of our world.[47]

In looking at the state this accent on materiality has been particularly rewarding. It helps us understand the nature and history of the technostate. No one has been more important in this work than the historical sociologist Chandra Mukerji.[48] In her recent book on the state-sponsored canal system of seventeenth-century France, *Impossible Engineering*, she distinguishes

---

[44] For a brilliant and pioneering foray into the history of the technopolitical see Ken Alder, *Engineering the Revolution: Arms and Enlightenment in France, 1763–1815* (London: Princeton University Press, 1997); and "Making Things the Same: Representation, Tolerance and the End of the Ancien Regime in France", *Social Studies of Science*, 28:4 (1998). See also the fine work of Richard Biernacki, particularly on how the material forms of factories and of payment systems embedded different notions of human labour, in the process transmitting these over very long periods of historical time. Richard Biernacki, *The Fabrication of Labour: Germany and Britain, 1640–1914* (California University Press, 1995); see also the influential (but less original) James Scott, *Seeing Like a State: How Certain Schemes to Improve the Human Condition Have Failed* (Yale University Press, 1998). See John Law, *Organising Modernity: Social Order and Social Theory* (Blackwell, 1994) on astrolabes, and his *After Method* (Routledge, 2004).

[45] Bennett and Joyce (eds.), *Material Powers*, and Dan Hicks and Mary C. Beaudry (eds.), *The Oxford Handbook of Material Culture Studies* (Oxford University Press, 2011).

[46] Joyce, "What is the Social in Social History?".

[47] Richard Biernacki, "Method and Metaphor after the New Cultural History" in Victoria E. Bonnell and Lynn Hunt (eds.), *Beyond the Cultural Turn: New Directions in the Study of Society and Culture* (University of California Press, 1999).

[48] In Joyce, "What is the Social in Social History?" I give numerous other examples of this vein of scholarship. Chandra Mukerji, *Impossible Engineering: Technology and Territoriality on the Canal du Midi* (Princeton University Press, 2009), pp. 214–7, and Ch. 9. In distinguishing strategics and logistics, she adumbrates for logistic power (in distinction

between *personal* and *impersonal* rule, domination over people and dominion over things, the former involving what she calls a "strategics" of power,
the latter a "logistics". As the author remarks, impersonal and personal rule
each bring different kinds of power to social life: "Struggles among political
actors are clearly central to the political process, but so is land control.
Reworking the countryside requires different knowledge and logics of
action, which affect social order in distinctive ways."[49] My book works
with this distinction between personal and impersonal power in mind.
However, as will become plain, while there was a historical shift from the
former to the latter, this did not mean that personal power was superseded,
simply that it was continually placed in a new relation to impersonal power
and constantly reborn in new forms.

Both forms of power are invariably mixed but need nonetheless to be
distinguished: the canal system of France was built with strategic purposes
in mind but the logics of outcomes were shaped by the agency of material
things and processes (the natural qualities of stone and water especially),
and thus were often very different from political intentions. Outcomes
were also shaped by the particular and sometimes improvised processes by
which things were made – the actual making and not just the made thing.
As Mukerji has said, "For Foucault, the panopticon is a strategic instrument of power but how it is engineered does not matter: its power lies in its
design."[50] Power needs to be distinguished from agency therefore, even
if in everyday use we merge the two: things have agency, not power,
although when conscripted into impersonal rule they may serve the ends
of power, if not always or indeed usually performing to its script. Logistics
have their own thing-driven dynamics. In France the aim was that war-
ships should navigate the new Canal du Midi. This never happened.
Nonetheless, French state power, if by default, was still assembled, but
it lay now more "in the simple fact that water flowed through lands that
had been part of noble estates and now stood for France."[51] It was things
themselves that had taken a hand in preventing one outcome and shaping
another.

In similar fashion Mukerji refers to the "unintended state" in her account
of how political control in seventeenth-century France was made possible

to personal-strategic modes), the logical relationship between territory, dominion over
nature, the agency of objects and the "authority basis" of technique. Timothy Mitchell's
work as well as Mukerji's has as we have seen been important in thinking through the
materialities of the state, and Mitchell echoes Mukerji's emphasis on the agency of
non-human material things. Mitchell, *The Rule of Experts*. See also his *Carbon
Democracy: Political Power in the Age of Oil* (Verso, 2011) and "Society, Economy and
the State Effect" in Steinmetz (ed.), *State/Culture*, pp. 81–2.
[49] Mukerji, *Impossible Engineering*, p. 214.   [50] Ibid., p. 216.   [51] Ibid., p. 215.

through the means of territorial engineering.[52] This gave rise eventually to the development of "administrative stewardship". In France key servants of the King on the engineering side of land stewardship entered the collective world of engineers, masons, draughtsmen and other workers, and with them collectively developed new forms of expertise and new understandings of this expertise and its possibilities – expertise and understandings which could be at variance with their own ostensible purpose, namely the augmentation of the government of the Royal will. A new kind of state therefore emerged in unintended fashion out of the logic of practice evident in land stewardship, a logic that was proto-technocratic. What turned out to be an early incidence of the modern form of state administration involved multiple "entanglements" of things and persons, human and non-human agency.[53] Once again there is no Weber here it should be noted, no overarching historical drive to rationalisation. But there are unintended consequences (and the human and extra-human logics that make them up) as well as the intended ones. Therefore, in the account of administrative paperwork that follows, the emphasis is on how a particular logic of bureaucratic practice – in which human agency and the material agencies involved in writing were combined – brought into being a new kind of state, born in large part out of a new concern with system and systematicity. Rather than territorial, this state was now extra- or trans-territorial, in the shape of the British Empire. However, a particular logic of practice led to results which were anything but functional for the new bureaucratic institution of the India Office.[54]

ii.   *The coming of the technostate*

Mukerji's discussion of impersonal, logistical power opens the technological powers of the state to view. "Technostate" is a rather grand term it must be admitted; nonetheless by the middle of the nineteenth century technology was rapidly becoming key to state power, so that the term is warranted. Technology had always been important of course, especially in its most fundamental forms such as writing. Michael Clanchy's work on

---

[52] Chandra Mukerji, "The Unintended State" in Bennett and Joyce (eds.), *Material Powers*.

[53] Andrew Pickering, *The Mangle of Practice: Time, Agency and Science* (Chicago University Press, 1995).

[54] Penny Harvey and Hannah Knox in analogous fashion show the various convergences and divergences of different logics of practice at work in Peruvian state formation, as interpreted through the means of road building, the logics that is of engineers and workers. Penelope Harvey and Hannah Knox, "Abstraction, Materiality and the 'Science of the Concrete' in Engineering Practice" in Bennett and Joyce (eds.), *Material Powers*.

the English medieval state has for example shown how intimately the state in its early forms was related to writing and its technologies, and writing continued to be probably the central mode of state political technology.[55] Nonetheless, by the middle of the nineteenth century the things of the state had begun to form the state of things, the technostate. The natural world, and the knowledge and technology that operated upon it, became increasingly significant for states. This was an age of revolution in industry and communications, and thus of the state's deployment of scientific expertise. The government inspector was one evidence of this.[56] From around the mid-nineteenth century everything began to seem more "technical" than before. The terms of science and technology began to migrate into everyday life. In scientific discourse "objectivity" became a single word for what was now a single concept, one folding together a previous multiplicity of meanings. Beyond science but echoing it, as Thomas de Quincy remarked, the words "objective" and "objectivity", unintelligible in 1821, by 1851 were so common as not to need explanation. By the 1840s "objective" seems to have attained something like its modern meanings in England, France and Germany.[57] Over this same period the word "expertise" entered the English language, and became established by around 1860.

Later on in the book, however, I want to use "technical" in a broader sense than normally, to describe how state government, chiefly in the form of administration, was made technical. Much more than hitherto, around the mid-century bureaucracy in Britain became the object of conscious deliberation and organisation, and in this broad sense "technical". Not yet a "science", as it became in some places – not in Britain – it still developed its own elaborate techniques, standards and routines. Elite education went through a similar process around this time. Standards, systems, routines; these were the marks of both government and technology, in different but also overlapping ways. These changes had implications for people's beliefs about the state. For, in making governance seem more technical they also made its practitioners seem more politically neutral than before, and therefore the state itself seem more neutral, in fact now as something distinct from society, existing in its own right. The broad and

---

[55] Michael Clanchy, *From Memory to Written Record: England 1066–1307* (Blackwell, 1992). Also his "Does Writing Construct the State?", *Journal of Historical Sociology*, 15:1 (March 2002).

[56] Edmund Sneyd-Kynnersley, *HMI: Some Passages in the Life of One of HM Inspectors of Schools* (London, 1908).

[57] Lorraine Daston, "Scientific Objectivity with and without Words" in Becker and Clark (eds.), *Little Tools of Knowledge*; and Lorraine Daston and Peter Gallison, *Objectivity* (Zone Books, 2007).

the narrow senses of "technology" and "technique" began to converge therefore.

Mukerji's account helps us understand the great significance of calculability for the state, in this case as it operated upon land, water and their management. Standardisation was central to the capacity to calculate and became more and more critical for government, just as it has always been central to science, and technology in the narrow sense of the term.[58] Being so closely linked to standardisation, state processes are therefore dependent on the production of space and time as things that can be calculated and measured. When things can be more easily measured they are made "objective" and abstract, and so more easily governed. Just as the medieval state was technical, so was it calculating. It too depended for its adequate functioning, and for its authority and legitimation, on standardisation – that of writing – but also the standardisation apparent in the unified ranks of armies, law-keepers and bureaucracies, and that manifest in standardised forms of mensuration, particularly that of money.[59] The great French sociologist Pierre Bourdieu points to this in his work on the state and the "state nobility" (the high bureaucracy) in much later manifestations.[60] In his terms the state produces and imposes "categories of thought" that have enormous implications for what people believe about states. For these categories are seen to be applied in everyday life, in what is called by Bourdieu the "habitus". This is the environment in which material powers are particularly apparent, though Bourdieu does not explore these in detail.

He writes of the state "as the culmination of a process of concentration of different species of capital: coercive, cultural, informational, economic, symbolic".[61] This process constitutes the state as the possessor of a sort of meta-capital, which he describes as "statist capital". Essential to this meta-capital is the claim that "the condition, or at least the correlate, of all the other forms of concentration (of capital) is the concentration of a

---

[58] Mitchell, *The Rule of Experts*, Ch. 2.
[59] However, in the very interesting symposium of which Clanchy's essay "Does Writing Construct the State?" is a part, there is still a very limited sense of what the technical and the practical might be. See the special number on the state in *Journal of Historical Sociology*, March 2002. As Clanchy argues, the supernatural authority of the state is followed by the post-supernatural authority conferred by "standardisation", but the extent to which these post-supernatural aspects of the state were a product of the material, the practical and the technical is not seen. See also Witold Kula, *Measures and Men* (Princeton University Press, 1986).
[60] "Rethinking the State: on the Genesis and Structure of the Bureaucratic Field", *Sociological Theory*, 12:1 (March 1994); *Practical Reason: On the Theory of Action* (Stanford University Press, 1998); *The State Nobility: Elite Schools in the Field of Power* (Polity Press, 1996).
[61] Bourdieu, *Practical Reason*, p. 46.

symbolic capital of recognised authority". It is in the bureaucracy that the "symbolic capital of recognised authority" is most concentrated.[62] However, this authority is in turn dependent on the state's claim to all "the operations of totalisation (censuses, national accounting) and of objectivisation (for example, cartography, the unitary representation of space from above, or writing)".[63] "Doxic submission" is the rather splendid term Bourdieu coins for the affects created by the regimes of "truth" so instituted by the state through its claims to totalisation and objectification. So, there were similar processes going on in science and technology and the state and educational apparatuses (we shall later explore in some detail this meta-capital of the high bureaucracy).

Perhaps the most important of these processes involved the creation of "systems" in both technology and the state. The recent work of the historian of science and technology Leo Marx enables us to explore this.[64] He shows how during the early phase of industrialisation technological innovations had typically been represented as single, free-standing, more or less self-contained mechanical devices: the spinning jenny, the power loom, the steam engine – by a single machine in effect. However, by the 1840s the discrete machine was being replaced, as the embodiment of a new power, by what were in effect nascent forms of what Marx calls "sociotechnological systems" and what historians of technology call large-scale technological systems. Technology itself was now lending its weight to people's perceptions of living in *systems*, and not only technological ones.[65]

The steam locomotive, for example, despite its symbolic stature constituted only a part of the operation of the railway system, which required:

(1) ... Several kinds of ancillary equipment (rolling stock, stations, yards, bridges, tunnels, viaducts, signal systems, and a huge network of tracks); (2) a corporate business organisation with a large capital investment; (3) specialised forms of technical knowledge (railroad engineering, telegraphy); (4) a specially trained workforce with unique railroading skills, including civil and locomotive engineers, firemen, telegraphers, brakemen, conductors – a workforce large and resourceful enough to keep the system functioning day and night, in all kinds of weather,

---

[62] However, what this perspective of Bourdieu's amounts to is rather unclear – the centrality of claims to legitimacy and "truth" in the making of the state is clearly recognised, but at the same time the state itself seems to have a sort of internal logic and a prescience of its own. Indeed, Bourdieu is often criticised for not having a theory of the state.

[63] Bourdieu, *Practical Reason*, p. 47.

[64] Leo Marx, "Technology: the Emergence of a Hazardous Concept", *Technology and Culture*, 51 (July 2010).

[65] There are some similarities between my emphasis on the diverse and extensive nature of systems and "systems theory" as exemplified in its most elaborate and sophisticated form, that of Niklas Luhmann. However, my work has not developed in relation to this. See Luhmann, *Social Systems* (Stanford University Press, 1995).

365 days a year; and (5) various facilitating institutional changes, such as regulations establishing standardised track gauges and a national system of standardised time zones.[66]

Such "tightly coupled" technological systems emerged rapidly from the mid-nineteenth century, first in the US and then in Europe.[67] What Marx most illuminatingly dwells on is what he calls the *congruence* of semantic terms concerning technology, on the one hand, and the concrete operations not only of technological systems but of the contemporary forms of capitalism as well:

> In advanced industrial societies, of course, most technological systems serve a predominantly economic purpose. In capitalist economies they characteristically take the form of private-sector manufacturing corporations, banks, or public utilities with large capital investments. It is noteworthy that the concept of *technology* gained currency during the "incorporation of America", when … machines became working parts of a dynamic system, and the motives for change, the source of industrial dynamism, lay not in the inanimate machine but in the economic necessities perceived by its owners … There is a compelling logic in the retrospective application of the nebulous adjective *technological* to these hybrid, dynamic, expansionary profit making enterprises It exemplifies the congruence of *technology* and corporate capitalism.[68]

This account is somewhat US-centred however: in many advanced industrial societies where the corporate path was slow to develop, Britain included, technological systems served not just economic but political purposes too, in the form of state direction and often ownership and control, whether by the central or the local state. As Thomas Hughes has shown in great detail for the case of electricity infrastructure, the British system, unlike the American one, saw political and technological power as highly integrated, particularly at the level of municipal provision.[69] In Germany political and technological power were more integrated than in the US case but less so than in the British: in the USA, in fact, the political and technological were integrated in another sense of the political, in that technology and politics were subsumed in a highly politicised ideology of American dynamism and free enterprise. Unlike in Britain, politics and politicians were infinitely pliable. Therefore, as will become clear, the line

---

[66] Marx, "Technology", 68.
[67] Erik Van der Vleuten and Arne Kaijser, *Networking Europe: Transnational Infrastructure and the Shaping of Europe, 1850–2000* (Science History Publications, 2006).
[68] Marx, "Technology", 575.
[69] Thomas Hughes, *Networks of Power: Electrification in Western Society, 1880–1930* (Johns Hopkins University Press, 1983); also Thomas Hughes et al. (eds.), *The Social Construction of Technological Systems: New Directions in the Sociology and History of Technology* (MIT Press, 1987); Michael Allen and Gabrielle Hecht (eds.), *Technologies of Power* (MIT Press, 2001).

between the economic and political in the actual operation of infrastructure was in Britain anything but distinct. Nowhere is this more apparent than with the Post Office, combining as it did the reproduction of the state *and* capitalism. Industrial capitalism and the state both seem to have arrived as "systems" at about the same time, or at least to have become much more system-like than hitherto.

Furthermore, as consideration of the already sophisticated Post Office of the *eighteenth* century will make clear, something not totally unlike a "large-scale technological system" was already in evidence long before the end of the nineteenth century. Also, before corporate capitalism earlier kinds of industrialisation had already taken on some of the aspects of systems, if not the later large-scale ones. Certainly so in the language of contemporaries, as with the emergence of the British "factory system", where machine technology expressed what was conceived of as a high degree of technological and social integration. However, this was still rather geographically localised, apparent as it was most dramatically in the factory system of the manufacturing districts of the 1840s in the north of England.[70] In a less geographically localised sense, but one nonetheless arising from the example of the new industrial areas, the idea of the machine served to embed the notion of the self-regulating system in the imagination of contemporaries, in the political as well as the economic sphere. The machine it was felt mimicked human labour, but transformed it into something rational and efficient, reshaping it as systematic and self-correcting.[71] This idea of the machine as emblematic of the system also involved the notion of demystifying the world of labour by subjecting it to the light of openness and the public gaze. In the primitive shape first of the eighteenth-century treadmill's regulatory gyrometer, then the so-called "governor" device regulating the steam engine, and eventually the "self-acting mule" in cotton spinning, the idea of the system as something seamless, stable and secure, as well as rational and efficient,

---

[70] The classic statement is of course Karl Marx, *Capital: A Critique of Political Economy*, vol. I (Penguin Books edn, 1976), esp. Ch. 15, "Machinery and Large-Scale Industry"; but see Marx's target, Andrew Ure, *The Philosophy of Manufactures* (London, 1835); also W. Cooke Taylor, *Notes of a Tour in the Manufacturing Districts of Lancashire* (1841; Frank Cass reprint, 1968). See also Patrick Joyce, *Work, Society and Politics: The Culture of the Factory in Later Victorian England* (Harvester, 1980) and Joseph Bizup, *Manufacturing Culture: Vindications of Early Victorian Industry* (University of Virginia Press, 2003).

[71] W. J. Ashworth, "England and the Machinery of Reason 1782 to 1830" in Iwan Rhys Morus (ed.), *Bodies/Machines* (Berg, 2002), and see the other contributions in this volume; also A. W. J. Ashworth, "System of Terror: Samuel Bentham, Accountability and Dockyard Reform during the Napoleonic Wars", *Social History*, 23:1 (January 1998). I. R. Morus, *Frankenstein's Children: Electricity, Exhibition and Experiment in Early Nineteenth-Century London* (Princeton University Press, 1998).

was gaining ground long before its ultimate expression in the "large-scale technological system".[72]

It was in terms derived from the earlier traditions that the technological system of the Post Office was in part understood by contemporaries, before the more "tightly coupled" sense of system particular to the large-scale technological system proper began to apply to the Post Office around the mid-nineteenth century. For the revolutionary British postal system was by then well on the way to being such a system, and not a commercial but of course fully a *state* system. In the older technological imaginary the body was the other great metaphor (a very old one of course) for the system. From the mid-nineteenth century the telegraph was equated with the body's nervous system, both seeming to transmit intelligence instantaneously. In relation to one another they offered a powerful vision of self-regulation.[73] The telegraph in practical fact made possible the temporal synchronicity upon which the railway system depended, so that the railways themselves became a system, a supposedly self-regulating one, in name and in part in deed.[74] The body and the machine therefore both emphasised automaticity and predictability, and encouraged new visions of order, control and regulation in society.

Of course, the entire conceptual and practical underpinning of liberal modes of governance, involving the idea of freely operating persons, economies and societies, was itself predicated on the idea of the self-regulating *system*, whether religious or natural. As will be seen in the Conclusion, the notion of a *social system* upon which governance should be based emerged in the early twentieth century, and this followed upon the older ideas of religious, moral and natural orders and systems. However "social", in a liberal state this too was freighted with ideas of self-regulation – of the individual, but also of the rhythms and regularities of "the social" and "society" – as in welfare state socialism. This, from the 1970s, was followed by the market as the template of the state in neo-liberalism, in part a return to older ideas of order and system. The idea of the template of governance as a system of course goes back a long way, as does the idea, in liberal regimes, of systems that are self-regulating. Otto Mayr has drawn attention to the simultaneous emergence of self-regulating machines and political ideas to do with self-regulation in early-modern Britain. In particular, there was a symbiotic relationship between ideas of authority and order and the

---

[72] W. Ashworth, "Memory, Efficiency and Symbolic Analysis: Charles Babbage, John Herschel and the Industrial Mind", *Isis* (1996), 87.

[73] I. R. Morus, review of Michael Faraday, Experimental Researches in Electricity, in *British Journal for the History of Science*, 34:4 (December 2001), 470 ff.

[74] Ibid., 474.

mechanical clock. However, Britain saw the rejection of the clock metaphor, unlike much of Europe, as for liberal mentalities this smacked too much of a predetermined universe.[75] Instead, as in the case of the postal system, particularly the telegraph, the model of the organism, including the human body itself, came alongside the machine to reflect notions of self-regulation in Britain. This has been shown in terms of ways of seeing and acting upon the social order in nineteenth-century Britain,[76] and in the infrastructural government of the body in urban Britain, particularly in the politics of public health in the shape of the "sanitary city".[77]

Therefore, there seems to have been a close relationship between, on the one hand, the human experience and material operations of technology (particularly in its large-scale capitalist, industrial forms), and the state on the other. I return to Leo Marx's important work on large-scale technological systems (abbreviated by historians of technology as LTS), for although Marx does not talk about the state, given that one of the first true LTS was the state-run British Post Office, we have to do so. I want therefore to adapt and extend Marx's work. First, he remarks that what occurred in these complex LTS was "the blurring of the borderlines between their constituent elements, notably the boundary separating the artefactual equipment (the machinery or hardware) and all the rest: the reservoir of technical – scientific – knowledge; the specially trained workforce; the financial apparatus; and the means of acquiring raw materials". It is this "blurring" I am interested in, for something similar seems to have been evident in how the *state* was conceived and lived out in daily life. This blurring was central to the emergence of what were perceived to be "systems", whether technological, economic, moral, social or *state* ones. Furthermore, in effect each of these domains reinforced the idea of the system in the others. This erasure of boundaries was evident in the old lexicon of the technological imaginary, based on the machine and the body, but became even more marked in the new, based on an understanding of *technology* itself. This is charted by Marx.

The modern-day meaning of *technology* did not in fact gain full currency until after the irruption of technolgical inventions that characterised the "second" industrial revolution (*c.*1880–1910), that which resulted in the electric light, the radio, the telephone, the X-ray, the airplane and so on.

---

[75] Otto Mayr, *Authority, Liberty and Autonomous Machinery in Early Modern Europe* (Johns Hopkins University Press, 1986).

[76] Mary Poovey, *Making a Social Body: British Cultural Formation, 1830–1964* (Chicago University Press, 1995); *A History of the Modern Fact: Problems of Knowledge in the Sciences of Wealth and Society* (Chicago University Press, 1998); *Genres of the Credit Economy: Mediating Value in Eighteenth- and Nineteenth-Century Britain* (Chicago University Press, 2008).

[77] Joyce, *The Rule of Freedom*, Ch. 2.

Marx writes of a "semantic void" as obtaining before then, eventually to be filled with the word and concept of technology as we know it today. However, this is only a "void" if we disregard the older senses of living in a system, and in fact Marx discerns many signs of "an inchoate, anticipatory sense" of living in such a world of system well before 1880. This is indeed so, for the period from the early or mid-nineteenth century until 1920 or so was a time when contemporaries were coming to terms with the increasingly apparent state, capitalist and technological (and state-technological) systems that were now governing their lives.

Learning to live in a *system* involved then this blurring of boundaries, so that in the end a new whole was perceived, that of respectively the state, capitalism and indeed "technology" itself. This whole was as vague as it was powerful. As Marx says, "The whole system, apart from the hardware, is so inclusive, so various – its boundaries so vague as to defy exact representation. This ambiguity evidently is what Heidegger had in mind by his paradoxical if telling assertion that 'the essence of technology is by no means anything technological'."[78] In the LTS there was not only the blurring of boundaries between their material elements and their bureaucratic and ideological components, but "Even more significant, perhaps, is the erosion of the 'outer' boundaries, as it were, those separating the whole technological system from the surrounding society and culture."[79] Marx's remarks on the boundaries of "outer" and "inner" are revealing, for if technological systems took on the attributes of the ambient world, and vice versa, then the technostate was similarly affected: for instance just as the electricity system of modern France took on the aura of French national identity,[80] so too did the British Post Office take on that of Britain as a nation, an empire, and later on a state that belonged to the "people", as in the ideas of the "People's Post".

At the same time the sense of living in a distinct and powerful *whole* that was central to the LTS also became central to the sense of living in a state, especially when the state embodied the technical system. The state was thereby given a distinct form, contributing to its reality as a distinct "thing", a whole autonomous from society. "Things" themselves in fact, in all their perceived "concreteness", served further to give the state form, contributing to both its separation from and identification with "society". Marx's emphasis on the "hardware" as being outside the ambiguity of systems is important here, for it was precisely the *things* of the large-scale technological system and the techno-systematic state that, as we shall see,

---

[78] Marx, "Technology", 574–5.   [79] Ibid., 575.
[80] Gabrielle Hecht, *The Radiance of France: Nuclear Power and National Identity* (MIT Press, 1998).

gave them a great deal of their reality as "solid" entities, whether the railway locomotive as a token of the railway as a technological system (and a token of what "technology" was) or the post office and the postman as tokens of the postal state.

"Hardware" came in many forms, and is better described by Marx's more generalised term, "artefactual equipment", which allows us to embrace micro-technology, for instance the common postage stamp and the letter-box. Low tech was in fact folded within the large-scale system, as in postal communications, where it exerted its own logics of operation not always consonant with the effective operations of the high-tech and the large-scale (for instance the "monster of correspondence", that of the deluge of ordinary printed forms and bureaucratic words, which destabilised the big communication systems of the British state in India). When attention to low tech is given new histories of technology, capitalism and the state emerge. For example Miles Ogborn has recently shown how writing helped construct the capitalist-cum-state enterprise that was the East India Company in the seventeenth and eighteenth centuries:

The aim was to construct a controlled space for writing and calculation which would seek to ensure the accessibility of the books, the orderly conduct of accountancy, the absence of the selfish interests of factory chiefs, and all that depended upon it. Understanding this specific and small-scale geography of writing and writing practices as an ordering of the relationships between power and knowledge in the making of global trade, means recognising the social and cultural relationships that lie right at the heart of the economic arrangements of mercantile capital. It is also the case that if the 'logic' of capital was felt by those engaged in these forms of exchange as a 'logic' – as an impersonal, inexorable, and determining force – then that was exactly the effect achieved by the separations, hierarchies, and controls instituted in the factories' writing offices as the sites of local practices of abstraction and standardisation performed upon chains and compilations of inscriptions and reinscriptions … It was within these restricted public spaces, and only within them, that the English East India Company could turn their concerns into an objective and controlling profit-seeking force external to their servants' private interests, into the 'logic' of capital.[81]

Quite so, low-tech, as in this Indian case, as well as high-tech systems created the sense of living in something that was very much like a system, a condition where the parts were cohering into a kind of whole, not necessarily a system in the fullest sense perhaps but a "thing" of sorts, something with its own logic, "impersonal, inexorable and determining". What went for the logics of capitalism went – and goes – for the "logics" of the state, particularly for the liberal state, closely linked to capitalist enterprise as it

---

[81] Miles Ogborn, *Indian Ink: Script and Print in the Making of the East India Company* (Chicago University Press, 2007), pp. 102–3, also pp. 88–92.

was and is. This was not least the case in the form of the East India Company itself, a capitalist enterprise and a state both. And writing practices were a direct reflection of this: both the Company and the new nineteenth-century state form of the India Office depended on controlling writing in novel ways, and the techniques they used in fact for a long time had much in common.

Putting the state and technology back together again also requires some periodisation of the relationship, and this I propose in terms of a transition between the territorial state and what I call the communications state of the nineteenth century, something apparent first in Britain. After this, in the twentieth century we can discern a shift to a more fully fledged technological state. The "second" industrial revolution can be regarded as ushering in this latter phase. As Lenin said at the start of the twentieth century, electricity plus soviets made socialism; and technological government has thereafter been the common theme of state development, up to the present day of government struggles to control internet technology and govern through this control. Two world wars have of course greatly accelerated this form of the state, as in the case of what has been called in Britain the "warfare state".[82] Andrew Barry has recently argued that technological government has in fact now replaced territorial government (he does not acknowledge the historical importance of a communications phase).[83] He persuasively shows how the European Union has developed as a political institution as much by technological as by directly political means, standardisation making possible the creation of what he calls technological zones, which operate across national boundaries and so create a new kind of state. Technological government operates through interoperable zones formed by means of the circulation of technical practices and devices, so that technological spaces take priority over physical ones in the form of territory. Whatever the future of the EU, if any, technological government is more and more likely to flourish, especially perhaps if "technocrats" are in control of nation or meta-states, as they currently are in parts of Europe.

In terms of the territorial state, historians have shown how in the case of the greatest early-modern European state the power of France was literally engineered into the French landscape in the seventeenth century, through major engineering and land management initiatives.[84] However, writing

---

[82] David Edgerton, *Warfare State: Britain, 1920–1970* (Cambridge University Press, 2006).

[83] Andrew Barry, *Political Machines: Governing a Technological Society* (Continuum Press, 2001).

[84] Chandra Mukerji, *Territorial Ambitions and the Gardens of Versailles* (Cambridge University Press, 1997); see also on canal construction *Impossible Engineering*.

was still crucial, for as Mukerji has put it, "Colbert built a more effective state administration not by rationalising state offices but by using public documents to increase the government's capacity to exercise logistical power and engage in territorial governance".[85] This emphasis on changing the shape of the *land* was of fundamental significance in materialising the territorial state. So too was *water* engineering, as in the German-speaking lands at this time, and later when it contributed greatly to the eventual formation of a German nation state.[86] In Britain, land and water engineering took on a similar significance in the manufacture of the United Kingdom and the British empire-state out of the matrix of a greater England. Ireland was particularly important in this respect,[87] especially the massive public works projects of the eighteenth century and later, designed to drain and bring under cultivation the extensive boglands of the country, and so in the process "civilise" the supposedly wild Irish landscape and by extension the wild Irish populace. In the nineteenth century the Board of Works was regarded by many contemporaries as the de facto government of the country. The roots of this lay earlier, and engineering was key to these. What contemporaries called "engine science" – apparent in the role of Irish intellectuals as early as the Scientific Revolution of the seventeenth century – became essential to the state. This "engineering culture" was a powerful influence in shaping the idea that government could also be designed according to rational, scientific principles, so forwarding the civilising mission of Britain. A "political science" was held to be achievable in terms of what was called "experimental government": the idea was that "system" and "design" could be found in government as well as nature.

Ireland's governance was not only a matter of land management, public works and engineering: the Irish National School system of the early nineteenth century was the first national system of government-funded education in the world; the Irish convict system arrived some half a century before it did on the mainland; and in relation to what Carroll calls the "data state" the Irish Ordnance Survey by the late 1840s was a state science

---

[85] Chandra Mukerji, "Jurisdiction, Inscription and State Formation". The quote is from her article abstract.

[86] David Blackbourn, *The Conquest of Nature: Water, Landscape and the Making of Modern Germany* (Jonathan Cape, 2006). On the extension of the Napoleonic state in the German lands, in the case of Baden, see Blackbourn, Ch. 2. This involved extensive mapping, the elaboration of legal codes, tax systems and systematic weight and measurement systems – in short, active state building through infrastructure.

[87] Patrick Carroll, *Science, Culture, and Modern State Formation* (University of California Press, 2008), esp. Ch. 6, "Engineering Ireland: The Material Design of Modern Statecraft".

project of immense size, without parallel anywhere in the world.[88] The normalisation of state coercion was apparent in all this, for in Ireland, as to a lesser degree on the mainland, even though Britain was not a militaristic state the military was unsurprisingly the dominant model of state coercion. The Irish police force was in effect a military rather than a civil one.[89]

The public health and the "sanitation" movements of mainland Britain in the mid-nineteenth century show how what were in essence political matters were rapidly becoming technological ones, and so notionally "outside" politics.[90] The same was true throughout Europe, and as European empires spread, throughout the world technological flows were going both ways between the metropolitan and colonialised state.[91] State powers increased markedly in all the major European states, especially between 1850 and 1880. It was then, and again Britain was ahead of developments, that the benefits of industrialisation began to accrue in the form of tax bases for states. Cumulatively from the early nineteenth century the state's power over everyday life deepened: its legal powers and apparatus; its power over life and death; its interventions into manners and morals.[92] Increasingly, "state building" became a conscious pursuit, giving expression to dreams of limitless sovereignty and of an ordered, technological society, dreams linked to the idea of civilisation and the perfectibility of the individual.[93]

In the British case this was also evident in the development, from the 1850s, of direct British rule in India, something to which technological governance was central, particularly in the form of the railways.[94] The Indian railways also signalled the emergence of what would later be a

---

[88] Ibid., Ch. 4 on the "data state". Patrick Carroll-Burke, *Colonial Discipline: The Making of the Irish Convict System* (Four Courts Press, 2000). On statistics and the state see also Adam Tooze, *Statistics and the German State, 1900–1945* (Cambridge University Press, 1991).

[89] Carroll-Burke, *Colonial Discipline*, p. 236

[90] Christopher Hamlin, *Public Health and Social Justice in the Age of Chadwick: Britain, 1800–1854* (Cambridge University Press, 1998). See also Tom Crook, "Power, Privacy and Pleasure: Liberalism and the Modern Cubicle", *Cultural Studies*, 21:4–5 (July/ September 2007). See also Tom Crook and Glen O'Hara (eds.), *Statistics and the Public Sphere in Britain, c. 1800–2000* (Routledge, 2011) on aspects of public health.

[91] See the synoptic Daniel R. Headrick, *Power over Peoples: Technology, Environments, and Western Imperialism, 1400 to the Present* (Princeton University Press, 2010). Christophe Bayly, *The Birth of the Modern World, 1780–1914* (Blackwell, 2005), p. 251. Chandak Sengoopta, *Imprint of the Raj: How Fingerprinting was Born in Colonial India* (Macmillan, 2003).

[92] Bayly, *The Birth of the Modern World*, ibid., pp. 261–5, 473–5.   [93] Ibid., p. 253.

[94] Laura Baer, *Lines of the Nation: Indian Railway Workers, Bureaucracy and the Intimate Historical Self* (Columbia University Press, 2007), pp. 21–6. The state micro-managed the Indian railway system from its early days, although ownership was ostensibly private, with the exception of the (extensive) sensitive military sections. The whole system was taken into state ownership after 1900.

massive, centralised and autocratic state bureaucracy.[95] Once again we witness the birth of true large-scale systems in state as well as economic form. Christopher Bayly ascribes much of the motive power of the state-building activity at this time to the reforming zeal of the middling ranks of society, both within and beyond Europe, something he calls "godly methodism".[96] However, the "godly methodism" of reformers was more often a methodism concerned with techniques of governance themselves – making these and the things and persons that practised them methodical – than a methodism apparent in religion. Lord Dalhousie, the governer-general of India at this time, and a confirmed utilitarian, exemplified this technological methodism in his avid and hands-on encouragement of rail, postal and telegraphic communication.[97]

From around 1800 in Britain one can discern a new prominence for communications, in which the state became more and more involved. The new railway systems exemplified this shift from territory per se to communications, although in Britain the state regulated rather than owned the railway system. As a long-established trading state the salience of communications in Britain is obvious, and in the nineteenth century this was expressed in the governmental gospel of "free trade". The infrastructure that mattered here, of vital importance for Britain's new world economic dominance, was global and not simply national or even imperial. Continental Europe was to follow the communications route somewhat later and in a different fashion from Britain. Consequent upon later industrialisation, the transition from a taxation regime based on land to one depending on income, consumption and trade took longer to implement in Europe.[98] The global reach of British trade meant state involvement in facilitating the financial instruments of trade, the control of postal and telegraphic communication, and not least the encouragement of British shipping (to the extent that by 1911 Britain controlled the world shipping market, dominating its top and bottom ranges).[99]

In mainland Britain itself communications and territory came together in the great civil engineering projects of the late eighteenth and early nineteenth centuries. This was apparent for instance in Thomas Telford's

[95] Manu Goswami, *Producing India: From Colonial Economy to National Space* (University of Chicago Press, 2004).

[96] Bayly, *The Birth of the Modern World*, p. 474.

[97] On Dalhousie see Thomas J. Misa, *Leonardo to the Internet: Technology and Culture from the Renaissance to the Present* (Johns Hopkins University Press, 2004), Ch. 2.

[98] Daniel R. Headrick, *The Tentacles of Progress: Technology Transfer in the Age of Imperialism, 1850–1940* (Oxford University Press, 1988); also *Power over Peoples*. Peter J. Hugill, *Global Communications since 1844: Geopolitics and Technology* (Johns Hopkins University Press, 1999).

[99] Headrick, *The Tentacles of Progress*, Ch. 2 on shipping.

massive public works projects in Scotland and England. Not understood as state policy, and indeed as political at all, Telford developed in his practice-based, experimental and rational forms of project organisation many of the techniques of the "scientific" public administration of the Benthamites.[100] Road building in Ireland too, and with it what was known by contemporaries as the science of "road police", were by the 1820s well advanced.[101] The foundations for this communications "infrastructure state" had been laid during the canal-building mania between the 1760s and 1790s.[102] The late-eighteenth-century state was only in part still a fiscal-military one, designed for war and the maximisation of state revenues. It was also becoming an infrastructural state, serving fiscal-military purposes still but increasingly open to the interests of trade and commerce, abroad and at home, especially in the newly industrialising provinces, as in the case of its facilitation of canal building.[103] People were thus brought into a new relation with the state, including people of quite humble background.[104] Questions of public faith in Parliament came to the fore, and thus questions of trust in the state.

The route to nationally co-ordinated communications systems was indirect and sometimes contradictory in Britain, where local concerns always mattered. The contrast with centrally directed France is often made. For some time Parliament and government departments facilitated rather than initiated action. This still involved increasing levels of state oversight and supervision, reflected in central and local state institutions establishing comprehensive project standards and plans, employing inspectors, and developing hierarchical management systems as was the case with inspectors of roads in the Highlands. Specialised parliamentary technical committees, Improvement Commissions, Turnpike Trusts and County Surveyors, representative of all levels of the state, became increasingly central to the political system as the state began to lose its old myopia towards technological government. Therefore, long before the regular civil service an *irregular* state bureaucracy was evident. One reflection of this was the growth of civil engineering as a "profession". The rule of technical experts became apparent, and for some time technical expertise floated in between civil society and the state before it became much more folded within direct state management in the course of the nineteenth

---

[100] Joyce, *Rule of Freedom*, pp. 69–70; Hamlin, *Public Health*, pp. 264–5, 305–6.
[101] Carroll, *Science, Culture, and Modern State Formation*, pp. 148–50.
[102] See the invaluable John Money, *Experience and Identity: Birmingham and the West Midlands 1760–1800* (Manchester University Press, 1977).
[103] Ibid., pp. 29, 30–2, 277.
[104] E. Joanna Guldi, *Roads to Power: Britain Invents the Infrastructure State* (Harvard University Press, 2012), p. 98.

century.[105] The line between technical experts and bureaucrats also remained blurred for some time, Rowland Hill being a good example of this. However, "technocracy" was not apparent, even if technical experts were often the agents of change, for the politicians and high bureaucracy continued to hold sway, the latter by making themselves into "experts" in the new world of state "administration". Political power was still key.

Despite these qualifications, by the early nineteenth century proper nationally co-ordinated systems were in place. This was most dramatically evident in the road system and the postal network. The great significance of road transport in British state formation has only recently been recognised.[106] The development of an integrated national road system was vital. Between 1726 and 1848 the entire road system was transformed from a network to something resembling a homogenised system. Throughout the eighteenth century Parliament had passively ratified legislation, however as calls for road improvement increased by the 1810s it had emphatically moved to a centrally managed, national network of expert-run roads. Thus it moved beyond the phase in which local interests held the balance of power and not the centre.

The road system also shows the deepening hold of more distinctively liberal forms of the technostate. This was apparent in the most fundamental of material developments in road construction: between 1817 and 1835 parliamentary Acts and legal rulings combined to finally erase variations in road *surfaces* across much of the country. The long reign of the pothole over free communication was now overthrown. The period between 1810 and 1835 saw the culmination of a process whereby the highly dispersed eighteenth-century road system was formed into a new "diagram" of communication, with London at its centre, from which the spokes of the communications wheel radiated out to the constituent capitals of a newly realised Great Britain. Direct state management of the actual roads themselves became apparent, with signposts and village nameboards now directing traffic on narrower and better-surfaced roads, for example the Holyhead Road, the second most important road in the country after the Dover one. This was one of the great post roads which were rapidly making up a new sort of British nation. Technical homogeneity thus resulted in a new degree of political and social homogeneity.[107]

The Post Office was itself the single division of government most involved with the redesign of the road network. The Post Office's expanding internal

[105] See below, pp. 93, 172–4, 176–9, 181–2, 191–3.   [106] Guldi, *Roads to Power*.

[107] This and the following two paragraphs are largely based on Guldi's account. For the immediate point see Ch. 1, "Military Craft and Parliamentary Expertise", and her "Introduction", esp. pp. ix–x.

bureaucracy reflected a new political drive for direct government intervention in transportation networks. As Guldi argues, parliamentary directives gave these tasks a nation-building agenda. At the request of the committees planning Britain's centralised highway network, the Post Office was charged with making recommendations for the improvement of English communications with Scotland and Ireland. Post Office surveyors became the major official consultants to every state building project, promotion of the road network being one of the Post Office's major goals, which also included the building of the port at Holyhead Harbour, the Menai Straits Bridge in Anglesey and the Highgate Archway in London, projects designed to improve transport links between London and Dublin. As Guldi writes, "The Post Office became, after 1800, the only government office with a continuous role in recommending 'improvements,' suggesting rival designs, promoting certain engineers, providing their offices with evidence, and so reshaping the built environment. Post Office endorsed designers were therefore precedent-setting in new forms of design, urban, rural, and suburban."[108]

The new road system changed the world of social relations on the roads themselves.[109] Contrary to liberal fantasies (for instance those of Macaulay's hugely popular 1848 *History of England*) the new reality of road travel did not produce a different kind of interclass social mingling and national cohesion. Rather, what seems to have been the case was the development of endless traffic, in which new conditions for the privatisation of the self were established by new forms and protocols of travel. In this the previous experience of socialisation in the old road system became diminished, and markers of class and the state in modes of travel and road use were accentuated. The conditions for a new sort of governing through freedom and the free subject had begun to emerge. In the extension of technology into the home, apparent in the provision of household utilities – gas, water and mains drainage – similar ends were in view.

The great mass of the people themselves began to be involved (although class differences were so rooted that this process was to take a long time). The city, and the local state in a new configuration with the central one, became pivotal arenas of governance, so that the rhythms and processes of city life became "naturalised" as themselves new spheres in which freedom could be seen to be apparent, and in which it could be politically realised.[110] The city was to be governed according to the immanence of its own being, for it was felt now to have its own laws and its own rhythms, to do with health, morals, crime and so on. These had to be respected for

---

[108] Ibid., Ch. 2, "Colonizing at Home".   [109] Ibid., Ch. 4, "Wayfaring Strangers".
[110] For a full account see Joyce, *The Rule of Freedom, passim.*

it was they that generated the truths, including the "problems", political governance now depended upon, namely those of a free self existing in a free society and economy, but also apparent in, and realised by, a city of free communication. The urban, in a densely urbanised Great Britain, was to leave a deep imprint on liberal government in Britain thereafter.

At the central state level the Post Office was a paradigm for all these changes in the first half of the nineteenth century, for it represented a massive extension of capacities for knowledge, information and free communication. These capacities government both encouraged and drew upon in radically new ways. Involving communication at the most basic level, that of the word, the Post Office was the most revealing of all forms of the communications state. Like domestic infrastructure, it penetrated and reconfigured the home and the domestic sphere. It also penetrated and changed the world of work. Like transport provision it embraced town and country, home and empire alike. Thus it reshaped both the private and the public spheres, giving new forms and meanings to "territory" and bringing new meanings and social relations into play. It reordered social life irrevocably, and with it the daily experience of the state. In the next chapter I will show how this worked, pointing to how social life was transformed by the technical only for the technical to be made social again. This was the ceaseless motion technological government now brought into the political world.

Part I

The state of things: connecting

2 "Man is made of the Post Office": making the social technical

> If the country people are slack in writing, it is not because they want matter or occasion, but they want, and therefore they must have a rural post office in every village. The village post office, like the village public-house, is to make its own customers; and people are to be led to take the trouble of writing, as they are led to the pleasure of drinking, by having the means at hand for the immediate gratification of their passion ... Thus in the opinion of Mr. Hill, "Man is made of the Post Office, and not the Post Office for man." Letter-writing is as much a natural propensity, and as incontrollable a passion, as love, avarice, or ambition. The object of seduction, the village or district Post Office, is only to be at hand, and the appetite runs headlong to its gratification. Men and women are only so many machines for writing letters, and can only be considered as fulfilling their destiny when "hourly" contributing to the penny fund. Give us a Post Office – *Virginibus puerisque – scribimus indocti doctique – passim.*
>
> (Anon., *The Administration of the Post Office* ... 1844)[1]

To understand what I call the ceaseless motion of the technical and the social which technological government brought into the political world we have to think about infrastructure. For the technostate rested upon the provision of infrastructure. In its communications form this state brought together transport, domestic life, work and information in a new and revolutionary configuration. Developments in these different spheres were themselves closely related: in the areas of information and transport for instance, the telegraph and the railway marched side by side across the land, and the letter was distributed along the new roads and transported in the new trains. Things, people and ideas were brought into a closer relation than ever before, and it was the state that brought this about. The communications form in which it did so

---

[1] Anon., *The Administration of the Post Office, from the Introduction of Mr. Rowland Hill's Plan of Penny Postage Up to the Present Time...* (London, 1844; ed. Col. H. W. Hill, 1949), pp. 101–2, 103. The Latin echoes Horace: "Each desperate blockhead learns to write."

was above all the postal service.[2] For it was this that dealt in the word, the prime essential of all human communication. In systematising the communication of words, and numbers, it enabled the development and the co-ordination of all the other infrastructural domains upon which the state increasingly rested.

As historians of technology have pointed out, one of the key things about infrastructures is that they should function *systematically*, operating as automatically and humanly "unaided" as possible. Infrastructures therefore have the central characteristic of *flow*.[3] They flow in and with us as we flow through life. The result is that they become "naturalised", their very reliability, durability and replicability giving them a self-evident quality which very often masks the fact that they have human designs built into them, even if in practice these designs are constantly thwarted by the agency of their own materialities, as well as by the failings of humans. "Technical" in operation in this way they work largely outside our conscious awareness, so that we become habituated to their existence and to what they deliver to us; things like running water to wash in or defacate with, electric light to see with, but also flows of connectivity to communicate through, so that posting a letter also becomes what our anonymous pamphleteer of the 1840s, more prescient than he was aware of, calls "a natural propensity". In short, infrastructures make the social technical, and it is this process we shall be concerned with in this chapter. "Man is made of the Post Office".

Of course, all this taken-for-granted character of infrastructure can be turned on its head pretty rapidly when things *don't* work: if the tap is dry when turned on, when road traffic comes to a halt or when the light switch fails to illuminate the dark. It is then that the potential frailty of infrastructures is revealed and we become more fully aware of the enormous mobilisations of resources that make them function. But by and large they do work, increasingly effectively as time has gone on, at least in "advanced" societies. So, in general it can be said that historically they have involved a separation of human life from direct, sensory experience of the world and thus a mounting reliance on standardised technological regimes in which abstract not concrete forms of knowledge are dominant. This abstraction transforms the power as well as the material relations of

---

[2] By the term "postal service" I should make clear here that in what follows I mean not just the mails but the whole communications system operated, and eventually owned, by what in the United Kingdom was known as the General Post Office (the GPO, which contemporaries usually described as the Post Office).

[3] Thomas J. Misa, Philip Brey and Andrew Feenberg (eds.), *Modernity and Technology* (MIT Press, 2003), particularly Paul N. Edwards, "Infrastructure and Modernity: Force, Time, and Social Organisation in the History of Socio-Technical Systems".

societies, for it means among other things that knowledge has shifted from the local and the immediate to the extra-local, making "government at a distance" possible. For example, when land is surveyed and mapped the site of knowledge about it, and therefore a stake in power over it, migrates from the original users and their customary practices to those who possess this abstract knowledge and the tools and techniques that enable it. In looking at the institution of European private property in colonial worlds where it was previously unknown historians of empire have long been aware of this. Politically, people and things became increasingly calculable, and therefore increasingly able to be regulated, down to the extreme form of the "audit society" of late-twentieth-century Britain.

The nineteenth-century state was the central player in the development of infrastructure, in the form above all of postal communications. The postal system in Europe and its empires, also in large parts of the Americas, became in the nineteenth century a, and often *the*, leading arm of "advanced" states: in some places the military might numerically be the state's largest expression, but if this was the case the post was usually not far behind. In Britain, lacking a great army, the post was by far the largest institution of the state for more than a century after 1850, as well as by far the largest single employer of labour. By 1920 the British Post Office had a total staff of 240,000,[4] and it peaked in size at almost half a million by 1970, to be replaced by the National Health Service as the greatest employer of labour in Britain.[5] In the USA, the home of what has mistakenly been seen as a weak or undeveloped central state, it was in fact the *central* state that consciously and determinedly developed a postal system, and this system was deliberately aimed at carving out a united national community. This happened long before the railway and a modern road system in America, *and* before many of the European states had fully set about the task. There, at the very heart of private capitalism, it was the US Mail that was the largest single employer of labour in the USA from the 1790s to the 1920s.[6]

However, if infrastructures become embedded in our lives they in turn enable new and often unforeseen uses and social interactions. New

---

[4] Martin Daunton, *Royal Mail: The Post Office since 1840* (Athlone Press, 1985), pp. 194–5.
[5] Duncan Campbell-Smith, *Masters of the Post: The Authorized History of the Royal Mail* (Allen Lane/Penguin, 2011), chart 3, p. 707. On the growth of the Post Office in war see Howard Robinson, *The British Post Office: A History* (Princeton University Press, 1948), p. 437.
[6] David M. Henkin, *The Postal Age: the Emergence of Modern Communications in Nineteenth-Century America* (University of Chicago Press, 2006), Ch. 1; also Richard E. John, *Spreading the News: The American Postal System from Franklin to Morse* (Harvard University Press, 1995); *Network Nation: Inventing American Telecommunications* (Harvard University Press, 2010).

technologies, in altering the ground of social life, impact on existing social relations and political life in new ways and so create new social worlds. They also create new problems, especially for the state. Therefore, just as the social was made technical, so too was the technical made social again, as it was lived out in everyday life. This is the side of the ceaseless motion of the technical and the social that I examine in the next chapter, when I consider how the postal system became a learned reality, something achieved through the actual *use* of the system. In this chapter I consider the long-term development of the postal network into something like a postal *system*, and the role of technology in this. It is by these means that I explore how the social was made technical in the first place.

All this goes for technology in general as well as for infrastructure, including "slow" and "low" tech, in particular the technologies that the post came to depend on, above all the invention of the steel pen. These technologies transform society which in turn transforms them. The steel pen was largely a creation of this time, as we shall see, and it meant that a thousand years of laborious quill paring and shaping became irrelevant. It also meant that more people wrote, at once introducing the skills of the physical, writing "hand" to untold millions while at the same time bringing in its wake an enormous range of "labour-saving" devices designed to make handwriting less physically arduous. These new writing, and reading, millions were a problem for the state. A new "writing public" was made by technology and this public developed the resulting technosocial possibilities in its own ways, albeit within parameters set by the state.

I   The postal network becomes a system

What are postal networks and systems? Let us begin with the first term, "postal". As has been noted, the *mass* use of both the telegraph and the telephone was much more limited than is usually thought.[7] Though the telegraph was of fundamental importance in the development of the capitalist economy and in political, news and military uses, the metropolitan as opposed to the colonial state's use of it was for long rather limited. As for the telephone, it was only by 1902 that the major government departments of the Treasury and the Home Office were connected to the General Post Office exchange system. In the same year the Home Office only had two telephones (which were, it was rather

---

[7] Even in the USA, as late as 1941 98 per cent of telephone calls took place within the same state, and it was only a good while after 1945 that calling abroad became anything other than exotic.

vaguely said, being "largely used").[8] The predominating form of communication remained the letter and its associated forms, including the parcel, things that were literally posted. "Postal" is therefore an accurate term in which to describe the system. At the same time however, the extraordinarily wide remit of the Post Office as a universal communications provider is evident. "Postal" therefore denotes something at once very broad and something very particular (in essence the letter).

As for the term "network", infrastructure systems do in fact tend in their actual operation and appearance towards the character of the web, the lattice or the net, for instance electrical, telephone and road "networks". The network has indeed been called the quintessential communications metaphor.[9] In actor network theory itself what is useful is the emphasis upon what are termed "mediators" and "translation" as opposed to simple intermediaries and transportation, the latter denoting just bringing something across instead of transforming it. What the concepts illuminate is the way in which key human and non-human actors have the capacity not only to extend but to refashion networks, successful action being informed by the capacity of particular actors to enlist, redefine and redeploy other actors or "actants" (non-human agents).[10] To enlist, redefine and redeploy other networks too, so that networks can also be regarded as successful to the extent that they incorporate these other networks. Thus the relationship between the postal network and other networks is apparent (other state networks, political and bureaucratic, plus business and social networks). What is revealing about the postal network is its capacity to incorporate and in turn reformulate these other ones. As for the state at large, beyond the postal network alone, it too is the sum and the outcome of the various "mediators" and "translations" that

---

[8] Jill Pellew, *The Home Office 1848–1914* (Heinemann, 1982), p. 97.

[9] Laura Otis, *Networking: Communicating With Bodies and Machines in the Nineteenth Century* (University of Michigan Press, 2001).

[10] Bruno Latour, *Reassembling the Social: An Introduction to Actor-Network-Theory* (Oxford University Press, 2005), pp. 128–9. See also John Law on "heterogeneous engineering": 'Technology and Heterogeneous Engineering: the Case of the Portuguese Expansion' in Wiebe Bijker, Thomas Hughes and Trevor Pinch (eds.), *The Social Construction of Technological Systems* (MIT Press, 1987); also *Organizing Modernity: Social Order and Social Theory* (Blackwell, 1994). He uses the example of the Portuguese oceanic expansion to India to explain how an actor network functions (and sometimes doesn't). In order for an actor network to become stable, the artefacts in the network have to be able to survive. Many elements in the network are difficult to control and may change. If this happens, the network collapses. Controlling or taming these elements is considered heterogeneous engineering. These elements may be ships, labour and navigation devices for oceans, but extend to other networks too, including the mobilisation of states and administrations.

either extend or inhibit its powers.[11] Because this is the case the operation of the UK postal network is followed in some detail below, including the agency of things, for a crucial part was played by seemingly
unimportant "mediators" like letterboxes, stamps and envelopes, and
the "translations" these brought about; and also by the agency of often
unheralded human beings, as will be seen.

This brings us to the question of networks and systems, for in the
present discussion I have deliberately avoided the latter term so far.
There is an important distinction between the terms "network" and
"system". A network denotes an element of openness, drawing on the
idea of the lattice or the web. A "system" denotes more what is closed and
can be self-referring or self-regulating. In fact common English language
usage is to employ both interchangeably. However it is necessary to keep
the two distinguished. For what marked the development of the Post
Office over this period was the attempt to turn a network into a system
proper. Networks are successful to the degree that they build durability
and stability into necessarily mutable material and human affairs. What is
revealing about the postal network is its gradual but effective achievement
of this durability and stability. Part of the process of a network becoming a
system involves the degree to which durability and consistency will have
been imparted to the network. They can then be controlled more easily,
even to the degree of self-control, so that the openness of the network can
be in some measure closed. Something like this seems to have been going
on over the long term in the Post Office. This system-building was however a slow and painful business. Systems in practice constantly tend back
to the condition of networks. The emergence of a system was therefore
spatially uneven and temporally irregular. Nonetheless, enough was
achieved to warrant the term system.

Turning to the history of the postal network-cum-system then, what
was involved was first the series of links which made up 'the Post Office'.
Thus it encompassed for example the paths, roads, seaways and railways
that literally made up the links. These pathways in turn connected and
aligned the locations or nodes that made up the network. The transport
and communication "devices" which traversed and connected these links
were also involved, as were the forms of what was transmitted. Because

---

[11] Historians of the state, as opposed to historians of science and technology, are now
beginning to appreciate this: see for example Rui Branco, "Fieldwork, Map Making and
State Formation: A Study in the History of Science and Administration" in Peter Becker
and Rüdiger von Krosigk (eds.), *Figures of Authority: Contributions towards a Cultural
History of Governance from the Seventeenth to the Twentieth Century* (PIE Peter Lang,
2008), pp. 218–25.

forms in considerable measure shaped content, so too was communication content also involved.

From the very earliest times, for instance the Roman Empire and the *positus*, postal networks functioned to facilitate power. They enabled the state to govern. For the state to exist at all it is essential that it knows itself and that which it governs. Indeed this act of knowing can be said to be a fundamental act of constituting the state, so that the state is always concerned to both control and actively fashion information and knowledge. The post has historically been at the centre of this. The state in its old sense of "in state" – the institution of royalty, the court and their embodiment in the person of the monarch – needed to know itself and the regions it desired to govern, and had to be able to communicate its wishes to them.[12] Until the seventeenth century the post was no more than a tool of state power through knowledge, a way for the monarch to observe the subjects of distant parts of his or her territory and simultaneously to communicate royal commands to them and check whether or not these were being carried out. Then, and for some time after, the distinction between state and society remained blurred. The postal service enabled the monarchy to govern over an area that exceeded the area governable by direct personal influence (that is, personal encounter), or rather it allowed direct personal influence from the monarch, the embodiment of the state, to be extended over great distance and time in the form of official communication. The post enabled the incorporation of the disparate territories and subjects of the kingdom into something like a unit (albeit often a fluid one). Thus there is a direct correlation between the state's ability to organise and communicate with itself, and its power and extent.

There was a close relationship between personal proclamation, royal authority and the act of writing. The royal word had to be proclaimed. Like God the monarch was the word. The use of the parish church for readings aloud in public of proclamations and other public documents saw this relationship in political practice. Before the eighteenth century the church was in fact a sort of post office, physically "the office" itself with the "post" being the royal proclamation. Royal "news" was the original staple, before what would later be "news" in a more modern sense, and then later still the postal function per se. The church – the *established* Church of England – was a state "office" in another sense too, reproducing the state in its built form from the outside and within the church doing the same, for example in the post-Restoration displays of royal and state insignia on its walls. This was another proclamation of the word.

---

[12] E. Watson, *The Royal Mail to Ireland* (Edward Arnold, 1917), pp. 1–2.

In monopolising communication the monarch was (generally) able to ensure that theirs was the most extensive network of power. The rationality of governance was very clearly that none other had business communicating over distance. To do so could only be an attempt to incorporate a wider array of actors into one's own network, which was a threat to the pre-eminence of the state and thus could not be allowed. In the seventeenth century this rationality altered significantly. At this point the use of the post began to be extended more widely to 'the public', although this was an uneven process, and the public to which it was extended was much more limited than later versions, indeed something of an afterthought. Nevertheless the state/society distinction thus began to emerge more forcibly.

There are several possible reasons for this shift, among which is the impact of Renaissance socio-political thought. The evolution of the concept of the state in political thought and in different degree political practice can be seen to parallel the effect of the processes I am concerned with here, so that we see how thought about the state has also contributed to how we have come to think of the state as a thing. In sixteenth and seventeenth century political thought itself the state became separated from both the rulers and the ruled. It became distinct from the person and the status of the prince, on the one hand, and from the prince's subjects and the territory they inhabited on the other. The "classical republican" and liberal traditions contributed to the separation of the prince from the state, its inhabitants and territory; and the absolutist tradition, on the other hand, to the separation of the prince from the ruled. The word "state" emerged to avoid republican connotations, but also the idea of the personal role of the prince.[13] This suggested that the public had a right to govern itself and was constituted as a body separate from the state.

The shift to "public" use was also brought about by a political desire to augment national wealth and power. This desire was represented in Britain by a limited monarchy, in the form of the taxation policies of what has been called the fiscal-military state of the eighteenth century. This state fought shy of subsidising the post as a public service until the nineteenth century, seeing revenue collection as still the motive for public use. In looking at the Post Office network from the eighteenth century I shall be considering three

---

[13] Quentin Skinner, "The State" in T. Ball et al. (eds.), *Political Innovation and Conceptual Change* (Cambridge University Press, 1989). On medieval antecedents of the modern concept of the state see Ernst Kantorowicz, *The King's Two Bodies: A Study in Mediaeval Political Theology* (Princeton University Press, 1957). For the German tradition of the history of political concepts, *Begriffsgeschichte*, which is somewhat more alert to matters beyond language alone than the Skinner-inspired Cambridge School, see the recent initiative: University of Bielefeld Collaborative Research Centre (SFB 584), "The Political as Communicative Space in History".

linked processes: firstly, one by which the Post Office department of state emerged and was consolidated as a state institution; secondly, how it became the centre not only of the postal network but of communications in general; and thirdly the changing geographical configurations of the network itself.[14]

London, since the earliest times, has been the centre of the postal service, and the whole edifice was consciously constructed to facilitate metropolitan knowledge and control of the subjects and regions outside it. There was nothing "natural" about London being the centre of the state. It was deliberately made so by human design. This design combined capitalist and state interests from the beginning. The General Post Office had its headquarters, from 1678, in Lombard Street, at the heart of the business City.[15] London was connected to the rest of the kingdom, and beyond to foreign powers, by the roads that had by 1800 been the main arteries of British communication for several hundred years. However it was not until the post was reorganised by the 'Proclamation for the Settling of the Letter Office of England and Scotland' in July 1635 and made available to the public that the permanent post roads were established.[16] Although these roads were critical for inter-state communication they served the internal post of Britain fairly badly (for this was not their intention, foreign communication being foremost in mind). They ignored such major developing centres as Cambridge, Manchester, Birmingham, Nottingham, Derby and Southampton.

The General Post Office in London housed the offices of the national (inland and foreign) and the local post for London.[17] By the 1730s there

[14] For the postal system prior to reform (c. 1850) see C. Calvert, A History of The Manchester Post Office, 1625–1900 (J. E. Lee, 1967); C. J. Cooke, Irish Postal History: Sixteenth Century to 1935 (London, 1935); M. Reynolds, A History of the Irish Post Office (MacDonnell and Whyte Ltd, 1983); K. Ellis, The Post Office in the Eighteenth Century: A Study in Administrative History (Oxford University Press, 1958); J. Gardiner, A Generall Survey of the Post Office, with Severall Useful Remarques to The particulars of it Most humbly presented To his Royal Highness James Duke of Yorke (London, 1677); J. W. A. Lowder, A Postal History of London 1635–1960 (publisher unknown, c. 1982); Robinson, Britain's Post Office; Campbell-Smith, Masters of the Post; C. Roeder, Beginnings of the Manchester Post Office (Manchester, 1905); T. Todd, William Dockwra and the Rest of the Undertakers: the Story of the London Penny Post, 1680–82 (Cousland and Sons, 1952); Rowland Hill, Post Office Reform: Its Importance and Practicability, 2nd edn (London, 1837); R. C. Tombs, The King's Post: Being a Volume of Historical facts relating to the Posts, Mail Coaches, Coach Roads, and Railway Mail Services of and connected with the Ancient City of Bristol from 1580 to the present time (Bristol, 1905); E. Watson, The Royal Mail to Ireland: or an Account of the Origin and Development of the Post Between London and Ireland through Holyhead, and the Use of the Line of Communication by Travellers (London, 1917).
[15] Robinson, The British Post Office, pp. 55, 56.   [16] Ibid., pp. 13, 14, 31.
[17] The strength of the establishment of the different branches of the PO can be traced through Post Office Archives (POA), POST 59: Staff Establishment Books, 1691–1983. On internal organisation see also POST 59/1, 59/3, 59/22 and 97/1. POST 97/1, Private Collections: Walsingham Papers, 1787, pp. 160, 87. Also POST 58/1, Orders, April 13th 1774, p. 28.

were over 600 receiving houses in London, located in most main streets.[18] The network at this early eighteenth-century stage involved the relatively crude technology of trustworthy post boys, a series of equally reliable horses and innkeepers, and a number of chartered boats at the harbours. In addition to this there were agreements with foreign powers to transport one another's letters through their respective countries. The Post Office did not own any of the above items, nor did it employ any of the servants along the route. Rather, the state contracted with a series of private individuals in order to maintain a passable network. The function of the GPO was however also to *service* the post roads, for which purpose each road had a Clerk with a staff to assist him. Every road also had dedicated surveyors, who were in addition the eyes and ears of the GPO throughout the country.

As with the Post Office surveyors, the postal network as a whole was concerned with surveillance and security, and therefore with much more than the efficient passage of the mails themselves. Through the eighteenth century the postal network continued its old function as the eyes and ears of the state, collecting from its staff information on "all material transactions and remarkable occurrences".[19] In the eighteenth century the Post Office therefore served as a gauge of what was coming to be known as "public opinion".[20] This also involved the extensive opening of mail "on suspicion", and there seems to have been a considerable amount of interference.[21] In the early nineteenth century this operation passed to the Home Office. Secrecy and a reputation for probity continued side by side, however, as so often with the British state. The right to open mail was strictly guarded by the GPO in London and only the most senior officials could open mail on suspicion. This reputation for probity and for the privacy of the mail was, however, engineered mostly through the highly regarded institution of the Dead and Returned Letter Office,[22] rather than

---

[18] Todd, *William Dockwra*, pp. 19, 31, 53. On the volumes of the London Penny Post see also POST 19/4: Miscellaneous Mail Statistics, 1814, *28th March 1814, No. of Twopenny Post Letters delivered E & W of the Post Office for one day – delivered & put in*; also POST 19/36: Miscellaneous Mail Statistics, 1838, *Estimated Total Number of letters posted at every Post office in the United Kingdom founded upon an account taken for the week commencing the 15th January 1838*; POST 19/75: Abstracts and returns of mail items delivered and posted in the United Kingdom 1839–1855.

[19] Ellis, *The Post Office in the Eighteenth Century*, Ch. 5.

[20] Ibid., App. 11, "Freeling's Observations on the Press 1798".

[21] From 1714 the Hanoverian monarchs instituted a policy of close inspection and very extensive copying. They were regarded as innovators in the creation of intelligence, importing German experts to assist in this. This activity seems to have been highly efficient and characterised by considerable technical skills. Ibid., pp. 71, 74–5.

[22] POST 14/1, Bye and Cross Road Letter Management, Reports 1757–1826, *Instructions*, p. 30, and POST 61/5, GPO Memorandum, *10th September 1766*.

by any real openness about what was regarded as a state secret. Outside Britain too, what happened to the letters that could not be delivered became the litmus test of the privacy of the mails.

The very unusual if not unique legal status of the letter once it was posted reflected the character of the British state, for as with the balancing act of secrecy and probity the power of a strong central state tradition was manifest. For once posted the letter became the property of the Crown, unlike other national systems where it remained the property of the sender. The eighteenth-century Post Office, rather like the political use of "news" by the US Congress, also had a significant role as a distributor of official propaganda, which was sent as free state franks.[23] Nonetheless, by 1792 the Post Office was delivering free opposition as well as government newspapers and pamphlets, a process that had been gathering pace for some time.[24] Thus postal communications were linking into the functioning of the political system as well as the press, the Post Office network building aspects of these other networks into its own growing system as well, and as a result deepening its hold on the activities of society. This was apparent earlier in the introduction of the Penny Post system in London by Robert Murray and William Dockwra in 1680.[25] London in fact had a Penny Post some 160 years before the national institution of one in 1839. This operated only within London itself and was chiefly for business purposes. The government acted quickly to take it into the state system. Therefore the financial City itself can be seen as an important harbinger of the communications state, business as well as political networks being enlisted into the state postal network.

Penny Posts existed in other cities and sizeable towns from relatively early on and by the 1830s there were 295 of these in Ireland, 81 in Scotland and 356 in England and Wales, most of them of recent origin however. These pioneered a postal system not dependent on distance, weight and number of pages – the conditions of the national post – conditions which as will be seen were the chief impediments to change. The proliferation of the urban Penny Post meant that in effect there were two postal worlds, one for, and within, the cities and towns (itself chiefly for

---

[23] Ellis, *The Post Office in the Eighteenth Century*, p. 47. See also L. Hanson, *Government and the Press, 1695–1763* (Oxford, 1936), p. 116, and A. Aspinall, *Politics and the Press, c. 1780–1850* (London, 1949), p. 177.

[24] Ellis, *The Post Office in the Eighteenth Century*, pp. 49–50, 59.

[25] Anon. [William Dockwra], *A Penny Well Bestowed, Or a Brief Account of the New Design contrived for the great increase of* Trade, *and Ease of* Correspondence, *to the great Advantage of the Inhabitants of all sorts, by Conveying of LETTERS or PACQUETS under a Pound Weight, to and from all parts within the Cities of* London *and* Westminster; *and the Out Parishes within the* Weekly Bills *of* Mortality, *For One Penny* (London, 1680), p. 1. Todd, *William Dockwra*, p. 12.

business interests, and sometimes private and sometimes state run), and one – inferior – for the rest. In the early eighteenth-century network the state still had a limited interest in the local area and in interurban communications outside the well-worn routes.

This changed with the increasing number of what were called Bye- and Cross-Posts (cross-country routes) from this time, which meant that even if the urban areas remained isolated islands of cheap postage the United Kingdom as a whole slowly came to be organised in a network form.[26] In 1711 the Bye- and Cross-Posts were officially recognised, which led to greater government control of the network. This represents one of the most important developments of the postal network, extending regular postage between major urban centres, increasing its speed and in consequence increasing the general volume of postal traffic. Nonetheless the network was still by later standards limited, being mainly for business purposes, and slow and expensive between cities, and so not fully connecting the kingdom, particularly the rapidly changing parts of it; also those parts least easy to control, above all Ireland.

In order for Britain to develop as a united kingdom, new centres within the British Isles had to be established in addition to London. Perhaps the most difficult and the most necessary to set up was that in Dublin, capital of a quasi-colonial Ireland. The great technical problem was of course carrying the post across a very difficult sea as rapidly as possible, and added to that encompassing a relatively large land distance. This involved a plethora of technological changes: sail and steam packet technology; harbour development; turnpike roads; and improved mail coaches. However, the London to the port of Holyhead journey had been brought down to twenty-nine hours by 1828, and with the advent of steamships and the railway shortly after to a remarkable three-and-half-hours. A critical engineering achievement in this was the completion of the Menai Bridge in January 1826.[27] By 1840 Holyhead was the third largest receiver of letters in Britain.

At this time the postal revolution of the nineteenth century was beginning to get into its full stride. Clearly, this revolution was not an *ex nihilo* change. Nonetheless it is the limitations of the pre-reform postal system prior to 1840 that are striking. In the 1830s a Londoner still received mail from three separate offices, involving three different organisations: the Penny Post, the Inland Post and the Foreign Post. Islands of communicability the cities indeed were, for rates for post *outside city limits* were

---

[26] On Manchester see Calvert, *Manchester Post Office*, p. 13, also pp. 38, 51.

[27] Watson, *Royal Mail to Ireland*, p. 123, and see pp. 71, 79, 84, 87, 101, 104–5, 111, 121, 129, 151, 161–2, 209 for technological developments.

inordinately expensive. The rate before reform for a single-sheet letter was four old pence up to a distance of fifty miles, going up to one shilling for up to three hundred miles. A letter of two sheets cost twice this, and one of three sheets three times as much. A single-sheet letter to Liverpool from London cost eleven old pence.

It was above all the coming of the railways that transformed the speed of the post, and Manchester was the first city to utilise this system. The mail from Manchester to Liverpool was carried by the new service very early on, and by 1838 the London line was completed and mail travelled the entire distance from London to the north by rail. The extent of the change for Manchester after the coming of the railways, and the institution of the Penny Post, can be gauged by the fact that by 1865 there were five pickups and deliveries a day in the city, mail being collected between 5 am and 7 pm. In terms of stamp revenue, in 1858 the largest revenue from postal stamps in any British city outside London was that of Manchester.[28] However, in the 1860s the postal revenues of London were between eight and ten times those of Liverpool and Manchester (Liverpool, Manchester and Birmingham were the three leading postal cities after London). In 1853 400 million letters were delivered nationally, 675 million in 1864 and 800 million in 1870; plus, in 1871, 75 million post-cards and 125 million newspapers. Parcels, packets and books signifi-cantly added to the figures.[29] The sheer scale of the long-term national change after the institution of the Penny Post is quite staggering, as are the consistent long-term growth after the mid-nineteenth-century take-off and the spectacular growth after 1901, as Figure 2.1 shows. The total number of postal packets of all kinds sent is equally striking and is as follows:

> 1839 – 82,000,000;
> 1840 – 169,000,000;
> 1860 – 646,000,000;
> 1880 – 1,662,000,000;
> 1900 – 3,723,000,000; and
> 1920 – 5,716,000,000.[30]

In 1871 the German Postal Union invention of the postcard took off spectacularly in the UK, at the halfpenny rate some 75 million being posted in that year. Valentines cards enjoyed a similar popularity, as did book packets, samples and circulars. In 1870 the stamp tax was finally abolished from parcels. In the 1870s the number of letters delivered and

---

[28] *Postage Stamps Sold, 1858*, Post Office Archives.
[29] Robinson, *The British Post Office*, pp. 366–7.
[30] Figures based on *Post and Postal Services* by F. H. Williamson, POST 72/211.

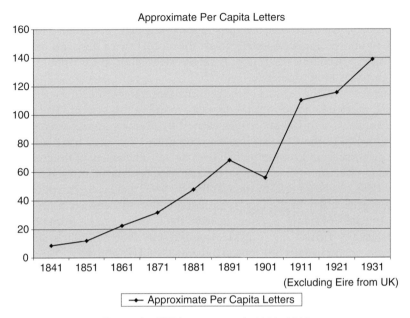

Fig. 2.1 Per capita UK letters posted, 1831–1931

posted *within* London amounted to fully half of all mail posted in the USA! Letter deliveries in London by 1908 averaged as many as twelve per day from head offices, starting at 7.15 am and finishing at 8 pm. Considerably before this time one could already post a letter home from the office in the afternoon saying that one would be late, and have it delivered well before reaching home.

It is the sheer density of connectivity in the British network that is so revealing. This is apparent in Table 1 (the relatively high density of offices in imperial India and modernising Japan might also be noted here, despite their low per capita figures). This can be complemented by figures for the ratio of post offices to people, although for a later date (1902–3):[31] by this time the proportions were: New Zealand 1:465, New South Wales 1:635 (the post office was most of all the instrument of white colonial settlement); followed by Switzerland 1:916, USA 1:1,017, Germany 1:1,482, Britain 1:1,858 and India 1:15,897. Obviously, in comparing these figures, precocious Switzerland aside, the greater size of Germany and the

---

[31] D. S. Virk, *Indian Postal History 1873–1923* (Indian Postal Association, 1991), p. 221.

Table 1: *Comparative density of Post Office coverage, 1883 (figures from the* Encyclopaedia Britannica, *1885, p. 585)*

	Number of letters and postcards to each inhabitant	Square miles (English) to each post office
Great Britain	41	8
Austria	13	29
France	17	32
Germany	19	15
Italy	7	27
Russia	1	1,829
Spain	6	74
Egypt	1	1,501
India	1	142
Japan	2	27

vastly greater size of the USA and India need to be borne in mind. In compact Britain one never had to walk far to find a post or telegraph office.

David Vincent has compared European postal flows and comparative social and economic development for 1890.[32] As expected, the countries of north-west Europe took the lead, with Britain at the top of the table by some distance for postal deliveries, and very high up the list for literacy levels (93%, only beaten by Switzerland, with Germany at 90% and France at 87%) and elementary school attendance (13%, this time behind Germany, at 15.9%, with France at 14.6%). However the really striking correlation is that between per capita postal deliveries and the extent of the railway system and the number of railway passengers. Here the British lead was phenomenal: in 1899 it handled half as many rail passengers again per annum than the US and Germany, and almost three times as many as France.[33] Britain was also the nation with the biggest postal organisation; in 1890 the employment figures for the post offices of the following countries were: India almost 37,000; USA 69,020; Italy 18,790; France 52,636; Germany 79,384; and Britain 91,002. Britain was without doubt the most connected state in the world at this time, so connected that

[32] David Vincent, *Literacy and Popular Culture: England 1750–1914* (Cambridge University Press, 1993), p. 47, Table 2.2 European postal flows and comparative element in 1890.
[33] Thomas J. Misa, *Leonardo to the Internet: Technology and Culture from the Renaissance to the Internet* (Johns Hopkins University Press, 2nd edn, 2011), pp. 112–26, esp. Fig 4.4.

people were now living their lives in networks that simply had to be controlled, and therefore in some measure be "closed", in opposition to the open nature of the network.[34] In short, people were living their lives now in "systems" of one sort or another, in which durability and stability were built in by technological means. Such systems were also becoming self-regulating or at least aspiring to this condition, as we shall see in the next section of this chapter.

However striking all this is it also conceals important developments. Firstly, national disparities: England and Wales generated far more revenue than Ireland and Scotland: of total postal income in 1874, 84% compared to Scotland's 9% and Ireland's 7%.[35] In 1854 the average number of letters per person delivered in England and Wales was 19, Scotland 15, Ireland 5; by the early 1870s this was 33 per person for England and Wales, 25 for Scotland and only 13 for Ireland.[36] These disparities continued. Secondly, class disparities: letters per person delivered in 1863 were as follows: London 48, Birmingham 28, Bradford 26, Brighton 48, Bristol 29, Cardiff 29, Leamington 57, Liverpool 31, Malvern 103, Oxford 36, Sheffield 16, Southport 52 and Windsor 40.[37] We see something of the social constituency of the new postal democracy from these figures: clearly it was the big population and business centres that led the way, but also the elite's educational centres, watering holes and residential enclaves – towns like Southport, Malvern and Leamington. At the other end of the scale were the new textile factory districts of the north: Bolton recorded 11 deliveries per person in 1863, Burnley 8 and Oldham and Ashton-under-Lyne only 6. Likewise the national per capita figures for delivery: only 4 in 1839, 8 in 1840, though increasing dramatically thereafter to 32 in 1871 and 60 in 1900.[38]

The postal society that emerged from the communications revolution of the nineteenth century was a class society, as will be seen more fully in the following chapter. The labouring majority of the population only joined the party after about 1900, and even then were less involved than the better off. This revolution reflected but also reproduced in new forms the *social* networks class consisted of. Once again it is apparent that what was rapidly becoming a postal system and not simply a postal network was folding within itself new kinds of networks. It prospered, or not, according to the success of this process. It articulated middle-class networks especially – social, economic and political ones – in a new way. In this process,

[34] Vincent, *Literacy and Popular Culture*, pp. 46, 49.
[35] Robinson, *The British Post Office*, p. 367.   [36] Ibid., p. 368.   [37] Ibid., pp. 368–9.
[38] Given in Vincent, *Literacy and Popular Culture*, pp. 39–40, also pp. 40–2, and Table 2.1 on p. 40.

class was not something that existed outside communication systems and outside the state. On the contrary, class networks and identities were the product of the state, in this case the communications state, something that has for the most part not been recognised in the social history of the state, nor the social history of class for that matter.

As well as social, regional and national variations the increase in postal flows after reform has to be seen in the context of the "underground post", the name given at the time to the vast unofficial postal traffic that had been going on in Britain for decades, indeed centuries, before the institution of cheap postage in 1840. The official postal system before the Penny Post was just too expensive for the great majority of people, and before the expansion of 1839 to the 1870s sizeable areas of the country were not covered at all, despite the local Penny Posts. This 'black' post was of great extent by any measure. In the parliamentary commission on the Post Office in 1838 the Secretary of the Post Office was forced to admit that between a quarter and a half of all UK postal traffic went through unofficial means.[39] According to the contemporary historian Justin McCarthy, "almost every kind of public conveyance" was used to transport what he called the "underground post".[40] People either used entirely separate means of conveyance from the Post Office, or they used the postal network in illegal ways. These took a multitude of forms, often highly ingenious. What was called "clubbing" was commonplace, people organising together to send bundles of letters, either officially or unofficially. Newspapers were regularly written on, or free delivery was exploited to send the virgin newspaper merely as a signal to the recipient. Within the law, the expedient of cross- and over-writing on letters was commonplace. Coastal ship traffic and steamboats on the Thames were regularly employed to transport letters "illegally", and "ship letters" to the USA were commonly sent outside the official system.[41]

It needs to be emphasised that this underground post office was not only extensive but deeply involved with the economic, social and cultural structures of the country. By far its greatest users were the business interests, of all sizes, including the very large, as apparent in the City of London. This use was totally unashamed, by users great and small, people simply feeling that what they were doing was neither wrong nor illegal. As has recently been shown, letter writing and use of the mails, especially the

---

[39] *Minutes of Evidence Taken before the Select Committee on Postage*, 1838, Col. Maberly Evidence, and see the report *passim* for details of the unofficial post.

[40] Justin McCarthy, *A History of Our Own Times* (London, 1880), vol. I, pp. 90–1.

[41] Derek Gregory, "The Friction of Distance", *Journal of Historical Geography*, 13:2 (April 1987).

underground post, was more widespread among the labouring classes than has previously been thought, though this was mostly restricted to their highest reaches.[42] The feeling that people had what almost amounted to a "right" to a decent post had by this time become common, and there is no doubt that the postal network itself played an important role in developing a civil society able to criticise the state. The principal communication corridors in the black post seem however to have been somewhat limited, namely those between the big cities and London rather than between provincial cities. Nonetheless, those connections within the areas around the big cities to a radius of about twenty miles were extensive. In the textile factory manufacturing districts in particular the carrying of post within these local settings had for long been a vital part of the putting-out systems that had preceded factory production. This system was utilised for personal mail also, though seemingly to a lesser extent, but it also took political form in the shape of the circulation of the radical, illegal "Stamped Press" in the early nineteenth century. What has to be appreciated here is how the new technological changes occurring in the shape of the Penny Post simply sidelined all this, obliterating a centuries-old and deeply embedded system of economic and cultural communication. This "disembedding" of old social relations was part and parcel of making the social technical which was evident in the technology of the new system.

The exclusions and inclusions of class can be compared with those of empire, and in this case India is the best example. However, it is first necessary to look to Ireland in order to further consider the exigencies of constructing a United Kingdom. Ireland as has been noted was very much a poor relation in terms of postal activity. Nonetheless, attempts made to maximise the speed and security of the postal connection between Ireland and the British mainland make it clear that Ireland was a vital strategic priority, if not as much as on the mainland a matter of constructing a mass postal community.[43] After Anthony Trollope's labour in the 1840s and 50s however, and parallel to his massive reorganisation of the rural mail in England, a predominantly rural Ireland began to catch up somewhat after mid-century. The network had always tended to predominate in the Anglophone and more literate south and east of the country, but in the west, for example, the remote parts of counties Galway and Mayo, and

---

[42] Susan Whyman, *The Pen and the People: English Letter Writers, 1660–1800* (Oxford University Press, 2010).

[43] Gary Prenderville, "*Correspondence, Power and the State: An Historical Geography of the Irish Postal Service, 1784–1831*" (University of Dublin Ph.D., 2006). Also see Cooke, *Irish Postal History*; A. R. G. Griffiths, *The Irish Board of Works 1871–1878* (Garland, 1987).

further into Connemara and the Joyce Country, the system from the 1880s penetrated in step with the development of popular education and the English language.[44] However, these developments were also in step with the protracted agrarian unrest of the region, in the form of the "Land Wars" of County Mayo in the 1880s. Security was therefore perhaps still uppermost, though the spread of education to which the post was of course always closely linked was in this Irish case, and to some degree on the mainland too, itself designed to secure the realm.

The situation in India differed in that the postal system was entirely outside GPO control, being part of the Indian revenue system and controlled by the Government of India. Ruthless technopolitical engineering predominated, and the system as regards its "public" use was chiefly designed for the British in India, along with at least some "educated Indians", those included in the very attenuated native public sphere engineered by the British.[45] The system highlights the jarring distinction between the actual practice of the Indian post and the liberal values of unfettered and universal freedom of communication. Although many technopolitical developments travelled from the empire to the metropole, this one moved the other way. The Indian Post Office, fully established in the 1850s and 60s, completely followed the lead of the GPO and the initiative of Rowland Hill.[46]

The various Indian vernaculars took a decided second place in the subcontinent, in terms of delivery and (revealingly) in the return of dead letters, where the vernacular was barely recognised. The authorities laid down that telegrams were only to be in the Roman alphabet, thereby disadvantaging native languages.[47] Of course, the difficulties of deciphering the great range of these languages were immense, likewise the parallel problem of non-English-speaking Indians having to process the English language post for delivery. The delivery problem seems to have been solved by an elaborate system of hieroglyphics conveyed to and by the so-called postal "peon" who was involved in delivery.[48] It was he who had to penetrate the neighbourhood

---

[44] See James O'Connor, "Aspects of Galway Postal History 1638–1984", *Journal of the Galway Archaeological Society*, 44 (1992), App. A for a list of dates and locations where post offices were established.

[45] Patrick Joyce, *The Rule of Freedom: Liberalism and the Modern City* (Verso, 2003), pp. 246–53.

[46] D. S. Virk, *Indian Postal History 1873–1923*; Nathanial Staples, *Observations on the Indian Post Office and Suggestions for its Improvement* (London, 1850); Devabrata Mukerjea, *The Post Office* (Calcutta, 1919).

[47] *The Indian Postal Guide*, 1861; the *Guide* started only in 1858.

[48] D. S. Virk, *Indian Postal History 1873–1923*, pp. 158–161.

in the form of the phalanx of servants that stood between him and the recipient of the letter (the Indian Post Office could never know for sure if the letter had reached its intended recipient). It was he who also had to negotiate the complexities of local religious and ethnic differences that made up neighbourhoods. The system was clearly poorly adapted to contemporary Indian culture and society: street naming and house numbering had not developed much, and there was therefore great reliance upon local knowledge and word-of-mouth inquiry. Indians were very reluctant to employ prepayment, addresses on envelopes were highly idiosyncratic, and envelopes were frequently filled with writing. In the later part of the century education departments began to start teaching the use of the post system in primary schools, but it is clear that the service was predominantly shaped for British use.

The elaborate system of getting the post to India (one of fast steamships, on-ship sorting, the construction of canals, eventually the laying of cables) once it reached the subcontinent was dependent on the on-the-job initiative of people such as the postal "peon" and the relative slow motion of transportation in India. Mail came across country from Bombay to Calcutta by bullock cart, although walking was the predominant form of letter transportation within India as a whole. These systems were often highly sophisticated, but the contrast with Britain is still striking. However, the post was used with considerable success by the British in the administration and governance of India. It was employed in collecting rents and taxes, providing money orders and savings banks (the first was set up in 1882) and for the provision of medicine (chiefly quinine). It also had a very strong military function: following the campaign in Egypt in 1882 "field post offices" were thereafter set up to service the Indian Army in its various engagements in and beyond the subcontinent. The system remained somewhat self-contained however: it was only in 1903 that India accepted a cheap uniform parcel post with the rest of the empire (it became part of the Imperial Penny Post scheme in 1898). Nonetheless, the network now extended from the entirety of the metropolitan state to the whole of empire.

In Europe and the USA technological innovation was continuous and very rapid, each nation borrowing from and contributing to the others technologically.[49] The British technological and organisational lead did

---

[49] For the various European Post Offices see the *Encyclopaedia Britannica* entry on the Post Office, vol. xix (1885 and 1905 editions); also www.postalhistory.org and the Wikipedia entry on postal history. The information in the first of these three sources is greatly superior to the others.

Fig. 2.2 GPO Headquarters, St Martins-le-Grand (GPO East), n.d., 1890s?

not last long. The reformed system after mid-century demanded increased international uniformity and integration. The outcome of this was the 1863 International Postal Congress, and in 1874 the Treaty of Berne, followed later the same year by the Universal Postal Union. However, what is equally striking is that within the context of shared knowledge and uniformity in organisation and technology, each nation developed its own system in distinctively different ways. These ways were mostly about nation building, something most visible in the built forms of the new postal empires, for example the spectacular Post Office headquarters buildings of the capital cities, like St Martins-le-Grand in London and the stupendous ones in Madrid and New York (see Figures 2.2 and 2.3).

Innovation and nation building were apparent in formal empires too, markedly so in the Austro-Hungarian one, the Hungarian Post Office being deliberately Magyrised in the ever-present attempt to

Fig. 2.3 Spanish Post Office headquarters building, Madrid, contemporary photograph

govern an empire of diverse and fractious nations and cultures.[50] In the German-speaking lands after the Napoleonic Wars there were forty-three different administrations fighting for control over the postal territory of what had formerly been the *Reichspost* of the Austro-Hungarian Empire.[51] The "postal wars" that resulted were a consequence of this extreme fragmentation. It was not until the 1850s that after Austrian and Prussian moves the old 400-year-old Thurn and Taxis aristocratic imperial postal monopoly was rescinded. Prussia's became the largest German postal system after this. After unification the German system in the form of the *Reichspostverwaltung* developed similarly to the British one, and it was this institution that consolidated German state power after unification. Bismarckian social reform and centralising political power crucially rested on the postal system for it was through the post offices of the new *Reichspost* that social benefits were channelled and social services provided. The postal system was

---

[50] See the exhibition guides to the Hungarian Radio and Television Museum, Budapest Post Office, and *Postai es Tavkozlesi Museumi Alapitvany Evkonyve, 2001* (Budapest, 2002), which includes an English summary.

[51] Information taken from website of Deutsche Post AG/Company Profile, 17 November 2010.

now completely under the control of the state, beating off potential private opposition after the First World War. Like the British system at about the same time it expanded into a whole range of new technological areas, including in the 1920s radio and television transmission. The first public radio show was broadcast in Germany in 1923, the first television transmission in 1928, and regular broadcasts only a little later. The parallel developments in Britain will be examined in the Conclusion.

II   Writing and postal technologies

Before turning to the technologies of the British postal system it is necessary to appreciate something of the everyday world of writing in which they eventually became so deeply embedded. In order to do this writing technologies are first considered, and then postal ones.

i.   Technologies of writing

> In times begone, when each man cut his quill
> With little Perryian skill:
> What horrid, akward, bungling tools of trade
> Appeared the writing instruments home made!
> What pens were sliced, hewed, hacked and haggled out,
> Slit or unslit, with many a various snout . . .[52]

In 1830 James Perry's "Patent Perryian Pen" helped establish Birmingham as the world capital of mass-produced, machine-made steel pens. These and the products of other city manufacturers flooded the market, in a matter of a few years usurping the near-two-thousand-year reign of the quill pen.[53] Thomas Hood's lines capture the inadequacies of the quill: the production of a writing point on the quill was laborious and very difficult to get right, especially for the copperplate hand then used. Pens might last only a week. For contemporaries the steel pen was yet another wonder of an increasingly wondrous age, "The knitting needle of civilisation" as it came to be called.[54] Birmingham, as opposed to factory Manchester, was the British centre of small-scale and less highly mechanised forms of capitalist mass production. Once again the model of technological development that mattered is seen to be low technology

---

[52] Thomas Hood, quoted in Donald Jackson, *The Story of Writing* (The Calligraphy Centre, 1981), pp. 133–4.

[53] Ibid., pp. 130–6.

[54] Asa Briggs, *Victorian Things* (Sutton edn, 2003), pp. 179, 182–7 on the history of the steel pen.

rather than high, that is the technology of the Birmingham model, as much a part of the British industrial revolution as the great cotton factory or the shipyard. Not that the consequences were any less revolutionary in this case: the new pens and nibs were cheap to produce, and could be customised for a vast range of uses and users. The steel pen has been called the world's first throwaway commodity. In this sense the new technology was "democratic".

The adjective also applies to the range of developments of which the pen was a part, and which it reflected as well as drove, namely the contemporary "March of Intellect". This was a contemporary cliché for the parallel development of mass literacy, mass education and a mass reading press and public, which came to a head towards the end of the century. These were inconceivable without "the knitting needle of civilisation". Like all revolutions this was a mix of the old and the new: the new technical order was a slave to old methods in that it had for some time to be able to reproduce the then established form of the written hand, copperplate. Copperplate itself became democratised. The new writing public that the steel pen ushered in eventually meant the development of new and more simplified styles of writing more appropriate for its use than copperplate. "Practical penmanship" became highly popular, and this seems to have spread from the USA to Europe in the 1860s, as a consequence of the very rapid development in the USA of the mail-order business in that decade.

A range of developments accompanied the mass manufacture of the steel pen and radically transformed the nature of written communication: new kinds of paper were developed adapted to the new pen, and new kinds of ink that were alternatives to the old acid-based ones, which corroded steel pens, did not run freely and smelt bad.[55] The development of aniline dyes from 1856 further improved inks. As will be seen in Chapter 5, the consequences for government of paper and ink now capable of new levels of legibility and durability in state documents were considerable. By the 1850s, pen, paper and ink had reached levels of development not surpassed until the coming of the ballpoint pen after the Second World War. The attempt to bring the ink to the pen, rather than the pen to the ink, in the form of a fountain pen, while meeting some technological success did not fully begin to realise its mass potential until 1900–1920.

On the other hand, the mass production of pencils developed rapidly if a little later than that of the pen (entering mass production in the USA after

---

[55] Jackson, *The Story of Writing*, pp. 133–42; David Carralho, *Forty Centuries of Ink* (London, 1904); www.inventorsabout.com; www.officemueum.com; Henry Petroski, *The Invention of Useful Things* (Vintage, 1994).

the Civil War, a little behind Britain). Germany and then the USA developed as leading world suppliers of writing tools, and of office equipment more generally.[56] In the USA Charles Goodyear invented vulcanisation in the manufacture of rubber, and the first eraser attached to a pencil was available in 1858. The French claimed the first modern mechanical pencil sharpener in 1847. Following on from the development of the pencil and the pen, an enormous range of inventions designed to meet every eventuality of domestic and office use ensued. It is difficult to do justice to the enormous ingenuity of this inventiveness, involving bespoke technologies now buried in the historical record and forgotten, but then of revelatory novelty. The result of this enormous explosion of little technologies of writing was to be felt after the inauguration of the cheap post in 1839.

It was not until the 1860s and 70s that a practical typewriter was developed, and again the USA was in the lead (the "qwerty keyboard" was developed in the late 1870s). A stenographic typewriter emerged after this time, also touch typing, but it was not until the last two decades of the century that typewriters became important for business and for the state, again in the USA. Even then, the up-strike typewriter meant the typist could not see the text when typing. After 1900 the front-strike machine made things easier and more efficient. Electric typewriters only arrived in any number after the Second World War, although dictating machines and copying technology developed rapidly from the late nineteenth century.

In the British Home Office, for example, it was only after 1887 that the use of the simple, mechanical technology of copying presses and carbon copies became widespread (it was introduced to the Board of Trade in 1850), reducing the need for human copiers. By 1890 only two typewriters were in operation, used by boy clerks, it being thought that "Lady typewriters" should not be subject to the unsavoury subject matter of Home Office letters. Nor could they be housed somewhere suitably removed from the Home Office male staff, gender segregation being the order of the day in office organisation. By 1898 all letters were typewritten, although a great deal of copying by hand was still done. The first telephone appeared in the Office only in 1896, and telephone use was not extensive

<hr />

[56] Henry Petroski, *The Pencil: A History of Design and Circumstance* (Alfred A. Knopf, 2000); Joyce Whalley, *The Pen's Excellence* (Taplinger, 1982); and *Writing Implements and Accessories from the Roman Stylus to the Typewriter* (David and Charles, 1975); Edward Tenner, *Why Things Bite Back: Technology and the Revenge of Effect* (Fourth Estate, 1996); also his *Our Own Devices: How Technology Remakes Humanity* (Alfred A. Knopf, 2003).

until a good while later.[57] Nonetheless, if of considerably more limited impact in Britain than the USA, a revolution in office technology had by 1914 fairly completely put in place the elements that enabled large-scale technological systems of all sorts to function, postal communications included. In Britain, marked by a combination of elaborate and sophisticated low tech and high tech, office and writing technologies and infrastructure were certainly sufficient to meet the ultimate demands of world war with considerable success.

From earliest times there has been a close connection between handwriting and the exercise of power. Three great traditions of calligraphy have been identified in relation to religion and political power: the Western, the Arabic and the Chinese.[58] The state itself has been seen to emerge out of writing,[59] for writing means that knowledge and information may be made durable and hence collected and organised in one or several locations, around which power subsequently coheres. Actual writing itself was for most of history closely guarded as the preserve of those who governed or influenced the state and society, whether the clergy, the state officials or eventually the men of business. Handwriting involves leaving a mark, literally an inscription. Historically this mark has been taken as a primary sign of authenticity, chiefly in the form of the signature,[60] for each signature is held to be unique. In India, where literacy was limited, especially in the period of British government, the signature was much less prominent in the activities of government than at home. It was there that fingerprinting first developed in the nineteenth century, as a major technology of identification for the British government.[61]

In the 1850s in Britain the evidence of handwriting "experts" was for the first time allowed in the law courts.[62] In the previous century, France had been the pioneering centre of a new science based on handwriting, graphology, part of which was involved with the use of writing in the analysis of personality.[63] Therefore writing was deemed to be uniquely personal. Yet handwriting was also de-anonymising. It testified to the unique individual but also exposed that individual to the eyes of the world, enabling the citizen to be known and traced, but also in this now

---

[57] Pellew, *The Home Office 1848–1914*, p. 94.
[58] Albertine Gaur, *A History of Calligraphy* (British Library, 1994).
[59] See above, p. 42.
[60] Chris Hawkins, *A History of the Signature* (Createspace, 2011); Jane Caplan and John Torpey, *Documenting Individual Identity: The Development of State Practices in the Modern World* (Princeton University Press, 2001), excellent on the history of documents, identity and the state.
[61] See above, p. 45, n. 91 on fingerprinting.
[62] Jane Caplan, research paper delivered at Manchester University, 2007.
[63] Renna Nezos, *Graphology: The Interpretation of Handwriting* (Rider, 1986).

public role to have entitlements to recognition as an individual by the
state. It has rightly been said that legibility produces illegibility, and does
not simply emerge from it. In the same way, literacy produces illiteracy
and does not emerge from it. What this means is that the achievement of
literacy and therefore legibility paradoxically create their opposites
because they produce an entirely new set of conditions with which government has to deal. It is only when literacy begins to extend beyond pos-
session by an elite that illiteracy becomes a political question and
frequently a political problem.

This paradoxical character highlights the importance of handwriting,
an importance which has not been given the recognition it deserves by
historians, certainly as compared with the attention given to the history of
reading.[64] Historically, the Secretary Hand of the sixteenth and seventeenth centuries developed out of clerical Book Hand, also from the Court
Hand that represented the other pole of power in earlier times. Secretary
Hand itself, practiced in both business and government, came to be linked
to notions of status and authority. As the *Universal Penman* of 1741 put it:
"Writing, much practised ... will insensibly arrive at Perfection and
Dispatch; and give in Writing what we admire in fine Gentleman; an
easiness in gesture, and a disengag'd Air, which is imperceptibly caught
from conversing with the Polite and Well-bred."[65] The same manual, one
of the most popular in England at the time, firmly based its claims upon
morality: it was publicised as "a compendium of moral precepts and
councils of prudence". The content of such manuals was invariably uplifting, in the double sense of the activity of writing as itself moral, and the
content of the material used in teaching and practising writing as being
moral.

School writing manuals in Britain over this whole period were concerned to teach the right way of sitting, holding the pen and moving the
body in the actual practice of writing. Manual co-ordination, the use of the
eye and hand, were instilled with rigour and rigidity (including the invariable attempt to "cure" left-handedness). In the British case as elsewhere
there was a strong connection between the state and the teaching of
handwriting. Prime Minister Palmerston for example was quite obsessed

---

[64] However, on writing see René Ponot, *De Plomb, d'encre & de lumiere: essai sur la typogra-
phie & la communication écrite* (Imprimerie Nationale, 1982); Roland Barthes, *Writing
Degree Zero: Elements of Semiology* (Hill & Wang, 1977); Florian Coulmas, *The Writing
Systems of the World* (Blackwell, 1989); Jack Goody, *The Logic of Writing and the Origin of
Society* (Cambridge University Press, 1986); Roy Harris, *The Origins of Writing*
(Duckworth, 1986).

[65] George Buckham, *The Universal Penman* (London, 1741), quoted in Jean Georges,
Writing: The Story of the Alphabet (Thames and Hudson, 1992), p. 150.

with handwriting. He worked long and hard at developing a legible hand himself, and was minutely concerned with the handwriting of his state officials. This is not surprising, for government business as we shall see was predominantly carried on in handwriting, something which long continued to be the case. De Vere Foster was Palmerston's Private Secretary, and it was he who developed a form of handwriting that was to be the model not only for the civil service and business, but also for the elementary schools which the state was increasingly involved in providing for the labouring mass of the population. De Vere Foster also experimented by developing a hand designed to benefit Irish emigrants to the USA. His Copy Book was in use in parts of the state system up to the 1950s.

Looped Cursive was designed to produce a simpler and more accessible style than the elaborate Copperplate. Nonetheless, the form still required the joining of all the letters within a word, including the capital letters, something it retained from Copperplate. It was taught almost exclusively in British schools until the Second World War. Eventually it came to be regarded as "the only real adult handwriting", something which reinforced its popularity and endurance.[66] As a reaction against this, so-called Print Script developed after 1906 as a hand believed to be more sympathetic to the child. It was based on the elementary forms of the Roman alphabet without unnecessary loops and flourishes, and without the joining of letters. Despite being as quick as its predecessor, in Britain it never attained the status of an "adult" hand. Round Hand was developed in British schools from the 1930s and was more child-centred, and by the 1990s it had become the most commonly taught hand in primary schools. Much earlier forms of Round Hand in the nineteenth century, not regarded as adult, were however regarded as suitable for women. The "hand" was the person therefore, especially in the class society of Britain where manual work – literally work with the hand – had the lowest status. However, the hand of the state frequently guided the writing "hand", quite literally so when the writing teacher took the hand of the taught, which he and she increasingly did.

As David Vincent has shown, compositional rather than just handwriting skills were taught in state education after 1871, although then only to a very small minority of pupils.[67] However, the teaching of writing and reading had gradually developed as an active rather than a passive skill

---

[66] On the various writing "hands" see Joyce Whalley, *The Student's Guide to Western Calligraphy: An Illustrated Survey* (Shambhala, 1984).

[67] Vincent, *Literacy and Popular Culture*, Chs. 2–4, 6. The following account is based on Vincent's work.

before this time, although it was still not linked to the development of the child's imagination. The use of "look and say" methods in reading and the use of better trained teachers were accompanied by a thawing of the prevailing anathematisation of the child's home environment and by the slow secularisation of the curriculum. After 1862 the Revised Code of Education put literacy at the centre of the curriculum. The new steel pens of the writing revolution flooded the state market.[68] Looped Cursive was an attempt to go beyond the old restrictiveness. However writing acquisition was for the most part divorced from the world of the home, also that of work, and despite the thawing of the old class hatred of the poor there was a systematic attempt to eradicate the popular culture of home and work from the school itself. For most, before at least the 1880s and then only partly, manual dexterity allied to the crude inculcation of religion and morality was the dominant experience. The state attempted to enforce a terrible uniformity on the child, with things only changing slowly thereafter.

For a minority of educated working men and women, writing was a key to the expression and development of an inner consciousness and an inner life. How big this minority was is unclear. The recent work of Susan Whyman has indicated how before 1800 levels of quite accomplished literacy in letter writing were achieved among some farmers and artisans,[69] and these were avid users of the Post Office network. Even though as we have seen letter-delivery figures for the "classic" manufacturing towns of the nineteenth century were strikingly low, the rate of increase in postal deliveries from this level was afterwards fairly considerable.[70] In working-class politics and social organisation, above all the trade unions and friendly societies, writing of both simple and developed kinds was vitally important. However, it seems clear that the post was not a truly mass working-class phenomenon until at least the late nineteenth century, when it caught the tide of increased literacy and state schooling.

There were also pronounced national differences in the teaching and acquisition of handwriting. Writing was profoundly linked to the obtaining culture: in Japan writing excluded erasure and repetition, and there was no equivalent invention to the writing eraser there.[71] Cultural value in China and Japan was even more inscribed in the writing hand than in the West, where the spoken word, as also in India, was comparatively more

---

[68] Whalley, *The Student's Guide to Western Calligraphy*, pp. 87–129, and on the twentieth century, pp. 129–171.

[69] Whyman, *The Pen and the People*.

[70] Vincent, *Literacy and Popular Culture*, pp. 43–9, 273–4.

[71] Patricia L. Machlachan, *The People's Post Office: The History and Politics of the Japanese Postal System, 1871–2010* (Harvard University Press, 2011).

significant than the written. Writing in China was independent of phonetic evolution and linguistic change and for this reason the character in
Chinese writing has had a vast significance. In an analphabetic culture, as
in Chinese society, the role of good writing and of being well read has been
immense. In alphabetic cultures handwriting was still greatly significant
and there is no clearer case of this than in its place in forging and developing the nation state in Europe.

Here Germany is a good example outside Britain, although the postal
system in Britain also formed the sense of national identity there too, and
imperial identity (as well as the infrastructure of connectivities that undergirded identities). Gothic Script had this nation-building agenda in
Germany, and as we have seen already the gradual amalgamation of the
many postal organisations of the German-speaking lands was of fundamental significance in this. Gothic Script was only abandoned in the
interests of another kind of nation building, that of Hitler: anathematised
now as the "so-called Gothic type", and as a product of the Jews, Gothic
Script was replaced by Roman in January 1941 as the Nazi regime
attempted to reach beyond German speakers alone.[72] Unsurprisingly, in
liberal Britain there was greater diversity of handwriting styles than elsewhere, France for example developing a national copybook for the teaching of handwriting in schools early on.[73] Even the USA is generally
regarded as having a more easily recognisable national style than the
UK.[74] Spelling reform was everywhere driven by the state, and it is to
the state that I now turn in order to consider the second theme of this
section, the technology the Post Office itself deployed as it strove to shape
its network into something like a system.

ii.   Postal technology

The postal system depended on technological innovations that attempted
to remove the postal network from the human intervention that had
previously characterised its existence, with the (ultimately vain) idea that
it could become a technically self-regulating system. Politically, this was
part and parcel of facilitating not now the powers of the sovereign but
those of a civil society supposedly capable of being realised without direct
government intervention. For technopolitical innovators like Rowland
Hill this was quite explicitly the intention, though for other less ideologically driven people the political motive was more muted. Nonetheless,
what I have called organised freedom now began to result on a mass

[72] Steven Roger Fischer, *The History of Writing* (Reaktion Books, 2005), pp. 281–2.
[73] Ibid., pp. 306–7.   [74] Whalley, *The Student's Guide to Western Calligraphy.*

scale.[75] The liberal state was rapidly taking shape, whether we think of liberal in the conventional sense or as the systematic technomanagement of freedom.

What were these technological innovations and when did they become apparent? It is impossible to discuss all of these of course, and I concentrate first on what arguably was the greatest transformation of all historically, the one linked with the coming of the railways, namely that associated with the 1839 Uniform Penny Post as it was called. There were two other major periods of transformation, those of motorisation and the automation of the service, occurring respectively either side of the period spanned by the two world wars.[76] Looking at the entire period covered by this book, as well as cheap and uniform postage I shall deal with transport, telecommunications (chiefly the telegraph) and finally the staff. The latter is particularly important, as it was in this period that the Post Office began to treat its staff as an object in a system, something to be improved, maintained and cultivated, rather than simply employed. In this sense, as in the civil service more broadly, human agency was made technical. Again it is often the little tools that mattered – stamps, postboxes and so on – and it was bespoke, purpose-built and in-house technology that was in evidence. To function properly the Post Office had itself to develop a whole universe of punches, stamps, inks, papers, bags, belts, paper forms, sorting devices, furniture, offices, transport devices and so on. I can only give a small selection of these.

The most significant feature of the Post Office in the period *c.* 1800–1920 is the way in which the service begins not only to deliver letters but to become a *universal* communications system, delivering parcels (from 1883, resulting in the renaming of letter-carriers as 'postmen') and controlling telegraphic communications (from 1870) and telephonic communications (in 1912, establishing, like the telegraph, a uniform system for the whole country). And then came the "broadcasting" of information and entertainment, in the early form of the BBC. It also acted as the actual "office" of the state, in transacting all kinds of social and economic state business, the state office being invariably right at the physical centre of communities. It controlled more and more of its operations *directly*. This was not a particularly overt goal of the Post Office, but a feature that accumulated as the services it received from railway companies, private telegraph companies and so forth were found to be inadequate or not those it required. Where it was not

---

[75] See above, pp. 5–6, 28–9.
[76] See below, pp. 313–14 and Campbell-Smith, *Masters of the Post*, pp. 391–3.

operational or financial concerns that drove absorption of other communication networks it was the government itself and its political
choices, although sentiment in the institution itself was usually quite
strongly favourable to public control.

Indeed, one of the most able of all senior officials in the Post Office,
Frank Scudamore, the man who drove state adoption of the telegraph
service and the savings bank, was of the opinion that state ownership
was a case of "the nation working for itself".[77] This expression says a lot
about contemporary attitudes: the sense of communal purpose in the
state as the expression of the nation, the value of work and of working
for oneself, so that the state was not seen as contrary to but as a source
of a personal independence that also had a marked collective character.
Here we have a striking and very typical example of how the naturalisation of the state, which I later consider more fully in terms of its
"learning", could lead to outcomes that if compatible with social liberalism also pointed to a sense of collective ownership of the state in
which the gap between state and society lessens, so that more socialised
versions of the state may emerge.[78] In this case, why should the nation
state not work for itself if others were not up to the mark? This comment
by Scudamore is essentially no different in spirit from the pride in the
state that motivated the radical and Labour Party sentiment behind the
post-1945 welfare state. It too was about independence through work,
drawing mightily still on Victorian notions of freedom. It both fitted
liberalism and pointed to possibilities beyond it.

However, as the next chapter shows, becoming a universal communications provider had rather more to do with creating capitalism than
socialism. For it was the postal system that, perhaps more than any
other state body except the Treasury, probed and shaped the market-
state relationship in new ways, structuring it politically while at the
same time preserving the fiction of the market's free operation.
Economically it extended its function to that of a bank in 1861, with
the replacement of the Money Order Office by the Post Office Savings
Bank. With over nine million accounts by 1913 and fourteen thousand
branches by 1900 it was the largest banking system in the country.[79] In
1864 it also provided an insurance service to encourage self-help
among the lower classes. It also collected state revenue from licenses
for animals (in 1869, dogs), and for guns, carriages and in 1902 motor
cars (and later on of course for radio and TV). After 1908, as in
Bismarckian Germany, the Post Office was also used to pay old-age

[77] On Frank Scudamore see ibid., pp. 161–3, 175–84, 197–8.
[78] See above, p. 10, and below, p. 311.   [79] Campbell-Smith, *Masters of the Post*, pp. 178–9.

pensions and the other new state benefits of the time.[80] As we shall see in the following chapter, the medium and the message merged, in the sense that the state was realised in everyday *practice*, in material, practical and bodily forms. Letters, parcels, forms, bills, money management, state benefits and so on, a good part of the social and economic management of everyday life in fact, *were* the state, the state *performed*.

The Uniform Penny Post   Firstly, however, I will turn to the Penny Post, in the context of which around 1839 a series of key technologies began to draw more and more actors into the postal "loop". The following passage is from the most famous of all reformers of the post office, Rowland Hill, the architect of the Penny Post and the man generally regarded as the founder of the modern postal system (it was written in 1837):

It is believed, therefore, that the proposed reform, if undertaken by Government, would not meet with opposition. Its object is not to increase the political power of this or that party, but to benefit all sects in politics and religion; and all classes, from the highest to the lowest. To the rich, as to the less wealthy, it will be acceptable, from the increased facilities it will afford for their correspondence. To the middle classes it will bring relief from oppressive and irritating demands which they pay grudgingly ... And to the poor it will afford the means of communication with their distant friends and relatives, from which they are at present debarred. It will give increased energy to trade; it will remove innumerable temptations to fraud; and it will be an important step in general education: the more important, perhaps, because it calls on Government for no factitious aid, for nothing in the shape of encouragement, still less of compulsion; *but merely for the removal of an obstacle, created by the law, to that spontaneous education which happily is extending throughout the country*, and which, even the opponents of a national system will agree, ought to be unobstructed in its progress.[81] [my italics].

This is the language of liberalism (and of course the language of class): it is only necessary for artificial obstacles to be removed for the spontaneous operations of society to occur, in this case spontaneous education. It should be remembered that Hill was first an educationalist, from a family of noted educationalists. This interest, and the Hill family clan, established strong links with the leading liberal reformers of the day – with the Mills, Bentham and Chadwick – and with the political lobby for educational reform and the "March of Intellect".[82] Beside the connectivity of mass communication was then a much older form of connection, that of family (the Hills were indeed a clan: they had a "Family Fund" and ran a

---

[80] A. Clinton, *Post Office Workers: A Trade Union and Social History* (George Allen and Unwin, 1984), p. 32.
[81] Hill, *Post Office Reform*, pp. 66–7.   [82] Daunton, *Royal Mail*, pp. 3–35 on Hill.

"Family Council" to forward their joint interests).[83] The claim presented by Hill is the familiar one that the reformer's scheme is above politics and religion, and so in accord with the natural operation of things.[84]

The liberal possibilities of the post for Rowland Hill involved the psychological assumption of the time, shared by the utilitarians but by many others too, that when the preconditions for freedom were set up the object of that freedom would be drawn mechanically into action. This was part and parcel of Enlightenment thinking in the late eighteenth century. These assumptions were satirised in a pamphlet attacking Hill, the gist of which is conveyed in the quotation that opens this chapter: as his anonymous opponent put it, "Thus in the opinion of Mr. Hill, *Man is made of the Post Office, and not the Post Office for man*" (my italics). Laicised in common sense as "The March of Intellect", or the operations of Providence, rather similar views characterised all shades of opinion, conservative as well as liberal, opinion very far removed from Enlightenment and utilitarian views.

The technological underpinnings of the mass, uniform Penny Post rested upon the prior development of several technologies. One of these was the stamp. The history of the postage stamp has an enormous and detailed secondary literature, much of which assumes that the stamp in its modern separate, adhesive form was central to the development of the Penny Post. In fact the modern stamp, and other systems of stamping that were also new at the time, were only one element, the graduated payment of letter costs irrespective of weight and number of pages being equally important. It is worth dwelling for a moment on the technology of stamping, however, for a series of concerted and inventive technological innovations were at a practical level quite crucial for the emergence of the postal system as, at least in theory, a self-regulating communication system. It was necessary in the bespoke technology of the stamp to maintain the following objects in view: security from forgery; convenience of public use; facility for rapid checking; and the expense of production and circulation of the stamps – all elements that would help facilitate a homeostatic system of communication.[85] To discourage forgers a system of extensive, costly and delicate machinery had to be established. For the printing it was felt a combination of embossing and printing at the same moment in production would present forgers with the greatest difficulty.

[83] Adam Kuper, *Incest and Influence: The Private Life of Bourgeois England* (Harvard University Press, 2009).

[84] For the counterarguments of the old order see the pamphlet of which the prefatory quote to this chapter is an extract, cited at n. 1 to this chapter.

[85] D. N. Muir, *Postal Reform and the Penny Black: A New Appreciation* (London: National Postal Museum, 1990), p. 79; also p. 87.

Hill agreed that "there is nothing in which minute differences of execution are so readily detected as in a representation of the human face", for which purpose the face of the Queen was advised.[86] The patriotic sentiment which might be expected to lie at the heart of the placement of the Queen's head on the stamps was, therefore, only a part of a process designed to prevent fraud. A human face was the most recognisable object and the Queen's probably the most recognisable of all faces. In turn, the stamp certainly made it so. Thereafter Britain was the only state not to present its name in some written form on its stamp. The representation of the nation state as the monarch's image, alone and unadorned, therefore drew symbolic power from the purely visual in a unique way.

Rowland Hill and his assistant Henry Cole adjudicated the entries for the public competition for the new stamping procedure – the fusion of the bureaucrat and the technologist is apparent, as with so many of this and to a lesser degree the next generation. Cole was in fact a competition entrant, and Hill and his family inveterate inventors. The Hills were among those responsible for the contemporary development of the envelope in a new form suitable for the new postal system, the outcome of their labours being the self-adhesive envelope, one also capable of being folded by machinery. The importance of this is fairly obvious. The letter could now literally be enveloped in a way that packaged up the privacy of its contents – and hence the privacy of the author – in an easy and convenient way. The consequences of this for an increasingly privatised subjectivity will be considered later. Economically, in mass-production terms, the envelope machines had important consequences for business, also increasingly for politics, in the forms of advertising and electioneering.

In the event, the plans adopted were not those of any one competition suggestion, but a combination of several. The adhesive stamp emerged as the most convenient and widely used form of stamping, and by the end of January 1841 sixty-eight million Penny Blacks had been printed and the instant popularity of the penny stamp demonstrated. However, of equal importance was the change to charge by flat rate dependent upon weight, the system already in use in some parts of Europe. Most importantly, as far as communication in general is concerned, the Penny Post transformed the way the Post Office was used to communicate. Before the Penny Post the vast majority of letters were, of necessity due to cost, one-sheet communications giving short, vital pieces of information (the well-to-do could write at length if they so wished). British letters were generally sealed sheets, paid for by distance and per sheet, so that the customer

---

[86] Ibid., p. 97.

was charged double rate for one extra sheet of paper. The introduction of the Penny Post had two key implications for communication, therefore.

First, the penny rate made use of the official post far more attractive. Much of the increase in postage following the introduction of the Penny Post was doubtless due to illegal mail being transferred to the postal network. This benefited the sender greatly as it would doubtless have travelled more quickly and securely through the Post Office. It also signified the Post Office gaining more (practical as opposed to official) control over the postal network. Secondly, the charge by weight rather than sheet and distance meant that longer letters could be written. This in turn enabled greater personal communication and transformed what was written in the letters. The opportunity was provided to move beyond the simple communication of vital information towards the more meditative letter (though illegal letters may have already been of this nature, and the letters of the wealthy certainly were).

At every step new technology was employed, in this case a technology of more exact measurement. Rowland Hill was also involved in the production of new weighing machines, one such machine being designed by his brother Edwin.[87] The creation of accurate machinery was essential to the operation of a successful charge by weight, for it was necessary that the public could not attempt to reclaim their money by alleging incorrect measurements. This would render the whole system inoperable. A considerable trade grew out of this shift. Some enterprising merchants not only made weights for the Post Office, but sold them for public use so merchants and others could weigh their letters before sending them.

These technological developments helped refashion the social. Letter delivery before the Penny Post of 1839 depended on local knowledge and face-to-face contact because delivery was dependent on the payment of costs by the addressee. In creating prepayment in much more convenient forms than hitherto the postage stamp in its various incarnations was a key element in taking the previous, and very high, level of human interaction and human agency out of the communication system. The system of cheap state postal delivery which the stamp facilitated served to link names to addresses and residences in a way which depended on formal and impersonal systems of information (for instance the commercial postal directories that developed so rapidly at this time, and which while specific to each city were published in uniform editions by national concerns). In turn, the Penny Post served to accelerate the numbering of

---

[87] POST 100/1, *Rowland Hill's Private Journal*, vol. I, 1839–41, p. 35.

house doors and the fixing of street signs, and of letterboxes on doors[88] (the latter was something the Hills also had a role in developing).

Bernhard Siegert describes the Prussian postal system of the same time in a very illuminating way, emphasising a shift away from territory as a defining element of the state to the communication dimension that I have described regarding Britain.[89] Graduated by distance, weight and number of pages, in the old system proximity and the centre were emphasised, what has also been called "the friction of distance". In the new system the permeability of borders and new centre–periphery relationships became apparent. This transition from what Siegert calls the "route" to the "relay" is apparent everywhere.[90] In the form of the bureaucratic and paperwork governance of the British empire it is considered in Chapter 5. In the Prussian example compulsion in the use both of the state post and the state school were long apparent, the two always being closely linked. The Prussian authorities were intent on making, as one put it, "every citizen an individual",[91] so that in helping constitute a new kind of cognitive subject the postal system enabled the bodily performance of a new sort of civic privacy for the subject. However, in Prussia this individual did not yet govern itself, as in liberalism, but was part of an intensely governed bio-political "population" (Siegert does not seem fully aware of the distinction here between different sorts of political subjectivity forming around this new configuration of the individual).

The Penny Post can on the one hand therefore be understood as conducive to the growth of privacy and to the individuation of the subject, enabling the fabrication of a free society as well as a free economy. House and person were attached, defining individual identity in a new way, just as the folded, and literally "enveloped", letter enhanced and protected individual identity and liberty. However, on the other hand, the logic of the Penny Post was conducive to the creation of the collective as well. Names were taken out of the context of the locality, circulating in a new sort of "public" arena. This version of organised freedom explicitly emphasised privacy and represented and consolidated a sphere of freely circulating information, yet for all the emphasis on privacy was openly dependent on transparent procedures, procedures not linked to local, and hidden, forms of knowledge. The cultivation of the individual self was intimately related to new forms of collective subjectivity, and these became implicated in governance. Perhaps the key dimension of the postal system in this regard was

---

[88] Joyce, *The Rule of Freedom*, Ch. 1.
[89] Bernhard Siegert, *Relays: Literature as an Epoque of the Postal System* (Stanford University Press, 1999).
[90] Ibid., Chs. 6, 7.   [91] Ibid., Ch. 11.

addressability. Individuals came to be known in terms of their addressability. As Siegert puts it, the address was delivered by the letter, rather than the letter being delivered to the address.[92] Eventually the legal definition of the person came to be defined in part in terms of this addressability. To be without addressability came to be synonymous with being outside the realm of civil rights and civil identity. In Britain "no fixed address" popularly denoted a situation where the core of identity itself was put in question, for to have "no fixed abode", as it was also put, denoted rootlessness and being outside the norms of society.

Transport   The Uniform Penny Post was developed at much the same time as the railways. The railway carriage of mail together with a uniform, cheap postage combined to consolidate the postal system as essential to the whole communications structure of Britain. The use of the railways embodied certain ideals about speed of delivery and the extent of the service that are implicit in many other developments. This is emphasised by the fact that in 1855 it was calculated that to transport mail by railway cost 10d per mile and only 2¼d per mile by any other method.[93] Clearly the willingness to sacrifice cost-effectiveness to speed shows that the rapid transport of mails was as much a postal priority as cost. The most directly postal innovation in the history of the railway however is the Travelling Post Office ('TPO'). This device not only allowed the post to be distributed more rapidly *via* rail, but accelerated this process by providing the facilities for sorting mail *en route*. It is this, combined with the speed of rail travel in general, which produced the great acceleration witnessed in mid-nineteenth-century communication. Before this development provincial towns had been served with the mail in a matter of tens of hours, or in terms of days.

The first equipment for picking up and putting down mail bags from a train represents a largely unconsidered although very significant development in making the postal network increasingly technical, freeing it from direct human intervention, and so making it more like a self-sufficient system. It was designed by Nathaniel Wordsell, Superintendent of the Coach-building Works of the Grand Junction Railway, who had assisted his father in building the tender for the Rocket in 1829.[94] Wordsell was a Liverpool Quaker, and both the son and the father of railway engineers. His was an educational world very different from the high civil service, that

---

[92] Siegert, *Relays*, Ch. 12, "The Standards of Writing".
[93] Clinton, *Post Office Workers*, p. 29.
[94] H. S. Wilson, *The Travelling Post Offices of Great Britain and Ireland: Their History and Postmarks* (The Railway Philatelic Group, 1996), p. 2.

of the famous Ackworth Quaker school near York, considerably influential in its own way but not to be compared with the commanding heights of Winchester or Eton (though another Ackworth "old boy", John Bright, did erupt into high politics for a time). Not that the Wordsells did not help shape Britain and the empire more than many Old Etonians. Wordsell is part of a rather different cast of characters than is present in most state history. This included those who created and ran state networks, from bureaucrat-technologists like Rowland Hill to the unsung and largely unrecorded people who designed and largely purpose-built the vastly complex technology of the Post Office itself, and the paperwork technologies of great bureaucratic offices that are considered later. The labours of these people made them every bit as much authors of the state as the leading politicians and bureaucrats. Their agency was vital in forming the state even if their formal authority and their real power over decision-making were often and indeed usually circumscribed.

Further refinements and devices were associated with the TPO, and by the end of 1852 there were 30 sites alone on the line between London and Perth. A return of 1905 shows that 171 of the 216 total sorting coaches had the catching apparatus fitted (see Figure 2.4). This was the

Fig. 2.4 A late-Victorian Travelling Post Office team (note the mail-catching device on the right of the picture)

peak of the TPO,[95] although the apparatus only ceased work in 1971.[96] In August 1838 a parliamentary Act was passed to compel railway companies to carry ordinary or special mail at times the Postmaster General directed, and to provide carriages for it.[97] The Post Office could place mail on any train, demand special trains at their convenience and ask for bespoke rolling stock (it is to Post Office initiative that we owe the creation of corridor connections between carriages). In return the railways were paid a fixed sum: over £1 million in 1869.[98] The extension of the railway, and thus the Post Office, into every far-flung part of the country, resulted in the further extension of postal services and post offices themselves into every town and, following Trollope in the 1850s, every village.[99] The railway network was incredibly extensive and allowed post to be carried to most towns of any significance. In addition the efforts of Hill and Trollope meant that a near-universal coverage was achieved, only the most isolated areas lacking a post.[100]

The railway postal service met with great success and its political significance was widely recognised. W. M. Ackworth noted in his *Scottish Railways: Their Present Position* (1890) that 'The Postmaster General, with his omnipresent mail bags, and his yet more obtrusive parcel-post hampers – I saw six huge ones landed from the Orkney steamer one evening last June – is a far more efficient representative of the central government than any Secretary of State for Scotland, and is doing more to cement the Union than any Scottish Home Rule League can do to break it.'[101] The Post Office by mid-century was the most visible aspect of the central state – it was not until 1856 that every county and town was compelled to have a police force, and even then these were under the control of local not central authority.[102]

Telecommunications   After the state took over the UK telegraph system in 1870, by the end of 1873 there were an astonishing 15 million

---

[95] Watson, *The Royal Mail to Ireland*, p. 4.
[96] Peter Johnson, *Mail by Rail: The Travelling Post Office* (Ian Allen, 1995), p. 13.
[97] Ibid., p. 10. This fixed sum was the subject of some controversy in years to come and was felt by the PO to be very high; however they had little alternative.
[98] Ibid., pp. 47, 48–9.
[99] On the extent of the railway network in 1840 and 1852 see M. J. Daunton, *Progress and Poverty: An Economic and Social History of Britain 1700–1850* (Oxford University Press, 1995), p. 312.
[100] Clinton, *Post Office Workers*, p. 31.   [101] Johnson, *Mail by Rail*, pp. 16–17.
[102] For the extension of policing and the response to it see amongst many others D. Taylor, *The New Police in Nineteenth-Century England: Crime, Conflict and Control* (Manchester University Press, 1997).

messages a year and by 1885 this figure had doubled.[103] Overseas telegraphs were however not controlled. The Post Office also took up wireless
telegraphy in the 1890s and by 1909 all coastguard stations had an office.
It was also responsible for the development of submarine telegraphs.[104]
The Post Office took over regulation of the telephone system in 1880
under its power to monopolise electric communications, and by 1911 was
running the entire enterprise after earlier operating it by licence to private
companies and municipal authorities. From this time the Post Office
controlled the entire telephone network, which it was able to run at a
considerable profit, controlled, from the 1920s, by an electronic exchange
system.[105] The importance of telecommunications is relatively obvious, in
that it provided ever more rapid means of communication, the indirect
but almost immediate communication of the telegraph replacing the delay
of the letter, even if in practice the letter was very fast. The instant and
direct communication of the telephone opened up a new era.

However the telegraph functioned to communicate only small amounts
of information very rapidly. Initially the telephone merely seemed to be an
even more rapid method for achieving the same thing and it was not seen
as the great innovation it became after 1910 or so. The early use of the
telephone was designed for rapid communication of information, perhaps
with more clarity than the rather brief telegraph. It was not until much
later that it developed into a cheap-enough medium to be a tool for general
long-distance conversation. So much so, in fact, that it was often not
considered necessary to extend telephone communication in the early
years where there was already a telegraph, unless the destination was a
particularly vital one. It was not until the 1920s that the full potential of the
telephone came to be realised and the telegraph really declined.

The significance of state ownership and direction was widely recognised. As Disraeli put it regarding the telegraph: "For the first time in
history the government proposed to enter on a strictly private
enterprise ... now it was overthrowing preconceived notions, as well as
the cherished views of our better political economists."[106] Even the free-
trade *Economist* felt that "By 1868 ... the distrust in State competence to
do profitable work is generally diminished. The Post Office is admitted to
do its work very much better and more cheaply than any company."[107] By
then the state had demonstrated in a variety of areas that it was capable of
operating systems such as the Post Office and the police extremely well.

---

[103] Clinton, *Post Office Workers*, pp. 33–5.   [104] Ibid., p. 35.   [105] Ibid., pp. 35–8.
[106] David L. Kieve, *The Electric Telegraph: A Social and Economic History* (David and Charles,
1973), p. 138.
[107] Quote from *The Economist*, 26 (11 April 1868), 412 in Kieve, ibid., p. 145.

Through *practical* demonstration the state had made a case for its authority.

By the end of 1872 there were 5,000 telegraph offices (1,900 at railway stations) and 22,000 miles of overhead telegraph line, 83,000 miles of wire and 6,000 instruments sending 12 million messages (already 50 per cent more than under the company telegraphs).[108] A step change in communication patterns followed this.[109] In the 1870s each telegraph wire could only carry one communication per channel. By 1900 the Duplex system was sending two messages per wire and ultimately four messages could be sent through each (the Quadruplex).[110] By the same year message speed had increased tenfold. By 1898 wireless communication had been extended to shipping. It was also eventually possible to fit the system in cars and aircraft. The potential impact of wireless telegraphy was immense, offering instant communication over vast distances with far less infrastructure than traditional telegraphy. It also allowed far greater flexibility in use, enabling mobile communication. One of the drawbacks of the telegraph was that it was a fixed system.

Between 1919 and 1939 the number of telephone calls rose from 719 million to 2.236 billion, with trunk calls up from 46 to 112 million.[111] The telephone handset had been patented by Bell in 1876 and the automatic telephone exchange itself, patented in the USA in 1891, was to lead all the wires for communication to one place from where any subscriber to the network could connect to any other.[112] This was a great advance from the fixed lines and roundabout communication of the telegraph system. The telephone spread telecommunications to a general audience in a new way. It was a far more flexible network that could connect any point to any other and the handset was small enough and simple enough to be placed, ultimately, in every home that could afford it. The telephone returned communication back to the private sphere, like the letter, where the message was transmitted directly between the sender and receiver from their own houses (or initially any other telephone point) using the Post Office only as a system of transport. The telegraph, in contrast, was a very public system where the user had to travel to a fixed point, of which there might be only one in a town, to make a short message which contained only important information and which was necessarily transmitted publicly through the medium of the telegraphist. However in 1920 all this still mostly lay in the future.[113] Nonetheless, by 1920

---

[108] Ibid., p. 178.   [109] See Clinton, *Post Office Workers*, App. 6, p. 623.
[110] Kieve, *The Electric Telegraph*, p. 234.   [111] Ibid., p. 248.   [112] Ibid., p. 200.
[113] See below, pp. 314–17.

the Post Office had a complete monopoly of the communications system of the UK, and this is another marker of how *systems* became embedded in British life: in the very monolithic nature of the state monopoly itself the citizen encountered a reality which appeared a seamless whole. As we have seen this whole might take the form of the state or of the capitalist system in its large-scale technological guise,[114] although given the steadily increasing hold of not only the central but the local ("municipal") state over the provision of public utilities, especially transport from the 1880s, the state was probably the strongest realisation of living in a system.

The postal staff The technical was as much about humans as non-humans. The telephone and telegraph involved the Post Office creating its own factories so that formally skilled staff now necessitated many different and new sorts of training. The Post Office's own Engineering Department was set up in 1882 and immediately built more than 740 miles of cables under London, eventually splitting the country into a series of engineering districts, each with its own surveyor, and with its headquarters at St Martins-le-Grand.[115] Instead of a network of persons and objects traversing the country the Post Office had now become a fully technological and engineering *system*, one which contributed to how the country was in ever new ways being technologically organised, standardised and bureaucratically classified. However, this edifice was built upon the solid foundation of a human staff that was for long before this time steadily being made "technical".

The changing qualifications of the crucially important letter carrier, among the least "skilled" but the most numerous of Post Office workers, reveal something of this, the period after 1850 marking a new departure. It was the same general picture for sorters, clerks and other low-level staff (see Table 2).What lay behind this was the desire to establish the most appropriate physical human resources for the Post Office (flat feet and poor sight excluded). There is a real sense in which the Post Office was selecting men of a particular physical character to slot into its system and testing them to ensure they were of durable enough material. Some of the most important and revealing developments in relation to the Post Office staff concerned the telegraph staff. The first was that a large proportion of them were women. By 1880 the Post Office was employing 5,611

[114] See above, pp. 36–43.
[115] See POST 76: *Post Office Engineering, 1882–1984* for a history of this service.

Table 2: *Changing qualifications for junior Post Office staff, 1798–1896*

1798	Letter carriers to be appointed outside the 20–35 year age range.
1803	Boys under 16 years not to do any Post Office duty.
1839	Clerks and sorters to be between 16 and 30 years.
1854	Auxiliary letter carriers not to be over 28 years; re-examination at the end of probation.[116]
1855	Letter carriers to be between 17 and 30 years; health examinations introduced by the Civil Service Commission.[117]
1855	Auxiliaries over the age of 28 when appointed will not be considered for permanent letter carriers.[118]
1856	Letter carriers to be no less than 5'5" (feet/inches) and must be able to lift two weights of ½ hundredweight each.
1857	One-third of letter carrier applicants were rejected on medical grounds. Their strength is classified as generally less than that of labouring men, but adequate; letter carriers' height to be no less than 5'3"; postmasters in that year were to be between 21 and 31 years when appointed.[119]
1858	The Civil service examinations are made more difficult for rural postmen; the Civil Service Commission wants letter carriers to be appointed through open competition, which is done;[120] the test is literacy, a physical examination and height is to be 5'5" or more.[121]
1872	Provincial letter carriers to be a minimum height of 5'4" and their chest to measure no less than 30".
1885	Provincial letter carriers minimum chest measurement to be 29½", weight at least 116 lb.[122]
1889	Men with flat feet taken as postmen.
1890	Short-sighted sorters admitted, provided they wear glasses.
1896	Minimum weight of letter carriers in the provinces to be 126 lb.[123]

telegraphists, of whom 1,556 were women.[124] This was not entirely novel as the Post Office had long been dealing with women as subpostmasters. However these were not usually employees of the Post Office in the strictest sense. As important as this, however, is the change the incorporation of the telegraph wrought on staff structure. The telegraph forced new employment techniques on the Post Office and changed the role of all its staff.

Clearly, the need to develop technical skills was one aspect of this. However there was no need for the Post Office to involve all its staff; this was a strategic choice (again brought about by a desire for economy). From 1881 it was required that new entrants to the Post Office be qualified on both post and telegraph duties as far as possible, at least at a

---

[116] POST 64/1, p. 975.   [117] Ibid., p. 974.   [118] Ibid., p. 976.   [119] Ibid., p. 978.
[120] Ibid., p. 979.   [121] Ibid., p. 980.   [122] Ibid., p. 982.   [123] Ibid., p. 983.
[124] Kieve, *The Electric Telegraph*, p. 190.

basic level. This training in both tasks was termed 'dual training'. The following year it was decided that candidates for jobs and for promotion must pass both requirements at every stage of the process, however basic these were at the lower levels. This was crucial, for it was at this point that Post Office work was definitively rendered *technical* for everyone – a milestone in the development of communications as systemic, the idea being that the Post Office would be taken into self-regulation, supposedly beyond the vagaries of human frailty.

Technical training for the higher grades required specialised instruction and it was with this in mind that the Post Office established a system of technical schools to train its operatives and engineers.[125] However, this was for organisational and financial reasons limited to the bigger post offices and never became general. Nonetheless, the nature of employment in the Post Office had changed and as such the organisation had changed with it. Working for the Post Office was now as much a matter of technical facility as personal presentation and good recommendations. While the establishment of the telegraph network involved the laying of thousands of miles of new line and wire and the use of machines that were fast and accurate enough to be practically useful, it also required that there be human resources capable of operating these machines at the desired rate while maintaining their mechanical performance. Part of the ambition of a self-operating telegraph network involved establishing a system that could repair and maintain itself to a reasonable level. Technically competent humans were, then, as much a part of the telegraph network as the material they operated upon. Like the apparatus, they needed to be fabricated; unlike for traditional Post Office roles good candidates could not be selected from any respectable walk of life, brought straight in and trained on the job. The kinds of skill necessary for the telegraph operator, and to some degree for all staff, were of a technical nature and required at least some degree of instruction and expertise.

By the 1930s experiments were being conducted to assess the way counter duties were operated. This work involved interaction with the public. Even the traditional Post Office skills of public interaction were being transformed into acquirable and accredited skills to be implanted in the staff. This was not an isolated practice, and indeed had long been the case. For instance on the introduction of the telegraph it was found necessary to utilise a system of messengers to carry the messages. The messengers were generally young boys, and were the subject of much concern. In 1891 a system for drilling

---

[125] POST 63/13, *Report of the Committee appointed to discuss the question of the Establishment of Schools, both for Manipulation and for Technical Instruction, and the question of the Allowances which should be given to learners in such Schools, and to Instructors* (London, 1870), p. 1.

Post Office boy messengers was introduced (from the 1880s the police had used military drill for recruits). One of the most public faces of the Post Office was being acted upon in order to generate a better relationship with the public. The messengers were to be paraded every morning when they arrived for duty, their uniform was to be inspected and they were to be put through a short drill. In 1892 a 'more regular' system was introduced.[126] The military was the model, as the following makes plain: "The physical drill for the Army, described in the Manual of Infantry Drill, was considered as excellent exercise for boys, and copies of the Manual were distributed to the offices where drilling was in force. In the first instance sticks only were used for the exercises, but subsequently a loan of disused carbines was obtained from the War Office and these were generally used, except by the smaller boys whose strength was not equal to handling them." As for the Post Office as a whole, when war came in 1914 the regiment of the Post Office Rifles was formed from the staff and fought at many of the major battles of the Great War (see Figure 2.5).

Fig. 2.5 The Post Office Rifles on parade (they are assembled in the yard of the Post Office's King Edward Building in London)

---

[126] POST 62/116, *Boy Messengers Official Drilling, 1891–1921*; also POST 63/13, p. 1.

The lives of Boy Messengers were drawn into the Post Office in more subtle ways than through direct drilling. As with the many large staff organisations of this type (considered later) the Post Office established clubs and activities, in this case for the boys to maintain their loyalty to the service, by providing a social link in their lives. The Post Office established and funded Boy Messengers' Institutes where the boys could socialise.[127] Boy messengers provided the foundation for the study Dr Bashford of the Post Office Medical Department made into 'The Physique of Young Londoners', published in *The Lancet* in 1931.[128] The Post Office Medical Department was the body most concerned with the physical wellbeing of the staff and acted to ensure that the labour force functioned to its maximum efficiency. A consequence of the Northcote-Trevelyan Report for the Post Office was a reconsideration of entry requirements. Age limits were to be 17–23 for all clerks and sorters entering the service and it was considered desirable to give potential recruits a medical examination.[129] A Medical Officer was appointed and the duties of officers from then on involved gaining the maximum possible service from the men. This was also in effect a disciplinary system to increase efficiency. Medical problems could seriously affect the Post Office as its staff worked in close quarters together in difficult conditions making them prone to epidemics.[130] "Efficiency" was thus increasingly at centre stage. To understand better this quest for efficiency it is necessary to turn once again to the earlier history of the institution and how it and its users were involved in making the technical social again after first having made the social technical.

---

[127] POST 62/116, *Minutes of the 94th Meeting of the Committee of the Headquarters Boy Messengers' Institute held on 6th December 1935; Minutes of the 96th Meeting ... 24th April 1936*; and *Minutes of the 98th Meeting ... 27th November 1936.*

[128] The article was published in *The Lancet* on 5 December 1931 and is reproduced in POST 62/116: The Physique of Young Londoners: Some Comparative Notes.

[129] POST 64/1, pp. 2, 8, 14.   [130] Ibid., pp. 32, 653–68, 752–3, 761.

3   Postal economy and society: making the technical social

> The Post Office is a wonderful establishment ... So seldom that the letter, among the thousands that are constantly passing around the kingdom, is ever carried wrong – and not one in a million, I suppose actually lost! And when one considers the variety of hands, and of bad hands too, that are to be deciphered, it increases the wonder.
>
> Jane Austen, Emma, first published 1815[1]

So far I have considered the development of the postal system and its associated technology. This has from time to time touched upon the economic uses of the Post Office. However, it is necessary to follow the economic aspect more systematically for it was not incidental but central to this state institution. So, I consider what I call the "postal economy" first, then "postal society". However, both are part of the same operation, the present chapter being concerned with that side of the process involving the uptake of the technologies of the state in the life of the citizen, which I term making the technical social, having in Chapter 2 considered the previous process whereby technology remade existing social possibilities. This chapter therefore involves the state as a learned reality, something which was the product of use and the realisation of what I have termed the performance of the state. This learning is considered in more systematic detail in the second section of the chapter, after the economic side of things.

Both the social and economic aspects involve the question of the relationship between types of political regime and types of technology. Fairly obviously, it is mistaken to equate particular kinds of political regime with a particular kind of technology, for instance postal technology. For example, postal systems across contrasting political regimes were often very similar, as were other infrastructural systems such as the railways. By 1914 most organised states in the world had comparable postal communication structures, complete with post offices, postboxes

---

[1] Cited in Susan Whyman, *The Pen and the People: English Letter Writers 1660–1800* (Oxford University Press, 2009), p. 1.

and cheap postage. Broadly similar postal systems fitted quite comfortably with different kinds of polity, whether old autocracy, monarchy, authoritarian and centralised democracy, or colonial regimes. With fascism and Stalinism too indeed: the Gestapo routinely summoned its victims by postcard. All that is required is a state capable of managing a bureaucracy that has some pretensions to efficiency and honesty and which can guarantee (more or less) the passage of information, people and things across its territory.[2]

Nonetheless, state materialities do have important resonances with particular sorts of political regime, in this case a liberal one. The secrecy of the mails was by no means self-evident in non-liberal regimes with highly developed communication systems, as in the instance of the routine opening of post in the East German political system, and also the widespread surveillance of telephone conversations. In parallel, in colonial situations the universality of access among the European populations was contrasted with a very curtailed access among native ones. So the maximisation of organised freedom seems to have been more in tune with the logics of some technological systems than others: as regards postal systems, these were very difficult to operate to maximum utility without maximum access, openness, trust and privacy, things more in evidence in liberal than in non-liberal regimes. As Andrew Barry has put it,[3] writing of the particular compatibility of liberal regimes and the telegraph, in an ideal liberal state there is no one centre, but instead multiple centres which will in theory enable the unimpeded circulation of people, goods and information. This will in turn enable the institution of a mobile and knowledgeable citizen, one with multiple perspectives. To develop this sort of state it is necessary therefore to secure free communication, particularly free circulation – so there is in liberalism a corresponding drive towards establishing the infrastructural preconditions for connectivity.[4] It can be said, then, that some technologies are more conducive to the

---

[2] My thanks to David Vincent for his help with some of these aspects of postal history. See his *The Culture of Secrecy: Britain 1832–1998* (Oxford University Press, 1999).

[3] Andrew Barry, *Political Machines: Governing a Technological Society* (Continuum Press, 2001), p. 12.

[4] Christopher Otter explores the relationship between liberalism and technology to wonderful effect in his study of light, vision and the political in nineteenth-century Britain: *The Victorian Eye: A Political History of Light and Vision in Britain, 1800–1910* (Chicago University Press, 2008), see esp. pp. 19, 260 and 259; and "Making Liberal Objects: British Techno-Social Relations, 1860–1900" in Tony Bennett, Francis Dodsworth and Patrick Joyce (eds.), *Liberalisms, Government, Culture*, Special Issue of *Cultural Studies*, 21:4–5 (July–September 2007).

organisation of freedom than others.[5] With this in mind, I turn to how the liberal state of freedom made the technical social in the economic sphere.

I   Economising the state and society

The capitalist economy and market were not "naturally" free and neither were they distinct from the state. The market did not exist outside political governance simply awaiting its delivery from subjection. The state can be said to facilitate the market but it is already clear that it went further, for it actively fabricated the supposedly free market, by law, by military might, by the fostering of economic knowledge[6] and by the creation of infrastructure, nowhere more importantly than with communications infrastructure. The same can be said for "society". The General Post Office enabled the disparate aspects of a free society to know and evaluate one another, thus aiming to make the economy and society self-regulating, as they should be and essentially were according to the fantasies of liberal governance.

There was a direct relationship therefore between the ideal of the free agent and the necessity for normative, standardised and civil conduct that would aim at this ideal. The idea and in considerable measure the material achievement of the Post Office was that it would create subjects capable of relating to others they had never met, so engaging in action at a distance with others, action both economic and social. It also refashioned the ties of friends and families as well as of strangers. Thus the liberal state necessitated the cultivation of subjects able to work by the rules of the postal game. One element of the liberal paradigm is of individuals acting by themselves, and in order for them to do this it was necessary that they be able to provide for themselves at present and in the future. This required them to exchange and communicate with a wide array of specialised services and to buy products on the market. In order to do this successfully they needed to be able to negotiate this impersonal and dispersed market, and the General Post Office was a major agent helping them to do this.

Michel Foucault has suggested that the essential element in establishing an autonomous art of government, one distinct from the unalloyed sovereignty and power of the prince, centred upon the "introduction of

---

[5] Also particular aspects of technology, such as durability. See Christopher Otter, "Making Liberalism Durable: Vision and Civility in the Late Victorian City", *Social History*, 27:1 (January 2002).

[6] Michel Callon (ed.), *The Laws of the Markets* (Blackwell, 1998).

economy into political practice".[7] He writes, "To govern a state will therefore mean to apply economy, to set up an economy at the level of the entire state, which means exercising towards its inhabitants, and the wealth and behaviour of each and all, a form of surveillance and control as attentive as that of the head of the family over his household and goods."[8] This establishes "the economy" as "a level of reality, a field of intervention", a natural process whose logic lies "in the things it manages and in the pursuit of the perfection and intensification of the processes which it directs".[9] Central to this process of the "autonomisation of government" was "the recentring of the theme of economy on a different plane from that of the family" and the recognition of the problem of *population*.[10]

Government began to have as its purpose "the welfare of the population, the improvement of its condition, the increase of its wealth, longevity, health, etc.; and the means the government uses to attain these ends are themselves all in some sense immanent to the population". The population rather than the power of the sovereign becomes the end of government.[11] Wars are fought to augment the powers of this new Leviathan of "population". Foucault terms this transformation of the "state of justice" into the "administrative state" the "governmentalisation of the state".[12] From the late eighteenth century in certain countries, especially Britain, this all took an increasingly liberal direction in which government became centred on retreating from direct involvement and allowing the immanent "logic" of the market to operate with a new degree of autonomy. A new but still an incomplete autonomy so that the government of the "economy", *pace* Foucault, did not yet lie "in the things it manages". The "economy", until the twentieth-century fictions of the autonomous market, still retained strong elements of the moral and the political.

Timothy Mitchell's work on colonial Egypt throws much light on how states construct markets, what he calls the "formatting", or we could also say the assembling, of markets by political interventions.[13] This happens most basically with the institution of private property, resting as it does at an ontological level on the state's employment and reproduction of perceptions of the natural world as abstract and uniform, in terms both of

[7] Michel Foucault, "Governmentality" in Graham Burchell et al. (eds.), *The Foucault Effect* (Harvester, 1991), p. 92. The essay is also in James D. Faubion (ed.), *Michel Foucault: The Essential Work*, vol. III : *Power* (Allen Lane/Penguin, 2001).
[8] Ibid., p. 92.   [9] Ibid., pp. 92, 95.   [10] Ibid., p. 99.   [11] Ibid., p. 100.
[12] Ibid., p. 103.
[13] T. Mitchell, *The Rule of Experts: Egypt, Techno-Politics, Modernity* (University of California Press, 2002), Ch. 2.

space and time (private property depends on dividing up the world in easily manageable and hence transferable chunks of space and time). This was for example evident in the imposition of these categories of perception in situations where they were not endemic, in this case in the day-to-day management of colonial Egypt. The colonising state in his example formatted the colonial economy as a unified entity on the model of a "national" economy, and this was facilitated by the creation of new forms of knowledge and of institutions designed to implement this knowledge. One of the results was the development of a new public for economic information and knowledge. The state formatted economic activity in such a way as to produce a distinct "economy", the very "national" boundedness and seeming reality of which in turn acted as a template for the further consolidation of the state. However, the nation is not the only such state "economic" model. This process went on at home too, in the colonising metropolitan British state, although Mitchell does not discuss this.

Equally or more important in assembling economies are the material interventions that occur in a particular political territory, especially those taking the form of infrastructures, for it is not only a case of the deployment of knowledge. Much of the power of these materialities comes out of their very materiality (as we have seen in relation to the "reality effect" brought about through the concreteness of the material artefacts and processes of technological systems[14]). This is more than just an "effect" in minds of course, for material interventions also operate outside how they are perceived, although the capacity to conceive of an economy as having material tangibility and what Mitchell calls "density" is inextricably linked to its material operations. We have also seen how the unique density of postal provision in Britain helped contribute to the sense of the state as an autonomous reality in the shape of a "system". The development of the idea and practice of the "national economy", in the metropole and the colony (where in the latter this occurred), in turn produced the "effect" of the state's reality. Therefore the "assembling" of the economy by the state that we see in this chapter contributed to the credence given the state as well as the economy itself as distinct agents. The assembling of "society" by the state had the same end as that of the economy, so that the economy, society and the state were mutually reinforcing. All three seemingly different entities were in fact part of the same political process.

I have described something of the transition of the postal system from instrument of sovereignty to an increasing element of economic provision.

[14] See above, p. 41.

The "Post Office Charter" of 1660, *An Act Erecting and Establishing a Post-Office*, effectively created the modern institution. The Act saw the purpose of the system as "the maintenance of mutual Correspondencies", remarking that "the well ordering whereof is a matter of general concernment and of great advantage, as well for the preservation of Trade and Commerce as otherwise".[15] Nonetheless, it was not until the later decades of the eighteenth century that the system was significantly reformed with the clear aim of creating a postal economy in mind. This idea of a postal economy will be seen in two somewhat different respects: firstly the introduction of economy within the institution of the Post Office itself; and secondly the extension of the process of "economisation" within society at large. Each was closely linked to the other. Obviously the Post Office was only one of a number of institutions assembling the economy in this way (the courts, fiscal institutions, Poor Law and health policy being among the many others). However, without the role of writing and its communication all these others were pretty meaningless. Also, in the form of the liberal state there has, as has been seen, always been a close affinity between free communications and liberalism.[16]

Taking the first sense of postal economy, within the institution itself, there were twin aims of economy in mind. Firstly there was the drive for simple economy within the service, in the sense of saving money, but there was also the introduction of the principles of political economy into the daily organisation of the Post Office, and more widely into the state as a whole. We have already seen something of this for the Post Office in the late eighteenth century marketisation of the employment relationship, and after this time the organisation of the Post Office staff as a carefully shaped tool of management.[17] This was not only a way of economising in the parsimonious sense, but a system of "economisation" in the sense of making the organisation work internally according to the rationality of the market. "Economical government" in this internal sense is more fully considered in Chapter 5, when I consider the daily life, and what I term the "common knowledge", of the bureaucrat.[18]

The promotion of economy in the form of "economical government" within the institution and beyond it in society is a story that in both aspects greatly concerns the Treasury department of the central state. So, before in this chapter turning to how this process of economisation was gradually extended from the Post Office as an institution to the totality of society, the place of the Treasury needs consideration, not only in relation to the

---

[15] *Journal of the House of Commons*, vol. VIII, App. 175 (12 Carl. II cap. XXXV, *An Act Erecting and Establishing a Post-Office*).
[16] See above, pp. 46–7.   [17] See above, pp. 95–9.   [18] See below, pp. 193–216.

Post Office but in its general significance for the British state. Within the inner circle of the high civil service there was another inner circle, that of the Treasury. This innermost circle drew its power from its control over departmental civil service appointments, and its firm financial control of individual government departments. The Civil Service Commission itself, set up in 1855, was in fact a sub-department of the Treasury. It was the body concerned with the recruitment and regulation of the new civil service. Commissioners had legal independence and made their own personnel selections, but recruitment policy and overall financial control were in the hands of the Treasury. The Treasury traditionally picked the best civil servants from the individual departments, whereas the departments had to rely directly on the civil service examination. From 1919 the consent of the Prime Minister to vital appointments in all government departments was required. However, as the Prime Minister had no direct knowledge of civil service personnel, in practice the Head of the Civil Service, who was the Permanent Secretary of the Treasury, had the power of appointment.[19] In addition Treasury people tended to become permanent secretaries. There was, therefore, a sense in which high civil service knowledge was ultimately Treasury knowledge.

Recalling Pierre Bourdieu, this very much looks like the meta-knowledge of the state that he writes about, the Treasury possessing the meta-capital of the state, the monopoly of the state's and society's other capitals being expressed in what was at once the most symbolic and most real of all forms of capital – the capital of managing monetary capital. This was the capital that counted. This bears greatly on the basic question of how the ensemble of government departments and institutions that at one level make up "the state" is stabilised and given direction. The question of how what I earlier called state "centres" are created comes up here. This making of "centres" is not at all self-evident, especially when we think of the state and society in the more fluid ways of process I advocate rather than in the old static ways of structure. What keeps the institutional state show on the road in the first place, then, is the question. This is taken up in numerous places in this book, depending from what angle of vision we view the state. In Chapter 5 it is given the closest attention, in the case of the India Office. There it will be seen how paperwork, paper, filing systems, the materialities of these and of the "centres" and "systems" that they help create, are collectively one vital way of approaching how the heterogeneous institutions of the state are held together.

---

[19] Thomas Balogh, cited in Hugh Thomas, *Crisis in the Civil Service* (Anthony Blond, 1968), p. 15.

The Treasury is another way, through its materialities too of course, its own paperwork, as well as its institutional controls (which ebbed and flowed and were never complete). Looking at the stabilisation of the state in terms of how the individual elements of its institutional apparatus were tied into the institutional ensemble of the state as a whole it is clear that the institution of Parliament represented the formal "centre" of the state, as it was "the Crown in Parliament", generally perceived as the "centre" of the "constitution", that was the bearer of sovereignty. However, it was the Treasury that connected the apparatus itself. Its role should not be exaggerated. It had a limited role in governing the empire, especially India, as indeed did Parliament. It also had little role in the work of the Foreign Office, which remained strongly aristocratic and Etonian long into the twentieth century (and immune to Parliament a lot of the time).[20] India, its armies and its administration, were paid for out of India's revenues and the Treasury had no control over these. Nonetheless, in most other realms of government the Treasury was as often as not a major part of what brought coherence to the state.

The years between 1660 and 1702 saw the emergence of the Treasury out of the old Exchequer as a distinct department of state. This increasing hold on power was due to the development of new material technologies, especially accounting ones, which established the *efficiency* of its methods for governance. Government became increasingly accountable, and hence knowable, at least in theory. If the foundations of Treasury power were laid then, these became more firmly embedded in the organisation of government in the liberal state of the mid-nineteenth century. The Treasury began to operate in tandem with the liberal principle of "publicity", the need now to make the workings of government "transparent".[21] Treasury controls went hand in hand with Parliament's overseeing of finance and administration, which involved the annual presentation of reports, and a new relationship with Parliament's Public Accounts Committee. Public accountability was refined, moving from the merely negative idea of financial propriety to the idea of standards that guaranteed the wisdom and efficiency of public expenditure.[22] At the same time, the secrecy government needed was continually strengthened by Treasury control. There were limits to "transparency". Before the Northcote-Trevelyan reforms, in the 1830s, the Treasury had strengthened the bonds of administrative secrecy by limiting disclosure

[20] Zara Steiner, *The Foreign Office and Foreign Policy, 1898–1914* (Cambridge University Press, 1970); Raymond Jones, *The Nineteenth Century Foreign Office: An Administrative History* (Weidenfeld & Nicolson, 1971).

[21] Patrick Joyce, *The Rule of Freedom: Liberalism and the Modern City* (Verso, 2003), Ch. 3.

[22] Henry Roseveare, *The Treasury 1660–1970: The Foundations of Control* (George Allen & Unwin, 1973), Chs. 1, 2.

of government inspectors' reports and the information civil servants could give parliamentary committees.[23]

Nonetheless, as an arm of liberal economic governance, fiscal governance, like "economical" governance in general, worked to produce efficiency by producing accountability.[24] This accountability, like "efficiency", was for most contemporaries never far removed from moral questions. As has been argued,[25] the political economy of the time, if in some measure seen in terms of the operation of an autonomous system of laws and their expression in a distinct "economy", was not separated from moral and political concerns. This separation from the extra-economic was to come later, particularly with the advent of the application of mathematics and economic modelling in the twentieth century. Political economy was still linked to moral economy: this was so most famously for Gladstone, with his populist programme of "Liberty, Retrenchment and Reform".[26] Fiscal governance in this understanding meant the inculcation of the good moral habits of frugality. Money in Gladstonian terms was by such habits to fructify in the pockets of the people. The controls of the Treasury, if having a moral motive and outcome, were nonetheless engineered through paperwork technologies of accounting.

Between 1850 and 1870 Charles Trevelyan and Gladstone were instrumental in making the Treasury a "professional" institution, something accomplished contemporaneously with their invention of the modern civil service.[27] Trevelyan's reform of the civil service involved extending Treasury control over it, so that the good governance practised by a newly created and "neutral" civil service would be guaranteed by the operations of economical efficiency. The Permanent Secretary of the Treasury from this time was traditionally regarded as the head of the civil service, something taking official form in 1919. Of course, Treasury control of the civil

[23] David Vincent, *Literacy and Popular Culture: England 1750–1914* (Cambridge University Press, 1993), p. 123.

[24] Philip Harling and Peter Mandler, "From 'Fiscal Military' to Laissez-Faire State: Britain 1760–1850", *Journal of British Studies*, 4 (1993); Philip Harling, *The Waning of "Old Corruption": The Politics of Economical Reform in Britain 1759–1846* (Oxford University Press, 1996).

[25] Frank Trentmann and Martin Daunton, "Worlds of Political Economy: Knowledge, Practices and Contestation" in Trentmann and Daunton, *Worlds of Political Economy: Knowledge and Power in the 19th and 20th Centuries* (Hargrave, 2004); Keith Tribe, "Political Economy and the Science of Economics in Victorian Britain" in Martin Daunton (ed.), *The Organisation of Knowledge in Victorian Britain* (Oxford University Press, 2005).

[26] Eugènio F. Biagini, *Liberty, Retrenchment and Reform: Popular Liberalism in the Age of Gladstone, 1860–1880* (Cambridge University Press, 1992).

[27] Roseveare, *The Treasury*, Ch. 3; R. A. Chapman and J. R. Greenaway, *The Dynamics of Administrative Reform* (Croom Helm, 1980).

service and of other government departments was in fact often contested and circumscribed, but of its central role in the new form of political rationality then emerging there is little doubt.[28] As Treasury Secretary between 1849 and 1854 Trevelyan (and his assistants) secured financial control by establishing a modern system of forward accounting and budgeting. The Audit Act of 1866 subsumed these developments and it has been said that after this time there were no major innovations in public finance until PAYE in 1940.[29]

The system of public finance that emerged in Victorian Britain, and continued well into the twentieth century, hinged on the idea of a "naturalised" economy, in the sense that the economy was held to be outside the operations of politics, subsisting in a state of self-evident (and highly moralised) truth. Civil service self-understanding, and its public promulgation in the form of a supposedly impartial civil service, were in turn sanctioned precisely by this operation of a putatively "neutral" economy. This is nowhere clearer than in the system of taxation.[30] The dismantling of the fiscal-military state of the eighteenth century made local government particularly important, as realised in governance of the nineteenth-century city.[31] The central state could instead concern itself with the regulation and administration of a dynamic economy, something which could be done by a small and expert cadre of administrators, together with the law courts and chartered professional bodies. What Martin Daunton calls the "delegating-market" state had by the mid-nineteenth century, through the income tax, helped create a "fiscal constitution" which established trust between state and people – at least some people, the kind who paid income tax, a highly influential but relatively small group. The income tax was introduced in 1842, and combined collection at source with self-assessment by members of the taxpaying public.

Institutional methods were also developed to maintain strict controls on state expenditure generally, "retrenchment" as it was called creating trust in the competency and efficiency of government. The fiscal system was designed to remove the claim that it favoured the interests of particular groups. The high measure of probity and transparency achieved in managing the new fiscal constitution seems to have impacted widely at this time. The permanent officials at the Treasury and the Inland Revenue

---

[28] Maurice Wright, "Treasury Control 1854–1914" in Gillian Sutherland (ed.), *Studies in the Growth of Nineteenth-Century Government* (Routledge & Kegan Paul, 1977).

[29] Oliver McDonagh, *Early Victorian Government 1830–1870* (Weidenfeld & Nicolson 1977), Ch. 2.

[30] Martin J. Daunton, *Trusting Leviathan: The Politics of Taxation in Britain, 1799–1914* (Cambridge University Press, 2001).

[31] Joyce, *The Rule of Freedom.*

were adamant that taxation should be above class and sectional interests, believing that the state had its own interests (the security of governmental revenues, the consent of taxpayers, the stability of the financial system). As Daunton notes, the influence of career bureaucrats in maintaining the new, liberal fiscal constitution was very great.[32]

Taken out of politics in this way, the "fiscal constitution" in the course of the nineteenth century contributed greatly to the perceived neutrality of the state and of those who operated it. Fiscal policy, it has been said, conquered the middle classes for the state. However, workers were influenced at the time too, popular radicalism responding enthusiastically to Gladstone's policy of "liberty, retrenchment and reform", the economic middle term of this populist platform being just as important then as the other two.[33] Economic affairs in other fields at the time also had major consequences for how the state was perceived at a popular level: this was reflected after the mid-nineteenth century in the state's acceptance of collective bargaining and its gradual and qualified rapprochement with the unions. It was also seen more widely in the new post-Chartist climate in which industrial capitalism was increasingly accepted at a popular level as at least dictating the rules of the economic game.

Labour was now viewed at a popular level as one economic "interest" among others in the new economic system of free-market industrial capitalism. As the economy came to be taken out of politics in this way, the state benefited because its personnel were now viewed as the guardians of fiscal rectitude, and more widely the custodians of a capitalist system that could when properly reformed be made to work efficiently and justly.[34] It is in fact from this time that one can trace the failure of the working class, just as the rest of society, ever to mount a radical challenge to the institutions of the British state. Politically, it also needs to be remembered that Chartism did not for the most part challenge the institutions of the state itself, least of all a Parliament it sought access to through the vote, but rather the perceived corruption of the state, something personalised in the central role given to a supposedly corrupt and privileged ruling class. As I have elsewhere argued at length, the "populism" that informed popular politics and populist sentiment was rooted in the struggle against the perceived "privilege" of the

---

[32] Daunton, *Trusting Leviathan*, p. 378.

[33] Eugenio Biagini, *Liberty, Retrenchment and Reform: Popular Liberalism in the Age of Gladstone, 1860–1880* (Cambridge University Press, 1992).

[34] Patrick Joyce, "Work" in *The Cambridge Social History of Great Britain, 1750–1950*, vol. II (Cambridge University Press, 1990).

governing classes, not against the state itself.[35] By 1900 however the
strains on the "fiscal constitution" system were apparent, given new
"welfare" and military expenditure. The eventual outcome was a questioning of the Victorian consensus, but then its subsequent reassertion,
as will be considered in the final chapter of this book.

In regard to the Post Office and its disciplinising by economical governance, the relationship between it and the Treasury is important to an
understanding of the economic assumptions that underpinned the system
as a whole. The Post Office was always administered as a branch of the
revenue and thus fell directly under Treasury control. As such, all its
income and expenditure passed through the Treasury's hands. From the
1840s the Treasury instituted a complex procedure for the introduction of
any new service or position in the Post Office, all of which, however minor,
required its assent.[36] Matters as small as the temporary hire of a bicycle or
the employment of a part-time cleaner were submitted by the postmasters
to the surveyors, who then sought authority from the Secretary in
London.[37] A survey of the Treasury Letter Books in the Post Office
Archive bears this out, there being a constant and detailed interaction
between the senior officers of the Post Office and the staff of the Lords of
the Treasury.[38] It must be remembered that Rowland Hill's postal
reforms were brought in while he was a Treasury official, and the general
trend of this reform can be seen from this perspective as an attempt to
mould the Post Office according to the Treasury's assumptions about
economic necessity and desirability.

In this capacity the Post Office's collection of statistics for the Treasury
was of great importance. The Post Office was more obsessed by statistics
than any department of state, partly because letters could be so easily
counted. This counting showed an inexorable upward progression in the
march of civilisation, unlike disobliging crime or health statistics.
Uniquely amongst government departments the Post Office both promoted a government procedure and defined its consequences, a wonder-
fully self-obliging way of proceeding that contributed immensely to the
almost universal perception of the incredible success of the organisation.
The Post Office established probably the most complex set of bookkeep-
ing procedures of any department, bringing its own bespoke technologies
into play here as in all other areas. The Treasury role at this time was to act

---

[35] Patrick Joyce, *Visions of the People: Industrial England and the Question of Class, 1840–1914*
   (Cambridge University Press, 1991).
[36] Maurice Wright, *Treasury Control of the Civil Service 1854–1874* (Oxford University Press,
   1969), pp. 2, 3; see also Roseveare, *The Treasury 1660–1870*.
[37] Martin Daunton, *Royal Mail: The Post Office since 1840* (Athlone Press, 1985), p. 274.
[38] POST 1, *passim*.

in order to establish greater postal coverage and provide an essential infrastructure for its ideal economy. It was however a source of complaint in the early twentieth century that Treasury control was excessively restrictive and was detrimental in that it reduced the freedom of the Post Office and led to excessive centralisation.[39] These contradictions showed up in all areas of Post Office activities. In the pre-1914 years the demands of business directed decentralisation, the demands of uniform government and of bureaucracy (and the pressure of the unions) centralisation.[40] The state was caught between the two, a frequent dilemma.

Turning to how this process of economical government was gradually extended from this institution and from the state to the totality of society, over the course of the eighteenth and early nineteenth centuries the Post Office underwent a paradigmatic transformation. Although the necessity to generate revenue persisted into the twentieth century, the service function of the Post Office gradually expanded until in the late nineteenth century net profit for the Treasury, while considerable, was only a small fraction of turnover. There are two aspects to this extension of the economy from the institution to society: the creation of an infrastructure that facilitated economic freedom; and the encouragement of the kind of subject capable of acting in this new sort of free society. I shall consider the first in terms of what I call postal economy, the second in the next section in terms of postal society.

Adam Smith suggested in *The Wealth of Nations* that "All systems either of preference or restraint, therefore, being thus completely taken away, the obvious and simple system of natural liberty establishes itself of its own accord."[41] The only role for the sovereign in this circumstance is "the duty of erecting and maintaining certain publick works and certain publick institutions, which it can never be for the interest of any individual, or small number of individuals, to erect and maintain".[42] The Post Office was one of these public institutions. Smith defined the Post Office as an institution like coinage, "for facilitating commerce" and generating revenue.[43] However it is clear that the Post Office had many economic applications, for not only did it establish the conditions whereby

---

[39] C. R. Perry, *The Victorian Post Office: The Growth of a Bureaucracy* (Royal Historical Society, 1992), p. 29.

[40] See for example the Postmaster General's Annual Reports, particularly the 10th Annual Report, 1864 and the business statistics collected in POST 17 and POST 19.

[41] Adam Smith, *An Inquiry into ... the Wealth of Nations*, ed. Campbell, Skinner and Long (Liberty Fund, 1981), IV.ix.51, p. 687. See also Graham Burchell, "Peculiar Interests: Civil Society and Governing 'The System of Natural Liberty'" in Graham Burchell et al. (eds.), *The Foucault Effect* (Harvester, 1991), p. 139.

[42] Smith, *The Wealth of Nations*, IV.ix.51, pp. 687–8.   [43] Ibid., V.i.d.3, also V.ii.a.5.

economic society could operate, but commercial society more broadly – where commerce implied intercommunication and civilisation as much as economic exchange. This required a system of uninterrupted *flows* of information, goods and labour. Without these flows the "system of natural liberty" would be unable to regulate itself. As we have seen, it is precisely the production of *flow* that is so important in infrastructure.

This was recognised as an aim by contemporary Post Office propagandists. Henry Burgess, advocating *More Speedy Postage Communication Between London and the Distant Parts of the Kingdom* in 1819, saw the purpose of postage as the improvement of commerce. Improving commerce would have the effect of "restoring us to general prosperity and happiness", for "Nothing has contributed more to this effect than those establishments instituted for the rapid transmission of merchandise and intelligence."[44] Burgess proposed a postal system for the rapid transit of "pure" information about prices and markets: "[t]o vary the quality of every commodity or convenience, to adapt it to the varying desires of the people, with a corresponding variation in its price, is a principle of political science recognised in all commercial transactions"; and "[t]here is no matter or convenience purchased by man, in which the truth of this principle would be so manifest as in that of a power to obtain quick or slow information by post".[45] In order for markets to work it was necessary that there be as many interconnections between their different aspects as possible, and that these would be as rapid and instantaneous as they could be made.

The main advocate in Parliament of postal reform, Robert Wallace, elected MP for Greenock in the first Reform parliament of 1832, claimed in 1833 that the Post Office should be "conducted on more liberal principles" and that free trade should apply to the transmission of letters.[46] Wallace and his associates, with whom Hill was closely connected, skilfully engineered a series of reports and enquiries into the Post Office between 1835–8, brazenly appropriating the machinery of state. Parliamentary Select Committees were packed with picked witnesses, including spokesmen of the Mercantile Committee, a business lobby group.[47] The Society for the Diffusion of Useful Knowledge was also mobilised, involving the "popular" publisher Charles Knight (who

---

[44] Henry Burgess, *A Plan for Obtaining a More Speedy Postage Communication Between London and the Distant Parts of the Kingdom* (London: Printed for the Author, 1819).
[45] Ibid., p. 54.
[46] Howard Robinson, *The British Post Office: A History* (Princeton University Press, 1948), p. 248.
[47] *Parl. Papers, Minutes of Evidence Taken Before the Select Committee on Postage, 1838.* Also Derek Gregory, "The Friction of Distance", *Journal of Historical Geography*, 13:2 (1987).

published Rowland Hill's famous pamphlet on reform).[48] The postal economy took the form of extending the infrastructure upon which the new economy depended. This meant moving beyond the letter and more immediate forms of information, also moving beyond writing alone. The first ancillary service offered by the Post Office was the Money Order. This service was provided from the 1790s and was a laborious but secure way of sending small amounts of money, banks dealing only in more substantial sums. The only other way to transmit small sums over a distance was to send them through the post, a risky business. The Money Order became a full Post Office service in 1838 and the cost was reduced in 1841 leading to much greater use of the service.[49]

The reform of the Money Order system represented a divergence of opinion about the nature of the Post Office and economic reform. The question was: which was more important, the service and infrastructure provided by the Post Office that enabled society to function economically, or the principles of economy that even Hill felt it was necessary to enforce throughout society in all its institutions if market forces were to be in genuine operation? Again the state was caught in the contradictions of its own making. Hill lost out to those willing to run the Money Order system at a loss. After this the Post Office became unashamedly a public service, complete with cross-subsidies across its different branches, something Hill was bitterly opposed to. Men like the innovative and enterprising Frank Scudamore pushed the Post Office in this new direction;[50] also Stevenson Blackwood, Secretary from 1880–93. He was aided in the early 1880s by Henry Fawcett, the blind Postmaster General and a renowned Professor of Political Economy at Cambridge. Some indication of the dense web of interconnections existing within the governing classes is evident in the fact that Fawcett was also deeply interested in the administration of India, even being known mockingly at Westminster as the Member for India.[51] Fawcett was a close friend of Leslie Stephen, the first modern university "don", whom we shall meet in a later chapter. Stephen was the father of Virginia Woolf; Woolf was at the centre of the Bloomsbury Group as was John Maynard Keynes, and so the story, and many other stories of British power, go on. Along with Blackwood, Fawcett pushed forward the parcel post, the issue of Postal Orders and a

[48] Rowland Hill, *Post Office Reform: Its Importance and Practicability*, 2nd edn (London, 1837), pp. iv–v and 8–9; see also J. R. McCulloch's remarks in 1833, cited in Robinson, *The British Post Office*, p. 247. William Lewins, *Her Majesty's Mails: An Historical and Descriptive Account of the British Post Office. Together with an Appendix* (London, 1864).
[49] Daunton, *Royal Mail*, pp. 85–6.   [50] See above, p. 84.
[51] Duncan Campbell-Smith, *Masters of the Post: The Authorised History of the Royal Mail* (Allen Lane/Penguin, 2011), pp. 185–8.

range of other measures designed to develop the economic side of the service, especially the savings banks. These were designed to foster the development of a certain sort of economic man – frugal, acquisitive, entrepreneurial – so that the shaping of the economic and the social were in practice indivisible parts of the same process, one particularly aimed at the small-scale sector of the economy.

In 1874 George Chetwynd, the Receiver and Accountant-General of the Post Office, had already suggested an alternative system that would enable cheaper transfer of money. Chetwynd had in fact also been an innovator in the Post Office Savings Bank system. He suggested that "postal orders" should be cashed by the bearer on sight at the Post Office, removing the complex and costly accounting procedures. Postal Orders were introduced in 1881 in Fawcett's period, providing an easier method for transferring the small sums that were to underpin family security and small-business transactions for many years.[52] These services were invaluable for the small business because the banks only catered for the exchange of large sums between major businesses.[53] The Money Order and Postal Order systems underpinned the small-business economy, in fact. This was highly significant, as in the 1880s "big business" made up only about 15 per cent of the national economy.[54]

These measures established the conditions whereby it was possible for people to work at a distance from their families, making it conceivable for labour to be mobile, particularly for temporary periods. This was all the more important at this time in that labour mobility was just about the only structural solution to unemployment.[55] Like the penny letter the Money Order and Postal Order allowed families and social groups to maintain contact with one another over distance relatively cheaply, permitting different parts of a family to be separated and yet all (in theory) still connected and financially secure. The idea of mobile labour and its attraction to places of scarcity meant that different members of the family with different skills might be required in different places at different times. Without a way to transmit money this would be impossible, and would thus provide a serious restriction on mobility, or lead to either the undesirable break-up of families or to the impoverishment of one particular section of the labour force, defeating the object of the system as a whole. The letter itself, in enabling mobile labour, helped retain the morally essential institution of the family. David Vincent has argued that the Penny Post was seen by some at the time of its institution as a means to

---

[52] Daunton, *Royal Mail*, pp. 88–9.   [53] Ibid., p. 91.
[54] Leslie Hannah, *The Rise of the Corporate Economy* (Methuen, 1983).
[55] Vincent, *Literacy and Popular Culture*, p. 37.

relieve the economic depression of the 1830s and 1840s, the Select Committee on Postage citing the way paupers "clung" to their parish, preventing them from finding work, as a consequence of their inability to afford the cost of postage and so communicate with their families.[56] The letter was also thought to provide an essential means for maintaining control over distant youth. Rowland Hill wrote: "May we not presume that many young persons of both sexes, who are continually drawn into this metropolis from distant parts of the kingdom, and are thenceforth cut off from communication with their early guardians, might, under different circumstances, be kept from entering upon vicious courses, to which the temptations are so great and the restraints, in their case, are so few?"[57] What was chicken and what was egg here is not clear, however, modern evidence suggesting that mobility bred improved communications rather than the other way around.[58]

The connection between the post and education is apparent in the first important ancillary service introduced by Rowland Hill, the book post, in 1848. This was a clear attempt to "civilise" the public, encouraging them to read and educate themselves, especially with the "non-political publications" that comprise what was called "useful knowledge" at the time, the kind of knowledge peddled by the Society for the Diffusion of Useful Knowledge and the Chambers brothers.[59] The Post Office Savings Bank was another service provided by the GPO intended to create the conditions of possibility for a free market. The Post Office had been involved in the savings bank system since 1807.[60] In 1860 Chetwynd, at that time a mere bookkeeper in the Money Order Office, building upon newspaper interest proposed a new system of Post Office Savings Banks. He saw this as "having for its object the security of money deposited in Savings Banks, and the encouragement of the working classes in provident habits".[61] Chetwynd is yet another unsung bureaucrat-technologist of great importance for the development of the British state.

Frank Scudamore, Receiver and Accountant-General of the Post Office, commented on this plan that "The facilities offered to the Depositors will be great, as they will have within easy distance of their houses a Savings Bank agency ... These facilities will be afforded in

---

[56] Ibid.   [57] Ibid.
[58] On the role of mass conscription and emigration in Europe, see Martyn Lyons, *Readers and Society in Nineteenth-century France: Workers, Women, Peasants* (Palgrave Macmillan, 2001).
[59] See James Kay Shuttleworth, cited in David Vincent, *Literacy and Popular Culture*, p. 6.
[60] H. O. Horne, *A History of Savings Banks* (Oxford University Press, 1947), p. 168.
[61] POST 75/2: 7 *Reports, Minutes and Memoranda Explanatory of The System of Post Office Savings Banks* (London: HMSO, 1871).

districts which at present have few Savings Banks", and even where they were available the Post Office system would probably be preferred "because they will afford, what other Savings Banks do not afford, complete security to the Depositors".[62] It was suggested that this would attract "a great number of persons who have never yet made use of Savings Banks".[63] He was right. The scheme was quickly introduced the following year and Gladstone claimed that it was one of the six government achievements of which he was most proud given the results it achieved.[64] Its enormous extent has already been discussed.[65]

The Post Office then extended this provision to insurance schemes, which provided for the individual or the family in case of injury or death.[66] A similar development in the postal infrastructure was the pattern post. This began in 1863 under business pressure. The pattern post was in effect a parcel post for the transmission of samples of one's product with no intrinsic value of their own. This enabled companies to advertise their products more effectively and to reduce costs by removing the need for representatives to travel or post large items at high cost to demonstrate their wares.[67] The parcel post itself was a quite crucial dimension of infrastructure: it involved a vast amount of material reorganisation in the Post Office to accommodate the enormous number, size and bulk of parcels. Again, bespoke technology to handle unprecedented and unforeseen circumstances was much in evidence. The result was the first parcel post to India in 1885, followed by the first to Europe in 1886. These parcels seem to have carried just about everything: the author remembers London childhood Christmases in the 1950s when a large turkey would arrive in the post from the west of Ireland. The fact that some part of the anatomy of the bird would frequently be sticking out of the parcel seemed not to offend the postman in the slightest, and dinner was delivered to the front doorstep as a matter of unremarked fact. The parcel post completely transformed the possibilities for commercial postage, especially in the shape of the mail-order business. On the establishment of the parcels service letter carriers were renamed "postmen".[68]

Turning to the major structural changes taking place in the economy over the nineteenth and twentieth centuries it is clear that many of them would have been impossible without the postal service. Although these

---

[62] POST 75/2: 20.   [63] Ibid.   [64] Horne, *A History of Savings Banks*, p. 181.
[65] See above, pp. 84–5.
[66] On insurance see Nikolas Rose, *Powers of Freedom: Reframing Political Thought* (Cambridge University Press, 1999), pp. 80, 81.
[67] Daunton, Royal Mail, p. 56; and for a history of these, C. A. King, *Historical Summaries of Post Office Services* (London, 1906).
[68] Daunton, ibid., p. 10.

developments could not have been anticipated by the postal reformers, nonetheless they were a consequence of their assumptions about the nature of the market. The importance of the postal system for the small business sector has been seen, and micro-capitalism's importance in the economy as a whole. The system of Smith's "invisible hand", it is argued, was changed from the late nineteenth century into the "visible hand"[69] of managerial capitalism, which saw the creation of the modern corporation. The paradigmatic study of the emergence of big business and the "culture of management" understands this process to be driven by the communications revolution as much as by the transport one. The divorce of ownership and control in managerial capitalism that characterises twentieth-century commerce generally also occurred in Britain, reaching its height in the 1920s.[70] The Post Office was central to this, through the uniform postal rate and even more so the telegraph. Cheap rates and certain communications greatly facilitated long-distance business communication.[71] In particular, as business became more complex and more specialised, in order to run a successful enterprise it was necessary to co-ordinate a great range of different services, products and markets. Rapid communication and distribution was essential in this.

The business world and the liberal state were symbiotically related in terms of bureaucratic organisation and the powers inherent in organisational techniques and technology, both sides freely borrowing from one another, historically the state being in the van in the nineteenth century and business in the twentieth. This was apparent in the USA as well as the UK, the large railway companies of the USA adapting the numerical registration of documents practised in Whitehall departmental registries at the time. State bureaucracy greatly shaped early corporate capitalism, with its top-down, de-individualised model of control, each strata of management governing its own behaviour according to clear rules, and with open lines of communication and accurate, copious record-keeping. The "expert" movement for office mechanisation in UK administration as it developed from the early twentieth century was on the other hand influenced by notions of systematic management coming from the USA,

---

[69] See A. D. Chandler Jr, *Strategy and Structure: Chapters in Industrial Enterprise* (MIT Press, 1962).

[70] Leslie Hannah, "Visible and Invisible Hands in Great Britain" in A. D. Chandler and H. Daerns (eds.), *Managerial Hierarchies: Comparative Perspectives on the Rise of the Modern Industrial Enterprise* (Harvard University Press, 1980), pp. 41, 42.

[71] Chandler Jr, *Strategy and Structure*, pp. 195–6; *The Visible Hand: The Managerial Revolution in American Business* (Harvard University Press, 1977); C. Lee, "The Service Industries" in R. Floud and D. McLoskey (eds.), *The Economic History of Britain since 1700*, 2nd edn, vol. II: 1860–1939 (Cambridge University Press, 1994).

and it incorporated these ideas into its model of British administration thereafter.[72]

The various postal services were particularly useful to individual industries, the telegraph being most influential in the trades of cotton, corn and perishable goods, particularly fish, fruit and vegetables. It was also important in shipbuilding, insurance and the metal trades.[73] In the mid-1850s it appears that 50% of telegraph messages related to the Stock Exchange, 37% were commercial and only 13% related to family or personal business.[74] International stock exchanges would not have happened without the telegraph. The press utilised the telegraph, and business utilised the press. The Press Association was formed in 1865 to lobby the telegraph companies for lower rates, receiving a subsidised service until the 1950s.[75] Large companies covering a national market, provincial and national stock exchanges, insurance and ship-broking, the police and fire services, and international trading as a whole also benefited.[76]

However, the structure of business was social and cultural as well as economic, and as H. L. Malchow has noted, "The commercial middle class was in fact becoming a national community in the three or four generations from the Industrial Revolution to the First World War."[77] Leonore Davidoff has argued that in the late eighteenth century there were only 3–400 politically notable families in Britain. By the end of the nineteenth century this "elite" had increased to 4,000,[78] and business was increasingly integrated within it. The large business class itself also increased but tended toward "a cultural homogeneity as sharp regional identities – small town origins, language and manners, and religious particularisms – merged. Similarity of enterprise, the growth and concentration of businesses, intermarriage and common schooling had their effect."[79] This was in good measure driven by the relationship between the culture of the letter and that of business. The letter was central to the creation of the new kinds of business self emerging from the business system. As Malchow observes,

[72] Jonathan Agar, *The Government Machine: A Revolutionary History of the Computer* (MIT Press, 2003).

[73] Jeffrey L. Kieve, *The Electric Telegraph: A Social and Economic History* (David and Charles, 1973), pp. 236–7.

[74] Ibid., p. 119.   [75] Ibid., pp. 216–7, 228.

[76] Ibid., pp. 217, 236–8, 245; and pp. 239–40 on the press.

[77] H. L. Malchow, *Gentlemen Capitalists: The Social and Political World of the Victorian Businessman* (Macmillan, 1991), p. 6.

[78] See Leonore Davidoff, *The Best Circles* (Ebury Press, 1986), pp. 2, 61.

[79] Malchow, *Gentlemen Capitalists*, pp. 1–2.

The respectable bourgeois often used the written word as a way of communicating that gave the appearance of intimacy yet was safely and distantly controlled – in which the "authorised version" of self could be presented. Diaries were written to be read and perhaps published, letters conveyed both surface information and much else – in the coded formulas of expression, the black borders, the feel and costliness of the paper, the crests suggestive of an heraldic authority, sometimes not perhaps possessed. The very act of writing contained a message which is both personal and public – the self-importance of the broad and hasty strokes of the businessman's pen; a spinster aunt carefully crossing her letters . . . determined not only to save paper but to convey to nephews and nieces the virtue of economy.[80]

This distanced presentation of the self was an important aspect of late-nineteenth-century communication in general, where the increased scale of social and commercial transactions meant that the kind of face-to-face deals and interaction common in earlier generations, between people who were generally known to one another personally, were becoming more a thing of the past.

As has been seen, in imperial terms the Indian economy, like the Egyptian one, similarly saw the "formatting", or assembling, of markets by political interventions. This was part and parcel of the global role of Britain and its place as the chief power in telegraphic communication. In the third quarter of the century the telegraphic cable was extended to Europe, to the Ottoman Empire and then to Africa and India. This was mostly the activity of private companies, driven by the market opportunities that the state opened up for them. The topmost levels of the Indian administration were directly involved,[81] although unlike in Britain early government control gave way to private enterprise. The Eastern Telegraph Company was the greatest beneficiary, becoming one of the first true global corporations. It dominated the world market to the interwar years and at one time controlled 40 per cent of the world's telegraphs.[82]

II   Postal society: learning the state

If people were to be "freed" in the realms of the market this was also so in civil society. Yet the "freeing" of these zones was accompanied by the invention of a whole series of attempts to shape and manage conduct within them in desirable ways. On the one hand, the public activities of

[80] Ibid.
[81] Headrick, *The Tentacles of Progress: Technology Transfer in the Age of Imperialism, 1850–1940* (Oxford University Press, 1988), Ch. 4.
[82] Dwayne R. Wiseck and Robert M. Pike, *Communications and Empire: Media, Markets and Globalization 1860–1930* (Duke University Press, 2007), esp. Ch. 1.

free citizens were to be regulated by codes of civility, reason and order-liness. On the other, the private conduct of these citizens was to be civilised by "equipping them with languages and techniques of self-understanding and self-mastery".[83] As well as being one of the agents that facilitated commerce and industry, the Post Office was therefore also involved in the creation of the kind of subjects capable of existing and acting freely. The most crucial aspect of this was the ability to cultivate ethical subjects capable of self-subjection. The act of letter writing was itself an important aspect of this cultivation of self and external awareness.

One of the particular features of the Post Office we have identified is the way it acts to extend the connections between the state and the citizen, establishing its presence in every town and most villages in the country, embedding itself thoroughly in the practice of daily life. As connections were established over greater distance, the state and its systems of com-munication became essential to more and more aspects of the citizen's life. The state and its communications infrastructure were engineered into the lives of its citizens to the extent that much of the life of the nation came to depend upon its services. The transition from impermanent to perma-nent postal connectedness was of great significance in this regard. It meant that the network was always available, ever present, in the sense that postal communications are always open for use, even if in practice their use may be limited. The correspondent is in theory always accessible, even if the letter is not written. The routes, links and stations of the network are always there. This is in contradistinction to the sending of individual utterances by a messenger or to delivery that depended on the vagaries of personal inquiry, as in the system before the postal reforms of the mid-nineteenth century. In this sense therefore, as well as the others considered already, the network took on the shape of a system, something in fact decidedly abstract even if grounded in the concreteness of artefacts. The postal network in this form began to loom over contemporary life as a strange kind of entity, invisible and abstract, but real and concrete at the same time.

As has been seen, in the transition from impermanent postal connect-edness to permanent connectedness it was the development of address-ability that mattered. Addressability meant that one was now inevitably part of a new system of connection, like it or not (and in the early days there were many who did not like this at all, hating to be ever available to the letter carrier). The actual use of the system, its material embodiment

---

[83] Rose, *Powers of Freedom*, p. 69.

in human practice, performed the state. However, in doing so people also performed the kind of "society" formatted by the state (as in like manner the state set in place the essentials of, assembled, the capitalist economy). It did so in people's understanding then and since as something distinct from the state, as like the economy a "naturally" occurring reality. This depended not only on the state's projection of distance between state and society, but precisely the opposite in many ways, namely the reiteration of presence, but of presence in the British case as something restrained and conditional, dependable and firm. Something that was present but not overwhelming, illiberal and arbitrary.

Such can be said to be the characteristics of the British state over the long period of this book, of how the state actually operated a lot of the time, and of how it was felt to operate, at least by the more wealthy and educated members of society, and to an increasing if not similar extent by the working classes. The seeming lightness of being of the British state was only possible because it was anchored in such solid foundations. However, as I have suggested, these foundations might also have had the potential for socialised versions of the state that were in tension with liberalism and organised freedom. As the state became more and more akin to what I later call "a way of life", people felt it to be the "people's post" and so at some distance from the prevailing liberal power hegemony.

At the same time, it must not be forgotten that state violence and legal coercion were part of the foundations of the liberal state too. What liberalism could not rule by freedom it ruled by other means, as we have seen.[84] For the insane, the criminal, many women of all classes, and many of the ordinary labouring poor the weight of the state could be crushing. This was evident in the sanctions of legal codes, which underpinned *all* performances of the state – those which relied overtly on force and those which relied on active consent. If the majority of people were increasingly governed by consent of a sort, as the old and harsh penal codes were left behind after the mid-nineteenth century, legal coercion was still critical. Nonetheless, the foundations of the state were thereafter increasingly rooted in use, habituation and practice, so that the state got more and more under the skin of life as time went on. For these performances of the state – the state as *habitus* in fact – the theatre of the Post Office was particularly important. There especially the material and human performance of predictability, reliability and dependability in the end led to trust

[84] See above, pp. 5, 6–8, and below, pp. 303–7.

in the state, embedding it in British life in ways that have been characteristic ever since.

This involved that mutuality of the social and the technical I describe in
this and the preceding chapter, only now in the second phase, the socialisation of the technical. Technical operations were translated back into
human practice.

This process of interchange between human and non-human practices
is described by Bruno Latour with characteristic brio.[85] His work points to
how we can think of the new postal system in terms of what he calls
"translation devices", things with the capacity to enlist and transform
other actors and networks in the social. These were numerous. The postbox, even the mail aperture on the door, were of this nature. They offered
a training in "permanent connectedness" and in the new faceless communication that replaced the old post, whether the legal or the underground system. This sort of communication depended for its purchase on
focusing people's lives and their imaginations on the creation of space and
time as abstract. On a scale not hitherto achieved time and space came to
be realised as universal and abstract, and the postal system played a
critically important part in this. The standardisation of both after the
mid-nineteenth century was a joint product of the new railway system
and the new postal system. The steam engine has also been understood as,
from around this time, working in a similar way in determining the rhythm
of time in automatic fashion, independent of nature.[86] It inculcated
regimes of "homogenous and empty time".[87] We are here in the new
economy of "functional equivalence" described by Mary Poovey,[88] of a
new capacity to align erstwhile disparate elements of knowledge together
on the basis that they are uniform and interchangeable, something only
achievable when time and space were homogenous and uniform. New
sorts of abstraction made the world calculable and therefore manageable
in ways that had not previously been possible.

By 1856 Greenwich Mean Time was the official time of the Post Office,
although it did not become legally enforceable across the country until the

[85] Bruno Latour, *Pandora's Hope: Essays on the Reality of Science Studies* (Harvard University
Press, 1999), Ch. 6, "A Collective of Humans and Nonhumans: Following Daedalus's
Labyrinth".

[86] Christoph Asendorf, *Batteries of Life: On the Story of Things and Their Perception in
Modernity* (California University Press, 1993), Ch. 10.

[87] Donald M. Lowe, *History of Bourgeois Perception* (Harvester, 1982).

[88] Mary Poovey, *Making a Social Body: British Cultural Formation 1830–1864* (Chicago
University Press, 1995); *A History of the Modern Fact: Problems of Knowledge in the
Sciences of Wealth and Society* (Chicago University Press, 1998); see also Steven Shapin,
A Social History of Truth: Civility and Science in Seventeenth-Century England (Chicago
University Press, 1994).

1880s. The telegraph itself played a key role in the institution of GMT in 1843, for it was the telegraph that produced the simulation of instantaneity that the unification of time depended on. Two years after the Post Office took over the telegraph in 1870 it instructed all Post Office buildings in the country to maintain Greenwich time. GMT was adopted worldwide in 1883. By 1914 135 states and colonies were in the Universal Postal Union, a fruit of postal time, exchanging 25 billion letters a year. For Sir George Airy, the Astronomer Royal and the force behind GMT, mental labour could be as well measured as manual, and its "productivity" could be increased by attention to the principles of political economy. As Simon Schaffer has shown, the plan to link Greenwich to the telegraph network was for Airy the self-evident extension of the disciplinary hierarchy and division of labour already in place in the Observatory at Greenwich itself: putting the Observatory to work in this new way would help to reproduce this hierarchy in the country as a whole and so contribute to the efficiency of business "through a large portion of this busy country".[89]

The codification of time was part of a much wider process. As Witold Kula has observed, this was a period when the qualitative was eclipsed by the quantitative.[90] The state was a vital actor in a series of processes that embraced the codification of mensuration in all dimensions of life. However, these developments had begun much earlier than the nineteenth century, and postal systems were again to the fore. The Post Office had pioneered the unification of time and space: in 1747 it was discovered that the Post Office mile was much longer than the statute mile;[91] this spurred on the drive for accurate measurement, and the Mail Coach service after its institution in 1784 put a new premium on speed and time efficiency, with its sleek and sophisticated "patent coach". The coach mail guard carried a locked timepiece and a "time bill". The timepiece, in the absence of uniform time, was set for different times in the different towns passed through.[92] However, time standardisation only really came into its own when it could be systematically linked to space. In society as a whole spatial experience was reconstituted alongside temporal.

[89] Iwan Rhys Morus, "The Nervous System of Britain" in Iwan Rhys Morus (ed.), *Bodies/Machines* (Berg, 2002), p. 465.
[90] Witold Kula, *Measures and Men* (Princeton University Press, 1986), Ch. 21.
[91] C. J. Cooke, *Irish Postal History: Sixteenth Century to 1935* (London, 1935), p. 29.
[92] Robinson, *The British Post Office*, pp. 104, 110. PO Heritage Information Sheet No. 6, April 2002, "The Mail Coach Service", now online at the PO website, www.postalheritage.org.

Again, the coming of the railway was crucial. Wolfgang Schivelbusch dwells on the journey before the railway, linked as it was to the world in terms of concrete, immediate experience and how in the railway journey the sensuous experience of early travel was decomposed into an apprehension of the world as discrete and evanescent (a world now seen through the compartment window).[93] Perception was recomposed as "panoramic" and as "spectacle". The world seen from the carriage window became a distanced, objectivised panorama, a process akin to Simmel's account of the experience of urban life, where in the later nineteenth century the growing cities had become alien places, full of fleeting encounters and disrupted moments.[94] On the city streets Simmel perceived the creation of a new interiority as a way of handling this fractured experience. This predicated an external world which was seen as "objective", as opposed to subjective inner life, which allowed for individual expression. The state was both the beneficiary and the instigator of developments which complemented what Simmel called "objective life".

The systematic linking of space and time happened with the development of addressability and permanent connectedness. By the 1790s Manchester, ahead of the game, had numbered its houses, signed and measured its streets (in 1753) and published a directory. London did this about the same time but those parts of the country that had grown organically were far behind, for example Oxford, for which *Robson's Commercial Directory* of 1839 was the first directory of the town to show numbered houses. The inauguration of the Penny Post precipitated the almost universal numbering of town and city streets (villages managed without numbers until the 1920s, however, and many houses in the country continued with house names instead of numbers until the 1960s). A rational method of numbering new houses was implemented only in the 1880s, putting odd numbers on one side of the road and even numbers on the other.[95] If learning the new system of addressability was a gradual business, nonetheless these developments fit squarely with a totalising form of knowledge where each location can be known individually and assigned a place in the system, so that it can then be readily identified and accessed. Individuals can then be assigned to these places. In this way the entire territory of the state could become known and mapped and accessible from the centre with some precision. What this meant was that permanent

---

[93] Wolfgang Schivelbusch, *The Railway Journey: The Industrialisation of Time and Space in the 19th Century* (Berg, 1986), Ch. 3.

[94] Georg Simmel, "The Metropolis and Mental Life" in K. M. Woolf (ed.), *The Sociology of Georg Simmel* (New York, 1950); see also "The Stranger" in the same volume, and David Frisby, *Simmel and Since: Essays on Georg Simmel's Social Theory* (Routledge, 1992), Ch. 6.

[95] Oxford street history on www.headington.org.uk.

connectedness could now be more fully "taught", and learned. What evolved was a technology of trust in the state produced by human and machine-made predictability and reliability. Trust was performed in action, in use; trusting in the use of the postbox for example, a receptacle often lone and isolated, and seemingly unprotected from theft and vandalism. Embedded in things and practices – in offices themselves, in uniforms – the postal system became in time the object of a certain veneration, as something inherently British, efficient, unobtrusive and yet dependable, the ideal vehicle to represent the rights and liberties of the freeborn British letter writer.[96]

From addressability itself flowed huge consequences. First, it meant the enormous growth of information about the citizen and the necessity to process this information. Postal reform from the 1840s and the rapid growth of London's population meant that by 1871 about 100,000 houses had been renumbered to serve the needs of the new postal system. Also, 4,800 "areas" had to be renamed. Order was brought to the system by the adoption of postcodes after 1856, when – inevitably – it was Hill's plan that went forward. London was followed by other large centres, Liverpool being the first provincial city to be divided into districts, with Manchester following in 1867–8. An increasingly elaborate system of geographical subdistricts and numbers aided sorting and delivery.[97] Correct and honest postal operation became absolutely vital if trust in the new system was to be created and maintained. This was especially so after the repeal of the old draconian legal code, which in the case of the Post Office included capital punishment for defrauding the mails. The last Post Office employee to be executed was in 1832, and the Post Office authorities were active campaigners against the repeal of the death penalty when it came in 1835. Before this time it was a capital offence even to interfere with the mails. The violence of the state lay behind Jane Austen's "wonderful establishment". The Post Office supported the security of its operations with its own very active investigation departments, which changed in form over this period, becoming more specialised after the 1840s and 50s. The right to search either members of staff or of the public exercised the organisation greatly, for it might trespass upon the freedom of the person: investigators were clear that search upon demand was not a suitable practice for a public institution like the Post Office, but that because it held things in trust for the public it must nonetheless always have appropriate reserve

---

[96] On the "freeborn" English and British in the city see Patrick Joyce, *The Rule of Freedom*, Ch. 5, "The Republic of the Streets".

[97] The current postcode system in Britain, whereby the postcode is the vital key to other information about the citizen, originated in the 1960s, accelerating greatly after 1985 and successful trials of Optical Character Recognition. Royal Mail, Heritage Information Sheet No. 4, April 2002.

powers.[98] As we have seen, postal systems in every state were very concerned to trace missing letters and undeliverable "dead letters", so preserving the "sanctity" of mails.

Long before postal reform in the 1840s the Post Office had commissioned maps of its activities, and in the nineteenth century there was an enormous increase in this activity, so that the "network" took increasingly visual form, for the Post Office and for the public at large. The connecting lines on the numerous "circulation maps" of Ireland and the British mainland produced by the Post Office made it possible to envisage the character of the whole network at a glance, as a system in fact, enabling rapid calculations and increasingly sophisticated understandings of the network's operations (the striking visual form of the evolving network can be seen in Figures 3.1 and 3.2).[99] The Post Office drew on the sophisticated mapping of the Ordnance Survey, which itself dealt in abstract conventions conveying the world as "objective".[100] The increasingly abstract nature of the PO maps is much in evidence in the Post Office Archive (see Figure 3.3).[101] These circulation maps showed in spatial form and in considerable detail postal deliveries and collections by railway, mail cart, parcel coach, omnibus and tramway, mounted foot post and cycle posts (bi and tri-). Onto these maps temporal schedules could be transferred so that time and space were simultaneously mapped. In the end, almost everything in fact got mapped: air travel, the Travelling Post Offices, the location of letterboxes, the walks of postmen, bicycle routes, tidal activities – the list is seemingly endless.

Temporal and spatial scheduling of all sorts existed side by side with and complemented such mapping expression. This is apparent in the extraordinarily voluminous Post Office directories that appeared after the 1840s.[102] These brought into public view a vast amount of information about the functioning of towns and cities which enabled people to schedule their lives with a new exactness. This exactness could be utilised in the organisation of city life in new ways because the directories provided the names, addresses and occupations of city dwellers on a vaster scale than ever before. Commercial and political activity in particular prospered. The scheduling of times and spaces likewise became apparent in a host of daily postal

---

[98] PO/120, Investigation Department 1836–1993. For interesting cases, 120/411, file 16, "Conduct of Missing Letter Business in the London District".

[99] PO/21; the "Circulation Maps" exist for England and Wales, 1770 to 1912.

[100] See above, pp. 44–5.

[101] PO/21; compare Cary's 1790 "Survey of the high roads from London to Windsor", used but not commissioned by the Post Office, with the more conventionally abstract 1805 "Map of the mail post, branching, class and by roads for Ireland", and again with the "Circulation Maps" from 1835 onwards, especially the 1838 geometric map showing post rates in Ireland.

[102] Joyce, *The Rule of Freedom*, pp. 197–8.

Fig. 3.1 Circulation map of Ireland, 1912

encounters beyond the use of directories, from reading the schedules of
delivery and collection on postboxes (given the frequency of delivery these
schedules could be quite extensive) to the increasing use of the physical
offices of the Post Office itself. Scheduling was part of the public presentation
of an organisation that aimed at and generally achieved a high degree of
efficiency. The Post Office aimed for safety, accuracy and reliability and its

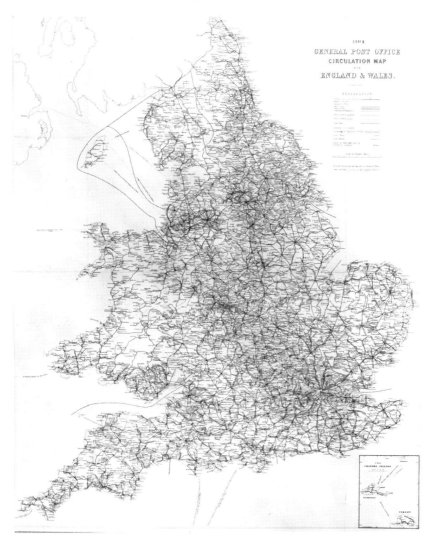

Fig. 3.2 Circulation map of England and Wales, 1904 (1 inch to 10 miles, original size 88 × 109 cm)

highly organised and finely honed routines rapidly became enmeshed in the routines of daily life. The institution also became more and more visible. It is to this combination of routine, dependability and visibility I now turn to explore the use of the system and so in more detail the learning of the state.

It should be remembered that the post was an invisible network and system as well as a visible one. This is in the sense broached earlier of the

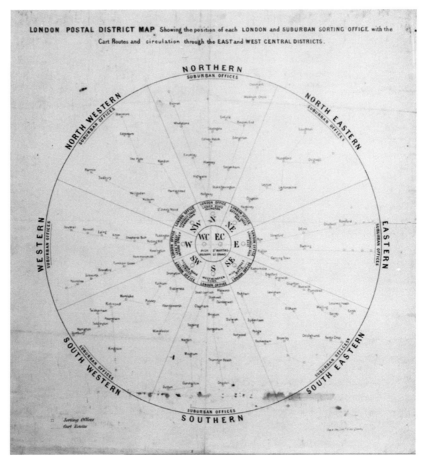

Fig. 3.3 London Postal District Map, 1838 (this maps the position of central and subsorting offices, with cart routes and circulation through east- and west-central districts)

system as made up of links and routes that are ever present, so that the post is always open for use and not dependent on individual users. Systems are ever present and inclusive, even if in practice their use may be limited. Both in its invisible and visible dimensions the post was embedded in lives through the materialities of its operations. Its visibility was manifest in many ways. First, there was the uniform. It seems the first Post Office employees to be issued with a distinct uniform were the mail coach guards who, from 1784, wore a scarlet coat with blue lapels and a black top hat with a gold band. The highly visible mail coach insignia, and the actual coach itself, also (dramatically) confirmed the existence of the state. As of 1793 the London General Post letter carriers were furnished with a scarlet coat with blue lapels, a blue waistcoat and a beaver hat with gold band. By 1834 this uniform was worn by letter carriers in Edinburgh and Dublin as well as London.[103] By 1851 letter carriers in the largest provincial towns were wearing uniforms. The first year that trousers were issued as part of the uniform was 1855.[104] By 1861 the all-scarlet uniforms had been replaced by blue, on each side of the collar the letters "GPO" being embroidered, above the officer's number. The growing uniformity of the uniform was relentless. Even so, London held onto some of its distinctiveness until 1910, when a committee on uniforms reduced uniforms to six classes, corresponding to six grades.[105] The model of the military became increasingly emphatic, for example in 1868 when a military-style tunic replaced the old frock coat and waistcoat. Thereafter the use of good-conduct stripes on uniforms became widely extended. All employees could be easily identified by the Office itself and by the public (see Figure 3.4).

Fig. 3.4 Postman with good-conduct stripes, 1897, Hurstpierpoint, Brighton

[103] See POST 61/7, and PO Information Sheets.   [104] POST 61/63.
[105] POST 61/11. For more photographs of uniforms see Daunton, *Royal Mail*, illustrations on pp. 142 and 143.

The postman became part of the landscape. His, and eventually her, public behaviour was highly regulated.[106] Long prison sentences were given for stealing letters, and suspicion might bring about dismissal.[107] The postman became an integral and highly valued member of the community. The postman's walk staked out his domain, which in rural parts could be especially extensive: in 1919 the average walk of the rural postman was sixteen miles a day. The ubiquity, and overwork, of the letter carrier/postman is conveyed powerfully by the following.[108] Charles Cooper, a letter carrier, was examined by an internal committee of the Post Office Circulation Department in 1860, one which included Frank Scudamore and Anthony Trollope. This is a description of his day (he was then five-and-a-half years in position):

Begins at 5 am with sorting: lasts 45 mins (used to be 20). Then arranges letters for delivery (in same location), for 1 hr 45 mins. Then delivers at 7.30 am. Delivery lasts on average 1 hr, when he has his delivery card signed and has officially finished work (for that period of the day) but then goes round again with registered letters and packets. Has to wait until the warehouses are open to deliver the registered letters. Goes to post office or to a coffee-shop to wait. Generally finishes about ten past nine. Goes round again separately (twice a week) to collect his postage [for unpaid letters], so sometimes walks his round 3 times. Cannot collect at the same time as often no-one there to collect from so has to give credit and collect later. Also does other duties: Mon Wed and Fri on duty again at 11, collecting and sorting London District Letters, collecting letters from pillar boxes, lasts till 12.15, otherwise next duty begins at 5 pm, where he obliterates stamps and acts as a messenger until 8 pm, when the mail goes out.

One letter carrier had five duties a day, walked twenty miles and was on his feet ten hours. Some of the men interviewed had very long service, one Edward Edmond more than twenty years, others sixteen, eleven and so on.

The visibility of the British postal system is often ascribed to the bright red pillarbox. The British use of pillarboxes was pioneered by Trollope in 1852 and after a period of regional and local variability in colour and design the "National Standard" pillarbox was introduced in 1859, becoming bright red ("pillarbox red" as it is known) in 1879, and not

---

[106] Edward Bennett, *The Romance of the Post Office* (London, 1919), esp. Ch. XXII; on the postman and the village post office, Ch. XXI.

[107] Alan Clinton, *Post Office Workers: A Trade Union and Social History* (George Allen & Unwin, 1984).

[108] POST/14: Post Office: Inland Mails Organisation and Circulation Records, 1757–1982. Post 14/232: Papers relating to internal arrangements in the Circulation Department, 1860–1867. Minutes of Evidence taken before the Committee appointed into the Internal Arrangements of the Circulation Department of the General Post Office, with Appendix. This committee was undertaken on the submission of memorials by the sorters and letter carriers disappointed at their lack of progress in the job, as promised them by previous Postmasters General. Excerpts taken from pp. 1–3, 5.

Fig. 3.5 First "National Standard" pillar box (with street lamp on top), London St, Rochdale, used 1859–66

changing much for more than a century after this (see Figure 3.5). The long familiar cylindrical box was first designed in 1857 by the new Department of Science and Art. Modelled on the Greek "Tower of the Winds" it was designed to be both useful and uplifting.[109] The old bellman, the previous agent for collecting mail, was rapidly superseded by this mini-technology of trust, the non-human box, with its anthropomorphised "mouth". Similarly, the post office itself became part of the landscape.

Again this was, and is, especially so in small communities, but even in very big ones sub-post offices became centres for communal involvement of all sorts, often places of recourse in emergencies, so that the subpostmaster became an important figure in the community. Memoirs about rural post offices in village Cornwall, some in the same family for generations, are good evidence of this.[110] The post office in the industrial village

[109] Jean Y. Farrugia, *The Letter Box* (Centaur Press, 1969); Martin Robinson, *Old Letter Boxes* (Shire, 1987).
[110] Natalie Allen, *Through the Letter-Box* (N. Allen, 1988), Chs. 9, 28, 29.

Fig. 3.6 Broadbottom, Cheshire, a village post office with assembled staff, *c.* 1900

had, and has still, the same role, as in the case of Broadbottom mill village post office pictured in Figure 3.6, on the Cheshire-Derbyshire border. The subpostmaster's conduct in turn was shaped by an unending flow of circulars from GPO headquarters. Post Office Circulars were first introduced in 1859 and were published weekly. They were used as a way of guiding staff in their duties and informing them (and through them, the public) of new postal services and operational changes. Crimes and incidents at post offices were also reported along with appointments of senior postal staff and changes to mail services.[111]

The Post Office itself was therefore also a "society" of sorts, even if one increasingly divided in terms of labour relations. It became visible as a kind of community, to its own workers but also to the public at large, especially the large numbers who, like family dependents, looked to it. This was in part due to the incessant circulars, but perhaps more to the steady growth of staff associations of all kinds concerned with recreation, welfare, benevolent societies, life assurance for postal officers, arts and sports; there was even the Post Office's own awards and honours scheme.

[111] On PO Circulars see PO/68, "Staff instructions", 68/458–472. "Post Office Circulars" are instructions issued to Post Office staff on alterations to existing services and introduction of new ones. See also POST 68/473–544.

By 1900 these were already highly developed, again the Post Office pioneering many developments that would later characterise large-scale capitalist enterprise. The Post Office is a department of the civil service, and therefore its employees are civil servants, so that there developed an element of job security; also the provision of pensions. It also published a wide range of its own publications, as well as the circulars, and distributed the publications of its various unions and civil service associations. From 1887–91 the principal organisations of post office workers were established: the Post Office clerks began the United Kingdom Postal Clerks Association in 1887, and postmen set up their own Postmen's Union in 1889. These were the predecessors of the Union of Post Office Workers which was formed in 1919.[112]

The visibility of the Post Office as a physical centre, an office, just as the visibility of the envelope logo "On His Majesty's Service", testified to the fact that the service state had arrived with a vengeance. The first post office was established in October 1635 in Bishopsgate Street, London. In 1854 the first post offices owned and run by the Royal Mail opened. These were known as crown offices while those run by agents were known as sub-offices. From the early days the Post Office dictated the shape of post office premises; even when not owning these itself uniformity had to be observed: as a surveyor put it to Hill, 'It is my practice, in all new Appointments, to require a Postmaster to construct the Office on the Counter principle, and also with a lobby for the Public, and in most Cases I . . . am not, therefore, inclined to recommend that any part of the expense should be defrayed by the Crown'.[113] Offices needed a proper counter for Post Office business and a "lobby" for the proper circulation of the members of the postal public. The number of post offices increased from 9,973 (935 head offices) in 1854 to 24,354 in 1913 (including almost 8,000 of the much larger head, branch and "Town sub-offices").[114] This number held steady thereafter and began to decline after 1970, precipitously so after 2000 until now British post offices, where they exist, are very often relegated to the shameful anonymity of supermarkets (see Figure 3.7).

The pattern of Oxford's growth was typical of the country. Oxford's only post office had been at the south end of the town hall on the other side of St Aldate's Street since 1842, but by 1878 it was no longer big enough.

[112] There is a vast PO collection of this associational material. See esp. POST/92: Post Office Publications [1855 to present].

[113] Post 14/17 (Post 14: Inland Mails Organisation and Circulation Records, 1757–1982); copy book of reports by Southern (formerly Home) District Surveyor John Henry Newman, 1854–1863, esp. Dorking, 18 July 1860, to Sir Rowland Hill, p. 231.

[114] Daunton, *Royal Mail*, pp. 276, 278–85, on post offices.

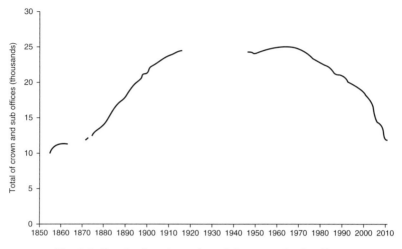

Fig. 3.7 Graph of total number of Crown and sub-offices, 1850–2010

Fig. 3.8 Oxford Post Office, 1878

The new post office, built by HM Office of Works, was of Chilmark stone on four floors and was clearly a considerable building (see Figure 3.8). Its internal use was divided as follows: basement – clerks', letter carriers' and sorters' kitchens, a battery room, boiler rooms, stores, coal cellars; ground floor – public office, a postmaster's room with a passage to a sorting room at the back that had lavatories for the clerks and letter carriers; first floor – telegraphic instrument room, clerks' rooms, messengers' room, lavatory; second floor – apartments for a resident porter, consisting of sitting room, bedroom and kitchen, and rooms for telegraph and postal stores. By 1903 the post office had again outgrown its space, and a large new sorting office was built at the back, as well as a new room for the postmaster, "retiring rooms" for the clerks and postmen, and new lamp and store rooms. Telephone and messengers' rooms were also added, and telegraph messages were conveyed from the instrument room to the boys' room by means of a pneumatic tube. Electric light was then brought into the old building and the extension.[115]

The Oxford office was itself a kind of community, self-sufficient in many respects, a house and a home of sorts, within an office. It had "retiring rooms" and eating as well as living spaces. The "house within the office" had been typical of state organisations for a long time and this importance continued. This will be seen in Chapter 7, where in the case of the India Office this quasi-domiciliary phenomenon took the shape of the upper-class house and home. The public school and the Oxbridge college, cradles of governance, were other instances of how the spatial locations of power should be central to our understanding of the state. Not at the meta-level of "disciplinary power" however, but in terms here of the most symbolic and materially all-embracing space of our intimate lives, the house. The state of this time took on the cultural and material colouration of its ambient world in a very direct way, one more direct than in later, more specialised and differentiated spatial forms, for instance the "purpose-built" departmental office. Oxford Post Office was a house of the state therefore. It reproduced the state in this most simple form of everyday life, serving to embed it in the postal workers' and the public's everyday world. It was like them. Another aspect of the state's capacity to adopt the character of its ambient world was the use of big city-centre post offices to reflect the supposed character of the history of local, regional and national life, the latter as in the case of Aberdeen Post Office, pictured in Figure 3.9.

The capacity to communicate with the wider world also brought the wider world more directly to communities that did not always particularly welcome its presence, for instance small, often isolated and conservative communities. Nonetheless, like most communication systems once in place, the post fairly rapidly became commonplace and unremarked.

[115] Detail from www.headington.org.uk.

Fig. 3.9 Aberdeen Post Office, 1907

This was also evident in the writing of letters, perhaps the single most important expression of how the liberal communications state had a role in configuring the sorts of subjectivity that would be conducive to its successful operation. It was here that habituation to the state through use was especially apparent. In order to write a comprehensible letter it was necessary to reflect upon what one was trying to communicate, learn how to express that and be able to place oneself in the position of another, to assume their perspective on the situation, and thus know what it was necessary to explain to them in order to make the letter comprehensible.

Jürgen Habermas has suggested that the eighteenth century was "the century of the letter". Research on Germany at this time has shown just how important was "the emancipation of writing" from state tutelage for the emergence of the idea of a civil society separate from the state.[116] As Habermas puts it, "In the intimate sphere of the conjugal family privatised individuals viewed themselves as independent even from the private sphere of their economic activity – as persons capable of entering into

---

[116] Ian F. McNeely, *The Emancipation of Writing: German Civil Society in the Making, 1790s–1820s* (University of California Press, 2003).

'purely human' relations with one another. The literary form of these at the time was the letter."[117] The letter, he argues, was a system of self-observation, best embodied by the diary which was in practice a letter to the sender. In fact much literature in the eighteenth century was epistolary in form. For example, Richardson's great outpourings of sentiment in his *Clarissa* took the form of a collection of letters.[118] The form of the letter was inseparable from the sensibility contained within it. The kind of self-knowledge and agonised reflection on one's nervous condition present in *Clarissa* helped foster the kind of self-analysis Habermas and others have perceived. In the eighteenth century the letter therefore had a particularly close identification with truth and immediacy. The presentation of such impassioned appeals to "truth" and the essence of the situation (as in Burke's *Reflections on the Revolution in France*) often took the letter form.

This kind of interiorised letter writing was, however, hardly a mass pursuit. The distinctive governmental enterprise of organised freedom in the nineteenth century lay in the attempt to extend this facility from the educated and leisured to the mass of people, and in the process help bring civility to them. One of the most obvious and important connections was that between the postal system, the letter and the development of literacy. The postal service supported the new interest in mass education, which in turn encouraged literacy. However, as David Vincent has shown, amongst many groups literacy was a communal knowledge rather than a personal skill. From the 1750s to the 1830s the literate-illiterate distribution was approximately 50:50 and no great effort was made to change this (for a variety of reasons including the widely held perception that education was dangerous). As he notes, literacy was for some groups until comparatively late in the nineteenth century a feature of the "functional social unit" rather than the individual.[119] Indeed, socially, for male groups, literacy was not of particular importance.[120] By the end of the nineteenth century this had changed radically and the vast majority of people were literate to some degree. This was achieved through standard state education and was brought about by the greater necessity, and possibility, of the communication of people, goods and words. As we have seen business led the way in letter writing, so pioneering new sorts of identity. As Roger Chartier, echoing Habermas and Malchow, suggests: "It is upon this fundamental link between 'business' and letter sending that a further

---

[117] Jürgen Habermas, *The Structural Transformation of the Public Sphere: An Enquiry into a Category of Bourgeois Society* (Polity, 1992), p. 48.

[118] James How, *Epistolatory Spaces: English Letter Writing from the Foundation of the Post Office to Richardson's Clarissa* (Ashgate, 2003).

[119] Vincent, *Literacy and Popular Culture*, p. 23.   [120] Ibid., pp. 30–2.

long-term shift – the emergence of a sphere of individuality and privacy – may be seen to hinge."[121]

The model of the private corresponding individual was intended to replace the communal nature of reading and writing. Civility was to be cultivated by self-examination and a crucial technique for encouraging this was letter writing. The written letter assumed a very particular form and was itself very much a technology of communication, involving techniques which must be taken seriously.[122] Not only does the teaching of literacy encourage the writing of letters in a particular form, with particular layouts and styles suited to particular subjects, but also, more fundamentally, it necessitates a common mode of communication. This was not always obvious. People unused to writing or receiving letters had no notion of reader response. It was often difficult for the uneducated to frame a letter that would be comprehensible to someone without immediate experience of the issues at hand. In addition, it was necessary to communicate in a way that was readable by others.

Firstly, it was obviously necessary that both correspondents either spoke the same language or were familiar with the other's. Thus the extension of the letter as a fundamental part of communication was an aspect of the standardisation of the language and the extension of the standard in spelling, grammar and idiom ever further throughout society. This standardisation was very evident at the time.[123] Secondly, it was necessary that correspondents could read one another's writing and this saw the development of a highly stylised and new alphabet, different from that in print. These changes in handwriting forms and in instruction in handwriting itself were considered in the previous chapter. Alphabetic reform was introduced during the Renaissance and had direct links to humanist scholarship.[124] From the Middle Ages, when writing was first extended outside the confines of the church and the ranks of administrators, there has been a literature whose aim is to regulate and control ordinary forms of writing.[125] In order to achieve the kind of standardisation necessary for communication, particularly business communication, a variety of state and non-state governmental strategies were deployed. These applied to the content and form of the letter as well as handwriting. This is too large a subject to enter upon adequately here. However, recent

---

[121] Roger Chartier et al., *Correspondence: Models of Letter-Writing from the Middle Ages to the Nineteenth Century* (Polity, 1997), p. 21.
[122] Vincent, *Literacy and Popular Culture*, p. 1.
[123] Joyce, *Visions of the People*, pp. 203–11.
[124] Henri-Jean Martin, *The History and Power of Writing* (Chicago University Press, 1994), pp. 293–4.
[125] Chartier *et al.*, *Correspondence*.

work on the history of the letter indicates some of the ways in which we might understand the outcomes of the letter revolution.[126]

These outcomes were of course often far from those envisaged by people like Rowland Hill. As the work of Henkin on the USA shows (and there is no reason to think a good deal of this does not hold for the UK also), the models of supposedly "personal" letter writing that continued to obtain were, unsurprisingly, the old ones. These were the models of the business letter, the letter as the bringer of news, and the letter in the shape of the continuing attempt to mimic talk. At the same time, letters were often addressed to several people and might be shared at both ends of the process, writing and reading. There was much fear of what private correspondence might bring, and consequently the monitoring of letters. Nonetheless, what he calls "epistolatory intimacy" developed, and behind it, as in the UK, there were strong political and economic ideologies at work.[127] By the 1870s in the USA the letter had developed as a major vehicle for the performance of the personal self.

Forms of "epistolatory intimacy" varied greatly. For the less educated, and for some of the educated too, what emerged was often, paradoxically, the very public "private" letter. The contents and expression of the letter were often highly conventionalised and formulaic.[128] They led as much in the direction of social uniformity and normalisation as towards real individuality. On the other hand, family correspondence itself was of great importance, serving to keep families together and negotiate an often hostile world outside, the world of liberal individualism. Refraction through earlier models had its effect here in creating the formulaic "private" letter, but so too did a great array of governmental strategies aimed at letter writers, coming from within and from outside the state apparatus as such. For example, writing manuals and composition books in schools and for a wider public, both in Britain and France, while moving towards the expression of an interior self, were suffused in formulae of address and expression which mimicked prevailing social hierarchies and had a role in reproducing them. The forms of intimacy and individuality recommended

---

[126] David M. Henkin, *The Postal Age*. Susan Whyman, *Sociability and Power in Late Stuart England: The Cultural Worlds of the Verneys* (Oxford University Press, 1999); "Letter Writing and Literacy in the North of England 1700–1800" (Manchester University research paper, May 2008). My thanks to Susan Whyman for her help on this subject.

[127] Henkin, *The Postal Age*, pp. 99–118, 199–200.

[128] How, *Epistolatory Spaces*; Chartier et al., *Correspondence*; George Sainsbury, *A Letter Book: Selections with an Introduction on the History and Art of Letter Writing* (London, 1922); K. Graham Thomson (ed.), *The Pan Book of Letter Writing* (Pan, 1961); E. M. Busbridge, *Collins Letter Writing and Etiquette* (1908); J. W. Marriott, *The Secret of Good Letter Writing* (London, c. 1943); Anon., *How To Write: A Pocket Manual of Composition and Letter Writing* (Glasgow, 1883).

were decidedly within the paradigms of liberal civil society, although of course actual letter writing was so various as not to be containable within any overarching paradigms of conduct.

However, the public-private letter had a long history, one in fact intimately connected with the formation and reproduction of elites, and as the character of elites changed in the nineteenth century, and as their values were disseminated down the social scale, this function continued. Susan Whyman has shown how childhood epistolary efforts amongst the wealthy in the seventeenth and eighteenth centuries were a right of passage that provided entry into polite society, and were "letters-in-training", teaching self-discipline and appropriate behaviour. The keeping of archives of family letters was part of this. As she remarks, "The significance of this overlooked pedagogical technique cannot be over-emphasised. It shows that letter writing was used as a foundational skill for all later learning. Furthermore, schoolboys also experienced this basic method for over three hundred years."[129] So they did, and far into the nineteenth century – indeed beyond.

Whether they concerned the state or "society" the realisation of new political collectivities that the Post Office made possible was not lost upon the politicians concerned. Cheap postage and uniform coverage of the entire island with post offices contributed to the establishment of genuinely national mass movements. Cobden wrote to Hill, following the success of the Anti-Corn Law League, to tell him his creation was "a terrible engine for upsetting monopoly and corruption: witness our League operations, the *spawn of your penny postage*".[130] The Prime Minister, Lord Salisbury, in speaking to the Institute of Electrical Engineers in 1889, enthused about how humanity was now technologically assembled on one great plane, where for the first time all could see and all could judge everything to be seen and judged.[131] Supposedly effortless and instantaneous communication had brought this about, equally the "ceaseless vigilance" of the state and of society over themselves that Salisbury spoke of as the new political reality of universal communication. Salisbury chose to forget that communication over enormously long water and land routes by cable was anything but instantaneous. Equally, his view was as much fantasy as reality.

As such Salisbury reminds us again of the unintended and refractory character of the state. Just as technological innovation in the India Office frequently led to unforeseen outcomes in which the work of administration

---

[129] Susan Whyman, *The Pen and the People*, "Advice to Letter Writers", p. 258.
[130] Vincent, *Literacy and Popular Culture*, p. 38 (emphasis in original).
[131] Iwan Rhys Morus, "The Nervous System of Britain", p. 458.

was increased and complicated rather than being decreased and simplified, so too in the Post Office. Once change was entered upon entirely new and unforeseen problems were created, and technical devices often worked in unexpected ways. In the case of postal communications, as David Vincent has shown, the achievement of public postal communication created new opportunities for secrecy.[132] Postal confidentiality itself gave new possibilities for disclosure and a new apprehension of the betrayal of confidence. What expectations surrounded the "private" letter? Should it be read in private only? In the Post Office as in the India Office the need for centralisation was frequently in tension with governing locally, on the ground; and in the liberal state as a whole, as in states in general, there were always tensions and contradictions, the drive in one direction leading to unforeseen problems in others. Political events constantly threw up new demands: for instance, and returning to the India Office again, setting up a new bureaucratic system for governing India – the "Indianisation" of the system in India between 1918 and independence in 1947 – meant the laborious dismantling of the old system and the creation of something that even so was, in operation, contradictory precisely because the old order still clung to it. The state therefore is never "finished" and always a work in progress.

Even so, Salisbury identified new departures for the proto-democratic state, after the recent Reform Acts of 1867 and 1884 had brought it into being. State regulation of broadcasting in the twentieth century, particularly in the shape of the BBC, was to realise some of these departures, as will be seen in Chapter 8. The Post Office therefore served to consolidate the presence of the state in new forms in the era of democratic politics. This was so for the governing classes as for the rest of the population. For both, however, as we have seen, it did so chiefly as embodied practice and as something achieved through use. As such, the state existed both within and often below conscious awareness, the latter because it was something realised in living itself, in carrying on from day to day. Therefore "discourse" about the state, whether "polite" or "popular", gets us only some of the way towards rethinking the state in new political terms. The same is true when it comes to the matter of communications and connectedness within the state apparatus itself. This will now be considered. As with the Post Office, this too was a matter of writing.

---

[132] Vincent, *The Culture of Secrecy: Britain 1832–1998, passim*.

4 Filing the Raj: political technologies of the imperial state

> The so-called "chancery double", a folded sheet of paper of prescribed dimensions and format, was perhaps the most indispensable requisite of the Austrian civil and military administration. Every report, every memorandum, had to be set down on this neatly trimmed form, which, owing to the uniqueness of its format, enabled official documents to be distinguished at a glance from private correspondence. From the millions and millions of such forms piled up in government offices it may one day be possible to glean the only reliable account of the history of the misfortunes of the Habsburg monarchy.
>
> Stefan Zweig, *Beware of Pity*[1]

It is to Zweig's millions and millions of forms piled up in government offices I now turn, for whatever offices these were in – those of the Habsburg or the British Empire – it is they that give, if not the only reliable account, then certainly one from which a reliable gleaning of state history can be made. We move in this chapter to the colonial and imperial aspects of the British state but with the focus on how centre and empire were connected, not on the operations of empire locally. It is therefore connections and communications that still occupy centre stage. However I begin to consider the people of the state here, chiefly bureaucrats, but these are still in second place to the things of the state. The human state proper is considered in the second half of the book. In the first section of this chapter, under the title "Making centres", I discuss the development, out of the East India Company, of the India Office. This takes up some important questions about the role of writing in general, and bureaucratic paperwork in particular, in creating the connectivity necessary in governing an imperial state; although what I have to say applies to other kinds of state too. The second part of the chapter, "The faculty of arrangement", goes into considerable detail about what the actual practice and material forms of writing and paperwork arrangement amounted to, for it is only by understanding these that we will properly appreciate how bureaucracy and the state worked and were effective.

---

[1] Pushkin Press edition (London, 2008), pp. 257–8. Originally published 1939.

144

I   Making centres

Partly in line with some of the theoretical and methodological emphases evident in this book, a good deal of the historical literature on empire and colonialism has come to be interested in networks and flows, dispersal and disconnections, so that the contingency of empire is now highly marked in many accounts. This is how one recent one puts it:

... the shape and politics of the growing and changing British empire from the seventeenth century onwards is not adequately captured by simple models based upon the assumed centrality of Britain within a hierarchical set of relationships to discrete overseas colonies, territories, and trading zones. Instead, alternative models of "networks" or "webs" seek to explore a different geography that allows a range of competing and contradictory relationships to come into view. These alternatives emphasise the vulnerability of empire as well as its dynamism ... Investigations of this complex whole refuse, both as impossible and undesirable, calls to provide totalising accounts of this reconceived British empire, or the global geography of which it was a part. Instead the focus is on analysing and tracking particular sites, connections, and movements.[2]

As the historian Kathleen Wilson has put it, "In one sense, empire as a unit was a phantasm of the metropole: all empire is local."[3] If the monolith of empire is no more and all empire is local, how then are we to think of empire at all? Was there one thing, that which we call an empire? Was there even "India" (or just a set of disparate jurisdictions and powers)? We are thus led to ask the same questions about a form of the state, the empire state, as about the state itself. How was the whole thing held together? In the new literature on empire the answers to this question are not at all clear, so that the central matter of how flows and dispersals are co-ordinated, and connections are made and stabilised over space and time, still remains opaque, the technics of stabilisation not receiving as much attention as those of dispersal.[4] Postcolonial history has forgotten the centre. Ann Laura Stoler's recent work on the "imperial archive" in the case of the Dutch in the East Indies is a case in point – important as the work is, it concerns the archive much more at the periphery than at the centre of

---

[2] Miles Ogborn, *Indian Ink: Script and Print in the Making of the English East India Company* (Chicago University Press, 2007), pp. 2–3.
[3] Kathleen Wilson, as cited by Ogborn, ibid., p. 3.
[4] See Ann Laura Stoler, Frederick Cooper et al., *Tensions of Empire: Colonial Cultures in a Bourgeois World* (University of California Press, 1997); Ann Laura Stoler, *Carnal Knowledge and Imperial Power: Race and the Intimate in Colonial Rule* (University of California Press, 2002); Frederick Cooper, *Colonialism in Question: Theory, Knowledge, History* (University of California Press, 2002).

empire.[5] Essentially an ethnography using government records, it covers the contents but not really the forms of the state record, at least in the sense that they will appear here. It is therefore important to, as it were, de-provincialise Europe once again after its recent and salutary provincialisation,[6] in the sense of thinking again how the imperial state was and is "centred" and what "centres" are. The important thing, as Miles Ogborn has observed, "is to find ways to treat metropole and colony in a single analytic field".[7] The analytic approaches that I have already indicated point clearly to such a field.

In particular, what a centre is is not at all self-evident when we think of society in the ways I advocate. The Treasury and Parliament are two of the candidates I earlier put forward for what a "centre" might be. However, this rather begs the question, for it can be asked in turn whether if society and the state are as "liquid" as I say they are, do not these institutions also collapse into a welter of contradictions and contingencies? What underpins these? What holds the institutions of the state together individually and collectively, collectively as the state itself? The answer I give has already identified the rule of money as important, in the sense of what was called "economical governance". This concerns one of the two elementary particles of the state – any state, empire or not – namely numbers. The other such particle is words. In what follows – and again it applies to any form of state, but especially polyglot empire states – I therefore consider the *words* of government (though numbers and words invariably combine in practice, of course). This concern also involves the things words are inscribed with and on: what we usually call paperwork, the systems through which it is organised and the implements that organise and inscribe (pens, filing devices, etc.). Studying the materialities of these and of the "centres" and "systems" that they help create is one vital way of approaching how the heterogeneous institutions of the state are held together. Once again we are concerned with what the state *did*, in this case govern by writing and the things of writing. "Systems", again, for these are the things from which systems are made.

The importance of information communication in empire has been recognised in terms of such things as the press but not so much the paperwork systems of the state.[8] The systems by which empire assembled

[5] Ann Laura Stoler, *Along the Archival Grain: Epistemic Anxieties and Colonial Common Sense* (Princeton University Press, 2010).

[6] Dipesh Chakrabarty, *Provincialising Europe: Postcolonial Thought and European Difference* (Princeton University Press, 2007).

[7] Ogborn, *Indian Ink*, pp. 1–12.

[8] For an influential information-driven account see Christopher Bayly, *Empire and Information: Intelligence Gathering and Social Communication in India, 1780–1870* (Cambridge University Press, 1996).

and processed its information undergirded the nature and quality of the information itself. Administrative paperwork systems themselves, their material forms, were anything but neutral tools employed by a directing governmental intelligence. In order to consider these systems in this chapter I shall mainly draw upon the example of the India Office, the government department set up in 1858 to replace the governance of the commercial East India Company. As such the India Office represented a new phase of colonial intervention in the form of direct political government from London. However, in looking at the state in its guise as part of a system of states, the state in its external life, so to say, I could have considered the Foreign Office or the Colonial Office. I concentrate on India however because empire was so much part of the "external" life of the state at this time, and because India was the part of the empire that mattered most. By and large the processes I describe at work in the India Office were characteristic of the other departments of state – both the home and the external state.

Comparing the Colonial Office, the Foreign Office and the India Office, one of these might be in advance of the others at different times when it came to pioneering administrative change. In the 1820s and 30s the Colonial Office made the running, under the vigorous leadership of the Permanent Under Secretary, Sir James Stephens, a vigour made necessary by the West Indies crisis of 1833. However, from the mid-nineteenth century the Colonial Office ceded primacy to the India Office and thereafter became the poor relation of imperial governance. Power in the colonial possessions of the empire which it governed tended to have strong centripetal tendencies and it always had problems in managing these.[9] In India, where there were also similar tendencies, after the institution of the India Office it was this office of state, effectively a government within a government, that was the most precocious in developing technologies of paperwork. For it was in India, a "paper empire" as it has been called, that this mattered most. J. S. Mill, an "Examiner of Indian Correspondence" in the India Office in London expressed this importance in answer to a parliamentary committee question in 1858:

Will you state more specifically the causes to which you attribute the satisfactory working of the Government? I conceive that there are several causes; probably the most

[9] Brian L. Blakeley, *The Colonial Office, 1868–1892* (Duke University Press, 1972); Sir Charles Jefferies, *The Colonial Office* (New Whitehall Series, Allen & Unwin, 1995); Sir Alexander Wood Renton, *The History of the Colonial Office* (London, 1889); Mandy Banton, *Administering the Empire, 1801–1968 – A Guide to the Records of the Colonial Office* (University of London, Institute of Historical Research, 2008); John Bramston, *The Colonial Office from Within* (London, 1901).

important is, that the whole Government of India is carried on in writing. All the orders given, and all the acts of the executive officers, are reported in writing, and the whole of the original correspondence is sent to the Home Government; so that there is no single act done in India, the whole of the reasons for which are not placed on record. This appears to me a greater security for good government than exists in almost any other government in the world, because no other probably has a system of recordation so complete.[10]

However writing mattered as much in Britain as it did in the empire, and the home government departments were not too much out of step with developments in the India Office. In all departments the *permanent* officials became the ones that mattered, rather than the political secretaries and under secretaries and even sometimes the political department heads themselves, the Secretaries of State. The *éminence grise* of the Foreign Office, Edmund Hammond, Permanent Under Secretary between 1854 and 1873, had his almost exact counterpart at the India Office in Arthur Godley, later Lord Kilbracken. The Foreign Office, like the India Office, was pretty much a world unto itself, although a different one: still aristocratic, heavily Etonian, aloof. Slow to change also, with very senior people doing quite menial clerical tasks even in the early twentieth century.[11] It resembled its cousin the diplomatic service, with which it had surprisingly little official connection. Nonetheless it moved with the times, if slowly, after 1871 the examination becoming more important in recruitment.

The British as well as the Indian Civil Service emerged out of the East India Company, a commercial organisation which depended in large part on patronage. The Chater Act of 1793 is sometimes regarded as establishing the first civil service in a modern sense. The idea of permanent institutional arrangements for the systematic training and higher education of servants of the state was developed in India after 1800, with the foundation of Fort William College.[12] The term "civil servant" in fact came out of this Indian experience, the so-called "covenanted civil servant". From 1813 the term was reserved for the graduates of the Indian Civil Service College established at Haileybury.[13] After 1855 the name was transferred to successful candidates of the competitive civil

[10] John Stuart Mill: Evidence before the Select Committee of the House of Lords on India Affairs, in John M. Robson, Martin Moir and Zawahir Moir (eds.), *The Collected Works of John Stuart Mill*, vol. xxx, *Writings on India* (University of Toronto Press, 1990), p. 33.

[11] See Zara Steiner, *The Foreign Office and Foreign Policy, 1898–1914* (Cambridge University Press, 1970); Raymond Jones, *The Nineteenth Century Foreign Office: An Administrative History* (Weidenfeld & Nicolson, 1971).

[12] J. M. Bourne, *Patronage and Society in Nineteenth-Century England* (Edward Arnold, 1986), Ch. 7.

[13] Bradford Spangenberg, *British Bureaucracy in India: Status, Policy, and the ICS in the Late Nineteenth Century* (New Delhi: Manohar Book Service, 1976).

service examination and embraced both the home and imperial civil service. Over this time, in India and London, an administrative cadre was built up, patronage and jobbery were curtailed, different departmental duties defined and salaries made proportionate to responsibility.[14] The foundations of the metropolitan system can be found in the colony therefore, in terms both of the practical development of civil service traditions and the impetus for reform.

If the new "rational" bureaucratic system emerged more naturally out of the old order than is sometimes recognised, then the significance of the reformers in codifying and so further directing change is clear. The Northcote-Trevelyan Report on the civil service, of 1853–4, the foundation of modern British administration, was inspired by the example of Macaulay's reform of the Indian Civil Service, which involved the use of competitive examinations as early as 1833.[15] Sir Charles Trevelyan himself, author of the Report, was educated at the Indian Civil Service college of Haileybury, and was Macaulay's brother-in-law. Whether or not this connection was an instance of the old patronage system, not only did the new order evolve slowly out of the old, but the old was not at all lacking in "rationality" and utility, as will be seen – subsequent history, initiated by the reformers themselves, having typecast it as moribund and corrupt. Posterity has sometimes too readily believed Trevelyan and company.

Paper and writing were especially important in the government of India, given that this involved governance at a distance, indeed multiple distances, so that the India Office in London ostensibly governed all of "India", from the central parts of the imperial administration – first in Calcutta and then in Delhi – to the individual political units that made up the complex political formation that was "India" (presidencies, provinces and so on). This complexity marked the whole edifice of British rule, down to the level of the individual District Commissioner, indeed the village itself as a political structure. Given the complexity and the distance of the British governance of India, the supposed head office in London in fact often had relatively little, if anything, to do with the actual governance of India on the ground.[16] The (white, British) execution of power in India depended not only upon the various bureaucratic organs of the Government of India, and the shock troops of the incongruously minute

[14] L. S. S. O'Malley, *The Indian Civil Service 1601–1930* (London, 1931), Ch. 2.
[15] Richard A. Chapman, *The Higher Civil Service in Britain* (Constable, 1970), Ch. 2.
[16] On the political and administrative structure of India, see David C. Potter, *India's Political Administration* (Oxford University Press, 1986); Arnold P. Kaminsky, *The India Office, 1880–1910* (Mansell Publishing, 1986); Martin Moir, *A General Guide to the India Office Records* (The British Library, 1988). See also "Memorandum on the Home Government of India", 1887, India Office Records (IO)/V/27/220/20.

number of officers in the Indian Civil Service itself, but upon a myriad of local intermediaries and arrangements, as well as a vast number of Indian civil servants in the lower ranks.[17] How, then, did empire cohere, in the face of these localist tendencies? Paper is the short answer: it was in the conditions of the time the only thing that could govern an empire which was numerically one of the greatest so far seen in history, thanks chiefly to some 300 million Indians. Imperial governance in general, and Indian governance in particular, was not only incredibly complex but also incredibly simple: India was run from London by the new India Office, with a total staff of about 300. The London numbers compare with the equally remarkable little over 1,000 "civilians" in the Indian Civil Service who ran things in India. It was only paper that made this possible.

If paper was the answer, this only sets up more questions, above all that of how what was known at the time in India as the "monster of correspondence" was to be controlled, a monster much less apparent at home but still a threat there too. In India there was always more of a premium on writing than in Britain. This was for a variety of reasons, including the multiple levels and institutions of governmental organisation in India, the distances involved (making personal communication difficult) and the calibre and status (non-gazetted) of lower-level recruits in India.[18] Lord Curzon, then Viceroy of India, complained of these lower ranks in 1898 as in comparison with their British equivalents not being part of the practical knowledge created by daily interaction in a coherent department with a spirit and identity of its own. As a consequence, these lower officials were always inclined to put things in writing, becoming addicted to writing at length, in part necessarily so given conditions, one of which

---

[17] Patrick Joyce, *The Rule of Freedom: Liberalism and the Modern City* (Verso, 2003), Ch. 6.

[18] Non-gazetted officials were not part of the official civil service establishment. In India, the effects of great distances and the complexity of political organisation were augmented by the seasonal peripateticism of the central administration, also sometimes its movement into military camp. The relatively small number of elite British officers, themselves constantly moving from post to post, added to the need to leave things in writing. The physical condition of government offices only added to the confusion. Until at least the 1880s the offices of some of the leading Indian administrative departments were inadequate, meaning that officers worked from home quite often, and what offices there were, in fact quite often rented ones, might be widely dispersed. In the case of some departments of the central Secretariat of the Government of India administration, the Military Department in particular, there was constant movement up and down the subcontinent in its liaison with the army. Unlike the home administration too, what was at home decided by committee had in India to go through the medium of extensive paperwork to be resolved by often highly dispersed officers. The increasing demand for accountability from London, especially of the financial sort, amounting to what one Indian official called "a thirst for the minutest information", involved the vast multiplication of correspondence. See E. H. H. Collen, "Memorandum, 6 June, 1899", p. 5; also P. J. Maitland, "Memorandum, 8 June, 1899" (IO/EUR.F. 111).

was also that writing was in India one of the main criteria for promotion. Curzon, as many before and since, saw this loquacity as the curse of the British Empire.[19] In like manner, a despairing Metternich had earlier tried, in vain, to have the reports of key officials in the Hapsburg Empire made orally, not in writing.[20]

Almost immediately after his arrival in India, Curzon confronted the terrible face of the correspondence monster: he came upon "prodigious files which start almost from the commencement of time", some being almost a foot high. He also wrote, in his usual laconic, patrician fashion of being in a "wilderness of diverse opinions", in which he was subject daily to "the dismal ordeal of irresponsible loquacity", in which the purpose of the file was entirely lost to view, becoming "mummified in the Departmental tomb". File circulation he likened to badminton and tennis, the purpose being to keep things always in the air. He looked approvingly back at London, where:

A well organised Department has only one mind, which is not necessarily, or usually, the mind of any single person. The duty of each officer, from the Chief to his junior subordinate, is to consider not what he would himself like to say, but what the Department has to say. If the clerk in the Colonial Office is asked to "look up" a certain question he does not simply record his own opinion: his note is, in effect, a draft of what the undersecretary may write and send out in the name of the Secretary of State ... I venture to suggest that in all written communications with other officers the mind of the department should be formally expressed.[21]

In India there was no such mind.[22] Working practices were endlessly made up on the spot, without the element of design or system evident

---

[19] British Library, IO/EUR.F.111.239 "Memorandum on the System of Noting in the Departments of the Government of India". For the correspondence arising from the memorandum see also the collection of materials under the same classification number, in particular Curzon, "Notes on an Address System of Conducting Official Business" (hereafter Curzon, "Memorandum"). See also "Office Order" No. 1 of 1892 and "Office Order" No. 20 of 1889, on previous rules on noting, referred to in Curzon's "Memorandum"; also Order No. 5 of 1896. See also IO/F111/158, letters of Secretary of State to Curzon, including letters from Sir Arthur Godley; IO/EUR.F.102/17, Letter from Curzon to Sir Arthur Godley, 12 January 1898. See also for the many administrative and other exigencies of governing India as seen from the Indian side, the forty-one-page printed Minute, EUR.F111./241A, A. P. Mcdonnell, October 1901, Taini Tal, marked "Strictly Confidential". See E. H. H. Collen, "Memorandum, 6 June, 1899", p. 5; also P. J. Maitland, "Memorandum, 8 June, 1899" (IO/EUR.F. 111).

[20] David Laven, *Venice and the Venetia under the Habsburgs 1815–1835* (Cambridge University Press, 2000), pp. 78–82.

[21] IO/EUR.F111.239, "Memorandum on the System of Noting in the Departments of the Government of India", Secretary of the Legislative Department.

[22] T. Raleigh, Secretary of the Legislative Department, letter to Curzon, 3 June 1899 (in EUR.F.111, Curzon, "Memorandum").

at home.[23] This was unlike the home administration, where inherited memory and the ethos of the department were at work, in a situation of temporal and geographical continuity where personal contact obtained.

As this picture indicates, power did indeed work itself out at local points in unexpected and often contradictory ways, but in order to operate at all British power had to be articulated at particular sites. Such a site, the really strategic one, was the India Office in London. The most important site of all, it served to articulate the government of India in India with the institutions and processes of the central British state, something which was not only an administrative but also a political and constitutional necessity. The governance of India was indeed governance at a distance. However, in one way or another government can be regarded as *always* involving "action at a distance". This is a term found in the work of Bruno Latour, where it serves to illuminate understandings of how material objects and processes, for example "immutable mobiles" such as navigation devices and maps, operate to co-ordinate and command dispersed entities, making them in the process governable entities. In this sense, "centres" can be understood to be what Latour calls "centres of calculation".[24] As an India Office memorandum of 1910 indicates, keeping open the channels of information from India meant the fullest possible extension of government by writing, something which was central to what was called the "superintendence of control".

The India Office was therefore very much a centre of calculation, or as John Stuart Mill put it, a centre in which the *accounting* of power through the means of writing could be carried on. Centres are however more than locations of calculation alone, extending to matters of decision and execution as well. All these three functions were functions of the India Office,

---

[23] Ibid., p. 4. On arrival in India Curzon immediately produced enormous and detailed considerations of Indian administration. He wrote to Godley almost at once: "I am engaged in studying the system under which papers are kept or filed here, and how the office work of writing, minuting etc. is carried on ... it seems to me at first sight cumbrous and faulty to a degree. The amount of writing is extravagant and persons are allowed to write whose opinions are not worth putting on paper. Important letters (which the Viceroy is bound to read) are abstracted in about equal length with superfluous comments by clerks. The files appear to me to be kept in the fashion much more clumsy than in our office at home ..." See IO/EUR.F.111.239 "Memorandum", in particular Curzon, "Notes on an Address System of Conducting Official Business". See also Office Order No. 1 of 1892 and Office Order No. 20 of 1889; also Order No. 5 of 1896. See also IO/F111/158, letters of Secretary of State to Curzon, including letters from Sir Arthur Godley; and IO/EUR.F.102/17, Letter from Curzon to Sir Arthur Godley, 12 January 1898.

[24] For definitions see Bruno Latour, *Pandora's Hope: Essays on the Reality of Science Studies* (Harvard University Press, 1999), pp. 304, 307, 311.

which was deliberately fashioned as a centre of empire at the time. It will be apparent that I extend the sense of "centre" beyond orthodox understandings (usually denoting the centre as the active, directive and sentient nucleus from which all power and decision flows). Clearly, it is difficult to find a single term that describes the multiple functions of the India Office as a "centre". Perhaps it might best be called a centre of connection, or of "connectivity", of the capacity to connect.

As such it was concerned with developing paperwork systems, in line with the other developments of systems already seen. The India Office made the bureaucratic *system* a reality, and – a variation on the same theme – made bureaucracy a *systematic reality*. Under the pressure of rapidly escalating demands upon imperial governance between the mid-nineteenth century and the First World War, it slowly and unevenly developed a paperwork system that met the new needs. However, it does not at all follow that this guaranteed control, least of all, as we have seen, control on the ground in India. Nor was the emergence of this new system, in the shape of a new centre of connection, the only reality of imperial governance. Quite often, just like the immediacies of power on the ground, it might not matter very much at all: what mattered was talk, informal connection – the talk of gentlemen very often – and so it will be necessary to analyse these "informal" dimensions of governance in some detail, including the materialities by which these gentlemen and their talk were formed.

Nonetheless, writing systems were the foundation. Writing had to deal with what were already the abstractions of administration and governance, namely reports, minutes, memoranda and things actually called "abstracts", in effect producing reports of reports and abstracts of abstracts. It piled abstraction on abstraction, so that questions to do with the systematisation and classification of information and knowledge are always critical for government. The operations of this centre of connection worked at a *systemic* level, but they can also be said to have worked at a *symbolic* one, involving in the case of the India Office the symbolic *performance* of its functions, a performance to the various "publics" involved in Britain, India and the rest of the empire.[25] Through its operations, in the display of the putative efficiency, coherence and eventually the openness of its paperwork systems, it can be said not only to have performed its functions to these publics, but also to have helped bring them into existence in the first place.

---

[25] In previous work I began to consider how the new administrative regime of the British state consequent on the changes at mid-century (themselves pioneered in East India Company days) ushered in the performance of transparency and "publicity" by various means, particularly in the form of the examination for different grades of the civil service. See Joyce, *The Rule of Freedom*, Ch. 3.

Thus the institution itself had a key role, through its performative actions, in fashioning the various constituencies perceiving it. This production of the institution through paperwork spoke to other constituencies as well as the public, first and foremost the bureaucrats themselves, then its various political constituencies (especially Parliament), the press, and eventually its scholarly (especially historian) constituency, of which this book is a fragment.

These symbolic-performative aspects can be seen at work across the long history of the transition from the old East India Company to the new India Office. Until 1833 there was no regular steam packet system between Britain and India, and even after this the time taken for documents to arrive in Britain and then be returned to India was great. Therefore, because of the long-distance nature of governance a premium was put upon accurate records, East India House in London constantly demanding more information from India. However, if there was a premium on information it was, relatively speaking, quite late in the history of the Company that it began to systematise this information in more sophisticated forms: it was only in 1791 that the Company was first in a position to offer regular accounts to Parliament. However, the 1780s saw improvements in the organisation of dispatches from India, so that the subject divisions given to documents corresponded to the new administrative boards of the Company established in each of the Indian presidencies. Dispatches began to be sent in numbered paragraphs, in two columns, so that replies could be placed beside their related subjects or questions (before the 1780s paragraphs were not arranged in subject headings or placed in order of importance). From the 1790s there also seems to have been a considerable improvement in company archiving.[26]

However, in the first quarter of the nineteenth century these developments did not always impress contemporaries. Thomas Monro, the Governor of Madras, reported that it was only when he inspected the Company's records in London did he fully realise "they contain such a mass of useless trash". His belief was that a distorted, anglicised picture of India was being presented in London: "Every man writes as much as he can, quoting Montesquieu, and Hume, and Adam Smith, and speaks as if we were living in a country where people were free and govern themselves."[27] As Jon Wilson has recently so revealingly shown, the government of India on the ground, at least in east India in the early nineteenth century, proceeded out of anxieties and insecurities about governing a

---

[26] H. V. Bowen, *The Business of Empire: the East India Company and Imperial Britain, 1756–1833* (Cambridge University Press, 2005), pp. 157 ff.

[27] Munro, quoted in ibid., p. 179, n. 103, and see discussion at pp. 179–80.

population of "strangers" rather than out of any preordained ruling plan, however much the Company liked to think it had one. Correspondence sent back home covered over these insecurities, though without this cover-up central government could not have functioned, depending as it always had to upon the fictions as well as the facts of government.[28] This was necessary if things were to fit into a system.

In 1814, a Company stockholder told the General Court that the Company had "undoubtedly the power of strength, but they had not the best power, the power of knowledge".[29] However, while it is true that the Company was obliged always to create a view that was based solely upon the written word and its accuracy, the later emphasis on information and system was at this stage probably less significant than the symbolic, performative and political aspects. As the most recent historian of the Company indicates, information was not the primary aim.[30] Instead, by seeking to establish control over all forms of written communication the Directors were attempting to demonstrate to their employers, to the politicians and Parliament, and to public onlookers in general, that they were able to control the empire, this at a time when they were frequently under criticism. The increasingly well-regulated paper empire they created inside East India House acted as a surrogate for the territorial empire that they had established, the hope and the aim being that the surrogate order of paper could be projected on the territory through the application of high standards of accuracy and attention to detail.[31] One can draw a parallel with the mapping of India, a cartographic India being central to the political imaginary not only of those who would govern, but also, if in different manner and degree, of those who were governed.[32] The Company in fact developed a great sense of institutional pride in its record-keeping and communication systems between the 1820s and 40s.

The old order, however, remained apparent in the new for some two or three decades after 1857. Those who developed the new institution sought as much continuity with the old East India Company as possible, seeing

[28] Jon Wilson, *The Domination of Strangers: Modern Governance in Eastern India, 1780–1835* (Palgrave Macmillan, 2007), and see the excellent review of the book by Philip Stern at www.history.ac.uk/reviews/review/790. The relationship between the necessary fictions of government and the countervailing pressures of subterfuge in the face of confusion and insecurity remains to be fully considered in the historical literature, especially as this was framed in the relationship between centre and locality.
[29] Bowen, *The Business of Empire*, p. 179.   [30] Ibid., pp. 178, 182.
[31] Ibid., pp. 180–1.
[32] Matthew E. Edney, *Mapping an Empire: The Geographical Construction of British India, 1765–1843* (Chicago University Press, 1999).

the old Court and the new Council as analogous.[33] The Office in the 1860s was said still to have the airs of the old Company, its "inherited casualness" and "benevolent paternalism".[34] It was not alone. As late as the 1880s government clerks, in this case in the Home Office, were wont to leave the office late each morning for a drink in the nearby Red Lion, a practice only eventually put a stop to by the expedient of sending a messenger across the road to the pub to bring back beer for all to be consumed in the office itself. It was also known for Home Office Registry clerks to have bottles of spirits in their desks to fortify them for their work. Cricket in the Registry corridors survived long afterwards.[35] However, by the 1880s the familiar comparison between the civil servant clerk and the fountains in Trafalgar Square – both played all day from ten to four – was rapidly becoming a thing of the past. In the India Office, first the appropriately named Sir Louis Mallet, Permanent Under Secretary from 1874 to 1883, and then the even more mallet-like Arthur Godley, the longest serving of all Permanent Under Secretaries, from 1883 to 1909, consolidated the new systems, making the Office even more a state within the state. They shifted the emphasis decisively in this new centre of connection from the performative to the systemic and they did this by means of the centralisation of paperwork.[36]

By the 1880s the work of the Office ceased to be widely dispersed within the departments and became retained by department heads, the scope for individual initiative at more subordinate levels being severely limited. First and Second Class Correspondence Clerks after 1880 ceased to be involved in drafting correspondence, their major function being collating and copying materials for the Assistant Secretary and Secretary of their particular department. The Lower Division Clerks became responsible only for routine work. Sir Charles Wood, in drawing up what was called the "Magna Carta" of the new India Office, put together in 1859 to establish new Office procedures,[37] made clear the power of the Permanent as opposed to the Parliamentary Under Secretary, the former having responsibility for the key

---

[33] On the "double government" see also the memo of August 1858 on the conduct of East India Company business which makes clear the very unwieldy nature of the Company's London administration (IO/L/PS/3/61). For Lord Stanley, an India Office founder, on the new institution, ibid., pp. 476–80.

[34] Kaminsky, *The India Office*, pp. 12–13.

[35] Jill Pellew, *The Home Office 1848–1914: From Clerks to Bureaucrats* (Heinemann Educational, 1982).

[36] Kaminsky, *The India Office*, pp. 19–20, also pp. 12, 14–15. In fact, Godley served as long in office as all the other Permanent Under Secretaries combined.

[37] "Directions for the Transaction of Business in the India Office", dated November 1859 (IO/L/PO/MSC5).

departments, especially the Secret Department.[38] In an era when the over-sight of India was of scant importance to Parliament, and of little public interest most of the time, centralisation and systematisation went on unim-peded. In India itself, also, the greater role of paperwork procedures of a systematic nature had at this time a similar effect, including at the points where British governance directly interacted with Indians.[39] Aspects of paperwork processing such as registration and archiving therefore became of central importance, but most important of all was the organisation of the file itself, in that the file can be considered as the basic unit of the whole system. However, before considering the structure of the file and aspects such as registration and archiving, it is necessary to turn first to the nature and technologies of writing itself.

At the most basic level bureaucratic authority, and hence the state, rests upon writing. We have seen how the very historical emergence of the state was inseparable from the power writing made possible.[40] Foucault recog-nised the central place of writing in this regard. The "disciplinary power" which he saw emerging in the seventeenth and eighteenth centuries depended upon institutions – armies, prisons, hospitals among others – and in turn institutions rested upon writing.[41] The central place of the particular and individual "case" was inconceivable without the keeping of files, the writing of reports, in general the keeping of records, whether or not the case in question was that of an individual, a body of medical symptoms or an institution itself. As such, as Foucault saw, bureaucracy and writing were part of a new "economy of visibility" already evident prior to the nineteenth century, in which power radiated *from* the centre and was no longer *massed* there, as in the old state of the royal will (where power, as Foucault put it, was immanent and expressed in "what was seen, what was shown").[42] This new power was in contradistinction to the previous form of power, monarchical power, which hinged upon display

---

[38] 'This department was always something of a law unto itself in the Office, Secret Department Correspondence going directly to the Secretary of State and remaining his near-exclusive concern. See "Directions for the Transaction . . .", ibid.

[39] The role of the District Officer seems to have been increasingly circumscribed from the third quarter of the century onwards, in the sense that more time was spent in the office, and less in camp. As one historian of British India remarks, this led to a reshaping of British governance in that the District Officer was decreasingly seen as the direct human embodiment of rule, and more as its representative. Sir Edward Blunt, *The ICS: The Indian Civil Service* (London, 1937).

[40] Michael T. Clanchy, *From Memory to Written Record: England 1066–1307* (Blackwell Wiley, 1992).

[41] Michel Foucault, *Discipline and Punish: The Birth of the Prison* (Penguin,1991), "Docile Bodies", esp. pp. 189–90.

[42] Ibid., "Torture"; and Ernst Kantorowicz, *The King's Two Bodies: A Study in Mediaeval Political Theology* (Princeton University Press, 1997).

and upon the projection of "majesty", earlier in the form of the monarch's body, and then in the Court of the monarch as in the palace and gardens of Versailles. This new emphasis on a radiating power from the centre led to retreat from the subjectification of the monarch to a new emphasis on the objectification of that which was now to be governed – the "case", the citizen – something only made possible by writing.

All discursive authority is obtained by *citational* practice, either by revelation (of an author) or by its opposite non-revelation, as par excellence in the case of the bureaucrat. In resting upon writing, bureaucratic authority inheres however in a special sort of writing, one that is "reiterative", dependent on repetition and rule.[43] In this sense bureaucratic writing, and bureaucratic practice in general, can be said to be self-referential: for instance, the authority of the file rests upon its relationship to other files and its place in a system of files. Only secondarily does the authority of bureaucratic writing rest upon something outside the system of which it is a part, even when that something is the state itself. Therefore it is never possible to recreate the full authority of the file, unless we have access to the plenitude of other files and documents of which it is a part, something which the selectivity of the archive always militates against.[44] We might then properly speak of the authority of bureaucracy as obtaining before its legitimacy, contrary to Weber, who maintained that all authority was legitimated domination. It is always at one remove that bureaucratic writing stands for the "something else" of the state, for its authority depends upon its systemic properties, hence the invariable bureaucratic anxiety about tracking papers removed from files, and files transferred from one system to another. Thus, in the very nature of bureaucratic writing itself, we see emerging the origin of the systemic qualities of the particular kind of "centre" which I consider here, just as of all other centres of the bureaucratic function. System inhered in the abstract character of paperwork organisation, and in its autonomy as a purely discursive process. In turn, rather like the abstract character of postal connection itself, it seemed to float free of that which it served, and in carrying its own authority helped create the sense of what was earlier referred to as "an impersonal, inexorable, and determining force", a "logic".[45] This was so in the case of the "logic" of capital, of the East India Company as the site of this logic. This is

---

[43] Ilana Feldman, *Governing Gaza: Bureaucracy, Authority and the Work of Rule, 1917–1967* (Duke University Press, 2008), "Reiterative Authority", pp. 14–20, on the ways in which the authority of writing produces the authority of bureaucracy. I wish to thank Ilana Feldman of New York University for her helpful assistance.

[44] Ibid., pp. 34–40.   [45] See above, p. 42.

how systems, in reality and perception, enter into the world, and it is the same for the state as for capital.

However, because bureaucratic writing is at one remove from the organisation it serves, in this case the state, the nature of the link between bureaucratic authority and the state was contingent, the authority of writing only secondarily resting upon something outside the system of which it was a part. The earlier discussion of the distinction between the state and the various powers it draws upon will be recalled, the state being perhaps more a centre where different sorts of power are connected together than itself an inventor of power – not only bureaucratic but religious, military and other forms of power.[46] This autonomy of bureaucratic authority is especially apparent in the case of weak states, but applies generally. In the case of a weak state, describing the history of twentieth-century Gaza under its various administrations, including the British mandate over Palestine, Ilana Feldman has shown how bureaucratic authority can survive detached from the state, so much so that the bureaucracy in Gaza perpetuated its own autonomous authority from the state by actively not drawing attention to the regimes of which it was a part.[47] In strong states the link to the state was correspondingly greater, but still inherently contingent and conditional.

Reiteration, rule following, systemic regularity – all make for the authority of the file, and hence form the basis of all bureaucracy. They are conducive to discipline and conformity of course, but by the same token productive of the often remarked ossification of bureaucracies. Also, by establishing authority in the way they do, in terms of regularities of rule, they make possible challenges to this authority based upon the perceived absence of system and regularity should this occur. In essence, they entail rights as well as enforce discipline. Because it is autonomous from political institutions in this way, the authority of bureaucratic writing reflects authority back upon the institution of bureaucracy and upon bureaucrats themselves, and the various institutions attached to these are the beneficiaries – in this case, the state. The *systematicity* of the file and filing organisation, contained in the materialities of writing, is probably the central element in this process, vastly intensifying bureaucratic authority and hence the authority of the state. This whole process therefore plays an integral part in how the state in the modern world has come to be "naturalised".

Bureaucratic authority is of course in practice related to different kinds of state regime, which are in turn dependent on writing to different degrees

[46] See above, pp. 28–30. [47] Feldman, *Governing Gaza*, Chs. 2 and 3.

and in different ways. In writing of Muslim society, Brinkley Messick's example of Yemen is of a state quintessentially based upon writing and textuality (those of Sharia law), so much so that the author speaks of the "calligraphic state".[48] While the nineteenth-century British state cannot be considered a calligraphic state, nonetheless what Messick calls "textual domination" was apparent there too, in the sense that the authority of the pen certainly concerned the conveyance of the message of "ruling ideas" and of the state. The power of state writing was amplified through other state institutions, especially the education system. Messick writes of how the power of bureaucratic writing is reinforced by this magnification of its underlying structural characteristics throughout society:

A textual habitus, a set of acquired dispositions concerning writing and the spoken word, and the authoritative conveyance of meaning in texts was repro-duced in homologous structures and practices across different genres and insti-tutions. It was the resulting, partly implicit, experience of coherence amid diversity, the reaffirming of basic orientations with multiple forms and sites of expression, that enhanced the natural qualities of the dispositions themselves. From domain to domain, the quiet redundancies of discursive routines were mutually confirming.[49]

Quite so, and "quiet redundancies" is a nice term, signifying how the reaffirmation of the most powerful orientations results in the desuetude of countervailing tendencies.

In the case of bureaucratic writing and bureaucratic authority, in Britain and elsewhere, homologous structures and practices across differ-ent institutional sites within the institution of state bureaucracy itself (cross-institution departmental structures say, or their common filing or registering practices) similarly reproduced the experience of the coher-ence, and indeed the inevitability, of the state. The results were often beyond the comprehension and control of bureaucrats, frequently help-less in the face of the brute materialities of the processes going on. This is all essentially the same as that learning and hence naturalisation of the state I have already charted for the postal system of Britain. This too depended in part on the elaboration of a writing "habitus", but also on much more, on a habitus reproduced in a complex set of bodily and mental dispositions acquired in the use of the network in quotidian life. The same thing was going on in both areas, namely, to follow Brinkley's words again, "homologous structures and practices across different genres and institutions [reproducing the] experience of coherence amid

---

[48] Brinkeley Messick, *The Calligraphic State: Textual Domination and History in a Muslim Society* (University of California Press, 1993).
[49] Ibid., pp. 251–2.

diversity" and reaffirming in multiple forms and sites of expression "the natural qualities of the dispositions themselves".

There was, then, a close correspondence between what we might call the logic of the state and the logic of capital. Each in large measure depended on controlling writing in a new way. The India Office – in fact the lineal descendent of what was an amalgam of the state and of capitalist organisation, the East India Company – was a new sort of what was referred to earlier as a "controlled space for writing and calculation, involving accessibility, order, the absence of selfish interest".[50] Such spaces also involved the absence of the political, it being stigmatised as a kind of selfishness, this being brought about by the institution of a rapidly emerging "professional" civil service at this time. Therefore, we can say that the authority of bureaucratic writing served to "format" not only the institution of bureaucracy, and hence the state, but also the bureaucrat himself or herself (at the time of course – and central to the bureaucratic ethos – overwhelmingly the former). Bureaucracy depends on the extinction of the individual personality of the bureaucrat and its replacement by what is designed to be regarded as the neutral personhood of the bureaucrat. Bureaucratic writing minimises the agency of the bureaucrat and bureaucracy, who do not appear as its personal authors. Writing was not the only means to this end: the powers inherent in the material forms of offices, the buildings that housed these offices, and the garb and demeanour of the bureaucrat, were some among many other means. However, it seems to have been writing that had the key role, and within this scribal world it was the file that had central place.

II   "The faculty of arrangement"

In his novel of 1850, *The Scarlet Letter*, Nathaniel Hawthorne wrote of the new government business of his day as having "the regularity of a perfectly comprehended system". This "perfectly comprehended system" was realised through paperwork techniques as well as the bureaucratic man. The technology of the man is considered in the next chapter, that of the file and of paperwork organisation in what follows now. Before the file could be assembled the individual papers that made it up had first to be referenced. And after it was assembled, it and its contents had to be kept and catalogued in such a way as to be of use to government. Therefore referencing, cataloguing and archiving were parts of file engineering. First, however, the file itself is considered, followed by these other aspects of "the faculty of arrangement".

[50] See above, p. 42.

The file

The file is the central unit by which state information is assembled and knowledge produced. However, this is not a matter of files in the abstract but of real files, real in the spatial organisation of the documents within them, the physical act of writing, the paper, pens and typewriters that did the writing, and so on. The file itself can in fact be understood in terms of the phenomenon of "black boxing" described in the science studies literature, the process of framing, and hence harnessing and redirecting, the various agencies of persons and things so as to give them new form, and hence a new capacity for action in the world.[51] Files are therefore concerned with excluding as much as including things, with what is in the box and with what is left out. They involve the "engineering out" as well as the "engineering in" of knowledge production and capacities for action. Hence the emphasis in science studies on how science and technological change is not a matter of cumulative progress but a series of stabilisations of agency that may be quite arbitrary,[52] or at least arbitrary in the sense that these reflect the particular dispositions of power and resources evident at the time. Therefore there was, and is, nothing necessary or inevitable about the ways in which files were composed and how information got into them and became "knowledge", so that it becomes necessary to look in some detail at how a file is actually made.

This is in two senses, firstly that of the arduous and decades-long process of invention and trial and error that marked the evolution of the file – file engineering as it might be called. This was almost invariably developed by relatively low-level bureaucrats, who were like many of the other technological innovators we have so far seen, the unsung engineers of empire. The business of becoming in any way an effective "centre" was dearly bought, and constantly undermined by the contradictions of different forces at work inside offices, in terms of individuals, departments, institutional traditions and so on. Although a measure of uniformity of practice within and across government departments in Britain emerged in the last couple of decades of the nineteenth century, heterogeneity was still marked.

This historical sense of file making receives consideration in the account of referencing and archiving that follows, but I concentrate first on the

---

[51] Bruno Latour, *Science in Action: How to Follow Scientists and Engineers through Society* (Harvard University Press, 1987); *Reassembling the Social: an Introduction to Actor-Network-Theory* (Oxford University Press, 2005), pp. 178, 181.

[52] On agency see Andrew Pickering, *The Mangle of Practice: Time, Agency and Science* (Chicago University Press, 1995).

second sense, that of what a file actually is, its makeup. The importance of the file, and the degree of historically cumulative expertise that had come by this time to mark its construction, are evident in the extraordinary level of attention given to questions of methods of arranging and submitting papers in the *India Office Procedure* of 1910.[53] The first and fundamental law of the arrangement of files in this document is as follows: "The papers in a file submitted under the Office Procedure Rules should be so arranged that the file, if read from top (the latest papers) to bottom, will present the history of each stage of the case in this Office in strict chronological order."

Therefore each file was a sort of miniature history that made up a "case". What the file "black boxes" is "the case", and each case is strictly arranged not only in temporal but also in spatial form – from top to bottom – just as in temporal form "in strict chronological order" (the horizontal filing system had not yet been invented). This chronological order in fact reproduces what is a historical ordering, so that the primary model here is history itself, this at a time when taxonomies of knowledge had taken on very powerful historical forms. These forms were organised around linear and progressive ideas of time, ideas emerging with particular force in the early nineteenth century.[54] However, in practice "each stage of the case in this Office" involved the active intervention of the Office itself, in that files were put together at different times and by different hands, so that "each stage" (and the very idea of a "stage" itself) was a post facto creation, something constructed over a time period the elements of which did not run in strict chronological order at all.

The other model of the file was the legal dossier, for in files minutes and proposals had to be accompanied by the papers and letters to which they referred. Either that or clear reference had to be made to their location. This was so that the "evidence" that supported a particular line of action was supplied, again in strict chronological order. Of course, just as was the case with the historical model, the "evidence" in this legal model was highly selective, for there was again a very high degree of post facto choice of documentation, dictated by the strict imperative to always manufacture a developmental path, a historical way, so as in turn to create a "case" or "subject", and so justify the final course of action, the so-called "decision". More than this, file construction involved the fabrication of "policy" itself,

---

[53] Note by the Under Secretary of State, "India Office Procedure", 1910 (IO/V/27/220/23). A striking contrast can be made between the detailed consideration given to paperwork procedure here, and the no less serious but extremely brief directions on procedure in the very earliest days of the India Office, in Sir Charles Wood (Permanent Under Secretary), "Memorandum on the Business of the India Office", 1859 (IOR/L./PO/MSC/5), and his "Directions for the Transaction of Business in the India Office", 7 November 1859.

[54] Joyce, *The Rule of Freedom*, Ch. 5.

which was not solely apparent in the heads of wise (or stupid) policymakers but in large part was the creature of file construction itself, one that altogether left out of the account, and indeed deliberately suppressed, the complex train of paper and of circumstances that had actually led to proposals.

Contemporaries were only too well aware of both the necessity and difficulty of achieving "policy" in the face of the correspondence monster and of the constant movement of people in India. As leading bureaucrats in the Government of India put it in 1899, the problem was one of achieving a system "whereby the perpetually changing individuality of those few persons can be made to represent the continuous policy of a great Government".[55] In this case, as so often, the key was correct note taking. And, just as securing the governance of India and of the empire more widely was at heart one of establishing connections, so here this was the case too, only now it was the connections between the countless paperwork contributions of those who were responsible for creating the documents and files "those few persons" depended upon. Only the creation of a clearly documented narrative would secure "policy" overall, something that in turn depended on securing the unity and coherence of the "case". Here are the same Indian bureaucrats, reporting to a newly arrived Curzon in India:[56]

We observe that His Excellency fully recognises the necessity of maintaining a permanent record of what may be styled the *inner history of a case*, which may be filed with the proceedings, but that he desires that this record may be limited to what is essential for the proper comprehension of this history at any future time by our successors, and that the practice of noting should be restricted as much as possible.[57]

As they further wrote, what was wanted was neither precis, paraphrase, opinion nor commentary, but statements of what they called "fact", something very difficult to achieve:

---

[55] "Joint note by the Secretary and the Joint Secretary, Public Works Department, on the system of noting in the Departments of the Government of India", signed Higham, Upcott and Gardiner, 13 and 14 June 1899 (EUR.F111.239), collection of responses to "Memorandum" of Curzon. See also "Memorandum on the System of Noting in the Departments of the Government of India", signed 29 May 1899, composed by Fraser, Finucane and Rivaz.

[56] Curzon was keenly interested in the subject of how connections were made. On arrival in India he asked the India Office for "a file of paper on any subject that you like copied out and sent me from my own showing how the papers are kept, to whom they go, who writes on them, who initials them, how the 'connection' of subject is maintained and so on. I am getting similar from FO and Col O at home and may desire some keeps from them". From 1899, EUR.F111.239.

[57] Higham, Upcott and Gardiner, 13 and 14 June 1899 (EUR.F111.239), collection of responses to "Memorandum" of Curzon.

When a case is submitted to an officer for orders, it should not contain more than one note from the Branch which submitted it ... the note submitted should represent the combined intelligence of the Branch ... When a note is required, what is wanted, either from the Branch or from the junior officer, who first deals with the case, is neither a precis nor paraphrase, opinion, nor commentary, but an accurate statement of facts, that is to say, a brief statement of the facts immediately required for the decision of the particular point under discussion, with correct references to the papers, which contain the facts. A statement of facts is not a precis, and if brief, complete and accurate, it is of the greatest value to the officer who has to decide on, or recommend, the action to be taken.[58]

To understand all this it is necessary to examine an individual file. Because file engineering was a continuing process the choice of any particular example becomes a little arbitrary. However, for this purpose I have taken one from the year 1900, when the file system of the India Office had developed a certain degree of sophistication and stabilisation (prior to further destabilisation and attempts at a new stabilisation later when, after 1918, the British government of India took on the new direction of the "Indianisation" of the service). The individual file I shall look at is 2101/1900 of the Judicial and Public Committee of the India Office, concerning – as it is put on the top page of the file – "Subject. ICS Final Examination – Proposed Inclusion of Indian History among Compulsory Subjects".[59] Files varied greatly in their size and content matter, which to some degree impacted upon their basic structure. For example, there were many files of a "technical" nature, in the received science and technology sense of the term, in which the principal points of the subject were merely summarised, and vast amounts of information of a supposedly technical character were hived off into appendices, replete with statistics and tables.[60] However, almost all of this information in practice involved the making of "policy", it being secured, and obscured, by this designation of material as "technical". However, variation among files notwithstanding, the document of 1900 is fairly standard, the basic structure of files by this time being uniform.

Looking more closely at file 2101/1900, 1900 refers to its year, the first number to the file's place in a chronological sequence over that year (see Figures 4.1 and 4.2). The arrangement of the file follows the pattern of the India Office Procedure of 1910:

---

[58] Secretariat Instructions, p. 2; Curzon EUR etc, on the role of the "clerk".
[59] To be found in IO/PJ/6/554, Part I.
[60] For an example of a technical file like this, see IO/L.PWD.6.404, File 246/93, comprising a list of enclosures to "Despatch No. 2 Public Works 1893", twelve in total, on irrigation projects in different provinces and states. These are made up of extensive "technical" matter on costs, estimates, mapping, engineering design and so on.

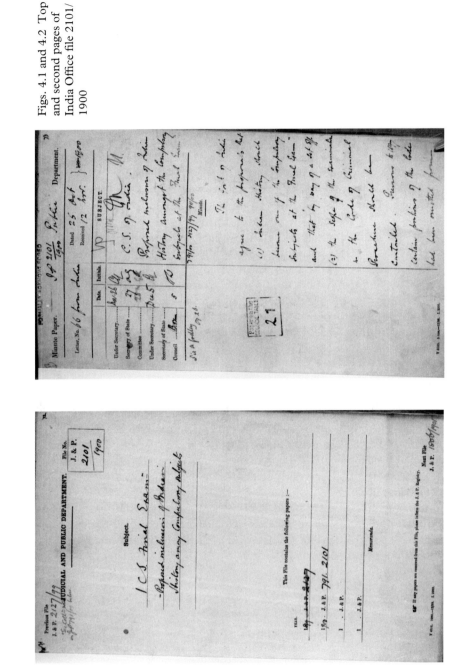

Figs. 4.1 and 4.2 Top and second pages of India Office file 2101/1900

The arrangement, in detail, should be as follows;
  (I)   (Top Paper). The submission docket.
  (II) (a) Departmental minute.
        (b) One or more blank foolscap sheets, when necessary.
  (III) Draft letters, telegrams or despatches with half margin.
  (IV) The despatch or other documents with which the file originates.
  (V)   "Previous" papers, among or below which (and not among papers I to IV)
        any papers added in the course of inter-departmental reference should be
        placed.

The physical layout of the file is therefore itself a self-ordering device, for
the first page as well as including the subject also makes reference to
previous files,[61] as well as the "next file" in the system. It also indicates
what papers were included from outside the file itself. As can be seen from
the illustration, there is also reference to paper 791.2101 of 1900. Already
the composition of the file is complex, for it includes *another file*, 791/1900,
so complicating considerably the whole process of tracing files and combining their contents. The file numbered on the top paper is immediately
referred to other files and file numbers, in relation to which its existence
depends, so that the business of accurately relating it to other files in an
overall system is crucial. The role of handwriting is already evident here in
the referencing notations on the top paper, and comes dramatically into its
own in the submission document (see Figure 4.2).

In this the self-ordering form of the file becomes clear again in that
the left-hand column is reserved for the use of the Under Secretary and
the Secretary of State, while that on the right is set apart for a synopsis
showing briefly the progress of the proposal submitted (under the heading
of "Subject"). Here "the case" has already taken on the form of action as a
"proposal". The file has become that which actions the world, the paper
form of doing things, which if not the actual form in which these things
necessarily got done, is the form without which nothing could have got
done at all. On the right-hand side, "the first entry will be made by the
initiating Department at the time of putting forward the file; it should state
in terms as brief and precise as possible the nature of the action proposed".
The "file" can indeed be seen as *fundamentally* a post facto creation,
because someone in the department concerned (normally the Head)
had decided it would become such, a file, after the event of the initiating
papers, which might be very numerous and in other cases not regarded as
worthy of being made into a file at all.

---

[61] See Fig. 4.1; the top paper as described above – the "submission docket" – was in fact page 2
of the actual file.

The file as a self-ordering system is however most evident in what was called at the time "the ladder" (see Figure 4.2). This took precedence at the top left of the page. The right-hand division below the heading of "Subject" can be seen to be the actual file minute *in extenso*, running in rough, unamended hand-written order starting beside the space reserved for the major Office officials, and then continuing over two columns thereafter. The Office Procedure guidelines here were elaborate, being concerned with the perennial problem of the length and prolixity of minutes so that the order was that "minutes should invariably be as precise and brief as possible". Every minute should conclude with "a definite statement as to the nature of the proposal for which the approval is sought". The use of micro-tools of management is evident, for instance "flags of stiff paper" to indicate particular papers referred to in a file, or the "yellow slips" in the front of files to indicate which department a file had been forwarded to should it leave the "home" department.[62] The routing of documents in the India Office was tracked by many such tools – "flags" not only marked places in files, but might also carry directions – for example "Action", "Paper under Consideration", "Draft for Approval", "Important", "Immediate", which were in different colours.

The ladder itself was comprised of entries for the Under Secretary and Secretary of State, the Committee (of Council), and then the Under Secretary and Secretary, followed by the Council (the reference here is to a box number, box 5, boxes containing documents being left on the Council table for consultation should the Council want this).[63] The fact that the Council Committee minutes were not included in files, nor the deliberations of the Council itself, is very striking, and even more striking is the fact that these Committee minutes were in fact not even retained by the India Office archival systems: given this and other omissions the highly selective nature of much file construction is again apparent. Nor did it much reflect the long and meandering passage of paperwork through the Office. A contemporary estimated that paperwork spent 90 per cent of its time circulating around the office, and 10 per cent of its time divided between the direct attention of officers.

The "ladder" that helped construct this vision of order had to be followed strictly so that the movement of the file could be traced from date to date and person to person. Another such device, with hindsight seemingly quite obvious and inevitable, but in fact elaborated over what

---

[62] Note by the Under Secretary of State, "India Office Procedure", 1910 (IO/V/27/220/23), p. 11.

[63] On the role and function of the Council see Moir, *A General Guide to the India Office Records*.

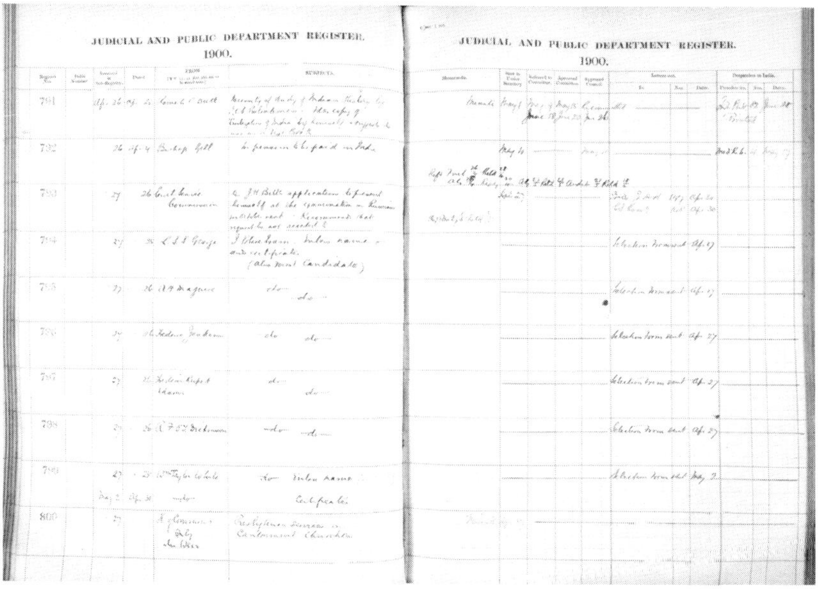
JUDICIAL AND PUBLIC DEPARTMENT REGISTER.
1900.

JUDICIAL AND PUBLIC DEPARTMENT REGISTER.
1900.

Fig. 4.3 India Office, Judicial and Public Department Register, file(s) 2101/791/1900

appears in retrospect an inordinately long period of time, was the registry document, whether that of the Central Registry or of the Registry of particular departments. In the case of number 791 (see Figure 4.3) the passage of papers and the history of the file were traced in horizontal fashion, compared to the vertical of the ladder, only now in much more detail. The Judicial and Public Register follows the passage of paper from reception in the Sub-registry (on 26 April 1900) to the resulting dispatches to India, *via* its passage through the authorities of what was now in effect a horizontal "ladder". There was nothing particularly novel about British developments, although different regimes seem to have each developed systems of their own: for instance in Hapsburg Italy at this time the *filza* was placed within the *fascicolo*, which in turn was put in the *busta*, all in chronological order, and generally cross-referenced, the right-hand side of papers being left for annotations and other marginalia.[64]

However, these tools of knowledge production need always to be considered beside the original and still immensely powerful tool of handwriting

[64] David Laven, *Venice and Venetia under the Hapsburgs 1815–1835* (Cambridge University Press, 2002), and personal correspondence, July 2011.

itself. The profusion of handwriting will be apparent from the illustrations so far: these parts and the rest of the file involved the rough, much amended copies of letters, the frequent use of initials as devices for marking the passage and the history of paper, the marginalia, and above all the extended handwritten letter and note. This use of handwriting concerned the employment of the body, the personal imprint, in the form of a signature that had a known author. Handwriting played a complex role within British bureaucracy at the time. Its use in this document is evidence of the distinction within the relatively newly reformed civil service between auxiliary/ low/mechanical labour and primary/high/intellectual work, a distinction built into the whole civil service. For while the lower ranks of the civil service had to be anonymous, the higher ranks could be, and in fact often had to be, anything but anonymous. Hierarchies of the bureaucratic self were essential to the production of bureaucracy; in particular the differences and the transitional zones between the monitored and the self-monitoring self, the former in the shape of the lower levels of bureaucracy which had to be *directly* disciplined and monitored, and so were minutely policed by rules and regulations. These involved not being able to employ their own hands and so divulge their identities. In this way a great many office practices and material forms, from the most humble aspects upwards – pens that worked, handwriting styles, ruled paper – were in fact means of cutting out room for mistakes, but also room for manoeuvre, latitude and initiative on the job.

Looking more closely at file 791.2101, it begins with a (handwritten) letter from R. Palme Dutt, a former senior Indian civil servant, then teaching history in University College London. Palme Dutt was a very significant Indian political intellectual and activist, and of great significance in the history of Indian nationalism. In the, retrospectively conceived, file system his letter is followed by the handwritten letters and notes of leading figures in the Office, including Godley and the head of the relevant department, who consult each other and conduct a sort of conversation *via* these means, making their own judgements on the proposal (not always complimentary to Palme Dutt), liberally deploying initials and handwritten dates on their own and other documents.

After this exchange the file next contains the handwritten form of a much cross-referenced standard, page 2 "docket", with a succession of dates indicating that it had gone through "the ladder" vetting system between 1 and 15 May. However, what this burgeoning file indicates – it is already quite lengthy and full of detailed information about past precedents concerning ICS examination subjects – is the actual "birth" of a file, in this case a fairly rapid one after the initial letter. The next in order in the file is the draft, handwritten form of a long letter from the Secretary of

State George Hamilton to the Governor General of India in Council, which capitalises on and develops the previous information. This, on the first page, is festooned with many signatures and comments, and in the top left-hand corner a hastily assembled handwritten "ladder".

The critical point here is that the file simply does not produce any evidence of what must have been the very considerable amount of labour involved in getting this subject information together, involving a great deal of paperwork, which was either simply not retained at all, or very rapidly got rid of (rather like the unretained Council Committee minutes). The file therefore frames or "black boxes" a greatly complex series of happenings. Some of the labour that went into the next stage of the file, which was the printed version of this handwritten draft letter to the Governor General, where 2101 bisects with 791 in fact, is at least indirectly indicated in the draft, by means of marginalia. However, the effect of the printed version of the draft is to further erase the labour that went into producing text for printing, so flattening out into a retrospective unity the many exchanges, personal and oral as well as written, that went into file making. This would have also involved the labour in the written documentation that supported the initial round of "conversational" handwriting between the high officials of the office.

However, the departmental head was by no means the only one involved in file making, for it was the case that the file was the construction of many hands, the role of the departmental head being not as magisterially directing as one might think, and in fact more one of co-ordinating, even controlling and curbing different inputs, some of which might be from a low level in the organisational hierarchy. Evidence from the Provincial Governments in India, as well as other government departments in Britain, makes it apparent that despite constant initiatives to expunge autonomy and initiative at the lower levels of bureaucracy, such room for manoeuvre continued to exist, and indeed would always exist given the reliance on a subdivision of administrative labour in which in practice the line between upper and lower divisions, and different mental faculties, was itself so often blurred.[65]

In the government of India within India itself, when a letter was received at a particular Provincial departmental secretariat it was first registered and then given to a Reference Clerk. He read it, noted all the references mentioned in the letter, and retrieved all the files in which those references were found, placing a slip at each reference. Even before the "birth" of the

---

[65] The FO's difficulty was one of hiring clerks with sufficient social status to handle FO material, it being felt that social status guaranteed the necessary discretion. See Jill Pellew *The Home Office*, and works on the Colonial Office cited above, n. 9.

file then there was a great deal of mostly hidden activity, as well as a fair measure of clerical initiative. The Reference Clerk then passed the papers on to another clerk, who composed a note on the gist of the letter, which was to set out and explain the connections between it and previous notes and papers on the matter, referring to any precedents that applied or might be relevant to the question in hand. The clerk was forbidden from making criticisms or comments, though in simple cases he was permitted to make a suggested course of action known. Nonetheless, these prohibitions notwithstanding, the various clerks involved had a decided input into file construction.

This input continued further up the clerical chain, the papers then being passed to a Superintendent Clerk (a superior officer in charge of a section of the office but still not regarded as a high-level, "intellectual", labourer) who would have read the note and then been responsible for editing it, rewriting it and passing it on, as he saw fit. The file would then finally go forward to the highest levels, crossing the supposed boundary between manual and intellectual labour and ending up with the Under Secretary or other very senior figure.[66]

When a decision had been made at senior level, a similar process is again evident in the execution of that decision. As one eminent Indian civil service officer put it:

> The clerk who writes (the reply) must always reproduce the sense, and if possible the words, of the order. Occasionally he overdoes verbal fidelity with disastrous results, for notes are sometimes expressed in terms more lucid than polite; or in his anxiety to make sure that nobody can mistake the meaning, he will reiterate the same phrase again and again. He rarely uses a short word if he can use a long one; and, by the time his draft reaches the under-secretary, it is often a mass of "grandiloquent and redundant verbiage" as he himself would call it.[67]

The Under Secretary might then have to amend or rewrite the draft before issuing it.

In light of this, we might consider imperial governance, and the state generally, in terms of what has been called "collective" or "distributed" cognition, the production of action being distributed socially between many authors (and in turn between these authors and material artefacts), authors in this case distributed in many layers of what was in reality collective and not individual governance.[68] This idea of the co-production

---

[66] Blunt, *The ICS*, pp. 158–9.

[67] Ibid., p. 159. See also "India Office Procedure" (IO/V/27/220/23) (marked "for official use only").

[68] The basic work, apart from Vygotsky, is Edward Hutchins, *Cognition in the Wild* (MIT Press, 1995).

of the state has been explored in relation to the enormously diverse and numerous forms of expertise actually called upon in great state enginee- ring projects, such as the Canal du Midi in seventeenth-century France.[69] Far from the state being the fount of the engineering knowledge required, it depended greatly on the (invariably unacknowledged) skills of artisans and peasants. Therefore we have an understanding of the state as not a unity, a clearly centred, entity, but as something distributed between many authors, arranged in many forms and layers of interlinked agency, including in this present British example the middle and lower levels of a bureaucratic hierarchy itself.[70]

Much of the business of governing, as in all states in fact, required a very difficult balancing act, that of permitting initiative and allowing input from below while ensuring that power and direction remained with the upper levels. This was achieved by numerous means, always with varying degrees of success. We have already seen this co-production of the state in evidence higher up the bureaucratic hierarchy, but below the very topmost levels in the form of the numerous bureaucrat-technologist innovators in the Post Office.[71] Also, in the same institution, how the attempt to make a single collective agent out of the staff was a product of the need to create discipline and curb initiatives at the lowest levels of the state hierarchy. If the lower levels of British bureaucracy undoubtedly had a subordinate role, the force of their agency, if limited, was real enough.

The manifold distributions of human and non-human material agency involved in co-production produced incoherence as well as coherence. This is clear in the cases of other bureaucracies as well as those of the British. Language was one aspect of this, the British in India contrasting with the Austrians in their empire, where they, unlike the British, sought to balance the use of German with deference to the employment of indigenous languages in government. In the administration of Habsburg Venetia, for example, bureaucratic Italian – which had been widely in use for centuries – remained after 1814 the official administrative language, but in practice much of the correspondence, especially with the centre, was written in the highly formulaic German of *Beamtendeutsch*, always in the correct style, *Korrentschrift*. There was a profusion of languages (and dialects) in use in the empire as a whole (as in India) which just as in Italy

---

[69] Chandra Mukherji, *Impossible Engineering: Technology and Territoriality on the Canal du Midi* (Princeton University Press, 2009), pp. 10, 12.

[70] At the higher levels of Indian government in India – before the India Office period when there was more control from London – schemes and rationales of governance were sometimes produced independently of London, developing as *sui generis* readings of the situation of the British on the ground in India. See Wilson, *The Domination of Strangers*.

[71] See above, pp. 90, 115.

had to be negotiated and formalised. In British India, for the central administration in London and India itself, the sole use of English and the rejection of native languages cut through potential complications ruthlessly. However, poor responsiveness to the periphery by the centre was the price paid, unlike in parts of the Habsburg empire.[72]

Nonetheless, the distributed cognition and so the co-production of the state that is in evidence here left room for movement from those below, necessitating accommodation or discipline from the higher levels. The dependence of the state on those lower down the chain is apparent for instance in the continuing reliance, given the difficulties of creating fully effective filing systems, on the initiative of clerks in finding as well as writing documents. Familiarity meant that staff often knew where to find documents anyway even if systems let them down. The individual bureaucrat could therefore impose his personality on the "system" despite the rituals of address, the formulaic nature of reporting information, and so on. Lower-level civil servants continued to express their own opinions, and bring all sorts of baggage with them to their jobs, but nonetheless theirs was a subordinate power, subordinate to the routines that increasingly made them cogs in the government machine. The logic of the system as a whole could anyway tolerate a certain degree of responsiveness to its subordinate and local parts; in fact it demanded a degree of responsiveness to peripheral needs. But they were in the end peripheral. Significant concessions did not usually have to be made, at least not until organised labour was strong enough to ensure them.

The incoherence of empire was nonetheless real and stemmed from its material workings as well as its human ones. These were *themselves* quite systematic, as once systems develop, their own irregularities and failures become built into them. The systemic qualities of centres of connection were dysfunctional as well as functional (this is one of the major ironies of all government). Sources of instability were a constant, in that the impetus for change and the reform of systems was driven by its own success, in the shape of the increasing volume of paper communication, which was forever threatening to overwhelm existing arrangements. As new systems were put in place to handle change they invariably ran up against the limits of the very changes they had instituted, or these changes were productive of unforeseen outcomes which generated more complexity and incoherence.

One very good example of this was the (in context) major development that led from the old folded system of papers to the new open- or flat-file

---

[72] Laven, *Venice and Venetia*.

system around the 1880s. This changed the age-old procedure whereby an incoming letter itself formed the file on its subject, being folded into four so that the blank front of the letter became the place on which the docket and minute were written. The inconvenience of this system was immense, for it involved the doubling, sometimes the quadrupling, up of papers, there being constant complaints about the crowding of the available space for writing, much of which was illegible. If correspondence was not itself used for noting, then small notebooks were placed in the four-folded papers, an even more inconvenient system. This was only abandoned in India in the 1880s. Papers and letters could now be attached as they were received, one after the other, heading them with a table of contents, and noting upon them freely.

In the instance of the Home Office only in 1885 did new papers begin to be put away flat in white jackets, the front of which formed the first minute, to which extra sheets could be added. This practice gradually led throughout the Office to "a modern, organised system of writing minutes: the illegible scrawls which had frequently been unsigned and undated, became neater, more expansive and more clearly initialled and dated".[73] However, precisely because the whole sheet of paper now became available for comment and notes, and because file contents became much more accessible and more easily itemised, a vast and almost uncontrollable increase in the amount of writing in India ensued.[74] This was compounded by the surprisingly late development, between 1900 and 1914, of the horizontal systems of filing which we take so much for granted today.[75] This was a true landmark in this micro-world of file engineering. Another revealing instance of the paradoxes accompanying the deepening systematic quality of paperwork involved printing: on the face of it the development of printing rather than handwriting documents would seem straightforwardly a case of bureaucratic advance. In some respects, especially in Britain, increasingly cheap printing was a boon, but in India its relatively minute costs, reflected in the printing of even the obscure remarks of lowly clerks, led to a profusion of documented material that again fed the monster of correspondence. Out of paradoxes and contradictions such as this was forged the qualified stability that these new worlds of paperwork brought to the governance of India and the empire.

[73] Pellew, *The Home Office*, p. 97.
[74] E. H. H. Collen, "Memorandum", 6 June, 1899 in EUR.F.111, Curzon, "Memorandum", and "Memorandum on the System of Noting in the Departments of the Government of India", signed 29 May 1899, composed by Fraser, Finucane and Rivaz.
[75] *Early Office Museum*, www.earlyofficemuseum.com.

From the file I turn to the referencing of incoming and outgoing papers. As so often, outside the India Office as well as within,[76] fundamental advances in managing paperwork came from the lower parts of the bureaucratic hierarchy. In the India Office such an advance was the achievement of one Charles Danvers, who worked his way up to be the head of the Registry and Record Department. It was he who conceived of a Central Registry as "the central and motive power to keep all the other Departments in full swing", also as the "brain" of the India Office, and one can indeed think of the Registry as the brain of bureaucratic offices, the place where information is assembled and recombined in new ways. In 1858, however, the brain of the India Office was still a somewhat undeveloped organ. A Central Registry had been inaugurated by Wood in 1857, but for two decades this simply continued the old procedures of the East India Company for the receipt and registration of letters. Individual departments, as well as the Registry, maintained separate registers of correspondence, and the resulting complexity of "double registration", in which some documents were entered while others were not, frequently led to a situation in which papers were spread all over the Office without any means of ascertaining where they were and what they contained.[77] As Danvers reported in 1878, each department had its own different practices and routines which evolved without reference to other departments.[78] The aim of producing a mechanism whereby officials would be instantly able to find the documents and information they wanted, in a form that was itself productive, was thwarted. It was also the case that each department made its own nominal and subject indices, while nominal indexing only was practiced by the Central Registry. While the departmental system was useful for future reference, the Registry system was in effect useless. There was no central co-ordinating "brain". Nor could there be until the documents were actually kept in one place.

A more elaborate and sophisticated Central Registry was developed in the years between 1878 and 1883 through the initiative of Danvers. In 1878 he reported 5,720 "letters" passing through the Indian side of the office, and 76,000 in the "home" correspondence. In 1893 the Registry

---

[76] For parallels to Danvers in the Home Office (namely A. Moran and B. Machonochie), see Pellew, *The Home Office*, pp. 96–101.

[77] Kaminsky, *The India Office*, pp. 16–18.

[78] On the development of a central registry see "Papers and Orders Relating to the Registry and Records Department" (IO/L/R/4/1), which includes a number of departmental replies to Danvers, but see in particular Charles Danvers, "Memorandum on a Central Registry Department for the India Office", signed Danvers, 30 March 1878, and the "Memorandum for Sir Lewis Mallett" by Danvers, Henry Waterfield and C. S. Colvin, dated 10 December 1878 (IO/L/R/4/1 f. 31).

logged 131,165 separate items. What is striking here is the preponderance of home over Indian correspondence, the empire in regard to the Indian correspondence side of it being run on the basis of some 6,000 "letters" in 1878, although these in practice varied greatly in length and complexity. Some "letters" were huge documents, files in themselves, as supporting documentation had to be sent to London from India. It is with these documents that we become most fully aware that the greatest task of bureaucracies is not so much accumulating information as economising it. So far we have considered documentation at the centre of empire in London; however it is the truly staggering size of the mountain of paperwork in India itself that has to be borne in mind. If large amounts of this information were sent to London, this was only the tip of the Indian mountain, and most papers were kept in the enormous Imperial Archives in India and never sent. The New Delhi archives alone are bigger than the total of all the India Office collections, as most of the supporting, evidential paperwork – called "Collections" and "Proceedings" – was kept in India, only one-third ever being available in London.One individual mountain of paperwork produced and kept in India can be considered.[79] The pinnacle of this particular example was the order of the Government of India Military Department in September 1887 that expenses of 76,000 rupees for a claim "preferred by the Nepal Durbar for expenses incurred on account of recruits enlisted in the service in Goorkha Battalions in India" should be paid. However, the file in which this was contained was of extraordinary complexity, comprising a list of accompanying "papers", which were not only listed but then presented in complete form. However, this was only part of the arrangement, for bridging the gap between the list and the papers were a number of what were called "Keep Withs", which presented the papers in précis form. There were three of them in this case, although there might often be many more, some of which were enormous. In this case two were printed and one not, the unprinted one not being attached; such unprinted material tended eventually to be lost in transit as a consequence of the prioritisation of printed matter.

This is another striking example of how, even with the enormous amount of material presented in the file, all the labour of producing and proofing handwritten manuscripts was lost to view, and with it much of the real business of "policy" making. What these extraordinary "Keep Withs" – few of which were sent to London – provide is a detailed natural history of the "case" of the file as it is born and travels through the bureaucratic labyrinth.

[79] The document is headed "Government of India, 1888, Foreign Department, Secret-E Proceedings, March, 1888", and begins with a list of papers, numbers 227–262 (Government of India Archives, New Delhi).

However this history is itself a selection and presentation of papers, put together by quite junior clerks, so that it is amply apparent from these documents that the initiative and intelligence of these people was crucial to the whole operation. It was their business to choose and make connections between all the relevant cases and documents. Everything might depend on the wit of the junior clerk; also, as always, on his prolixity or brevity. In addition, accompanying this reiteration of lists and their contents, there had to be correspondingly complex indices, often reproduced for several offices, and frequently handwritten, again by the clerks.

In the London India Office itself Danvers made clear there was no uniformity within and across government departments, and changes in paperwork systems were very much ad hoc, the situation being made up as administration went along its daily course, with departments continually borrowing from one another. He was impressed by developments in the Foreign Office and the War Department however, the external and military arms of the state being ahead of developments here, even if the Foreign Office was old fashioned in other respects. As late as 1900 the novelty in the Foreign Office of the Secretary of State not having to rely on his own memory or that of the chiefs of the Office was noted.[80] For long the Office did not have a Registry at all (although it did have good registration procedures), as to have one would mean socially inferior clerks gaining access to supposedly sensitive papers. The result was that the Foreign Office in 1900 was the only government department that still used the antiquated system of folded paper and minuting.

The Home Office, despite the new flat-file system of the mid-1880s, still had a defective cross-referencing system for papers. There were no effective subject indices and it was often impossible to look up previous Home Office decisions on a particular subject. By 1889 an alphabetical indexed "notebook" of precedents of all important cases had been developed by one enterprising official, whose enterprise was not matched by some of the old guard, who wished to keep the secrets of precedent in their own minds alone. This was one of the last vestiges (outside the Foreign Office) of the pre-reform days when precedents were few enough to be retained in the mind of a single experienced clerk, and when clerks fiercely guarded their own specialist functions.[81]

Again, the importance of minor officials in developing key aspects of file technology is apparent, for the enterprising official in this case, one A. Locke, was promoted in 1898 from a second-division post to the recently

[80] Raymond Jones, *The Nineteenth-Century Foreign Office: An Administrative History* (LSE monographs, 1971), Ch. 7.
[81] Pellew, *The Home Office*, pp. 97–8.

created Registry staff post of "Second Assistant Supt". Locke had "an uncanny nose for papers and a prodigious memory" which enabled him to set up an invaluable system of reference for the Office. By March 1901 he had, amongst other activities, cross-referenced all important precedents on about 4,000 cards. These were listed under headings such as "Home Office decisions on points of law", "Changes in Home Office practice", "Death sentences", etc. However he continued with the lowly job of Noter until 1911, when he was promoted to the august rank of Junior First Division Clerk.[82] Before the First World War, thanks to lowly paperwork engineers like Locke and Boemer at the Home Office, Registries had become much more efficient. In 1909, in a new building, the Registry was properly housed and its papers properly accommodated for the first time, although the Registry, like all Registries, continued to experience serious problems in keeping pace with the expansion of work and paper. The Home Office Registry came to be regarded as a model one, said to be "the object of envy to every other department".[83]

What was earlier called the "performative" or symbolic aspect of paper-work has been distinguished from the systematic. The paperwork systems of first the East India Company and then the India Office were seen to actively perform the functions of these institutions to the various con-stituencies involved. One can trace a broad historical shift of emphasis from performative to systematic paperwork, and to prioritising the collec-tion and analysis of information in the processing of state paperwork. However, the distinction is only a rule of thumb, for the performative continued later, and the systemic was always present. There were three primary dimensions to state activity in the shift towards system – the political, the historical and the administrative – the latter concerning the bureaucrats' own use of state papers. One of the chief uses here was in the assembling of "policy". All of these three dimensions concerned, however, the matter of open and public access to records, one becoming increasingly important. Different archival traditions obtained between different European states, in particular those bearing on the classification of documents and information. Europe, particularly Germany, had devel-oped registration practices and registries ahead of Britain, and this was reflected in greater sophistication in classifying systems. British archival traditions were more practical and rule of thumb than elsewhere, more related to each institution and its immediate needs, and this was reflected in the importance in Britain of the "policy" archive, as we shall see.[84]

---

[82] Ibid., pp. 99–100.   [83] Ibid., p. 101.

[84] T. R. Schellenberg, *Modern Archives: Principles and Techniques* (Chicago University Press, 1956), Ch. 8.

Firstly I turn to the political archive, as it may be called, and then the historical and administrative/policy ones. As the work of the present archivist of the India Office collections has shown, the use of archives by the East India Company Board to exert political control over the East India Company Council had by the inception of the India Office for long been common practice. Under the guidance of Sir John Kaye, Political Secretary in the India Office, paperwork procedures were similarly concerned with politics, but now the standing of the institution in the broader political sphere and not internally.[85] Archiving policy was very much concerned with the retrospective reinvention of the old East India Company, which was central to the development of the India Office in its early days. This involved presenting the Company not as a trading company but rather as a socio-geographical agent of economic empire, which the India Office was in fact then becoming. There was as much emphasis as possible on establishing continuities between the Company and the India Office. This was directly reflected in archiving: a vast number of commercial files were thrown out in Kaye's period. On the other hand, in order to establish the new political credentials of the Office, extensive keeping of land revenue records was instituted. In the late nineteenth century, this political use of archiving was evident in India Office attempts, extremely successful as they were, to resist parliamentary control and surveillance.[86]

The historical and the political functions of archives were closely related. As Moon observes:[87]

Appraised, weeded and promoted to historians, these records showed the East India Company as an efficient administrator of empire: when addressing their political masters, both Company and India Office also used the records to stress their competence in this role. The power of this kind of record, then, was well understood ... When, in the 1870s, the government of India began a programme to catalogue and to publish its own records, the Viceroy, Lord Northbrook, was frank about the reasons: "We are of the opinion that publication of all records is a matter of political importance and would do much to prevent misconstruction of the policy and motives of Indian governments."[88]

Previous to the 1840s the understanding of record keeping that seems to have dominated was one shaped more by a lawyer mentality than a

---

[85] Antonia Moon, "Destroying Records, Keeping Records: Some Practices of the East India Company and of the India Office", British Library unpublished research paper. Dr Antonia Moon is Lead Curator, Post-1858 India Office Records.

[86] This paragraph is based on Antonia Moon's paper, ibid. I should like to thank Dr Moon for invaluable assistance.

[87] Moon, "Destroying Records", p. 7, also p. 9; and on criteria for retention of documents see IO/z/f/4/1–18.

[88] Moon, "Destroying Records", p. 10, citing IO/L/R/7/201.

historical one. By the time of the new India Office Record and Registration Department of 1884 promotion of records to historical researchers had developed, with the publication of record guides and the development, just after the First World War, of proper storage facilities for documents (however, publicly available access to correspondence was still strictly controlled). Also, in the last quarter of the nineteenth century, a library, newsroom and museum were opened. The Company and India Office were always ahead of developments. The Public Record Office Act of 1838 had few regulations for the preservation or destruction of historical documents, although subsequent changes to the Act in 1877 and the Public Record Acts of 1898 increased the threshold for the destruction of documents from more recent times to 1715.[89] Sir John Kaye himself, like a number of Company and Office officials, was historically minded, and wrote a history of the East India Company.[90] It was however a very particular kind of history, namely the history of the Company as one of administration, a version of history as national pride based upon exemplary bureaucracy. The new post-1850s bureaucracy thus itself became a new hero of the national-imperial story, complementing earlier histories of Indian governance, pre- and post-1857, written by Company and Office officials.

The India Museum is a good illustration of how the India Office priority was, however, the development of knowledge for its own rather than for public use, although education remained important – education as propaganda that is (in 1860 200,000 people were said to have visited the (old) India Museum in the previous two years). The East India Company had set up the original India Museum, which was then taken over by the India Office and for a time housed within the new building of the 1850s before being transferred to the new South Kensington museum complex in 1874. Forbes Watson,[91] the first Museum Reporter, so-called, developed the museum first and foremost for bureaucratic use, as a "trade Museum", displaying raw products and materials, and the primary interest thereafter was in referencing and archiving material for the use of the India Office itself.

In the development of archiving in the India Office it was once again the lower ranks of bureaucracy that mattered. Clements Markham's work complemented that of Charles Danvers in the area of file reference and registration. Markham was interested in classification and cataloguing

[89] John G. Cantwell, *The Public Record Office 1838–1958* (HMSO, 1991). PRO (National Archives) website, www.nationalarchives.gov.uk.
[90] Sir John William Kaye, *The Administration of the East India Co.: A Story of Indian Progress* (London, 1853).
[91] J. Watson (John Forbes Watson), *Report on the Illustration of the Archaic Architecture of India, &c.* (India Musuem, 1869); *Report on Indian Wheat* (HMSO, 1879).

more than registration and tracking, and statistics was his hobby horse rather than the card indexes.[92] Departmental officials such as these developed their initiatives from within their practical experience of the Office, combining practical knowledge with a keen awareness of the necessity and the contingencies of *organising* knowledge. It was their constant everyday concern. In a memorandum written in 1878, Markham, eventually knighted for his services, noted how vast amounts of labour in the Office were being thrown away for want of a system of classification.[93] One example of this was that subjects needed to be considered with reference to all of India and not the separate provinces, as was currently the case. To Markham the records of the India Office still remained in a state of chaotic confusion. His memorandum was itself a model of clear analysis, being divided into paragraphs each with a list of numbers and paragraph contents given at the start in an "analysis of the paragraphs". The potential of classifying knowledge was more fully realised within the Office with the foundation of the Geography Department of the India Office under the leadership of Markham. The necessity of this knowledge was amply evident, Markham noting how the 1873 India census was woefully inadequate, as was statistical knowledge of India in general.[94] A self-driven "expert" (the amateur expert still being in evidence in this lower-level bureaucratic world), Markham actually designed the Geography Department itself, setting out its physical form as the material realisation of the classificatory systems he advocated.

As this indicates the Office priority was its own administrative knowledge, so that it was the systemic archive that increasingly mattered, especially what I call the policy archive. Archiving depended as much on getting rid of things as it did on retaining them, and government officials in all departments for long had a great deal of leeway in this, so that they often jettisoned paperwork with abandon. In 1908 for instance, Boemer, the Home Office Registry Superintendent, reported that he had so far dealt with 15 years' arrears of documents due to be considered for destruction and had destroyed in one period of 5 years "12 tons of correspondence".[95] On the changeover from Company to Office, no less than 180,000 files of the East India Company were destroyed in the 1860s by the India Office (amounting to 300 tons of documents). This was under the direction of Sir John Kaye, then newly appointed as Political Secretary.

---

[92] Sir Clements Markham, *A Memoir on the Indian Surveys* (London, 1871).
[93] Markham, "Memorandum on the Proposals for the Organisation Conduct of the Statistical Work of the India Office, from the Special Committee on Statistics", IO/x/4/28–29.
[94] Markham, ibid.   [95] Moon, "Destroying Records".

The peculiar constitutional position of the India Office meant that even more than other government departments it was a law unto itself when it came to the management of paperwork. Most government records came under the control of the Master of the Rolls, those of the India Office under the control of the Secretary of State in Council.[96] During Sir John Kaye's tenure of the Political Department, ignoring the Secretary of State, only those parts of collections that in his view showed policy making in action were retained.[97] A sense of his priorities is evident in the subjects on the receiving end of this destructive episode, namely files on national resources, public health, education and the "natives". Within the Office as a whole, powerful departments held onto their own records for their own purposes. Financial and military records were kept separately in the India Office, not in the Registry. The Political Secretary retained control of parts of the Secret Correspondence (this dealt mostly with frontier policy and political relations with Indian princely states).

The indistinct line between public and private as well as between politics and policy is also apparent.[98] The documentation of "policy" might take a distinctly unofficial line. "Dodgy dossiers" were things of the past as well as of the present in British political life. Some of the leading bureaucrats, also the political Secretaries of State, retained their own copies of some correspondence as their private property. Kaye's "demi-official" letter book was evidently taken out of the Office, and as early as 1859 Secretary of State Lord Stanley ruled that papers were not to be thus removed; obviously this rule was not always obeyed. Ministers and bureaucrats took papers home to work on, in India too, and it is not clear whether all these were returned, while there is certainly evidence in the India Office itself of papers being retained and "stored" in private offices for many years.[99] The papers of the Secretary of State regarding occasions "when he acted personally" were kept by Private Secretaries and not put in departmental files.[100] The idea of "private correspondence" meant that papers were taken away when Secretaries of State left office, including secret cipher telegrams, so that this correspondence was regarded as in some sense the "property" of the Secretary of State, the idea being that

---

[96] The 1914 Commission on Public Records included records of the India Office within the general governmental remit, but the Office still continued to steward its papers.

[97] Moon, "Destroying Records"; and Nihar Nandan Singh, *British Historiography on British Rule in India: the Life and Writings of Sir John William Kaye, 1814–1876* (Janaka Prakashan: Patna, 1986).

[98] "The Royal Commission on Public Records 1912, India Office Evidence", App. VI, No. 17, pp. 4–7, 51–3, 355–7, 661–3; also Moon, "Destroying Records", p. 9.

[99] Moon, private correspondence and "Destroying Records".

[100] IO/L/PO. The administration history at the start of the catalogue volume for this record series is drawn upon here. The volume catalogues official papers and files, 1865–1948.

outgoing officers should be protected against political successors. Up to the present day, sanctions against the public disclosure of correspondence said to be of a "secret and highly sensitive nature" have been especially severe in Britain compared to other states, and latitude for outgoing ministers is still considerable.[101]

At this stage of the discussion, then, we have some idea of how the liberal state worked, including its imperial dimensions, which were usually in practice far from liberal. Through the postal system we also have a viewpoint from which to understand the relationship between the state, society and the economy, and to think about the nature of liberal governance and of freedom in terms of this relationship. We have been dealing with "connections", and with how "systems" and their control in the form of "centres" were elaborated, within government itself – in the shape of the India Office – and in the links between state and society as manifest in the Post Office. We have been concerned with the power of writing, and the emphasis has mostly been on things, on the material state. However, the human state, the state of men as I have called it, has constantly made its appearance, including the discussion of the formation of the bureaucratic self in this chapter. It is now time, in Part II of the book, to consider the state of men more systematically than hitherto. Connections, systems and writing will continue to be our themes, and these, together with new ones, will be explored in terms of the formation of the bureaucrat and of the institution of bureaucracy. In particular, the educational foundations of the bureaucracy and of British elites will be considered. However, before this it is necessary to step back a little and present the formation of the governors – how they were governed and governed themselves – in the long-term perspective of the British state in its liberal manifestations.

---

[101] David Vincent, *The Culture of Secrecy: Britain, 1832–1998* (Oxford University Press, 1998).

Part II

The state of men: governing

5   The work of the state

There was one man, especially, the observation of whose character gave me a new idea of talent. His gifts were emphatically those of a man of business; prompt, acute, clear-minded; with an eye that saw through all perplexities, and a faculty of arrangement that made them vanish, as by the waving of an enchanter's wand ... the many intricacies of business ... presented themselves before him with the regularity of a perfectly comprehended system.

Nathaniel Hawthorne, *The Scarlet Letter*[1]

We turn now to the formation of state persons and the place of their work life in this, shifting emphasis to the men who embodied Hawthorne's "faculty of arrangement" (Hawthorne was writing of the government official). By my chapter title, "The work of the state", I point to its everyday realities, namely what bureaucrats actually did, and this I call their "common knowledge", a term used to give the first section of the chapter its title. This term has wider relevance, which I also discuss. The conduct of the bureaucrat is again explored in terms of practice and materiality, and the accent remains on writing for a time, for this was of equal importance in shaping the bureaucrat as in providing that faculty of arrangement that gave a centre to the state and to the institution of bureaucracy. However this was far from being a matter of writing alone, or of spoken language, important as these were. It involved the whole material world of the bureaucrat, particularly the built environment, so that I spend much time discussing the workplaces of bureaucrats – their offices, especially the India Office itself. These offices as much as anything else made the "office" of the bureaucrat.

The common knowledge of bureaucrats mentioned above was in Britain often termed "learning with Nelly", practical learning on the job. In the second section I turn almost exclusively to the high bureaucrat, whom I call the "civil service statesman". To a surprising degree his learning was also alongside Nelly, although Nelly was accompanied by

[1] Originally published in Boston, 1850.

the influence of the public school and an Oxbridge education. In that section I follow the occupational culture of the elite bureaucrat, one rather different to that considered in the first section, bringing out the links of this culture to ideas about the purpose and identity of the civil servant as a "statesman" – a man of the state who in actual practice was little different in outlook and character from the leading politicians; and little different in the degree to which he held power. I also consider the occupational culture and ethical stylisation of the politician. Shared outlook, social background and education united the two. Therefore, in using the term "governing classes" it is these people that we should have in mind, for contrary to some understandings, and to the doctrine of the separation of politics and administration, it was in both figures that the real business of government took place. The high bureaucrat, just as much as the politician, was involved in making state policy – in Britain, but especially in India. This power was so considerable as to properly merit the term "civil service statesman", a term indeed applied by a bureaucrat who was at one time head of the entire service. These men conceived of themselves as men of the state who had a particularly close identification with and knowledge of not only the British state but British society, and this further bolstered their power, as by convincing themselves of this they seem to have been able to convince many others too, then and since.

However, before considering this version of the "statesman", and the actual work of the state, it is first necessary to step back for a moment from the immediate argument to consider the wider historical context in which the figures of the bureaucrat and the politician – but also the technical "expert" – emerged. In eighteenth-century Europe the machinery of government was on the whole directed centrally, but in Britain it was more dispersed.[2] The eighteenth-century state in Britain was highly centralised in its military and fiscal dealings, yet depended on a bureaucracy that was amateur, if imbued with a strong sense of public duty.[3] Therefore to call it a military-fiscal state only is to neglect this other side of the state at that time, the side that governed society, especially at a local level. As well as an education in common with other sections of the governing elite this legacy of eighteenth-century "amateurism" was another factor preventing the later emergence of a "state service" caste in Britain.[4] Eighteenth-century bureaucracy was not only amateur but unlike its continental

---

[2] For the following account presented in more detail see Patrick Joyce, *Encyclopeadia Britannica* entry, "British History 1815–Present", 2008 revision.

[3] John Brewer, *The Sinews of Power: War, Money and the English State 1688–1783* (Unwin Hyman, 1989), pp. 4–21.

[4] See above, pp. 8–9.

counterparts neither venal nor particularly sizeable, although this did not mean that local government was not strong or intensive at a local level,[5] so much so that the familiar picture of strong European state traditions and weak civil society ones, in contrast to Britain, has been called into question.[6]

Nonetheless, communal and participatory elements of this local government were important, even if these went hand in hand with strong oligarchic tendencies, real power being largely restricted to the higher social levels. The late-eighteenth and early-nineteenth century state – at both central and local levels – was still marked by a strong sense of rights, enforceable at law, enjoyed by all members of the community – albeit unequally. Those with governmental responsibility did not generally try to exclude the mass of the population from some participation in the regulation of their own lives. In the courts by means of petition, through attendance at parish meetings, among other means, the poor could exert some influence. This influence, for both the high and low in society, was felt to operate at the level of the representation of communities, rather than of the individual, something reflected in the system of parliamentary representation itself.[7]

This was to change radically in the aftermath of the Napoleonic Wars. Thus the "rise" of so-called democratic government in the nineteenth century represented in many respects a *closing down* not an opening up of real democracy, or at least a closing down of the earlier opportunities for some participation in the political process. This was compounded by the switch from a communal to an individualised and representative, not participatory, proto-democratic system. Parliament, the executive, party and bureaucracy were refashioned so as to provide a framework within which individuals and institutions could operate with maximum safety and freedom. Politicians in the period between roughly the 1820s and 1860s can be understood as attempting to create a new and stable role for politics in the context of the decline of monarchical and aristocratic

---

[5] Joanna Innes, *Inferior Politics: Social Problems and Social Policies in Eighteenth-Century Britain* (Oxford University Press, 2009).

[6] Eckhart Hellmuth and John Brewer (eds.), *Rethinking Leviathan: the Eighteenth Century in Britain and Germany* (Oxford University Press, 1999). See also David Eastwood, "'Amplifying the Province of the Legislature': The Flow of Information and the English State in the Early Nineteenth Century", *Historical Research*, 62 (1989); James Vernon, *Politics and the People: A Study in English Political Communication, 1815–1867* (Cambridge University Press, 1993).

[7] E. P. Thompson, "Eighteenth-Century English Society: Class Struggle without Class", *Social History*, 3:2 (May 1978).

power.[8] Extension of control over the political process occurred by means of the development of a disciplined party system, the creation of a modern bureaucracy and the extension of the political franchise. The drivers of change seem to have been political, rather than, *pace* Weber, products of a general developmental process involving bureaucratic rationality.

The measures involved meant the delineation of a political sphere in which the parliamentary executive would dominate and the uncertainties manifest in the old institutional order would be minimised. It was political stability, and as far as possible continuity, that were aimed for – not democracy – although these could only be had at the price of a measure of democracy. The elimination of uncertainty that accompanied the clearer delineation of the political involved the development of accountability across all sectors of government, the civil service, patronage, the operations of Parliament, the taxation system, and so on. It was then that we see the inexorable rise of Treasury control in government (considered in Chapter 3). The clearer delineation of "administration" involved the idea of a civil service which was "non-political" and which regulated programmes of legislation developed by ministers and parties and vouched for by electorates.[9]

These developments were informed by the emergence of particular ethical stylisations that would be consonant with and indispensable for the operations of the new liberal state. They comprised, in effect, a series of moral economies of "office" that extended beyond bureaucracy alone to politicians, but no less to that twin brother of the bureaucrat, the pedagogue (the schoolteacher and increasingly the "academic"). The former was the high priest of the state, in the words of Karl Marx, and the latter in effect the high priest of civil society. The state depended on both sorts of priesthood, and on the much less saintly avocation of the politician. For all three, at least in their higher reaches, the end result was the outcome of their common educational formation and, secondly, of the material forms of the "office" they inhabited, which I consider first. Therefore, what Weber called *Lebensführungen*, deliberately fashioned forms or styles of life – moral economies of office in fact – were central to the technics of the liberal state.[10]

The emergence of centralised, regular bureaucracy in a modern form, which involved a more clearly delineated idea of the bureaucrat and bureaucracy themselves, occurred somewhat earlier in parts of Europe,

---

[8] Bernard Silberman, *Cages of Reason: The Rise of the Rational State in France, Japan, the United States, and Great Britain* (University of Chicago Press, 1993).

[9] Henry Parris, *Constitutional Bureaucracy: The Development of British Central Administration since the Eighteenth Century* (Allen & Unwin, 1969), Ch. 4, "Law and Administration".

[10] Paul du Gay, "Max Weber and the Moral Economy of Office", *Journal of Cultural Economy*, 1:2 (July 2008).

particularly but by no means exclusively in revolutionary France and its conquered territories.[11] It was then that "administration" and "bureaucracy" began to be conceived of as akin to an abstract principle. This was in great part because of the proliferation of written documents, the work of the state in fact, so that observation, cognition, decision-making and hence authority were becoming exclusively based on written documents. As the German legal expert Ludwig Von Jagermann put it in 1838, "*Quod non est in actis, non est in mundo*" (if it is not in a written document it does not exist).[12] In Europe the development of a professional civil service entailed a different way of being a state servant than in Britain, and therefore a different bureaucratic ethic, that of the *state* rather than the *civil* servant, the difference turning upon the distinction between centralised forms of the state (in autocratic Prussia and revolutionary "statist" France, say) and more politically liberal and less centralised ones. As we have seen, the military model for bureaucracy was also much more important in Europe than in Britain.[13]

The new understanding of the bureaucrat was entirely at odds with the eighteenth-century view that administration and politics were not separate things. Patronage bridged the two. The eighteenth-century administering apparatus in Britain was neither civil nor a service.[14] It lacked the uniformity, hierarchy and corporate discipline to be a service.[15] Neither was it "civil", for there was only limited distinction between civil and political affairs. Nor was the administration permanent. Officials might in effect be almost permanent fixtures but this was not systematic: the concept of permanence was meaningless outside the idea of a change of government, something only evident with the demise of the idea of the monarch's government after the 1780s.[16] From then we can trace the early history of the British civil service, evident for example in the slow beginnings of

---

[11] Peter Becker and Rüdiger von Krosigk (eds.), *Figures of Authority: Contributions towards a Cultural History of Governance from the Seventeenth to the Twentieth Century* (PIE, Peter Lang, 2008), esp. "Introduction", pp. 17, 19–21, 23. See also, in the same volume, Ben Kafka on the eighteenth-century French bureaucracy.

[12] As cited in Becker and von Krosigk, ibid., by Becker, p. 19.

[13] For magisterial/judicial rather than administrative traditions of bureaucracy see David Laven, *Venice and Venetia under the Hapsburgs, 1815–1835* (Oxford University Press, 2002) and on the comparative history of bureaucracy, Joseph C. N. Raadschelders, *Handbook of Administrative History* (Transaction Publishers, 1998), esp. Chs. 6 and 7 on the process of bureaucratisation and Ch. 9 on the state and nation building.

[14] Parris, *Constitutional Bureaucracy*, Ch. 2; Norman Chester, *The English Administrative System* (Oxford University Press, 1981); Pat Thane, "Government and Society in England and Wales, 1750–1950" in F. M. L. Thomson (ed.), *The Cambridge Social History of Great Britain 1750–1950*, vol. III (Cambridge University Press, 1990).

[15] Parris, *Constitutional Bureaucracy*, pp. 20–2.   [16] Ibid., pp. 22–7.

the replacement of remuneration based on honour and patronage by the rationality of the market, as we have seen in Chapter 3.[17]

This brings us to the role of the technical expert per se in the new political dispensation. Patronage was in one sense *extended* in the new administrative state of the nineteenth century. However this "new patronage" was of a different sort to that which had gone before, so that the new bureaucracy, the new inspectorates for instance, while being in part political appointees, depended not on patronage proper but on increasingly elaborate forms of expertise, ultimately answering to a bureaucratic ethic whose rationality was similar to that of the high civil service itself – one of merit rather than patronage. As historians of Victorian government have seen, the bureaucratic authority of the expert rested on an ideology of inquiry involving the discipline of rational inquiry and response to perceived "problems", a discipline in which the rhetoric of objectivity was embedded.[18] The new administrative state undoubtedly drew on what was perceived to be the ethical neutrality of science and technology, and scientists and technologists were called into central government with increasing frequency. The government Science and Art Department of 1853 was a clear sign of this. The drive towards standardisation in technical activities was accompanied by the proliferation of metrics of all sorts in public discourse, and these served as rhetorical as well as technical devices operating on the political world.[19] Metrics and standardisation became indelibly associated with the state and hence with the national interest. Civil servants increasingly tapped into newly professionalised knowledge directly, the Board of Trade having a statistical department by 1832, and statistics became widely used from the 1830s in the Poor Law Commission, War Office, Home Office and Privy Council on Education.

However, all this did not mean that the technical "expert" achieved the same salience as the politician and the bureaucrat, except that is the experts that serviced the new governing classes – the teacher and academic, ironically more the experts of art than of science. Technocracy and the *Lebensführungen* of the technocrat did not emerge. Briefly, we can trace two phases of the relationship between the new bureaucrat, the politician and the technical expert, corresponding to the shift from the fiscal-military state to the liberal technostate. The first phase took form in the

[17] See Ch. 3 above, pp. 105–6.
[18] Roy McLeod (ed.), *Government and Expertise: Specialists, Administrators and Professionals, 1860–1919* (Cambridge University Press, 1998); Valerie Cromwell, *Revolution or Evolution: British Government in the Nineteenth Century* (Longman, 1977).
[19] E. Joanna Guldi, *Roads to Power: Britain Invents the Infrastructure State* (Harvard University Press, 2012), Ch. 1.

representative figure of the civil servant, who was also in part a technical expert and in part a politician (for instance the Hill family in the Post Office). The second phase represented the disaggregation of this hybrid, the politician and civil servant becoming increasingly distinct ethical personae. William Farr, a high official at the General Register Office, was an instance of this, being a new kind of civil servant in whom the dedicated social scientist now became the dedicated bureaucrat rather than the dedicated lobbyist or opinion former.[20] The technical expert, therefore, tended to be swallowed up in the state machinery and unable to shape a public voice. The scientific expert, after the early days of zealot and lay scientific expertise, was therefore curbed by government, being completely submerged in government departments which relied on their own formal procedures and rules, and which were overseen by civil service mandarins in the shape of the Permanent Secretaries.[21]

The new sort of "expert" that mattered most therefore was this kind of man, the expert in administrating the centre of government, the expert of all the other experts as it were, the *capo di tutti capi*. It was not from science and technology that the personae of this kind of bureaucrat were fabricated, nor from this source that their perceived ethical neutrality and authority to administer were derived. These lay in two fields, their education and their work life. In respect to the former, we can see that in the new permanent civil service established by the Northcote-Trevelyan Report of 1853–4, Gladstone and others made a deliberate attempt to strengthen ties between administrative power and the existing upper classes, so that the code of the gentleman and his "honourable secrecy" came to epitomise the new bureaucrat.[22] However, this was now to happen by means of the code of "merit" as reformulated in the reformed public schools and a reformed Oxbridge. First however it is to the second of these two fields that I attend, namely the work of the state, and how this shaped the high bureaucracy but also lower levels in the hierarchy too.

I   The common knowledge of the state

Bureaucracy depends on the extinction of the individual personality of the bureaucrat and its replacement by what is designed to be regarded as the neutral, and therefore autonomous, personhood of the bureaucrat.

[20] John Eyler, *Victorian Social Medicine: The Ideas and Methods of William Farr* (Johns Hopkins University Press, 1979); and see Patrick Joyce, *The Rule of Freedom*, pp. 27, 32, 33.
[21] McLeod, "Introduction" in McLeod (ed.), *Government and Expertise*.
[22] David Vincent, *The Culture of Secrecy: Britain 1832–1998* (Oxford University Press, 1998), pp. 41–5, 46–50, 50–65 and Ch. 3, for continuing tensions and contradictions between secrecy and merit from the mid-nineteenth century onwards.

Therefore, in considering the mundane work of the state it is necessary to explore how this personhood is actually made. The bureaucrats as well as the institution of bureaucracy were produced through the routines and material practices of bureaucratic work. The civil servant examination entrant to the high civil service was turned into the finished product through the acquisition of *practical* knowledge (the product to be finished of course, at least at the top of the hierarchy, was public-school Oxbridge Man). Administrative knowledge was self-consciously a matter of the training of all mental and physical attributes. In a decided echo of the public school, initiation involved several years of active drudgery and self-abnegation, so that the power to what was called "drudge resolutely" and to train habit were prerequisites. In much the same way as in so much classics learning, the power to work hard at a subject one had no interest in was critical. What one analyst of the civil service has called the "drilling" of thoroughness, of accuracy, and of clarity of reasoning and language, were uppermost. Drilling was to continue until these became part of the civil servant's "nature". The "well written brief" helped authorise the persona of the "reasonable civil servant". Everything the young civil servant wrote was seen by a superior and subject to this scrutiny. The civil servant must always be able to show authority for what he writes, and to show correct reasoning. He experiences the "tough scepticism" of the experienced official. In the British civil servant a rigorous attention to writing and language for three or four years between the ages of twenty-four and twenty-eight "suffuses his mind and character permanently with a passion for precise facts and close inferences, and with a grim distrust of vague generalities".[23]

I have referred to this caste of mind with the term "common knowledge", and something more should be said about its use. Of course it echoes my general interest in the constitution of "common sense", of naturalisation, the *habitus*, and similar terms. It is striking how little attention has been paid to the sort of practical, everyday knowledge here called common knowledge. In the literature on governmentality it is usually conspicuous by its absence, for there the interest is either in highly generalised modes of power – disciplinary power or biopower, say – or the epistemic structures underlying the operations of government, especially liberal government. In other words, in freedom in the abstract, as opposed to, as in this book, freedom on the ground, in the dirt. The very opposite of "learning with Nelly", in fact, whether it be the male Nelly of the soldier's

---

[23] H. E. Dale, *The Higher Civil Service of Great Britain* (Oxford, 1941), p. 81, and *passim* for the qualities of the civil servant as described here. See also Vincent, *The Culture of Secrecy*, pp. 31–3.

mess room or that of the craftman's shop. Instead, as Mariana Valverde has argued strongly, a concentration on "high-status" knowledge has systematically ignored "low-status" forms, even though the latter have been (and are) used by the state in a great variety of situations.[24] As well as, and often instead of, considering single and general governmental logics across many fields and situations (a logic of high-status expertise), the significance of more specific sites of knowledge generated more locally is urged by Valverde.

This she calls local or common knowledge in the sense not only of it being tied to mundane contexts but also to common modes of reasoning and bodies of knowledge. Valverde considers what she calls "law's dream of a common knowledge" in terms of how legal knowledge is often highly reliant not on "expert" knowledge as such but on invocations of "common sense", on what is regarded as "common knowledge", that which a "rational person" could be expected to employ and act by. Local or common knowledge in its nature generates knowledge as it acts and does, as it goes along as it were, ironically rather like so-called hard scientific knowledge in fact. Ironic because, as science studies reveals, the knowledge a scientist thinks is being born *ex nihilo* is only one link in a chain of many actors (machines, inscription devices such as charts, living people, concepts etc.). Similarly, as Foucault saw in regard to "sex", knowledge is produced by the very processes that claim to discover and study it.

In terms of the instantiation of a textual and an institutional *habitus*, and so the production of bureaucratic authority and self-perception, one can first employ the idea of the bureaucratic "voice".[25] The term covers speaking as well as writing however. This is the position from which persons "speak", or seek to speak, what they consider to be "truth". It is the position from which in speaking or writing they claim authority: for instance, the voice of the scholar does not for the most part say "look at me" – the truth of what he or she does is to be got by leaving the writing subject out.[26] In this sense the voice of the academic and the voice of the bureaucrat are similar: both concerned to leave themselves out. The voice of the bureaucrat much more so, however, for his or her voice is strikingly monological, and not dialogical, so that it resists dialogue in the cause of shutting out other levels of experience pertaining to personal and

---

[24] Mariana Valverde, *Law's Dream of Common Knowledge: The Cultural Lives of Law* (Princeton University Press, 2003).

[25] "Who speaks? The Voice in the Human Sciences", *History of the Human Sciences*, Special Issue, 10:3 (August 1997).

[26] Ibid., 2.

individual life.[27] For instance there is the famous "plain style" of the bureaucrat's prose, and supposedly of their speaking, the style without style as it is supposed to be. As has been seen, particular "knowledge formats" such as the well-written brief authorise bureaucratic personae.[28] Prose style should be plain, judicious and terse. However printing also took a hand here, as can be seen from the vast array of printed forms that the Post Office was using by the 1880s, never mind the 1930s. The aim of the form was to simplify and standardise, to make things plain and terse, to the supplier of the form if not always in practice to the user. The simple fact that bureaucratic paperwork, of all sorts, came to be printed and so because of this further standardised meant that "form" determined content even more. Objectivised bureaucratic knowledge helped config-ure bureaucratic personae as objective.[29]

However the plain style can metamorphose into another monological style that is anything but plain, in the form of the convoluted mandarin-esque English satirised so well in the British television series *Yes Minister*.[30] This resists dialogue in a way contrary to the spirit if not always the practice of bureaucracy. The discourse of the bureaucrat is distinct from the dialogical style of the politician, which relies on projection of personality, *individual* personality, in order to secure power. However, if about the extinction of personality in one way, bureaucracy also partly depends on personality too, but on displaying personality as a surrogate code of *conduct*. For instance administrative ability in the British civil service was held to be about the arts of consultation, the efficient use of intermediaries, and so the employment of personal skills, but the end was the projection of a version of exemplary conduct. This exclusion of the individual self was designed to be inclusive at a fundamental level, for the bureaucrat's role was to be the voice of the state, of the public and of the common interest. Of course, this voice of the state was in practice anything but inclusive for the simple reason that it rested upon the views and prejudices of state servants who were and are always representative of their time and origins, thus in reality they are exclusive, not inclusive. Because this is so there can never be a truly "neutral" civil servant, for all

[27] Peter Becker and William Clark (eds.), *Little Tools of Knowledge: Historical Essays on Academic and Bureaucratic Practices* (Michigan University Press, 2000), "Introduction".
[28] Valverde, *Law's Dream of Common Knowledge*.
[29] Becker and Clark (eds.), *Little Tools of Knowledge*, "Introduction" on the role of paperwork in shaping the increasingly scientific forms of state bureaucratic knowledge apparent in the nineteenth century.
[30] See the substantial entry on *Yes Minister* in Wikipedia, also www.bbc.co.uk/comedy/yesminister.

bureaucrats in the end construct themselves in the image of the state they are in.

Within the regime of writing as well as the actual paperwork itself, as we have seen with the file and its processing, there were the written rules and regulations that governed the conduct of the officer. Looking at the making of conduct in this more direct fashion then, and remaining with writing for the moment, there was from the 1850s both in India and in Britain a proliferation of printed rules and regulations, all telling bureaucrats what to do and how to do it.[31] "Manuals", "lists", "calendars" and "handbooks" of all sorts abounded. What had earlier not been written down now increasingly was, so that writing to some degree replaced the fluidity of office precedent and custom. Promotion ladders, leave and rates of pay were made public, as were regulations governing conduct, including the economic and political activity of officers. These regulations are sometimes very extensive: the Ceylon manual of 1865 has 400 separate listed categories in the index.[32]

In India this "rule of the manual" was perceived to be evident from the 1840s.[33] The systematisation of the rules and regulations governing the operation of bureaucracy was in this case part of a more general move to exclude indigenous elements from high levels of government, so that Indians were limited to local rather than to provincial office, and so directed away from meaningfully political functions. Thereafter, the use of the English language itself served to demarcate upper and lower levels. The report was part of the same paperwork regime as the manual. The report legitimated the various administrative and cultural partitions of British rule, in part by being an "official" document and something authenticated as "science" if, as was so often the case, it contained statistics. Those outside these "official" and "scientific" worlds were excluded as bureaucrats drew the mantle of language, office and science around themselves. Beyond bureaucracy, and considering the object not

---

[31] For a fairly representative sample see *The Handbook of Civil Service: A Complete Guide, Etc to the Various Departments of the Public Service* (London, 1861); *The Civil Service Calendar, 1886, Containing the Official Regulations of Her Majesty's Civil Service Commissioners* (London, 1886); *The Ceylon Civil Service Manual, Being a Compilation of Government Minutes, Circulars, Etc, with an Appendix Containing a Summary of Colonial Regulations, a List of Legislative Enactments in Force, and a Glossary of Ceylon Terms. Corrected up to 30th of November 1865* (London, 1865); *Manual of the Rules and Regulations Applicable to Members of the Indian Civil Service* (Calcutta, 1887); *The India List Civil and Military* (London, 1882). It should be noted that only the 1897 item was published and printed by government, all the others being privately produced.

[32] *The Ceylon Civil Service Manual.*

[33] R. S. Smith, "Ruling-by-Record and Ruling-by-Reports: Complementary Aspects of the British Imperial Rule of Law", *Contributions to Indian Sociology*, 19:1 (1985).

the agent of governance for a moment, the importance of the government report in directly configuring rather than simply analysing the object of rule has long been recognised, for India and for the UK.[34]

The role of writing in governing bureaucratic conduct and bureaucratic common sense as well as the objects of rule has been recognised, in the Dutch case, by Ann Laura Stoler.[35] This role was however perhaps most evident with the examination. Very soon after the Northcote-Trevelyan reforms the examination became entrenched in ways involving conduct and not just learning, although the two were inextricably connected. The 1861 (privately published but government-endorsed) home civil service *Handbook* was itself highly opinionated and anything but ideologically neutral, inveighing as it did in its introduction against the "old" patronage order as government by the "incapable", assuring its readers, contrary to critics' claims, that examinations would not be at the expense of the "constitutional energy and vigour needed to sustain a robust manhood".[36] The conduct appropriate to manhood was complemented by the need for candidates to be what was called "naturally intelligent". This applied at least partially even to the lower grades. Down to the lowest levels of the government service ability now had to be *publicly* shown: this was the case for low-level clerks, but not however for labourers, even if the qualifications of the clerks were to be only in handwriting and orthography. A certain sort of new bureaucratic man was being engineered.

In India the examination mattered perhaps even more than in Britain. There promotion ladders were marked in advance by examinations, including the so-called "departmentals" in the early days of the career, quite apart from the initial examination that got one into the new "civil service" that was instituted by the Act of 1853. However, on-the-job

---

[34] For instance in India in the case of the Punjab. Here as well as being authentic and official the report has been understood to have helped create "a systematic understanding of the whole of Indian society", so "framing" India *in extenso* as the object of the bureaucrat's rule and the source of legitimation for his conduct. This happened in part through a change in the form of such provincial reports from being mainly a financial record of land revenue to a more "social" use involving the greater employment of statistics. This allowed the development of legal codes covering the population at large and not only those paying rents. The introduction of statistics entailed new forms and uses of knowledge about society, and these coalesced with the move from contractual to statutory government at this time. This process was complemented by other policies serving the same end, political and legal as well as bureaucratic. Ibid., 173–4. Martin Schaffner, "The Figure of the Questions versus the Prose of the Answers: Lord Devon's Inquiry in Skibbereen, 10 September 1844" in Becker and Clark (eds.), *Little Tools of Knowledge*.

[35] Ann Laura Stoler, *Along the Archival Grain: Epistemic Anxieties and Colonial Common Sense* (Princeton University Press, 2010). Also see above, pp. 12–13.

[36] *Handbook of Civil Service*, 1861. This handbook covered in all eighty-nine public offices, including those for Scotland and Ireland, the leading departments but also such as the Lunacy Commission and Metropolitan Police.

training mattered there as everywhere once onc was in. "Robust manhood" and examinations being in fact anything but incompatible, the
bureaucratic body and soul were involved as well as the bureaucratic
mind. As bureaucracy expanded there was a refashioning of how the
body of the bureaucrat was seen and presented, also a fashioning of the
senses of the bureaucrat himself or herself. This was evident in all
advanced bureaucracies, and among high and low levels of the hierarchy.
For example, there was the training of criminalistic observation, so that
in those sections of government concerned with expertise in crime after
the mid-nineteenth century there grew up what has been called the
"criminological eye".[37] In the account of the Post Office the uniform
and training of the letter carrier and postman were part of the training of
conduct of the low-level bureaucrat. As well as the criminological "eye"
there was the common postman's "walk", when the public behaviour of
this state official was closely monitored. There was also and perhaps above
all, as will be seen, the *place* of work, the office itself.

In addition, the extra-office environment was important of course,
especially in Britain. The London social-club life of the high civil servant
for example, and in India the social life of the civil servant. This involved
"learning with Nelly", but Nelly in India was a collective one – male and
female, native and British, the whole panoply of the social life of the Raj, in
fact – in which the British civil servant was forever on display, and so
forever on duty. On display to the natives, but also to fellow Britons, as the
novels of E. M. Forster and (on Africa) Graham Green make plain. This
display required a peculiarly intense training in social etiquette, which
was in practice a regulatory technology, the new arrival being actively
mentored by superiors as he encountered the social life of the club, the
house party, the visit and the use of the calling card. In India, far from the
personal life of the officer being rigidly separated from the job, as one part
of the logic of the public servant would suggest, it was an active part of it,
although a highly regulated part subordinated to the overarching bureaucratic code. Nor must we forget the material rewards of the high civil
service, in general and particularly so in India where the role was very
handsomely paid. The job was the means of a livelihood for the bureaucrat
in economic as well as social terms, so the civil servant at the high as well as
the low end of the spectrum was regulated by financial instruments.

---

[37] Hans Erich Bödeker, "On the Origins of the "Statistical Gaze": Modes of Perception,
Forms of Knowledge, and Ways of Writing in the Early Social Sciences", and Peter
Becker, "Objective Distance and Intimate Knowledge: On the Structure of
Criminalistic Observation and Description" in Becker and Clark (eds.), *Little Tools of
Knowledge*.

The training of the bureaucratic body has to be historically considered in terms of the overall transition from patronage to the examination and "merit", at home and in the empire. However this was slower than is often recognised. When the Order in Council of 1870 further extending the use of examinations was made it stipulated that they would be used only in those departments agreed upon by ministers, and these did not include the Home Office or Foreign Office. Only in 1914 after the McDonnell Commission on the civil service were examinations extended to all departments, and even then the Foreign Office only partly fell in line. And, even when examinations were implemented thoroughly, certification of good moral conduct had to be given in order to take them. This involved giving "proof", which in the circumstances of the time for those at the lower levels was only to be had from those of superior social standing. Men such as doorkeepers or domestic servants in the India Office, for example, regularly tapped into the patronage and family connections of existing and former Council members in order to obtain work. In the India Office itself examinations were less important than in India: Sir John Kaye, a leading Office official, was happy to extend patronage to his own son, and in doing this only echoed conduct that was widespread and largely unremarked.[38]

Caught between patronage and the examination Britain was a post-aristocratic society, and even if old-style patronage declined the country has remained post-aristocratic, unable to tear itself away from the burden of the past. The conflict, and rapprochement, of old and new rationalities of governance runs right through the period of this book, up to the present. In the early days the novelist Anthony Trollope, a very prominent Post Office official of the old mentality, derided the introduction of competitive civil service exams.[39] He was particularly vociferous about their effect: "As what I now write will certainly never be read till I am dead, I may dare say what no one now does dare to say in print, – though some of us whisper it occasionally into our friends' ears. There are places in life which can hardly be well filled except by 'Gentlemen'. The word is one the use of which almost subjects one to ignominy."[40] He went on, "The gates of the one class should be open to the other; but neither to one class or to the other can good be done by declaring that there are no gates, no barrier, no difference. The system of competitive examination is,

---

[38] India Office Records, L/P and S/19 (temporary number 244).
[39] Anthony Trollope, *An Autobiography* (Edinburgh, 1883), 2 vols., vol. i, pp. 18–19. See also Edmund Yates, *Edmund Yates, His Recollections and Experiences* (London, 1884), pp. 85, 85–6, 86.
[40] Trollope, *An Autobiography*, p. 39.

I think, based on a supposition that there is no difference."[41] Trollope's fears were to prove groundless. Those less than gentlemen did not storm the citadels of the British state, for Gladstone, Trevelyan, Macaulay and the others had done their jobs. Gentlemanly status was retained, remodelled and sanctioned and much the same sort of people continued to govern as previously. And so it has continued, at least in the sense that the ideology of "merit" in British society has been a cloak for the profound inequalities of that society. Or rather, more to the point, the "merit" machine has been the technological means by which these very inequalities have been reproduced, for given how deeply rooted social and economic inequalities are in Britain merit can essentially only have this role.

However, if patronage remained a feature of for instance the Post Office, it tended increasingly to be viewed as more of a burden than a benefit, as it was to MPs as well.[42] Even Trollope, with his strong emotional attachment to the old ways of doing things, recognised this.[43] It was finally abolished in 1895. As we have seen,[44] the sort of patronage that continued tended more and more to be based on merit anyway, especially on technical qualification. Even so, the definition of what "qualification" for a job amounted too was, and is, elastic, given the large areas of British government free of democratic accountability at the ballot box, the House of Lords most famously so. Irrespective of the whole public debate about examinations and "merit" the state had anyway for some time been moving away from older practices in a different way. This was previously seen in the long history of "economical government" within the Post Office, and it applied to government in general.

Bureaucracy and the bureaucrat were shaped by the wage and by capitalist rationality as well as by the examinations and gentlemanly conduct. The late eighteenth-century state was already "modern", "rational" and "capitalist" in this respect. Before the 1780s staff were paid according to seniority. Salaries were proportionate to length of service and the dignity of the office more than to the work that was undertaken by each officer. By paying staff for the performance of particular functions the costs of the service could be accurately assessed according to the principles of the cost of labour time and expertise. These were the standards appealed to in *The Wealth of Nations* and the assumption was that they

---

[41] Ibid., p. 40.
[42] Martin Daunton, *Royal Mail: The Post Office since 1840* (Athlone Press, 1985), pp. 2, 76.
[43] Trollope, *An Autobiography*, p. 39.   [44] See above, pp. 34–5.

represented the true cost of work.[45] It was taken as a given amongst the eighteenth-century postal reformers too that work should be measured according to the time taken to do it and the level of complexity and specialisation that was required to perform it.[46] Most importantly of all this would allow the costs of particular government services to be assessed according to the criteria that were becoming universal in all aspects of economic life.

We now take the divisions and remuneration of labour pioneered in the late eighteenth century as "natural", however they were and are anything but, least of all at the time of their invention. They did not however represent a movement from the "traditional" to the "modern", for instance from the irrational and venal to the rational and economic, but only a different way of doing things. The fiscal-military state was already "modern", perfectly efficient and "rational" in its own way. It is very important to recognise this: dichotomies of modern and traditional simply do not hold here, nor indeed in most places. Politically, they are very often the invention of interested parties, usually "reformers" of one sort or another. Capitalist rationality sat side by side with the retention of seemingly "traditional" ways of managing matters, and not only in matters of patronage, for the previously hidden history of the bureaucratic workplace tells the same story. The bureaucratic office does not see a progression from the household to the market model of social relations at this time. The historical trajectories of economic systems and the social relations of the built forms that housed these relations were not the same. Bureaucratic conduct and the training of the bureaucratic body took place most of all where the work of the state was carried on. These places, the places in common between state workers, served to further shape the common knowledge of governing. It is to these state places I shall now attend in some detail.

Not surprisingly for a great imperial state, when it came to the development of new Office buildings it was the Foreign Office and the India Office that led the way in the 1850s and 60s.[47] However, up to the end of the nineteenth century conditions in other government offices were fairly

---

[45] Adam Smith, *An Inquiry into the Nature and Causes of the Wealth of Nations*, ed. R. H. Campbell, A. S. Skinner and W. B. Todd (Liberty Fund, 1981), I.i.6, pp. 17–18, and I.iii.

[46] See the reforms of Lord Walsingham, the Post Master General, in POST 58/1: Orders, 1737–1774, 4 November 1772, pp. 7–8, also p. 90. See also POST 97/1: 1787, pp. 87–8 for Post Master General Walsingham on the abolition of gratuities.

[47] This discussion draws on M. H. Port, *Imperial London: Civil Government Building in London 1850–1915* (Yale University Press, 1995), Chs. 3, 8 and 13 on "battle of the styles". See also H. M. Colvin et al., *The History of the King's Works*, vol. VI, *1782–1851* (HMSO, 1973).

haphazard. The same department might have different locations and accommodation was often rented and not purpose-built, so that the adaptation of older houses and their stringing together to contain departments deserves the terms "warren" and "labyrinth", terms which were regularly applied to government offices. While centrally located in Whitehall, the War Office for example was spread out over ten different locations in the 1860s. Conditions were frequently cramped therefore, although for the higher officer compared with a century later individual rooms were actually quite big.[48] Economical government and legal and financial impediments, also political differences, retarded the development of government offices, but nonetheless a move of sorts to centralisation is evident, both of function within departments and in the evolution of the department itself.[49]

As the Post Office grew from the late eighteenth century the departments themselves became more specialised. Not only did different sections of the Post Office perform particular functions, but they were physically separated with different departments in different offices within the same building, as well as different buildings dealing with different aspects of Post Office duty. Again, a logic analogous to the market was in operation, in terms of the organisation and physical structure of the institution. In the seventeenth and eighteenth centuries the Post Office was run from a small headquarters without a particularly large staff. Staff eventually moved to more extensive premises on Lombard Street, until by the early nineteenth century the organisation was large enough to justify the construction of a dedicated building, St Martins-le-Grand. By the mid-nineteenth century even this was too small to handle the rapidly increasing business of the Post Office, so that the Money Order Office and the Post Office Savings Bank had their own separate offices in Aldersgate Street and St Paul's Churchyard.[50] Later the telegraph would have its own separate offices too. As regards the staff we have seen the attention to economy within the Post Office that extended to the treatment of the staff as what would later be called a "human resource".[51]

---

[48] Port, *Imperial London*, p. 32, Table 2.
[49] Ibid., p. 33; also *Parliamentary Papers 1856* (368), vol. XIV, p. 34; *Parliamentary Papers 1857*, (152), vol. XLI, "New Government and Offices", pp. 4–12; *Parliamentary Papers 1877* (312), vol. XV, Select Committee on Public Offices, App. A, Standard of Accommodation.
[50] William Lewins, *Her Majesty's Mails: An Historical and Descriptive Account of the British Post Office. Together with an Appendix* (London, 1864), p. 194.
[51] See above, pp. 95–100; and for further information on this, POST 64/1, pp. 7–8.

A number of factors spurred on developments in the nineteenth century, including the influence of business, where the labour-intensive "bank parlour" model of bank and merchant house division of labour became increasingly applied in government offices, clerks being massed together in large rooms. W. H. Smith, founder of the great office stationery and publications empire, was a leading politician of the time, and together with radical MPs and technocrats of bureaucracy developed this particular transfer of bureaucratic order from the world of business to the world of government. Once again, Charles Trevelyan was a major driving force. Trevelyan is claimed to have been the first to promote the notion of "administrative efficiency".[52] He had a clear understanding of the new government office as a disciplinary machine: when office labour was concentrated officers could interact personally, with the result that they would be able to evaluate each other's work and so emulate one another. The familiar distinction between mental and manual labour was once again apparent in his views, the idea being that the higher officers would work uninterruptedly in their own offices, while the lower orders would be concentrated together. This model developed rather unevenly, led by the India Office, but also implemented by the Board of Trade somewhat earlier. For all Trevelyan's innovations however it is quite apparent that in all these new developments there was very little comprehension of what an office building actually was, at least in the sense of the office building as we understand it.

It is here we begin to discern the central role of what I later treat more systematically as "domiciliary power", for it was the physical and symbolic form of the *house* – a crux of all human identity – that turns out to have been the critical site of human and governmental actions upon conduct. The new government office of the time (in this case the mid-to-late nineteenth century) was however only one of a number of spatial locations where the house and the home were brought together in new forms. The public school "house", the post-aristocratic high-bourgeois home, the Oxbridge College as a domicile, the Houses of Parliament, the new post offices themselves (as with the Oxford one), were all expressions of this, as well as the government office.[53] Each drew upon and magnified the potency of the others.

---

[52] Port, *Imperial London*, pp. 30–1. Trevelyan's promotion of economical government was part of a drive towards the concentration of revenue departments, designed to secure financial control, the idea being that such a concentration would bring to the fore the best officers so that these would go on to fill permanent positions in the Treasury.

[53] See above, pp. 9, 11–12, 26–7.

Two forms of this redeployment seem especially relevant for bureaucracy. These were firstly the collegiate one of elite education and the elite professions (the legal profession and the Inns of Court, and to some degree Parliament itself), and secondly the form of the private house of the wealthy, appropriations of the aristocratic house in neo-gentlemanly form serving to express the ideal of the gentleman as interpreted by the middle classes of the period. In practice these merged, the house being the ur-form of the college. The result was that the house of the Victorian wealthy served as the model framing (literally "housing") values about public service and the public servant. The much-vaunted "separate spheres" of Victorian culture, the house as home expressing private life only, tells only a limited part of the story. Somerset House, off London's Strand, is by common consent the first purpose-built government building.[54] During large parts of the eighteenth century the old, originally aristocratic Somerset House (the original was built in 1583) was used for a variety of government purposes. The demise of the old mansion coincided with a move to house government offices and the principle learned societies of Britain under one roof, an early example of concentration and the desire for efficiency. The new structure, built between 1776 and 1796, was also to be "a great public building … an object of national splendour".[55] However, the model was the house, the architect Chambers resolving the various purposes of the new structure by treating the offices housed in the building as what were in effect a series of town houses arranged in a quadrangular layout, extending across the whole site of the old palace and its gardens and out into the Thames, some six acres in all.

It should be emphasised that the new design represented a house in the full sense, a place where people lived. The new building had to provide living accommodation for the heads of the various departments housed there, also for the cooks, housekeepers, secretaries and others who serviced the civil service. At this time the Lords of the Admiralty also lived in parts of the Admiralty Building itself. A century later, the parliamentary inquiry of 1887 into the future War Office conceived of it in much the same way, in line with the "new" Foreign Office and India Office, namely as what it described as part government palace and part aristocratic house and household.[56] If the exterior took the form of the palace, then the interior took that of the household. In the case of the Post Office in the late

---

[54] www.somersethouse.org.uk/history. See also Port, *Imperial London*, pp. 43, 46.
[55] L. M. Bates, *Somerset House: Four Hundred Years of History* (Muller, 1967).
[56] Port, *Imperial London*.

eighteenth century, the model of the government office or department was also the household, not simply the house.

In 1691 the list of the entire staff of the GPO fitted onto one page of foolscap; however by the 1740s it had become more extensive and by the 1790s it was a complex organisation of several hundred staff. Even so, the structure at headquarters was both self-contained and secretive. The heads of the department had the title "Esquire" and had houses in the headquarters building. Their clerks had the title of "Gentleman" and had smaller lodgings in the Office, with quarterly salaries. The "outdoor staff" were on a wage.[57] Thus a distinction was made between the staff not only in salary terms, but physically in their location within or outside the building. Living apart from the rest of the community and keeping unsociable hours, the staff were segregated from the rest of the world. The active departments were housed on the lower floors while the apartments above ranged "from well appointed suites to overcrowded garrets".[58] Commensality was part of this, with "office feasts" at which "boastful songs about their own importance and efficiency" were sung. "A good Post Office education" was the aim, life and work merging into one. Dependants of the PMG (Postmaster General) were employed, starting in the office at the age of fourteen, frequently without pay but being marked out for promotion. Others came from more distant recommendations; none had been to university.[59] The staff had the parliamentary vote, but could not influence elections. In 1782 they were disenfranchised (except for the Patent Officers).[60]

If in government offices after the mid-nineteenth century government officers themselves had for the most part moved out of the workplace itself, many of the people servicing these officers had not, so that there is both discontinuity and continuity with the eighteenth-century pattern of the house and household as models for institutional governance. Contemporaries were themselves long aware of this hybrid character of the government office. For instance, a Treasury Study Group on government buildings in 1944 reported that before 1914 office buildings were either like architectural creations or private houses.[61] This is not surprising, when it is apparent that many of the new commercial office buildings designed at the time were themselves conceived of as little more than

---

[57] K. Ellis, *The Post Office in the Eighteenth Century: A Study in Administrative History* (Oxford University Press, 1958), p. 20.

[58] Ibid., p. 20; Post Office Archives, *Report on the New Post Office 1814* and *St Martins Le Grand*, Issue I, p. 234.

[59] Ibid., *The Post Office in the Eighteenth Century*, pp. 20–1.

[60] Ibid., *The Post Office in the Eighteenth Century*, pp. 22–3.   [61] Port, *Imperial London*.

relatively modest households.[62] As well as the domiciliary one, there are a number of other aspects of the government building that need consideration.

The move from the old Post Office building to St Martins-le-Grand in the 1820s was essentially the same as that from the old East India Company headquarters in the City's Leadenhall Street to Whitehall. Both represented a shift in the spatial centre of gravity of government from the old order of fiscal-military imperialism, the City, to the new liberal, communications state, though because the interests of the City and the Post Office remained so close the move from the old, inner-City warrens was in this case only to the edge of the City at St Paul's. However, the drift of government into the new pastures of a redeveloped Whitehall and Westminster was clear, pastures themselves opened up after 1840 to the London parks and the West End.[63] However, this shift only masked the fact that for all its assumed modernity government was coming back to its real home, to its ancient locations. Only now remodelled: between 1840 and 1860 the new Palace of Westminster was built, also the new Westminster Bridge. The Foreign Office and India Office were completed by 1868. Buckingham Palace started to function as the official London residence of the monarchy after 1837. This was followed by the redesign of the streets of Whitehall in the 1880s, which was fairly quickly followed by the second great phase of the building of imperial London around 1900, the building of Kingsway, the Aldwych, Admiralty Arch and the Mall.[64]

However, the Whitehall and Westminster concentration of government at the time was simply repeating what over the *longue durée* had been the extraordinarily concentrated nature of British government. It represented in spatial form the powers of a British state that was always Anglo- – indeed London- – centric. This was not just a remarkable spatial concentration but an equally remarkable concentration of *time* in a particular place, centuries of government being represented in the same location, so that temporal layers of the British state were laid down one upon another, in the same way as the streets of London have been created. "History" was

---

[62] Francis Duffy, "Office Building and Organisational Change: on the Sun Insurance Office in London, 1849" in A. D. King, *Buildings and Society: Essays on the Social Development of the Built Environment* (Routledge & Kegan Paul, 1980). See also Nikolaus Pevsner, *A History of Building Types* (Thames and Hudson, 1976).

[63] J. W. K., "The House that Jack Built", *Cornhill Magazine*, vol. II (July–December 1860), and vol. XVI (July–December 1867), "Of the House that Scott Built" on differences between the old Leadenhall Street office of the East India Company and the new India Office. See also Robert Machray, "The India Office", *India Magazine* (October 1900), 490 on the Office as a state in miniature.

[64] Jonathan Schneer, *London 1900: The Imperial Metropolis* (Yale University Press, 1999).

brought into play here, as with almost all the institutions of British government (law courts, colleges and schools, Parliament), the use of history in
art and architecture being an obsession of the nineteenth century. I have
elsewhere explored this "governance of time" in relation to the city,[65] and
this utilisation of time as a deliberate strategy of governance, as will be
seen again later when elite education is looked at. The same was occurring
in terms of the state. Whitehall and its environs, particularly the Strand
and the city of Westminster, were already ancient in the history of the
government office before the street took its various nineteenth- and
twentieth-century forms.

Therefore, it is not surprising that these ancient forms, as seen in the
government house as part palace and part private residence, were so
consistently reproduced. In terms of their grand public rooms, courtyards
and staircases, the Foreign and India Offices were designed as palaces of
government. So too was the Colonial Office.[66] The new St Martins-le-
Grand was similarly thought of; and as we have seen, across the world the
colossal public importance of Post Office headquarters was reflected in
the idea of the "palace of communications". In these respects, the outside
of buildings dominated over the inside. The result could sometimes be
ludicrous: preserving the window line which led from the Foreign Office
to the India Office (both were jointly part of the huge new complex of
government built by Barry and Scott) involved some of the windows in the
India Office being at floor level!

Most existing accounts of the bureaucratic office tend to deal with
cultural representations rather than practice and use, and in particular
with the external rather than internal structure, so almost completely
ignoring the material powers of the government office building. This is
the case with the India Office too.[67] The new India Office was in its
exterior designed to augment the affect of its paperwork technologies.
The design also aimed at expressing as much as possible continuities
between the old Company and the new institution. The narrative schema
of the building was also designed to smooth out all the inconsistencies and
contention of real empire, presenting "a natural, even seamless, rise to
power" (see Figure 5.1).[68] We know about the outsides of buildings more
than their insides because it is very difficult to understand their daily use
from this distance in time. India Office documents nonetheless take us

[65] Joyce, *The Rule of Freedom*, Ch. 4.
[66] Brian L. Blakeley, *The Colonial Office, 1868–1892* (Duke University Press, 1972), Ch. 4.
[67] H. M. Bremner, "Nation and Empire in the Government Architecture of Mid-Victorian
London: the Foreign and India Office Reconsidered", *Historical Journal*, 48:3 (2005).
[68] Ibid., 739.

Fig. 5.1 Photograph of the Inner Court, India Office, also known as the "Durbar Court", n.d., 1890s

some way towards understanding use and function. There is first the "Minute Paper 2" of the Clerk of Works Department, 1859, with the heading "The future household of this office and its domestic administration".[69] This is then supported by remarkably full documentation of the internal organisation and spatial distributions within the India Office.[70] This can be analysed floor by floor, quite literally upstairs/downstairs (to echo the

[69] Dated 30 November 1867, Folio 358, IO Records. This and the appendices are in the Accountant General's records at L/AG/27–30.
[70] Minute Paper 2 of the Clerk of Works Department, 1867, "The Future Household of this Office and its Domestic Administration". The memorandum of 30 November is then amplified in the form of appendices, as follows: "Appendix A., General memorandum of 1861 constituting establishment, meeting of the finance committee, 26th February 1861" (Folio 363 ff.); "Appendix B., Memorandum of the doorkeepers and messengers, their present and future duties; and temporary posts at new India office" (Folio 365 ff.); and most valuable of all, Appendix C., "List of rooms in the new India Office with the number assigned to each", 25 November 1867; "Appendix D., "Nominal list of office keepers, messengers etc according to class and those employed on outlying duties etc" (Folio 390 ff.); Appendix E., "Scheme showing extra messengers required and allotments of duties, etc"; Appendix F., "Showing allotments of messengers the stations answering bells and tubes" (Folio 396 ff.), a particularly useful document showing the whereabouts by name and room number of all who then worked in the India Office, 28 November 1867; Appendix G., "Diagram showing relative positions of rooms and messenger stations

title of the popular British TV series of that name on the class structure of Victorian Britain). The human geography of the government office represented that of the well-to-do house and household, and both represented the class structure of Britain with remarkable fidelity.[71]

We will look more closely at how the building worked. In 1867 the basement was first made up of the eighteen rooms where the infrastructure of the building was housed: coal cellars, boiler rooms and the maintenance spaces for the building's lifts. The basement, of sixty-one rooms in total, was the "downstairs" of the "great house" which the India Office truly was. Here was to be found provision for the large number of domestic servants and messengers, many of whom lived in: there were dressing and dining rooms, washing and waiting rooms, and kitchens (kitchens were separate for men and women). This was the level of human infrastructure, and it was here properly enough that wine, beer and food were kept. Above all, this seems to have been the domain of the head housekeeper, one Mrs Moores, who had her own group of personal rooms. So too did the head doorkeeper, Mr Badrick, who had a kitchen, scullery, bedroom and sitting room. Within the greater domestic whole numerous sub-spheres of personal domestic life are apparent therefore, sub-plots in the main story as it were. The pinnacle of the organisation, and the head of the house, was the Secretary of State for India, who had his own private entrance in the basement, one however keeping him away from unwanted contact with the servant class. However "below stairs" was not his domain but that of the lower orders, none of whom were lower than the charwoman: of sixteen charwoman eight lived in at a miserly salary of £40 per annum.

The complicated system of servant bells and speaking tubes began in earnest on the ground floor, although those in the basement "below stairs" also had channels of communication by these means. This communications technology, then common in the residences of the well-to-do, created internal connectivity in the building in ways that were highly sophisticated, and which are particularly revealing. It should be remembered that for long in Britain the telephone was called the "blower", and is sometimes called so today, a reference back to speaking-tube technology, as one had first to blow into the tube to activate the whistle at the other end before delivering the message (whistles were attached at each end of the

with which they communicate, the blue dots show the stations and names in red ink of the messengers on duty, as proposed" (Folios 397–400); this is the plan showing all the messenger stations in the building, floor by floor, with markings showing the connections between individual rooms and their inhabitants and the messengers who serviced these rooms (reproduced as Figure 5.4 in the text).

[71] The BBC TV series ran between 1971 and 1975; see the Wikipedia entry for this.

tube).[72] The importance of this technology has been overlooked. Tubes were widespread in offices as well as domestic houses, and had specialist uses on ships and in the emergency services.

The following is from the memoirs of the suitably named Sir Aylmer Firebrace, who was Chief of the Fire Service between 1941 and 1947: "internal house telephones were a long time coming in; speaking tubes were used instead. They were still in place – and some were in daily use – when I joined. The vicinity of the Chief Officer's desk literally bristled with speaking tubes, and at the quarters provided for me ... I had a voice pipe in every room, including bathrooms".[73] Communication was both made possible and limited by the characteristics of the speaking tube, which would allow communication only for fifty to a hundred feet.[74] Communication could therefore go up, down and through the building, a contemporary source talking of a six-room radius. Bells and their attendant bellpulls predominated over the tubes because of these limitations, and there was a complicated code of the number of pulls on a bell according to who was summoned and who was doing the summoning. The maximum seems to have been six pulls.

Servant communicated with servant, from floor to floor, the whole system being a series of "subcentres" helping configure the social relations that the building made possible. Mrs Moores and Mr Badrick were at the centre of one such system, that of the domestic servants and doorkeepers. Mrs Moores could connect directly by speaking tube to the female servants' bedrooms on the third floor from her "sitting room". On the ground floor, with its fifty-four rooms, were the public rooms of the accounting offices and the Auditor General's rooms. Here the density of connections and linking devices increased dramatically, supported by a system of clearly worked out messenger stations so that the availability of messengers would be better regulated (for a typical office room see Figure 5.2). On the ground floor were also the main entrance, waiting rooms and refreshment rooms. Here the higher levels of the hierarchy appeared in earnest, in the form of separate rooms for each Council member, each with its own messenger identified by name. The master–servant relationship, present throughout, was apparent here in male form, messengers and porters always being male. There were messengers operating between rooms that were quite close together, so that writing may have taken more

---

[72] For the speaking tube, also the bellpull, see the site of the online Early Office Museum, www.officemusuem.com.
[73] Sir Aylmer Firebrace, *Fire Service Memories* (Andrew Melrose, n.d.), p. 5.
[74] *The Manufacture and Builder*, March 1875.

Fig. 5.2 India Office, office room, n.d., 1890s?

of a role than might be expected, and talk less. On the first floor, with sixty rooms, were the military department, the clerical departments concerned with stores, a separate luncheon room and library for the Council members, who could connect directly from there by means of bells and tubes both to below stairs and to upstairs, as well as to the Council Room itself. It was here that the epicentre of the building was located, at least formally – Room 181, the room of the Secretary of State for India, at this time Sir Stafford Northcote. There was an impressive suite of rooms given over to his role, the grandest of which was the office itself (the Secretary of State had his own washing and retiring rooms) (see Figure 5.3).

The density of communication by bells and tubes thickened around the Secretary of State, extending to the various Private Secretaries and Under Secretaries in the immediate rooms (for the density of connections at this level see Figure 5.4). But what is striking here is how little the network extended beyond this nub on the second floor (obviously it extended to messengers, and the various levels below the Secretary of State could ring down to Council members and to the library and luncheon room on the first floor). Within this nexus the speaking tube was rationed out very

Fig. 5.3 Secretary of State for India, one of a suite of office rooms

carefully: speaking-tube connection was limited to that between the Secretary of State and the two Under Secretaries. The Secretary of State was favoured by a special floor bellpull positioned by his desk, the other bellpulls usually being arrayed either side of the fireplace. For this desk bellpull there is an elaborate diagram, so it seems that this part of the technology was designed by the Office people themselves.[75] As well as these forms of slow technology, there were the lifts (also slow) for letters, packets and general office use between floors.

There is then the mezzanine floor containing rooms for storing papers and books, followed by the sixty-six rooms on the second floor. Here was the public waiting room. Public access to the building at large was quite strictly controlled, public visitors coming up courtesy of the doorkeepers and messengers directly to the waiting room, and if not going to the waiting room were passed from one guiding messenger to the next until they reached their final destination. Visitors carrying parcels, boxes and

[75] IO Records, Minute Paper 2 of the Clerk of Works Department, 1859, "The future household of this office and its domestic administration" (App. D, folio 225C/377).

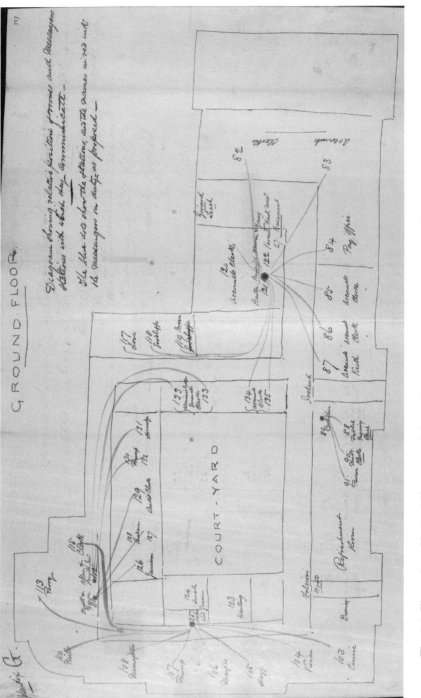

Fig. 5.4 Floor plan of India Office, ground floor (showing messenger routes and stations)

letters were to be admitted only if known to the doorkeeper. One of the senior messengers had to sleep in a downstairs office all weekend. Messengers and porters were dressed in uniform.[76] It was at this level that the rooms of the India Product Office were housed, especially notable that of the Reporter on Products; here also the museum and the room of the Geographer. These were the centres for the processing of information. At this level also were many other departments, including the Political Department. There were a large number of storerooms, also the bedrooms of the doorkeepers, even the third-level doorkeeper having his own kitchen and sitting room. The fourth and fifth floors were made up of towers, in which there were several servants' rooms; the sixth floor contained the cisterns, and the seventh the lumber room, storing office and correspondence books.

There are surprisingly few photographs of working rooms within the India Office, but what there are further reinforce the impression of the office as domicile. One photograph is of the room of George Birdwood, then working in the Revenue and Statistics Department (see Figure 5.5). The room is personalised, with photos, objects and cards on display. The domesticity of the interior is further emphasised by the mantelpiece. This is a home from home. Birdwood is dressed in a skullcap, reinforcing the impression of the scholar-savant, but he is also at his ease in what looks like a smoking jacket. Birdwood was knighted for his services and had previously been a professor of anatomy and physiology in Bombay. The room is also obviously a working space too, as the extraordinary filing system desk boxes make apparent. On the very large desk are bound volumes and large boxes of papers, also box files, and behind the desk is a rack containing very neatly folded copies of a series of *The Times* newspaper. Thus it is apparent that this building was the material expression of British class relations at the time as expressed in the upper-class home. Not simply expressed however, but also reproduced, so that once again we are aware how the state itself was a major player in fashioning class structures and divisions. In reproducing society in the form of the state the building also reproduced the nation, and this was of special relevance for "the civil service statesman", the elite bureaucrat. For him, and by him, there was felt to be a peculiarly strong and direct link between the work that he did, who he was and the purpose and identity of the British state, British society and the British nation.

[76] IO Records, "Office Keeping", L/AG/27–30.

Fig. 5.5 George Birdwood's office room, India Office

II   The civil service statesman

As early as 1857 the conditions of a permanent and secure service had partly been put in place, the Superannuation Act of that year establishing non-contributory civil service pensions, pensions lost if the service was left, so that the servant was tied to the service in this way. Hours and leave were usually pretty generous in the nineteenth century, a minimum seven-hour day having been laid down in 1910, and this generosity continued up to the Second World War. If a fortune could not be made in the high ranks of the civil service, at least compared to the law and to business, in return for a life of service a permanent, secure and well-paid career was to be had, as well as a pension. For the top-flight civil servant public honours were a significant part of the return made for the service vocation. These were given on a semi-automatic basis, strictly graded by civil service rank.

The 1870 Order in Council instituting civil service examinations across the civil service eventually led to uniformity of recruitment and to the grading of civil servants, which in turn hastened the development of a service consciousness. It also fostered professional groups and associations, especially in the lower ranks of the civil service, pressing for improved and uniform conditions of service. The idea of a service also emerged from below therefore, in the lower ranks, but given its professional and "trade union" character it was not there that power's centre of gravity lay as regards the public-service ethos that mattered most.

Within the Higher Division, variations in salaries and conditions continued up to the unification of the high civil service and the formal creation of the Administrative Class in 1919, under the guiding hand of Warren Fisher, Head of the Civil Service. Nonetheless, despite fragmentation, after 1885 the growth of "policy administration" out of "routine administration" was evident, as the move from a regulatory to an interventionist state gained pace.[77] While an increasingly strong sense of bureaucratic esprit de corps came into play, the department was probably the major focus of this before 1919, rather than a unified "service". After 1919, and following on the Haldane Committee's Report on the "machinery" of central government in 1918, the view of Whitehall not as a collection of government offices but as a coherent service, and a coherent structure of government, gained much more force. Treasury control was further enforced, and an "insider" civil service became increasingly marked.[78] Whether in terms of the department or the service, the highly masculinised nature of this conception of service is indicated by the fact that the marriage bar for women was not removed until 1946; up to then women who married had to leave the service.[79]

In addition to the influence of the elite pedagogic institutions that shaped the high bureaucracy and political class before 1918, the emphasis on the importance of practical, common knowledge was as important for the high as for the low civil servant. The department was the main location of this knowledge. Statements about this elite common knowledge of the state are relatively few and far between. By their nature high civil servants are persons of discretion and reserve. Therefore, Sir Edward Bridges' account of his own formation, and his personal and administrative ethics, is particularly valuable.[80] Bridges, born in 1892, was Head of the Civil Service and Permanent Secretary to the Treasury

---

[77] R. A. Chapman and J. R. Greenaway, *The Dynamics of Administrative Reform* (Croom Helm, 1980), Ch. 1.

[78] Ibid., Ch. 2.

[79] E. N. Gladden, *The Civil Services of the United Kingdom 1855–1970* (Frank Cass, 1967), p. 43, and Ch. 3.

[80] Sir Edward Bridges, *Portrait of a Profession: The Civil Service Tradition* (Cambridge University Press, 1950); and "Administration: What is it? And can it be Learned?" in A. Dunshire (ed.), *The Making of an Administrator* (Manchester University Press, 1956); Richard A. Chapman, *Ethics in the British Civil Service* (Routledge, 1988).

from 1945 to 1956. He was the son of the Poet Laureate and the architect Alfred Waterhouse's daughter, privileged connections by birth that were reinforced by his education at Eton and Magdalen College, Oxford. He ended his days KG, GCB, GCVO, PC, MC. Strictly speaking he falls outside the period of this book. Nonetheless, his whole formation was Victorian and Edwardian in character, and he also illustrates what we shall see were profoundly important continuities between the 1950s and the England of his birth. It was in this England that the collective ethos of the mandarinate he joined became strongly established.

In his account of his own formation the importance of what he calls "common sense" is made clear. A certain British, but more essentially English, penchant for "common sense" is revealed, something itself underwritten by the deeply important empirical idiom apparent in British cultural and intellectual life from the scientific revolution of the seventeenth century onwards.[81] This common sense had strong historical roots of another sort too, for Englishness and common sense were in his outlook seamlessly one thing. This Bridges expressed in his writing in terms of his professed love of precedent.[82] He allied this to a strong historical sense of the nation: the English village of his day he held to have grown out of this past, a knowledge of which would he believed increase affection and fellow feeling for, and a desire to serve, all who lived in that village. England is this village, not Britain. Influenced by the Oxford of T. H. Green, and inspired by the idea of an organic national past, Bridges also deploys the village as a metaphor for the civil service itself.[83] However, it is the individual government department that best exemplifies the village. Like the identity of the village, each government department has a "departmental view", which grows slowly out of precedent.[84]

It is essential for the civil servant, especially one who aspires to lead, to understand and respect this view. Getting to know it involves above all *acting* within it, in the sense that it can only be known through a style of proceeding based on personal knowledge and personal example – the empirical encounters of common service life. These work to the end of creating a consciousness of the collective, that of the department but also

---

[81] E. P. Thompson, "The Peculiarities of the English" in *The Poverty of Theory and Other Essays* (Merlin Press, 1978); Perry Anderson, *Arguments within English Marxism* (NLB and Verso, 1980); Patrick Joyce, "The Return of History: Postmodernism and the Politics of Academic History in Britain", *Past and Present*, 158 (February 1998).

[82] Bridges, *Portrait of a Profession*, pp. 160–5.

[83] On T. H. Green, see Thomas Geoffrey, *The Moral Philosophy of T. H. Green* (Oxford University Press, 1987).

[84] R. A. Chapman, *The Higher Civil Service in Britain* (Constable, 1970), pp. 285–91.

of the service as a whole.[85] As has been seen, accounts of actual decision-making in the higher civil service talk of the process as essentially "collective", being initiated by papers from below going up the chain so that authorship becomes occluded in the constant process of redrafting, and decisions "emerge". There is a strong sense that no one particular individual has a complete answer to a specific problem.[86] Common sense, common knowledge, precedent – these are what mattered.

Bridges' Quakerism gave him a strong awareness of the spiritual order and its moral imperatives, spiritual things in the Quaker code always requiring expression in real human conduct. However, this sense made him more rather than less typical of his fellows. Typical, for at the time of his educational formation the old evangelical ethic of the spirit realised in action and practical goodness was still strong, recast as it had been in the public schools and by the philosophical idealism of Green. This ascetic emphasis did not however seem to preclude in him the endemic clubbability of his peers. Their quite evident sociability likewise did not preclude their very frequent invocation of the simple life and of discreet and anonymous good *doing*. Bridges' belief in what he called "truth" is part of this spiritual and moral dimension, related always to action and doing, practical and commonsense things. For him what was so important about University was what he calls "the ardour of the chase" for truth, the practice of getting it rather than the end result. This search, and the life of action and service it implied, gave the searcher a particular insight into the mysteries of the British constitution.

The high civil servant, then as now, was regarded as the custodian of this constitution. It, and he, were practical, commonsensical, historical. Because it was unwritten the constitution too was the outcome of precedent, a thing of practice and not of theory, of the precedent-laden common law certainly but not of legal codes as in Europe. Precisely because the constitution was unwritten, professional and technical knowledge of governance was shaped in a particular way, so as to be by its nature not a rational-legal thing but a practical, experiential and historical one. In turn, in the absence of a Civil Service Act, the civil service was itself always regarded as a creature of precedent, and the forms of knowledge most prized were necessarily practical and historical. It was established and developed not by parliamentary statute but by the instrument of the Order in Council. Civil servants, like

---

[85] Bridges, *Portrait of a Profession*, pp. 160–5. See also Kevin Theakston, *Leadership in Whitehall* (Macmillan, 1999), Ch. 7.
[86] See also Chapman, *The Higher Civil Service*, p. 103.

government ministers in fact, were a product of prerogative. The civil servant therefore knew best what the civil service was and what was best for it. Bridges was representative in thinking of both himself and the service in general as proficient in knowledge of the constitution, and so it's real guardians. When the time came to put this knowledge into action he was ready. Bridges, and the so-called father of the modern civil service before him, Warren Fisher, were both at critical times invited to give the politicians advice on the constitution.[87]

At the heart of the advice they could offer was a knowledge of the nature of the political itself, in the sense of what was and what was not political (in practice, and above all for them, administration being non-political). However, this decision about what was political and what was not could only be profoundly political itself, not in the sense of the *parti-pris* political as they understood it, and indeed as British subjects and constitutional "experts" have for the most part subsequently seen it, but political in the deeper sense of where the line between the state and society should be drawn. This line was drawn by those *within* the state already, so that the drawing of it was an expression of *state* powers, and the interests, of the bureaucracy itself. Administration should be seen as, like politics, a way of governing people, for all the administrator's avowal that politics had the real power. The high civil servant was therefore a "statesman", like the politician but only more literally, a man of the state. But, as with Bridges, high-level bureaucrats were men of the state who were also devout Englishmen and devout imperial Britons.

At the heart of the demarcation of state and society, and linked to that of administration and the political, lay the constitution. Knowledge of the constitution took one deep into the nature of what the state was. The awareness of being able to see into the heart of the constitution was widespread among leading civil servants, for example Haldane,[88] who, rather like Bridges, saw the civil service as what he termed the "seams" of the constitution, the element holding the elaborate series of checks and balances together, precisely because of its capacity to know and be silent about the necessary fictions, and sometimes frauds, of the constitution.[89] The top civil servant, for Bridges, was a student of what he called the "national political outlook", in public opinion itself and in Parliament, and while he might hold party politics in contempt this was never the case for the political process itself, of which he was the servant.[90] Administrative knowledge was therefore practical and ethical, and this was strongly reflected in civil service attitudes to the systematic and formal

[87] Ibid., Ch. 4.   [88] *Richard Burdon Haldane: An Autobiography* (London, 1929).
[89] R. Thomas, Ch. 2.   [90] Chapman, *The Higher Civil Service*, p. 133.

study of administration, something that began to emerge in the late nineteenth century as the "science" of public administration. The absence of a written constitution meant that in Britain the study of public administration developed from the study of politics and government, and not from law as elsewhere.[91] The expertise of the top civil servant lay therefore in the practical workings of government, and not for example in economics or law, as in much of continental Europe. The distinction with the USA is interesting also: the study of public administration was in Britain a fragmented body of thought, found in economics, history, engineering, sociology, moral and political philosophy, and it was fragmented further at an institutional level. In the USA public administration was scientific, academic, and concentrated in particular institutions.

In the UK the parallel institutions to those of the USA were the public schools, Oxford and Cambridge, the civil service entrance exam, training on the job, and subsequently the London School of Economics and at Oxford the undergraduate degree in politics, philosophy and economics (PPE). However, UK universities lagged far behind the USA in the study of public administration. In Britain, there were for example hardly any academic texts on public administration before the inter-war years.[92] Even "public administration" intellectuals such as Graham Wallas combined teaching and writing with direct and practical involvement, in his case on the London School Board and on various Royal Commissions.[93] In 1970 a leading expert on the high civil service could write of there in

---

[91] Chapman and Greenaway, *The Dynamics of Administrative Reform*.

[92] R. Thomas, Ch. 4.

[93] What cohesion there was in the British case of public administration was owed to the Royal Institute of Public Administration and the Institute of Industrial Administration. Central government in fact gave little or no support to these, or to the study of public administration in general. Leading civil servants were certainly involved with the Royal Institute, but it is revealing how practical and experiential this involvement was. Addresses to the Institute were brief, direct, and designed always to convey the direct experience of the speaker, including his personality itself. Quite literally knowledge was about the active performance of expertise. Chapman, *The Higher Civil Service*, p. 86. The Civil Service Selection Board, founded in 1946 to "modernise" procedures, in fact made only very superficial use of contemporary management and psychological modes of evaluation. The civil service examination continued in its traditional, non-expert manner. Outside the high civil service, however, certain expert modes of knowledge were employed at other levels of the state apparatus, particularly psychology. Vocational psychology was used in industry and the armed services in and after the First World War, and in the inter-war years the National Institute of Industrial Psychology and the Industrial Health Research Board were formed. However, even in these services and especially in high civil service circles themselves, belief in this particular form of expertise was strictly limited, even though in the long term the sciences of the mind came to play an increasingly important part in the governance of the twentieth-century state. See Nikolas Rose, *Governing the Soul: The Shaping of the Modern Self* (Routledge, 1989).

effect being no real "training" at all in the civil service, the service doing almost exactly the same as it had done a hundred years previously.[94]

What is striking then is how practical, and politically and socially partial, knowledge authenticated itself in terms of particular versions of what in British history and society were supposed to be common values. There was a persistent belief in the top civil service, including the Foreign Office, that it was somehow representative of the real nature of British society. Dicey's *Law of the Constitution* had already helped to make all this official doctrine after its publication in 1885, for it was the role of convention that marked out the constitution of Britain, distinguishing its liberal freedoms from other nation states unlucky enough to have written constitutions. The Englishman and his constitution were both creatures of precedent and firmly rooted in the "middle ground". As Robert Colls has remarked of this faith in custom and precedent, "The English don't have to think about government, because they have cases and conventions that do their thinking for them."[95]

H. E. Dale, a child of Dicey, was born in 1875, and was a Whitehall insider and historian of the high civil service. In 1941 he gave revealing expression to such views.[96] If, as he says, the high official wields power, this is justified because "the beliefs of his intellect" and the "general temper of his mind are created by, and therefore adapted to, the invincible facts of life and government in a great and closely organised community". These "beliefs of his intellect" about "the invincible facts of life" exist above and beyond mere politics, the civil servant knowing the real feelings of the country. The ethos of bureaucratic detachment and scepticism is inextricably connected with this domain of the facts of life and government, a domain which is self-evidently true, for "would not its articles be accepted in private, by most men of sense and experience?"[97] The higher civil servant was quintessentially British as well as English (the former in practice usually amounting to the latter), for he was the same as the "ordinary sensible Briton" of the educated classes, as Dale put it. The class prejudices of the upper-middle class, of the public school and Oxbridge, were therefore the unacknowledged foundation of the common knowledge of administrative governance, and so a major foundation of the state.

The seamlessness of the link between elite, liberal pedagogy and the state is again apparent: Dale informs us that the ethical, political and social character of the higher civil service does not require lengthy treatment as it

---

[94] Chapman, *The Higher Civil Service in Britain*, pp. 70, 71–81.
[95] Robert Colls, *The Identity of England* (Oxford University Press, 2002), p. 82.
[96] Dale, *The Higher Civil Service of Great Britain*, Ch. 4 and App. C.
[97] Ibid., pp. 102 , 109.

is the same as that of the class from which nearly all high officials come, and this is the character formed in public school and Oxbridge.[98] The parallel outlook to this in the present day is apparent in the complacency of the view, held in Oxbridge too, that a profoundly inegalitarian Oxbridge is somehow an open meritocracy. We have here also the characteristic knowledge *style* of the high civil service, through which it authenticated itself, both to itself and to others – what the Balliol "don" Thomas Balogh, writing of the home civil service in the 1960s, styled "the mysterious part of Administrative Capacity".[99] This comprised an "effortless superiority, imbued with a cultivated scepticism", a style of office-holding deeply rooted in a particular kind of formal education which he termed "a purposefully useless, somewhat dilettante erudition" which would "keep dangerous thoughts away", a "tolerant scepticism (that) was obtained by . . . a formal kind of education, which developed powers of dialectical argument only",[100] especially in classics and maths. This was the education still on offer in his own institution.

To advance in the service, as well as this kind of education one also needed knowledge of the social world of the service and an acute perception of the official hierarchy, for this knowledge was an integral part of the cultivation of loyalty and discretion, "the subconscious instinct for what can be said and done and what cannot", as Dale put it.[101] In thinking about the "general temper" and training of the "administrative mind" at this level, it is necessary to recall how closed and intimate governing circles were in nineteenth- and, until relatively recently, twentieth-century Britain. These circles have always been small and closed (up to 1800 or so the individuals who made up the parliamentary class formed an even tighter group, made up of a few thousand individuals linked over several centuries by landholding, marriage and financial and commercial interests).[102] This is especially evident in recruitment to the higher ranks of the Permanent Secretaries in the civil service towards the end of the period studied here.

The dominance of certain public schools and Oxbridge colleges was immense – almost a quarter of all nineteenth-century Permanent Secretaries were old Etonians. Before 1914 just over half of all Cambridge graduates in the Open Competition for the civil service came from just two colleges, Trinity (with 39 per cent) and St John's.

[98] Ibid., pp. 82–3.
[99] Thomas Balogh, "The Apotheosis of the Dilletante in the Establishment of Mandarins" in Hugh Thomas (ed.), *Crisis in the Civil Service* (Anthony Blond, 1968), p. 12.
[100] Ibid., pp. 11–13. [101] Dale, *The Higher Civil Service of Great Britain*, pp. 89–90.
[102] Ellis Archer Wasson, *Born to Rule: British Political Elites* (Sutton Publishing Ltd, 2000).

Almost 20 per cent of all twentieth-century Permanent Secretaries came from just three Oxbridge colleges, Balliol and Christchurch at Oxford, Trinity at Cambridge. The significance of *Literae Humaniores* at Oxford, part of "Greats", is a further reflection of this. It accounted for no less than half the successful candidates at the Open Competition for the civil service before 1914.[103] Indeed, the civil service saw it as a model for the service as a whole. The overwhelming dominance of classics to 1914 is clear, and after this modern history took over a good portion of that old hegemony, so that a third of all those entering the Open Competition in the 1960s had studied modern history, the vast majority at Oxbridge.[104]

The closeness of the links between administration, politicians and policy needs to be emphasised. These were of many kinds, including their joint subscription to what was essentially self-taught economics, for the model of the economy they dealt in until far into the twentieth century was of a kind that able politicians and administrators with a traditional education could happily master and defend.[105] Similarities of culture and thought were complemented by similarities manifest in the actual practice of government. This was particularly evident in the empire. In India it was fed by institutional separations and safeguards for the autonomy of the India Office, unlike in the more dependent home civil service. Being independent of the Treasury Indian administration was paid for out of the revenues of India. With financial freedom, the Office in London and its officers on the ground in India were truly a government within a government. The London and Indian "administration" of India actively governed rather than simply administering, so that a vast number of decisions which would elsewhere have been considered political were ipso facto made unilaterally by "administrators". In India, in the absence of representative institutions, administration meant plain political power. The Indian civil service in India was shaped by its position as an instrument of foreign rule, in a way that the metropolitan civil service clearly was not.[106] Whether in terms of their relations with Indian subordinates, or their general views on empire and colonial administration, members of the Indian civil service regarded themselves and their work in the light of

---

[103] Peter Barberis, *The Elite of the Elite: Permanent Secretaries in the British Civil Service* (Ashgate, 1996).

[104] Chapman, *The Higher Civil Service*, p. 107, and pp. 40–2, 57–9, 134.

[105] Jose Harris, "Economic Knowledge and British Social Policy" in Mary O. Furner and Barry Supple, *The State and Economic Knowledge: The American and British Experiences* (Cambridge University Press, 1990).

[106] Clive Dewey gives a fair amount of prominence to this point in his discussion in *Anglo-Indian Attitudes: The Mind of the Indian Civil Service* (Hambledon, 1993).

the wider colonial encounter. The Viceroy, especially when he was a man of Curzon's inclinations, was the principal administrator as well as the political agent of the imperial state.[107] Godley, the Permanent Under Secretary in London, amalgamated political and administrative functions on the metropolitan side. He corresponded directly with the Viceroy on a fortnightly basis, and was as much involved in policy-making as in administration.

At home too the line between politics and administration was often so indistinct as to be meaningless, particularly when it came to "policy formation". This is quite aside from the rule of technical experts, where power was enmeshed in the silent operation of material processes and in the very designation of things as "technical" and so outside politics. For example, in the Home Office between 1848 and 1914 leading bureaucrats had a powerful role in making policy.[108] Unlike the situation of public administration in the USA for example, in Britain there was no clear distinction between policy and administration, it being widely recognised that the civil servant could initiate as well as administer policy, protected by the doctrines of administrative anonymity and ministerial responsibility. The American doctrine of public administration was that policy and administration were separate, and administration was a science. In Britain policy and administration were conjoined, and administration was a question of ethics.

Particularly after 1900, following the final rooting out of old-style patronage, there was less need to separate politics and administration, so that policy-making became even more a civil service interest. In figures like Haldane, Beveridge and Wallas the fusion of policy and administration was strongly promoted after the First World War.[109] Edward Bridges, the head of the civil service, drew the essential distinction between the "civil service statesman" and the "political statesman" precisely in order to draw attention to this administrative role in policy formation and to emphasise the meta-knowledge of the state that was the special preserve of the top bureaucrat.[110] For the bureaucrat was only a different type of "statesman" to the politician and both shared real power. This conception

---

[107] The distinction between policy and administration never seemed as problematic in India as it did in London – the ICS was an unashamedly colonial service and it was a comparatively small collection of men. The Viceroy therefore tended to dominate administration and the need for a politically neutral administrative class was less evident. The principal debates on this point concerned the most appropriate nature of colonial governance (on this point and these debates, see Dewey, *Anglo-Indian Attitudes*).

[108] Jill Pellew, *The Home Office 1848–1914: from Clerks to Bureaucrats* (Heinemann Educational, 1982).

[109] Hugh Thomas (ed.), *Crisis in the Civil Service* (Anthony Blond, 1968), Ch. 1.

[110] R. A. Chapman, *Leadership in the British Civil Service* (Croom Helm, 1984), p. 194.

of the "statesman", neither precisely politician nor bureaucrat, was a legacy of the eighteenth century. However, it was alive and well in the twentieth century, as Harold Laski was well aware.[111]

In 1927, writing the introduction to Henry Taylor's book of 1832, *The Statesman*, Laski remarked that it was perhaps the only exception to the absence in Britain of anything like the very old and very strong continental tradition of treatises on the art of government, starting most notably of course with Machiavelli's *The Prince*.[112] He remarked, "For neither the statesman nor the administrator in England has been prone to conscious deliberation upon the habits of his art", and that "the art of statesmanship remained a mystery unrelated to rule" in Britain.[113] As for Henry Taylor, a very influential administrator in the Colonial Office, he could easily have had a political career if he had chosen to. Laski recognises the continuing force of Taylor's account of the statesman into his own day, in the 1920s. In British history, from Taylor's time to his own day, the art of statesmanship for politician and administrator alike was a thing of intuitive knowledge, a "mystery" in the old sense of a secret knowledge.

Laski saw how the leading politicians and many of the leading bureaucrats in Britain up to his time had by and large been men of wealth and leisure, so that the craft of the statesman owed most to the "experience of handling men at an early age with some degree of executive responsibility", where "the business of government is the main preoccupation of his seniors", so that he "learns unconsciously that success therein is the highest ambition a man can have".[114] Whig, Liberal and Tory grandees had these proclivities in abundance of course, but in an age of unearned wealth, of servants and of strict class hierarchies this went some considerable way down the social pecking order as well, certainly as far as high civil servants.

To Laski, "few statesmen are likely to succeed who are either startlingly original or startlingly sensitive … The chief factor in their mental constitution must be the resounding commonplaces of their time".[115] As with the great Edwardian and Victorian politicians, what counted politically most of the time was the intellectually vapid politics of Duty and Principle. Equally, with the bureaucrats what counted was the public projection of conduct that would present themselves as beacons of Duty. Thus there were the closest of affinities between the civil service and political "statesman" (in Laski's view "the true government of the state, indeed, almost

---

[111] See below, pp. 326–7.
[112] Henry Taylor, *The Statesman: An Ironical Treatise on the Art of Succeeding* (Cambridge, 1927) (originally published in 1832), with an introductory essay by Harold J. Laski.
[113] Ibid., pp. xxi, xxii.   [114] Ibid., pp. xxvii, xxviii, xxix.   [115] Ibid., p. xxxi.

always lies in the hands of its administrators").[116] These affinities arose from their "common knowledge", in the sense of what each did, their job. They also arose from their common educational formation, for this was essentially about being taught how to govern, to govern themselves and to govern others. It was not that the moral economy of the office of the politician and that of the bureaucrat did not diverge, but this was far more at the lower than the higher levels of the political and administrative hierarchies. The bureaucrat aimed at self-abnegation, the politician at self-presentation, often self-promotion. The new party politics was organised around the figures of warfare, and its common knowledge was based on the idea of the campaign. The higher echelons of politicians remained however adept at creating the public expression of themselves as personified virtue, in contrast to the political personae emerging out of the new party organisational "machines", even though they relied upon the machines for securing election. On the Liberal side Elaine Hadley has recently shown how intellectuals and political leaders attempted to realise the liberal individual in a moral form based on political activity itself and not landed property. In practices like the signed journal article and the secret ballot they tried to establish what she terms "liberal cognition", a moralised way of realising politics that also involved the body, in what she terms in fact "liberal embodiments".[117]

In an age of intense moral and religious seriousness political leaders had to give party warfare a moral purpose, whether in the shape, to quote the political historian John Vincent, of the Tory Lord Salisbury's "intelligent traditionalism", the Liberal Lord Hartington's "public, practical sanity", Gladstone's "moral authority", or even Chamberlain's "energetic subversion".[118] Their actions were based not on what the electorate wanted but rather on what they thought it should have, and by and large the electorate came to believe that what they wanted was what the political leaders told them they should have. Party leaders were less concerned with talking directly to the electors, although they became good at this too, than with the organisation and direction of the political community in Parliament itself. In turn this involved utilising the medium of the aristocratic social round (the club, the country house weekend, the dinner table).[119] This was the "machinery and texture" of politics in a post-aristocratic age, the

---

[116] Ibid., p. xxv.
[117] Elaine Hadley, *Living Liberalism: Practical Citizenship in Mid-Victorian Britain* (University of Chicago Press, 2010).
[118] John Vincent, *The Governing Passion: Cabinet Government and Party Politics in Britain 1885–86* (Harvester Press, 1974), "Introduction"; also pp. 165 ff.
[119] Ibid.; and for an extremely revealing picture of the world of high politics and political management, continuing into the inter-war years, see John Vincent (ed.), *The Crawford*

materialities of which formed the common knowledge, the work life and the ethical personae of political leadership far into the twentieth century. As John Vincent describes the Liberal political class of the time:

The flowering of the political aristocracy which constitutes the successful and memorable part of Victorian liberalism was based on the happy absence of liberal ideas. It relied instead on conduct. The creed of rectitude in government, of administrative reform, derived from notions of how a gentleman should behave (especially when in public view in a situation of some class tension). The object of administrative reform in the state was to show the English gentleman to better advantage ... this was the answer, the only conceivable answer, to Arnold's question, "What was to happen when the aristocracy was gone?" The answer as most public men saw lay in the State, reformed and moralised, acting as an independent, underived, unaligned, but essentially popular and attractive social entity run by public spirited gentlemen of the old tradition.[120]

This description of the state accurately reflects the character of the British state far into the twentieth century. This state was rooted in the cultural forms shaped by its elite educational institutions, and these institutions shaped British elites in general and not simply bureaucrats and politicians, so that the state came to be grounded in habits of mind shared across the ranks of the wealthy . This made it all the stronger and all the more resistant to change. It is to the pedagogies of the powerful that I now turn.

Papers: The Journals of David Lindsay 27th Earl of Crawford and 10th Earl of Balcarres 1871–1940 during the Years 1892 to 1940 (Manchester University Press, 1984). Crawford was a leading Conservative insider, and for a time a Chief Whip.

[120] John Vincent, *The Formation of the British Liberal Party, 1857–1868* (Harpers Press, 1976), p. xviii.

6   The grammars of governance: pedagogies of the powerful

> In my beloved old school upon the Severn I can see now that we are not educated at all; no scientific methods were tried upon us. I doubt if any of the masters had even heard there was such a thing as a science of education. To them education was a natural process which all decent people went through, like washing . . . the masters were content to teach what they had learnt, and in the same manner. Most of them were Shrewsbury boys themselves, and because Greek had been taught there for more than three centuries, they taught Greek . . . of Greek our knowledge was both peculiar and limited. We were allowed no devices to make the language in the least interesting . . . the greater part of the school believed that Greek literature was written as a graduated series of problems for Shrewsbury boys to solve, and when a sixth-form boy was asked by a new master whether he did not consider the *Prometheus* a very beautiful play, he replied that he thought it contained too many weak *ceasures* . . . our sole duty was to convert, with absolute precision, so much Greek into so much English.
>
> Henry Woodd Nevinson, *Changes and Chances*[1]

Shrewsbury men and the many other kinds of "old boys" of the public schools governed Britain and its empire. Many of them still govern Britain. To understand how this came to be so it is necessary to step back in time and briefly consider the long English tradition of the shaping of those who would exercise authority and power in society and the state, those who I call the governors, for that simply is what they were. This is a story that takes us from the Renaissance to the modern implementation of the public school and university as machines for making governors, for it needs to be realised that the teaching of how to govern oneself and so how to govern others was not incidental but central to elite education. Therefore I extend the term "governors" beyond the state apparatus alone, in line with my overall argument. I title the first part of the chapter "Lineages of the liberal governor", and I again extend the meaning of terms, in this case

---

[1] London, 1923. As cited in Philip Cowburn (ed.), *A Salopian Anthology: Some Impressions of Shrewsbury Life during Four Centuries* (Macmillan, 1964), pp. 179–88.

"liberal", in line with my exploration of the liberal state and the nature of freedom.

Section I of the chapter also broaches the development of classics and what was called at the time and since a "liberal education", for it was this that chiefly comprised the education of elites, of whatever political hue. From classical times a liberal education denoted the education of the free man, as opposed to the enslaved one; also the education of the whole man, body and soul. While these aspects of a liberal education have been much considered the degree to which this sort of education always, then and now, involved the exercise of power and authority has been less well appreciated. If, as we have seen, the political exercise of freedom was inseparable from the exercise of authority, this was equally the case with liberal education.

Tracing the "lineages of the liberal governor" embraces not only "conduct books" about how to govern, and classics, but political thought and political conduct too, the grammars of governance becoming directly political at certain times, whereas at all times they are indirectly so. In the first part of section I, therefore, I consider how notions about independence and eventually liberal freedom came to inform ideas about what it was to be a man of authority. The second part of the chapter, "Classics and the remaking of liberal education", takes the story on into the nineteenth century, and looks systematically at classics as the heart of liberal education. This treatment of the subject has two aspects, spirit and body, in line with the two sides of the whole man which liberal education claimed to educate. This consideration of classics then leads to an account of examinations and the incorporation of "merit" into elite education, the study of the content and the form of liberal education in the shape of the curriculum setting the scene for the following chapter, which explores the totality of elite education beyond the curriculum alone.

I   Lineages of the liberal governor

Unlike the nineteenth- and twentieth-century institutional route to authority, namely the system of university qualification, there were many and diverse paths in early modern times. Education was only one of them, owning and working an estate and military prowess being others. However, from the Renaissance education counted more and more.[2] Learning the conduct required for authority became a process begun by the child's tutor

---

[2] For overviews see Ian Weinberg, *The English Public Schools: The Sociology of Elite Education* (Atherton Press, 1962), pp. 1–26; Gary McCulloch, *Philosophers and Kings: Education for Leadership in Modern England* (Cambridge University Press, 1991).

and continued in later life, chiefly through the medium of a series of manuals designed for the education of the young gentleman. The first English education manual to follow the all-conquering humanist format was Thomas Elyot's *The Book Named the Governor* in 1531.[3] Elyot's work is important because it defined the vernacular genre of gentlemanly education manuals, and because it linked them to the actual practice of government. It was sufficiently well respected to be used for the education of the future King James I of England and VI of Scotland.[4] *The Governor* was intended as a manual for the instruction of the future magistrates who were to enact the monarch's power. It was, of course, necessary that the youth under instruction should study classics and so learn Latin. They would then learn Greek through Latin.[5] Already the study of language, and especially grammar, in the new humanist grammar schools, was linked to power.

Gentlemanly status was crucial in defining the nature of early modern authority, and the people who were to administer the public and the common weal were chosen from the ranks of the propertied, especially the landed, for this would assure their independence. The humanist ideal of independence also involved the gentleman actively engaging in politics, gentlemanly independence being seen as a crucial determinant in the capacity for rule.[6] Independence guaranteed disinterestedness, and this nexus of disinterest and independence was a vital legacy in the shape of the disinterested "generalist". Specialisation, such as learning a skill, entailed dependence on another and constituted unfreedom.[7] The essential capacities considered necessary for governors of all types were *virtue* (a term subject to several definitions) and *authority*. The problem for the pre-liberal governor was how to cultivate these in order to perform his role convincingly (outside of the person of the monarch it was almost invariably a male role).[8]

---

[3] Sir Thomas Elyot, *The Book Named the Governor*, ed. S. E. Lehmberg (Dent, 1962), p. v.
[4] S. E. Lehmberg, *Sir Thomas Elyot: Tudor Humanist* (University of Texas Press, 1960), p. 79. Lehmberg suggests that the book was written as a standard humanist instruction manual for governors and that the passages praising monarchy were added later, possibly at the behest of Thomas Cromwell. See pp. 37–9, and for the passages justifying monarchy, Book I, Ch. ii.
[5] Elyot, *The Governor*, p. 6; and see pp. 1–2, 14.
[6] J. G. A. Pocock, *Virtue, Commerce, and History: Essays in Political Thought and History, Chiefly in the Eighteenth Century* (Cambridge University Press, 1985), Chs. 2, 3 and 6. Steven Shapin has shown that the status of a gentleman was directly linked to a capacity for virtue and truth telling, particularly through his capacity for rational, free action. S. Shapin, *A Social History of Truth: Civility and Science in Seventeenth-Century England* (Chicago University Press, 1994), pp. 42–64.
[7] R. Ascham, *The Scholemaster* [1570] in *English Works*, ed. W. A. Wright (Cambridge University Press, 1970), reprint of the 1904 edn, p. 190.
[8] Elyot, *The Governor*, p. 14.

Virtue was also strongly linked to existing notions of elite masculinity: as Elyot put it, "A man in his natural perfection is fierce, hardy, strong in opinion, covetous of glory, desirous of knowledge."[9] As he notes elsewhere, "A man is called *vir* in Latin, whereof, saith Tully [Cicero], virtue is named."[10] Virtue is necessarily a masculine quality therefore. Furthermore, the practice of government required a particular attention to the self, the cultivation of a particular appearance and certain ethical characteristics.[11] The would-be governor was directed to "know thyself", *nosce te ipsum*, particularly that part of man most his own, the soul. In focusing on the government of the soul Elyot recognised "that to him that is a governor of a public weal belongeth a double governance; that is to say an inward or interior governance, and an exterior or outward governance".[12] In order to perform his role the governor did not merely have to dispose of his public life properly (his material possessions and social relationships) but also to govern himself.

So, from these early times, we can see taking shape the various elements of governing that were bequeathed to the eighteenth century and would later be reformulated within liberal ideas about governance, which were not therefore a *de novo* creation of the nineteenth century. These were the elements of independence and the balance of authority and virtue. Virtue itself was closely linked to masculinity, and to what Elyot called "interior governance". This nexus was increasingly to be realised through a liberal education in the form of the study of classics, in which grammar itself had a central place.[13] Elyot and Roger Ascham were the templates, but following these there was a variety of manuals for the instruction of youths written by and for the tutors of young gentlemen. However, the school began to replace the private tutor as the place where the legacy of the earlier conduct book on governance would be developed. As M. L. Clarke reminds us, the Renaissance attempt to recover the classical world did not rest solely in learning to read Latin and Greek, but in following the classical way of life itself, the education of the whole man, involving virtue, authority and all the other attributes of being one who governed.[14] The grammar school, the template for what were later called public schools, was established upon the principles laid out in such classics as Quintilian's *Institutio Oratoria*, which became the general authority on education. The grammar school was distinguished from others, such as the private

---

[9] Ibid., p. 77.   [10] Ibid., p. 186.

[11] Ibid., p. 165; also pp. 99, 100, 102, 103, 104–22, 159, 164, 233.   [12] Ibid., p. 183.

[13] See Ascham, *The Scholemaster*, p. 189, for the kind of mind involved – not super-bright.

[14] M. L. Clarke, *Classical Education in Britain 1500–1900* (Cambridge University Press, 1959), p. 3.

and dissenting academies, by its classical curriculum and charitable function.[15] Education in the classical languages and their literature gradually became the main path to university, and university the path to learning self-governance and how to deploy authority over others. The nineteenth-century public school itself eventually became the gateway to a university education.[16]

The grammar school went through something of a decline in the eighteenth century.[17] However, the leading ones, in effect the leading "public schools", nonetheless educated the higher aristocracy and the political classes: one-third of MPs between 1754 and 1790 went to the handful of such schools, some deriving from the original "grammar" schools (Colet's St Pauls, for instance) and some, the most prestigious, being of royal foundation, most notably Eton and Winchester. As Clarke puts it, "The English grammar school as it was established in the sixteenth century, and continued for some three centuries after, was essentially the grammar school of the ancient world."[18] "Its curriculum and methods were not very different from those of the Roman Empire, and an Etonian under Keate would have felt quite at home in the schools of the time of Quintilian or Ausonius."[19] Like that of the schools, the eighteenth-century university system displayed great continuity. Cambridge was governed by Elizabethan statutes until the nineteenth century. Oxford had been reformed, but this took place as early as 1636 under Archbishop Laud. The presence of the classics at the centre of the curriculum continued from the sixteenth to the early twentieth centuries.

It was in the eighteenth century that ideas about independence and its associated attributes came most clearly to inform concerns about what it was to be a man of authority. This happened most publicly in the sphere of politics, involvement in the political process most dramatically highlighting what was involved in having a stake in the exercise of authority, both for the politician and the propertied citizen, who in participating in politics also took part in the exercise of responsible, public authority. Masculinity, virtue and "interior governance" took on new forms, and these in turn fed into liberal thought and politics in the nineteenth century. In general the most prominent division respecting the balance of authority and virtue was that expressed publicly in political argumentation, namely

---

[15] R. S. Thompson, *Classics or Charity? The Dilemma of the Eighteenth-Century Grammar School* (Manchester University Press, 1971), p. vii.

[16] Ibid., p. 1. The grammar school was however for many the most advanced level of education they would receive.

[17] James M. Rosenheim, *The Emergence of a Ruling Order: English Landed Society 1650–1750* (Longman, 1998).

[18] Clarke, *Classical Education in Britain*, p. 3.   [19] Ibid., p. 4.

the division between the "gothic" and the republican visions of authority, otherwise defined in the eighteenth century as "Court" and "Country" ideologies. The polemical exchanges involved between 1721–42 were to have a lasting influence on the definition of the ideal governmental persona, as did those when in the 1750s and 60s Pitt's supporters revived the language of Patriotism, first in opposition and then in government. In these debates the role of the *minister* or *governor* was defined in terms of public virtue, that is unselfish devotion to the public good, the opposite to faction and private interest.[20] The model of political conduct was Cicero. His treatise *De Officiis* was the most highly praised classical work at the time, one of the most widely read books after the Bible, and a major foundation of the moral personality considered ideal for the governor. It was also very widely taught in the grammar and "public" schools.[21]

The right to participate in politics at all levels of the political system, and so contribute to the common good, continued to be defined in terms of independence, founded as before chiefly upon property. Paul Langford has explored in detail the ways in which authority relied upon property in the eighteenth-century mind.[22] However, independence and property became more closely linked to gender from this time, as Matthew McCormack and others have demonstrated.[23] For it was the *familial* model of independence and its relationship to notions of social obligation and dependence that seems to have come into prominence, particularly in the context of the hierarchical system of clientage and patronage that was the basis of unreformed politics. The figure of the male head of the household proved to be an enduring one, influencing ideas about political participation long after the end of clientage politics, and indeed serving as the template for defining the political public sphere into the twentieth century. It was a figure that was also to be critical for nineteenth-century elite education and so for the inculcation of governance generally in British society, for the dynamics of family life and the symbolic economy of the home were at the root of an education in authority.

---

[20] The best introduction to political *virtu* is S. Burtt, *Virtue Transformed: Political Argument in England, 1688–1740* (Cambridge University Press, 1992); P. N. Miller, *Defining the Common Good: Empire, Religion and Philosophy in Eighteenth-Century Britain* (Cambridge University Press, 1994).

[21] On the Ciceronian nature of Court arguments see Ibid., pp. 88–102 and R. Browning, *Political and Constitutional Ideas of the Court Whigs* (Louisiana University Press, 1982), pp. 1–34. For the general significance of Cicero and his work in early-modern political thought, see Miller, *Defining the Common Good*, pp. 21–87, 89–94, 98–102.

[22] Paul Langford, *Public Life and the Propertied Englishman, 1689–1798* (Oxford University Press, 1991).

[23] M. L. McCormack, *The Independent Man: Citizenship and Gender Politics in Georgian England* (Manchester University Press, 2005).

As Francis Dodsworth has argued, in the eighteenth century these notions of civic virtue, independence and manly service of the public were central to the offices of *local* government as well as high political office.[24] Along with public debates about independence there were equally complex contemporary debates about the transformation of manners in Britain after the commercial revolution of the eighteenth century. The different positions need not detain us,[25] but in the broad centre of British political and social thought there was an accommodation between virtue and commerce based around the concept of politeness, a notion also bound up with gentlemanliness.[26] What occurred in the late eighteenth century seems to have been in part a rejection of prevailing notions and in part a reworking of them. There was a social broadening out of politeness, so that the new emphasis on merit beginning to emerge at the time was seen without sociability to lead to narrowness.[27] Effective action for the public man therefore turned on an idea of a form of politeness which embraced merit, while avoiding the narrow and the specialist viewpoint in favour of the urbane, the worldly, above all the "general", non-specialist view. This perspective contributed greatly to the notion of the nineteenth-century disinterested amateur (in our case, as has been seen, the high civil servant), but also to the ethos of elite education.

However, as Lawrence Klein and others recognise, the crucial drift of change into the nineteenth century was towards institutionalisation, particularly the institutions of education. Governance itself began to be institutionalised in the shape of professional bureaucrats and eventually academics, although because of the investment in sociable forms of merit this professionalism was of a particular sort, one inimical to the narrow

---

[24] Francis Dodsworth, "'Civic' Police and the Condition of Liberty: The Rationality of Governance in Eighteenth-Century England', *Social History*, 29:2 (2004), 199–216, and "Masculinity as Governance: Police, Public Service and the Embodiment of Authority, c. 1700–1850" in M. L. McCormack (ed.), *Public Men: Political Masculinities in Britain, 1700–2000* (Palgrave, 2007); also F. Dodsworth, "*Virtus* on Whitehall: The Politics of Palladianism in William Kent's Treasury Building, 1733–6", *Journal of Historical Sociology*, 18:4 (2005), 282–317, demonstrates that such strategies of political virtue and politeness extended beyond the argument in the pamphlet literature into the material culture of the Walpole regime.

[25] The apparent opposition of classical virtue and modern commerce is the subject of J. G. A. Pocock, *The Machiavellian Moment: Florentine Political Thought and the Atlantic Republican Tradition* (Princeton University Press, 1975), pp. 423–505 and *Virtue, Commerce, and History: Essays in Political Thought and History, Chiefly in the Eighteenth Century* (Cambridge University Press, 1985), esp. pp. 37–71, 91–123, 215–310.

[26] Klein and Carter are the best overviews of character and politeness in this period: Philip Carter, "Polite 'Persons': Character, Biography and the Gentleman", *Transactions of the Royal Historical Society*, 12 (2002); Lawrence E. Klein, "Politeness and the Interpretation of the British Eighteenth Century", *The Historical Journal*, 45:4 (2002).

[27] Klein, ibid., 875, and on the complex social operations of politeness, 880.

view. The ascendance of the liberal technostate, as represented by the figures of the bureaucrat and academic, but also the politician, involved from this time the marking out of distinct *Lebensführungen*, or ethical styles of "office", in the matrix, partly of this sort of gentlemanly politeness. Only partly, for politeness itself went through another transformation. What happened in the late-eighteenth and early-nineteenth centuries was that the attempt to combine an inner and outer life, morals and manners, had under the onslaught of war, revolution and reform broken down. These dealt a death-blow to the eighteenth-century man of "feeling and good sensibility", and the outcome was a divergence of inner and outer, which the Victorians, largely successfully, brought together again, fusing the two in terms of "character" and "sincerity". The attributes of character, those of the *inner*, moral person rather than solely its external foundations in sociability and property, began to be promoted. I shall return to Victorian "character" when looking at the public schools.

"Character" was in great measure shaped by the Evangelical Revival. Religion was however always of the first significance for the formation of modern ideas about governing others, so the Evangelical Revival of the early nineteenth century was not unique. One can perceive a particular form of political subjectivity emerging out of religion, above all the established religion of the church, Anglicanism. After the Act of Uniformity of 1662 the confessional state became established. In this, to be a full citizen, one had to be an Anglican; however this Anglicanism was defined as a particular middle way, the famous *via media* of the Church of England. In this belief was formulated in a latitudinarian fashion, as symbolised by the practice of occasional conformity (attendance at Anglican worship three times a year). This "English way", the way of the middle ground, has recently been given extensive treatment in terms of what is aptly called the "rule of moderation".[28] To be a citizen until well into the nineteenth century was to evince a political subjectivity defined in opposition to the perceived "enthusiasm" of Nonconformity, and the supposed "mysticism" and irrationality of Roman Catholicism. Therefore, "moderation" came to be inscribed on the soul of many Englishmen. Not on the souls of Nonconformists necessarily, whether in England, Scotland or Wales. Religious Nonconformity it has often and rightly been said represented the British equivalent of European political radicalism, but only up to a point: aversion to a "foreign" Catholicism fed what was, for all the recalcitrance of Dissent in general, a strong identification with the symbols and practices of

---

[28] Ethan Shagan, *The Rule of Moderation: Violence, Religion and the Politics of Restraint in Early Modern England* (Cambridge University Press, 2011).

state authority in this successfully decentred but still Anglo-centric state. The Catholic Irish were, however, another matter.

Dogmatic anti-dogmatism was to be important subsequently in several ways. It was a major element contributing to the notion of a distinctive "national character", one marked greatly by the Anglican version of moderation and toleration. As Paul Langford has argued, notions of independence, emanating from ideas of independence linked to property (the "great enchantress" of the eighteenth century), were closely connected to ideas about reserve, decency and moderation. This constellation of ideas and values had as he puts it by 1850 "cemented" themselves into the idea of the "national character".[29] They are still how the British, especially the English, like to think of themselves. They therefore make up British common sense about Britishness. However, they also make up ideas about what common sense *itself* is, namely something always in the middle, avoiding extremes, the sense of what is, or should be, held in common by all "fair-minded" people. Common sense is the common sense of the British, and as we have seen in the discussion of "common knowledge" and bureaucracy, this form of endemic self-congratulation was central to the operations of the state.

However, because the political liberty that gave expression to the English virtues of tolerance and moderation was as we have seen inseparable from the exercise of authority, self-congratulation needs to be tempered by the awareness that English liberty and English virtue were embedded in hierarchy. In British history there has never been much distance between authority and hierarchy – witness the British state's very own subservient church, the by law Established one. Even though the confessional state was dismantled in the first three decades of the nineteenth century, this did not mean that the institutional arrangements constructed over several centuries were no longer effective: the process of getting rid of religious and political disabilities was tortuously slow. Roman Catholic worship was not permitted at all until as late as 1778, and a full century later non-Anglicans were still not admitted to Oxbridge. There, until this later time, university tutors had to be ordained Anglican priests, and if not priests then members of the Anglican faith. Nor was there full Jewish emancipation until 1890, and the bitter political conflicts over the established Church in Wales, Ireland and England marked politics into the twentieth century. Much of popular politics in the UK was imbued with the tripartite tribal loyalties of "Church and State" Anglicans, Nonconformists and Roman Catholics,

---

[29] Paul Langford, *Public Life and the Propertied Englishman, 1689–1798* (Oxford University Press, 1991), also *Englishness Identified: Manners and Character 1650–1850* (Oxford University Press, 2000).

well into the twentieth century, and not only in Northern Ireland.[30] The confessional state lived on symbolically of course, in the panoply of monarchy, Parliament, the law, Oxbridge and the public schools (especially, as we shall see, the royal foundation of Eton College).

All the varied and complex currents of thought and behaviour so far considered eventuated in the outlook of liberal governance in nineteenth-century Britain therefore, and liberalism was not simply a new beginning. It, and the meanings of the freedom it espoused, and then politically engineered, were heavy with the freight of earlier ideas about authority and how to exercise it. In the same way liberalism did not mark a complete break from the idea of state regulation, quite the opposite in fact.[31] Here as elsewhere Britain was not as different from its continental neighbours as people have liked to think. Contemporaries in late-eighteenth-century Britain understood freedom not as simply freedom from interference, but as freedom from dependence or domination.[32] To be free one had to live in a free state governed by the rule of law. The greatest threats to civil liberty were usually seen as faction and patronage, which would draw the public and the state into dependence on the interests and wealth of a few individuals. Regulation of the social order according to law that had been granted public consent was not seen as a restriction on liberty, rather it conditioned it.

Arguments that defined intervention in public conduct as essential to the liberty of the state were therefore not at all uncommon in eighteenth-century Britain. Freedom was defined as a state between tyranny and anarchy, governed by the rule of law, where liberty was opposed not to interference but to popular license. The significance of liberal government was not that it broke the link between regulation and government, but simply that it argued against the idea of the maximum of regulation as the optimum form of government. Underlying the liberal concept of government was of course the sense that "the economy", also "society", constituted separate spheres, internally coherent, with laws of their own. However in order for these laws to operate, regulation – often close

---

[30] Patrick Joyce, *Work, Society and Politics: The Culture of the Factory in Later Victorian England* (Harvester, 1980) on the sectarian politics of north and west Britain.

[31] In what follows I draw on the joint introduction of Tony Bennett, Francis Dodsworth and Patrick Joyce from a recent Special Issue of the journal *Cultural Studies*, "Liberalisms, Government and Culture", *Cultural Studies*, 21:4–5 (July/September 2008). I am greatly indebted to Francis Dodsworth for his advice on the eighteenth century, which I draw on here.

[32] Philip Pettit, *Republicanism: A Theory of Freedom and Government* (Oxford University Press, 1999), pp. 17–50; Quentin Skinner, *Liberty before Liberalism* (Cambridge University Press, 1998). See also on dependence and independence, Miller, *Defining the Common Good*, pp. 73–149. And on freedom and state interference, Pettit, *Republicanism*, pp. 41–50; Skinner, *Liberty before Liberalism*, pp. 77–84, 96–9.

regulation – was essential. Rather than denying the importance of the common good, critics of the *ancien regime* argued that the old order was itself factional, governing for its own interest, not that of the nation. Mid-Victorian party political liberalism remained imbued with many of these classical values that are usually seen as characteristic of a previous age.[33] Commitment to laissez-faire was always conditional.

However the common good, and liberal freedom, were not usually conceived as conditions of equality and democracy. Rather, they were imagined as an orderly, hierarchical state, based on property and governed by the rule of law and norms of civility inculcated by government. The liberal governor, a propertied, educated and civilised man, would administer government impartially for the public good, a common good the unpropertied, the uneducated and the uncivilised could not know and had to be taught. Liberals sought to regulate passion, suppress barbarism and encourage character and public morality, which would be achieved by application of the correct laws to fit the human personality.[34] The ideal of a small state depended always on the creation of the capacity for self-government amongst the subjects of government, but also, as we shall see, amongst its practitioners.

With this understanding in mind we can better proceed to a first look at the public schools, which together with a reformed Oxbridge were to be the principal means by which governors were to be fashioned in the liberal polity in the two centuries after 1800. The creation of governance was everywhere apparent in the public schools. Indeed their essential task was teaching the business of governance. In the reformed public schools of the 1860s and after, inspired by Thomas Arnold at Rugby, the link between education and power was nakedly apparent. Arnold conceived of his *educational* role as inherently involving "government". For Arnold "the great work of government" was "the highest earthly desire of the ripened mind".[35] The Christian school was a representation in miniature of the Christian state.[36] This work of government involved governing the

---

[33] Eugènio Biagini, "Neo-Roman Liberalism: 'Republican' Values and British Liberalism, circa 1860–1875", *History of European Ideas*, 29 (2003), 55–72, and *Liberty, Retrenchment and Reform: Popular Liberalism in the Age of Gladstone, 1860–1880* (Cambridge University Press, 1992), pp. 83–93; and on the older legacy within nineteenth-century liberalism see J. W. Burrow, *Whigs and Liberals: Continuity and Change in English Political Thought* (Oxford University Press, 1988); Jonathan Parry, *The Rise and Fall of Liberal Government in Victorian Britain* (Cambridge University Press, 1993), pp. 14–15, 73–8.

[34] Parry, *The Rise and Fall*, pp. 6, 18.

[35] Asa Briggs, *Victorian People: A Reassessment of Persons and Themes 1851–1867* (Penguin, 1965), p. 163.

[36] John Raymond Honey, *Tom Brown's Universe: The Development of the Victorian Public School* (Millington, 1977).

school itself, but was above all about the boys governing themselves in accordance with the traditions of British liberty. For Arnold the public school was a "national institution" because it was rooted in the past and therefore in British freedoms, actively practicing these in the shape of boy self-government. The public school and the public schoolboy became each a miniature universe of the state, one in which all the political virtues so far considered came to rest. Self-government was a precursor to governing others. For the Clarendon Commission, which reformed the public schools in the 1860s, the English people should be indebted to the public schools "for their capacity to govern others and control themselves, their aptitude for combining freedom with order".[37]

Governance should be regarded as intrinsic to the schools, the most important object of their existence in fact – *all* public schoolboys, the bright and the dull, were taught the business of what was called "leadership", so that the formation of the high Administrative Class of the bureaucracy was of a piece with that of the well-to-do in all walks of life. It is nothing short of astonishing how the British upper and middle classes, almost alone in Europe, surrendered their boy children en masse, and some of their girls, to the private boarding school, making the break from home, and their trust in the school, almost absolute. What developed in the second half of the nineteenth century needs to be differentiated from what went before, however – the unreformed order.[38]

As late as 1860 Eton boys were reported to be idle as well as rich: the boys organised their own games and not the masters, and games were not compulsory. The idea of responsible discipline by the older boys was said to have gone.[39] Even daily service was discontinued and the choir was no more. Reform meant a frontal assault on the perceived anarchy of the boys' old school subcultures. However, one man's anarchy was another man's freedom and it should not be thought that the unreformed schools lacked their own ways of making governors. The old order was to be replaced by what was hoped to be a new closeness between masters and boys. The notion of boy self-government was however always central to teaching how others were to be governed, but the term meant something different in the old order than it did in the new. In the unreformed school order "boy government" is to be distinguished from the *disciplinary* boy self-government of Arnold and the other reformers. In the ancien regime

[37] Clarendon Commission, cited in George R. Parkin, *Edward Thring, Headmaster of Uppingham School: Life, Diary and Letters* (London, 1898), p. 41.

[38] Frederick How, *Six Great Headmasters* (London, 1905), for the mid-nineteenth century generation, and the role of the reforming headmasters as well as the Clarendon Commission.

[39] Tim Card, *Eton Established: A History from 1440 to 1860* (John Murray, 2001), Chs. 14–15, and *Eton Renewed: A History from 1860 to the Present Day* (John Murray, 1994).

boy self-government involved a real degree of autonomy for the pupils, and occasionally open rebellion. Discipline was corporeal and often savage. Nonetheless, boy autonomy was still a premeditated mode of pedagogy, although this could hardly be called liberal, however loosely. For in this system there was very little interest in the boys' character and personality, the active idea being that the best way to educate a boy was to leave him alone, so that the boys' own subcultures were seen as part of pedagogic experience. In the old days a boy might for example wander unescorted in the countryside in his very ample spare time. The idea was that one could only be a free man if one had experienced real freedom in youth.[40]

Boys were seen to be neither inherently good nor inherently bad: in the new order, Thomas Arnold struggled against what he called "the bond of evil" of the small boy group. In England he felt he was surrounded by a "mass of evil" that had to be reformed.[41] This evil was at once a social evil, requiring social action to make school society a social community, but it was also in particular a sensual evil in the boys, something requiring action on the senses and the body.[12] The training of the flesh went hand in hand with the training of the mind therefore. As Basil Willey saw, Arnold's great gift was to make ideas real, realising the Christian Society at Rugby in *practical* terms, the terms of the training of the whole person.[43] The idea of an active moral and physical creation of the individual was therefore new, in the old regime boys being unbenignly neglected. In the old order there was also a very wide age range, wider than later, and this included therefore a greater range of sexual maturity and presumably sexual activity, but not the obsessive interest that developed from the 1860s. Before 1850 it seems to have been the case that it was common and unremarkable for boys to share beds, two or more boys sharing together, as at Eton.[44]

As one historian of the public school has put it, reform can be characterised as a transition from freedom for boys to discipline for men, the state of childhood being subordinated to the idea of creating ordered and disciplined men.[45] Disciplinary self-government was interested in shaping the inwardness of the boy – reforming his character – through the means of premeditated regimes of discipline and surveillance of a

---

[40] T.W. Bamford, "Thomas Arnold and the Victorian Idea of the Public School" in Brian Simon and Ian Bradley (eds.), *The Victorian Public School: The Development of the Educational Institution* (Gill & Macmillan, 1975).

[41] Honey, *Tom Brown's Universe*, p. 3.   [42] Ibid., pp. 6–7.

[43] Basil Willey, *Nineteenth Century Studies: Coleridge to Matthew Arnold* (Chatto & Windus, 1949).

[44] Honey, *Tom Brown's Universe*, Ch. 11.

[45] John Chandos, *Boys Together: English Public Schools, 1800–1864* (Oxford University Press, 1985).

new sort. Character came to the fore therefore, in characteristic Victorian fashion. Arnold's version of disciplinary boy self-government became one of the organising principles of the Clarendon Report, in which it was stated: "The principle of governing boys through their own sense of what is right and honourable is undoubtedly the only true principle."[46] This principle was one of several defining characteristics of the schools after Arnold and Clarendon. These included the headmaster's independence from the governors, the new emphasis on the corporate identity of the school, and the fostering of this identity through "emulation", competition, and the identification of the boy with the teacher in a new system of pastoral care.[47] These elements will now be considered in more detail.

II   Classics and the remaking of liberal education

The major change in the nineteenth century was that the reformed educational institution itself became the main and usually the sole means for shaping those who would govern others – the bureaucrats who would govern the state and the wealthy and powerful who would tell society what to do. From around the 1840s the transformation of "character" became the chief moral objective in the public schools and Oxbridge, echoing the contemporary fixation. Character was pitted against "habit" in an almost Manichean battle for virtue and order. This battle was aimed at securing new sorts of political as well as moral subjectivity, for instance among the "working classes" of the 1860s, who according to Liberal politicians deserved the vote because of the moral advance their educational "cultivation" had made possible (the Tory Disraeli was more guarded but just as aware of the need, as it was put at the time, to "educate our masters"). Liberal education, suitably presented and carefully measured out, seeped into the education of the majority too. "Character" received expression outside education as well of course, for example in municipal self-government and the techno-governance of the city, for securing character was at the centre of producing the sort of person able to practice freedom responsibly.[48]

---

[46] Clarendon Report, *Parl. Papers, 1864, XX*, Public School Commission, First Report of Her Majesty's Commissioners, Section 13, "Discipline ... Moral Training in General".
[47] Honey, *Tom Brown's Universe*, p. 7.
[48] Joyce, *The Rule of Freedom*, Ch. 3, for further discussion of "character" and "habit"; and Tony Bennett, "Habit, Instinct, Survival; Repetition, History, Biopower" in Simon Gunn and James Vernon (eds.), *The Peculiarities of Liberal Modernity in Britain* (California University Press, 2011). Mariana Valverde, *Diseases of the Will: Alcohol and the Dilemmas of Freedom* (Cambridge University Press, 1998).

Ploughing a furrow worked by Weber and Foucault before him,[49] Thomas Osborne has recently identified some of the processes involved in the dissociation of the bureaucratic "officer" and "office" from the extra-official (personal, communal and political) loyalties that informed earlier kinds of state organisation. The patronage system in Britain exemplified these "extra-official" aspects. As Osborne indicates, the cultivation of ethical detachment and disinterest through the means of classics was central to the cultivation of the new civil service personae coming into being at the time. In creating bureaucracy as a "vocation" there are what Weber called the "spiritual" conditions of a distinctive life course or *Lebensführung*.[50] Equally there are the bodily conditions. However, in elite educational practice and theory "body" and "spirit" were one single thing. A liberal education encompassed both, and so did classics, at the heart of this education as it was. It is this paradox of elevated spiritual aspiration and ethical detachment, on the one hand, and a highly formalist and indeed authoritarian bodily discipline on the other, that I explore in what follows. This bodily discipline was to be had in the famous cult of sport in the public school, but I wish to emphasise how this concerned the curriculum as well and therefore liberal education as a whole. First I will consider "spirit" in shaping elite education, and then the body, which will also be considered in the next chapter.

Spirit

The emergence of elite educational reform was part of a wholesale refashioning of education by the state at this time. First the "ancient universities" were reformed, and then the "middle-class" endowed (and mainly grammar) schools, through the means of the Taunton Commission. This was followed in the 1860s by reform of the "public schools", in the form of the Clarendon Commission, which dubbed them "public". Although, unlike these, the Newcastle Commission on elementary education did not result in a great deal of immediate reform, the momentum for reform in elementary education grew after 1870 and was later apparent in secondary education in the Bryce Commission of 1895. The various Commissions that reformed the British educational system were themselves deeply infused with the tenets of a classical education. The Bryce Commission, for example, was informed by the Platonism that came into fashion in

---

[49] Thomas Osborne, "Bureaucracy as a Vocation: Governmentality and Administration in Nineteenth-Century Britain", *Journal of Historical Sociology*, 7:3 (1994).

[50] Paul du Gay, "Max Weber and the Moral Economy of Office", *Journal of Cultural Economy*, 1:2 (July 2008), 134–41.

Oxford from the 1860s and 70s.[51] This was especially indebted to Benjamin Jowett, "the great Tutor" so called, father of university and civil service reform, Master of Balliol and Regius Professor of Greek. He was the spider at the centre of the web of umpteen high bureaucratic careers, and one of the foremost guardians of the spiritual side of liberal cultivation of the whole man.

Jowett in turn educated the Balliol philosopher T. H. Green, whose Hegelianised Platonism had a profound effect on the Bryce Commission and on educational opinion generally before the First World War. His ideas about an enlarged remit for the liberal state influenced many of the leading social liberals of his day. His influence on the educational mandarins who made up the Board of Education in the 1890s was considerable.[52] These men were the architects of the Balfour Education Act of 1902, which extended state school provision from elementary (compulsory from 1881) to secondary education. Robert Morant, Permanent Secretary of Education in 1903 and later chair of the parliamentary commission implementing the National Insurance Act of 1911, was a Winchester and New College "man" who was influenced by Jowett and Green. He helped put in place a faint version of liberal elementary education in the mass education system as well as higher up the school social scale.[53] The Platonism of such men was based upon a view of British society as an organic community held together by differences, the hierarchy of the organism being reflected in and reproduced by the hierarchy of schools. The system of the public school, the grammar school, and the state sector of first elementary and then secondary school, would, as newly instituted, in this view cement the hierarchy of differences into the edifice of British society.[54] This hierarchy reflected another one, that between Greek in the public schools, Latin in the grammar schools and nothing at all for the vast majority of the rest.[55]

As a recent historian of classics in Britain puts it, Jowett and Green between them constituted a "high-level public discourse" which consciously encouraged the creation of Platonic Guardians for Britain and the Empire.[56] As a student Jowett had himself been part of the sort of charmed

[51] See the essays in Harry Judge (ed.), *The University and Public Education: The Contribution of Oxford* (Routledge, 2007).
[52] Robert Plant, "T. H. Green: Citizenship, Education and Law" in Judge (ed.), ibid.
[53] B. M. Allen, *Sir Robert Morant* (London, 1935).
[54] Christopher Stray, *Classics Transformed: Schools, Universities, and Society in England, 1830–1960* (Oxford University Press, 1998), Ch. 7.
[55] Richard Jenkyns, *The Victorians and Ancient Greece* (Basil Blackwell, 1984), p. 247.
[56] Stray, *Classics Transformed*, p. 22; R. Symonds, *Oxford and Empire: The Last Lost Cause?* (Oxford University Press, 1992).

circle he later encouraged. Frederick Temple (later Archbishop of Canterbury), yet another disciple and a favourite of Thomas Arnold, was headmaster at Rugby between 1858 and 1869. He helped form seminal members of the British governing classes, including Jowett. During one seven-year period of Temple's headmastership Matthew Arnold, Benjamin Jowett, Dean Stanley and Dean Farrar, all of critical importance in the history of British educational reform, and in the contemporary reformation of a liberal education, were in residence at Rugby together.[57] The circle turned again: for a similar period in the 1870s, at Balliol, Jowett numbered among what he liked to call his "men" Asquith, Curzon, Milner and Baden Powell.[58]

The "intellectual aristocracy" that Noel Annan wrote about many years ago was a part of these charmed circles.[59] Urban in temperament, evangelical in outlook, and public moralists in action, these opinion-forming intellectuals were nonetheless moulded in the cultural worlds of the public schools and Oxbridge – those of the high bureaucracy and the political class. They attended the same schools and colleges as these people, read the same books, competed for the same prizes and were taught by the same tutors. They were in fact often conscripted from the ranks of public-school headmasters and the fellows of Oxford and Cambridge colleges. They thoroughly embraced the "godliness and good learning" that were in the first place critical in the reform of the public school, the universities and the civil service.[60]

T. H. Green's philosophical idealism itself emerged out of the study of "Greats" at Oxford.[61] For Green and his pedagogic acolytes the nature of social ties was "displayed not in abstract theory but in the actual functioning of society".[62] The spirit and the flesh were to be drawn closer. Diverging from the earlier materialism and utilitarianism of J. S. Mill, and without requiring uncritical acceptance of established religion, Green's metaphysics was in practice a substitute for religion, one informed by a

---

[57] How, *Six Great Headmasters*, Ch. 5.
[58] Noel Annan, *The Dons: Mentors, Eccentrics, Geniuses* (Harper Collins, 1999), Ch. 6 on Jowett.
[59] Noel Annan, "The Intellectual Aristocracy" in J. H. Plumb (ed.), *Studies in Social History: A Tribute to G. M. Trevelyan* (Longmans Green, 1955), and Stefan Collini, *Public Moralists: Political Thought and Intellectual Life in Britain 1850–1930* (Oxford University Press, 1993).
[60] David Newsome, *Godliness and Good Learning: Four Studies on a Victorian Ideal* (John Murray, 1961), p. 250.
[61] *Literae Humaniores* roughly translates as "higher humane letters" and was grounded in the study of Roman and Greek language, history and philosophy.
[62] W. H. Walsh, "The Zenith of Greats" in M. G. Brock and M. C. Curthoys, *The History of the University of Oxford*, vol. II, *Nineteenth-Century Oxford*, Pt. 2 (Oxford University Press, 2000), p. 319.

still pervasive evangelical seriousness in which its adherents must not only change their views but strive to make the world better. This interest in action and the actual nature of society was very much part of Greats. In fact Green's influence has been seen by scholars to reflect the curious balance of Greats, which involved not only familiarity with the modern world but distance from it too, so that an interest in the ancient world cultivated a free and disengaged mind.

In the English-speaking world the sense of social involvement has always been an integral part of liberal education. Traditionally, the Greek ideal of wholeness has been kept alive by attaching it to the broad social world rather than to narrow occupational cultures. This solved the problem of the utility of liberal education by freeing its recipients from the world of toil (one had to have long years of schooling and hence be free from the need for employment). As we have seen, over the centuries there was a strong link between liberal education and high social standing, so this education has always been thoroughly involved in the formation of social and govern-ing elites.[63] In Plato the state is just and well ordered to the extent that its citizens are assigned positions for which their capacities best fit them, so that those who are most rational rule and those (the majority) who act on impulse are *ipso facto* the ruled. In Aristotle only those with the leisure and time to think are capable of citizenship, effectively debarring manual workers, and unquestionably slaves. Turning to the civil service itself, the idea always implicit in civil service reform was that the reform of Oxbridge education, centred on the Oxford study of Greats, would prepare men to run the liberal state and its empire. Likewise the reformed public school: like Plato's Guardians the public school men of England were to be in youth separated from their parents and raised in Spartan conditions, where they would aim to subordinate personal desires to securing the greatest possible happiness for the community as a whole[64]

Classics always had the most direct and urgent political relevance there-fore: first Greek civilisation and later Roman.[65] As Jowett put it, "The idealism of Plato is always returning to us, as a dream of the future; the politics of Aristotle continue to have a practical relation to our own times."[66] Aristotle was the dominant element before Plato and continued

[63] Sheldon Rothblatt, "The Limbs of Osiris: Liberal Education in the English-Speaking World" in Sheldon Rothblatt and Bjorn Wittock (eds.), *The European and American University since 1800: Historical and Sociological Essays* (Cambridge University Press, 1993); R. L. Archer, *Secondary Education in the Nineteenth Century* (London, 1921).

[64] Richard A. Chapman, *The Higher Civil Service in Britain* (Constable, 1970).

[65] Geoffrey Faber, *Jowett: A Portrait with Background* (Faber, 1957), esp. Section 3, Ch. 16, "The Heart of the Matter", pp. 359–60.

[66] Benjamin Jowett, *The Politics of Aristotle* (Oxford, 1885), 2 vols., vol. I, pp. xiii, xv.

to be very important. From Aristotle's *Politics* was taken the idea that the political constitution is essentially the full way of life of the citizen. The figure of the politician-administrator in Aristotle is that of the weaver or craftsman, who made noble actions possible for the citizen to achieve. Thus in his *Ethics* the good human being involves the *practice* of life in its full wholeness, body as well as soul, virtue or character being about real and practical behaviour and good conduct and not about abstraction and contemplation. Good conduct arose very much from good habits, which were only acquired from repeated action and correction. The governance of the state was something that could be learned, therefore. Evangelicalism and ancient Greece taught the same lesson.

It was Jowett who introduced *The Republic* to Oxford schools for the first time in 1847. Sir Stafford Northcote was part of Jowett's circle as, most important of all, was Gladstone. Northcote was educated at Eton and was a Balliol contemporary of Jowett (both had firsts in "Greats"). He was also Gladstone's Private Secretary at the Board of Trade. For Jowett the ancients taught that ethics and politics were inseparable (Jowett actually taught Political Economy himself in his earlier career, before turning fully to classics).[67] For Jowett the state was "the highest community". To this circle of reformers intellectual excellence was *ipso facto* moral excellence. Those who did best at intellectual work would prove to be "superior men".[68] For such men, eventually the generalist civil servants and the elite political class, classical language and thought became in effect a private language binding them together and serving as a template for their own society.[69] Earlier, in the Cambridge of the 1820s and 30s Julius Hare and Connop Thirlwell had been of critical importance for the transmission of German classical scholarship to England. Thirlwell's *History of Greece* was the first work in English to incorporate German scholarship. He in fact thought of himself as a new Socrates consciously training the best minds to feel romantically and think sceptically, reflecting the great influence of the Romantic poets at that time. A sort of romantic scepticism was the result, and this has been seen as a major part of the ethos not only of nineteenth-century Cambridge liberal education but also of the "intellectual aristocracy" that so much shaped British political reform over the long term.[70]

---

[67] See Evelyn Abbot, *The Life and Letters of Benjamin Jowett, M.A.* (London, 1897), 3 vols., vol. I.

[68] Ibid., pp. 27–8.

[69] Martin Bernal, *Black Athena: The Afroasiatic Roots of Classical Civilization*, vol. I, *The Fabrication of Ancient Greece 1785–1985* (Vintage, 1991), Ch. 7.

[70] See above, p. 245.

One of the central figures in this aristocracy, the great reformer of the Indian and British civil service T. B. Macaulay, had a critical role in promoting Greek civilisation and history. The cultic dimensions of this were apparent, Greek civilisation subsisting in a sort of moral and intellectual empyrean beyond earthly criticism. Greek was for him and his fellows the language of reason and civilisation, so that the study of the ancient world imbued the student with an ethic of detachment, a degree of separation from the world of the present which was first necessary so that ultimately one could govern the world more wisely. However for the great public-school headmaster Thomas Arnold's son, Matthew, Greek also put one under what he called the "empire of facts". Greek favoured practicality over speculation, also fostering scepticism and the virtue of a sense of tolerance of the real world that was the fruit of scepticism.[71]

Beyond the civil service the importance of ancient Greece for Victorian Britain has been frequently emphasised.[72] In its anglicised, post-Romantic guise Greek language, history and culture became associated with freedom, in distinction to Roman discipline and order. Mid-Victorian Hellenism became strongly linked with versions of liberal freedom as essentially British and English, defined as these were against supposedly Latin-oriented French expansionist authoritarianism.[73] Latin and the Roman models of order and civilisation came more powerfully to the surface at the end of the century, very much in line with the expansion of the British Empire. Latin also came to the fore in the public schools, although the hierarchy of Greek/public school, Latin/grammar school remained for some time. Greek was not abolished as a condition for university entrance at Oxford and Cambridge until just after the First World War. However, differences between Oxford and Cambridge classics should be noted: Oxford was more philosophical and cultural than philological and analytical Cambridge. Classical literature and history were already part of the Oxford syllabus by the 1830s. In line with its analytical traditions mathematics was far more important at Cambridge than at Oxford. Though, as we shall see, mathematics in nineteenth-century Cambridge was not at all inimical to the practical castes of mind involved in the political and administrative vocations.

In the Anglophone world therefore there was from early on a bias towards the social and political, rather than to other currents also present

---

[71] Osborne, "Bureaucracy as a Vocation".
[72] Richard Jenkyns, *The Victorians and Ancient Greece*, Ch. 4; Stray, *Classics Transformed*.
[73] Ibid., Chs. 3, 4.

in liberal education, ones which emphasised reflection and philosophy, and the intellectual before the civic. These were stronger in the tradition of *Bildung* (self-formation) within German elite education.[74] Nevertheless, in the course of the nineteenth century there was a shift to the training of the mind as the key to the training of character, something eventually issuing in university "research" in a modern form. Nonetheless, true to the British way the more cerebral turn of liberal education did not mean a dissociation from the socio-political world, manifest in the older tradition of the training of character.[75] Classics retained its central pedagogic role until well into the twentieth century by adapting to the rise of new intellectual disciplines in the universities in the second half of the nineteenth century, as well as to the historicism that increasingly marked its own pursuit. These developments gradually brought with them the idea of a content-free education, in the sense that one could pursue truth irrespective of the subject one studied. Instead of the idea of a general truth, uniquely located in classics, if truth could be pursued by many routes then this pursuit itself was seen to be where truth lay. In short, truth was method. The new notion of academic "truth" was progressive, historical and "scientific".[76] In some respects research therefore threatened the old idea of liberal education. The life of research was specialist, intellectualist, concerned with method, seemingly at variance with the holism and civic consciousness of a liberal education.

However, finding truth was still uppermost. What happened was that truth itself became sanctified, in classics as in the other disciplines of liberal education. As the historian of classics Christopher Stray puts it, if truth was now detached from value, it in turn itself became a value.[77] Only now truth was to be realised in its pursuit, this pursuit becoming a sort of moral journey (Bridges' idea of a classical education as the *pursuit* of truth will be recalled).[78] At Oxford the tension between research and the holistic ideal of liberal education was played out in terms of the arguments between Mark Pattison's and Benjamin Jowett's ideas of education, the former emphasising research, the latter the teaching tutorial, and with it a more outward, socially aware notion of the self. However, the old tradition

---

[74] W. H. Bruford, *The German Tradition of Self-Cultivation: "Bildung" from Humboldt to Thomas Mann* (Cambridge University Press, 2010).

[75] Ralph White, "The Anatomy of a Victorian Debate: An Essay in the History of Liberal Education", *British Journal of Educational Studies*, 34:1 (1986), 38–65; and Sheldon Rothblatt, *Tradition and Change in English Liberal Education: An Essay in History and Culture* (Faber and Faber, 1976).

[76] Sheldon Rothblatt, *The Revolution of the Dons: Cambridge and Society in Victorian England* (Faber and Faber, 1968).

[77] Stray, *Classics Transformed*, Chs. 2 and 6.   [78] See above, pp. 217–21, 225.

left its powerful mark on the new, for Mark Pattison, the prototype of the new "don" of the 1860s and 70s, regarded the true life of research still to be a means of connection back to the underlying wholeness of knowledge.[79] For Pattison, just as much as for Benjamin Jowett, a university education was "liberal" by virtue of the fact that it educated the whole person, the character and the will as well as the mind. Therefore "character" in its old and new forms still held power. Its inculcation remained the essential preparation for governing.

The difference lay in Pattison's more inward notion of the self, manifested in a dislike of what he saw as the university's capitulation to undergraduate teaching. However, for Pattison education still had a necessarily outward form, involving as it did the absorption of the educated into "the extant habits and ideas of the community or the class".[80] This absorption was to involve the teacher and the taught in the role of custodians and leaders of the values of "the community or the class". The essential element in both perpetuating the old and introducing the new understandings of character lay then in the resanctification of learning. This was itself apparent in the new post-1860s role of the don, the development of the tutorial and the emergence of the college in a new form.[81] Donnishness moralised the search for truth by embedding it in the reinvention of the college.[82] Resanctification was also apparent in the antiquity and beauty of Oxford and Cambridge and of many of the leading public schools. The deliberate cultivation of an aesthetic of antiquity therefore became an integral part of new ideas of what a liberal education might be, strengthening the love of learning for its own sake that was becoming part of a liberal education. These changes are considered at more length in the next chapter when the everyday life of the school and the college are considered. This life involved the world of things, and the body as a thing.

Body

So far this account of liberal education has been one of people's views, of what they thought, an approach mostly based on written texts. This is largely for reasons of necessity for thus has the history been written so far, as one of what is often called "thought". In academic writing about the history of governance this is particularly the case, most notably in the

---

[79] Stuart Jones, "The Scholar as Saint: Mark Pattison on Intellectual Culture" (draft research paper, 2007), and *Intellect and Character in Victorian England: Mark Pattison and the Invention of the Don* (Cambridge University Press, 2007).
[80] Jones, "The Scholar as Saint".   [81] Stray, *Classics Transformed*, Ch. 5.
[82] Rothblatt, *The Revolution of the Dons*.

history of political thought. The dominant position here is probably still the contextualised analysis of intellectuals' discourse about politics, power and the state evident in the work of Quentin Skinner and the so-called Cambridge School. In terms of its own field of operation, that of the workings of texts, this approach was long ago subject to searching critiques of its limited understandings of what text and context actually are.[83] However, one needs to go beyond this sort of critique to consider the material conditions of textual production and the materiality of texts themselves. There is also the need to go beyond texts alone, which I do in the next chapter. In doing so one draws attention to what "thought" actually is in the first place. The example of Shapin and Schaffer's great work on the social and political constituents of seventeenth-century science is enough to make us aware of the materiality of thought and of thought's bodily dispositions.[84]

However, a more recent and directly relevant example of how material and cultural practice impacts upon the constitution of thought is to hand, one that takes us back to nineteenth-century liberal education and nineteenth-century Oxbridge. Wainwright's *Masters of Theory* shows how even the most abstruse sorts of thought, in this case mathematical and analytical physics, which seem on the surface far removed from mundane experience, in fact emerged from the material and bodily routines apparent in the pedagogical practice of Victorian Cambridge.[85] The intrinsic character of the science itself was involved here, so that the practice of the Cambridge student in everyday life was not epiphenomenal but at the centre of what "thought" was. Theory was made "bottom up".[86] The

---

[83] See for example John Keane's formidable response to Skinner's work, which has not served to budge Skinner and his associates from their seemingly predestined path, in James Tully (ed.), *Meaning and Context: Quentin Skinner and His Critics* (Cambridge University Press, 1988). The work of Stefan Collini represents an advance on text-based approaches, in that he considers the institutional, economic and cultural elements at play, in for example the making of Victorian intellectuals and their writings; see *Public Moralists: Political Thought and Intellectual Life in Britain 1850–1930* (Oxford University Press, 1991), esp. Ch. 1, "Leading Minds: the World of the Victorian Intellectual". See the discussion above, p. 227, with reference to the work of Elaine Hadley on Victorian liberalism, which in turn critiques and moves considerably far beyond the Cambridge School.

[84] Steven Shapin and Simon Schaffer, *Leviathan and the Air-Pump: Hobbes, Boyle, and the Experimental Life* (Princeton University Press, 1985).

[85] Andrew Warwick, *Masters of Theory: Cambridge and the Rise of Mathematical Physics* (University of Chicago Press, 2003). There is also the work of Becker and Clark, considered earlier, on the micro-technologies that have helped fashion the liberal state, in the form of two of its principal components, the bureaucrat and the academic. Peter Becker and William Clark, *Little Tools of Knowledge: Historical Essays on Academic and Bureaucratic Practices* (University of Michigan Press, 2001).

[86] In Wainwright's account of Cambridge physics he identifies how a distinct tradition was marked out that was separate from and hostile to continental analysis. In Cambridge it was

actual concepts of physics themselves were shaped by such things as the physical rigours of the examination, and the mental but especially physical ("muscular") preparation for success in mathematics apparent in the daily routines of the undergraduate. Wainwright charts how the eighteenth-century idea of liberal education, which involved students in the subservient emulation of masters, was replaced by the new regime of nineteenth-century Cambridge, one which in its rigour and competitiveness encouraged both introspection and assertiveness. One critical area Wainwright charts is the transition from eighteenth-century explosive sport to nineteenth-century "exercise", particularly the obsessive contemporary involvement in walking and rowing. This mirrored the world of academic work, one also marked by the "cramming" that went into preparation for examinations. Academic success, or otherwise, was reflected in eagerly anticipated tables of merit and newspaper accounts of university ceremonies. Competition was intense, and took an enormous toll on the body and the mind. This everyday world of the academic institution is considered in the next chapter, although it gives us our cue here, for the mobilisation of the body was intrinsic to classical liberal education.

From Renaissance times this education was built around certain organising principles arising from adaptations of the Greek idea of an education for public service, principles concerned with the operationalisation of rhetoric, oratory and public declamation. In turn however the canon upon which these principles operated involved the exercise of drill, memory, repetition.[87] This was fully apparent in the grammar schools, historically the next layer down from the "public" ones in the hierarchy of educational organisation.[88] It was also evident in the "preparatory" schools that preceded the public school experience, the age range of the latter varying considerably, anything from ten to seventeen or eighteen years, though "day boys" might attend even earlier. The "prep schools", with boarding and day attendance, themselves varied in age range between five and thirteen years, and expanded greatly in number after the reformation of the public schools from the1860s, when the boarding side mushroomed. Both before and after this time they were designed essentially to feed the public schools, the culture of which they seem, not unnaturally in the

felt that although mathematics gave one fundamental principles from which to argue it did not guarantee these principles, and for that an "intuitive" element was needed, so that "muscular effort" came into play as part of scientific thought. The concept of "force" in physics in these contemporary formulations was understood as an intuitive, underlying and practical conviction (*Masters of Theory*, Ch. 3 and p. 221).

[87] Stray, *Classics Transformed*, Ch. 2.
[88] Ralph White, "The Anatomy of the Victorian Debate: An Essay on the History of Liberal Education", *British Journal of Educational Sociology*, xxxiv:1 (February 1986).

circumstances, to have sedulously aped. Some had "houses", but others were too small for this.

The formalism of classics involved the training of habit, for habit was precisely that aspect of being where body and mind were intrinsically connected. It was therefore a particularly sensitive locus of governance. As students of liberal governmentality have noted,[89] particularly in the case of the government of the will (as in the control of alcohol), the category of "habit" seems of particular importance in liberal regimes in that it is there that body and mind are joined politically, habit being the critical site where desire and compulsion are mediated. Classics was taught as much for the "moral value of exact scholarship" as for its intrinsic moral content. The training of habit takes on a particular relevance in relation to the great significance of "the language of character" among Victorian political intellectuals and educated opinion more widely,[90] for habit took physiological and psychological forms as well as moral ones, so that for contemporaries "thought" and mind were already corporeal in character. The language of character was embedded in Victorian Protestant evangelicalism, which brought to it an intensification of the sense of inward and physical struggle. Romanticism, and even religious agnosticism, contributed to this widespread moral psychology, one in which the problem of adequate moral motivation was the central issue. This often highly pessimistic view of human nature was marked in some of its varieties by what amounted to the *necessity* of moral struggle. However, the category of habit makes it possible to conceive of optimistic solutions also, for it embraces both stasis and change, both the "problem" and its solution, for if habits are ingrained in nature they can nonetheless be broken by the power of the will in its action upon, and through, the body.

The formalistic aspects of the teaching of classics applied to all pupils. There is no clearer expression of the centrality of classics to liberal education than that of the Report of the Clarendon Commission.[91] For the education of boys in large schools there should be one principal branch of study invested with a recognised and traditional importance, and that is classics. The highest office of education was said to be "training and discipline", though education was also to awaken capacities and taste, and teach one how to bear oneself in "cultivated society". On the one hand, classics is seen as the "key" to all aspects of modern civilisation, the source of all that is of enduring cultural and moral value. On the other, grammar, as

---

[89] Valverde, *Diseases of the Will*.
[90] Within evangelicalism itself there were divergent strains: a voluntarist one, but also a very strong deterministic element too. See the discussion in Collini, *Public Moralists*, pp. 105 ff.
[91] Clarendon Report, *Parl. Papers, 1864, XX*, Section 8, pp. 38–9.

"the logic of common language", is enthroned as the key to training and discipline. The logic of classics teaches regularity and lucid expression and embeds a capacity for understanding in terms of general laws. In practice, in the daily experience of children and young people, what this meant was that merit was to be found in hard and unrelenting work, above all in the very dullness of the "grind" of grammar in which the memory was actively trained to function ("grammar grind" first appeared in the Oxford English Dictionary in 1890). In contemporary understandings of "mind training" evident in ideas about classical education, what was called "the transfer of training", classics taught one how to learn.[92]

The sheer volume of classics teaching in public school contributed to the relentless "grinding" of the boy, and of course it is the boy one is dealing with in the public school until the very late rise of girls' education towards the end of the nineteenth century, although girls were exposed to the same sort of grinding. The body as well as the mind was governed by the curriculum: in the Harrow and Rugby of the 1830s and 40s classics occupied two-thirds of the curriculum, and time did little to change this preponderance. In the 1860s as much as 80 per cent of the boys' time was spent on classics.[93] At the turn of the twentieth century classics still kept its essential place, indeed for some time after this.[94] It was and continued to be central to the examination system, for entry to the public school, the universities and the civil service. Classics was entrenched in this way also because of the closed world of public school classics teaching, the school here as so often bearing the marks of the "total institution", one affecting the totality of the person's life.

As H.W. Nevinson put it in his account of Shrewsbury which opens this chapter, the masters "were content to teach what they had learnt, and in the same manner. Most of them were Shrewsbury boys themselves, and because Greek had been taught there for more than three centuries, they taught Greek." This did indeed mean that the boys' knowledge was, as he put it, "both peculiar and limited". In public schools in general teachers were frequently recruited from those who had attended the school, and the close link between particular Oxbridge colleges and particular schools contributed to the same effect. Leading public schools, such as Eton, produced their own textbooks, especially classics grammars. Habituation was furthered by the longevity of textbooks, most notably *Kennedy's Latin Primer*, which after its introduction in the 1880s and its

---

[92] Stray, *Classics Transformed*, Ch. 8.
[93] Thomas Bamford, *Rise of the Public Schools: A Study of Boys' Public Boarding Schools in England and Wales from 1837 to the Present Day* (Nelson, 1967), p. 62.
[94] Honey, *Tom Brown's Universe*, p. 169.

subsequent modifications continued to be the bible of grinding into the present day.[95] Latin and Greek grammars were in fact the fundamental tools of classics, and dominated the curriculum. The "peculiar and limited" education they gave rise to was well expressed by Nevinson, for in his experience "the greater part of the school believed that Greek literature was written as a graduated series of problems for Shrewsbury boys to solve". Grinding mind and body was the only way to mastery in this world.

The Eton grammar, appearing first in 1758, dominated for much of the time before Kennedy. Its formalism became associated with Toryism and power, uniformity in grammar being associated with uniformity in religion. Pedagogic challenges were aimed against the rote learning of established classical grammars such as this, by both philosophical and popular radicals, challenges made in the name of a more child-centred approach, and of grammar taught in the native language of the learner, not the ancient languages themselves. These had little impact on elite education. The grammar book was also a direct concern of state policy – the Clarendon Commission involved itself with the creation of standard and common grammars, eventually turning the matter over to the headmasters of the leading public schools.[96] Kennedy's *Primer* was the outcome of the controversy that ensued between liberals and traditionalists, an outcome that was far from liberal. The accent remained on "grinding", for Kennedy still concentrated on the logical rather than the philological analysis of Latin.

Once one left the "gerund grind" and entered the sixth form, it was not the case that the training of habit was left behind. Rather, in the form of verse competition, it came to a sort of logical conclusion as "a graduated series of problems" to be solved. What was involved has been called, kindly in the light of the Shrewsbury experience, a form of "puzzle and prayer",[97] a "semi-sacred" knowledge which was at once an aesthetic exercise and a training in logical, formal and analytical thinking – grinding made aesthetic. Henry Salt at Eton said that as boy and man, coming out of the "verse manufactory" that was the College, he had composed over 30,000 lines in imitation of Ovid and Tibullus, an experience the scope of which was not unusual.[98] In Winchester, as at all public schools, the voluminous College slang itself involved a form of "memory work", for this had to be mastered

---

[95] Christopher Stray, "Paradigms of Social Order: The Politics of Latin Grammar in 19th-Century England", *Bulletin of the Henry Sweet Society*, 13 (1989). For thirty years headmaster of Shrewsbury, Kennedy later became Regius Professor of Greek at Oxford.

[96] Christopher Stray, *Grinders and Grammars: A Victorian Controversy* (The Textbook Colloquiam, 1995).

[97] Stray, *Classics Transformed*, p. 71.

[98] Henry Salt, *Memories of Bygone Eton* (London, 1928), p. 87.

on pain of ostracism. The Winchester slang was called "Notions" and its mastery was regarded as essential to school identity. The parallels between classics and slang were recognised by one College historian, for both were said to be conducive to the kind of mind a liberal education should produce. Both involved not only memory work, but deductive reasoning and "an appetite for the ordered detail of a past tradition". Notions, like classics, was in this rather acute view rationalistic but it also venerated tradition. It thus represented a powerful appeal to emotional conformism.[99] The machine-like character of the content and the activity of the learning going into classical composition is illustrated by the building of the Eureka machine in 1845, a clockwork randomising automaton which produced Latin hexameter lines (see Figure 6.1). This elaborate construction, subsequently put on public exhibition in London, underscored the essentially political nature of verse composition, which was a training in the rhetoric and analysis of dead languages preparing men for lives as virtuous citizens and leaders.

To some degree the study of modern history came to complement classics prior to the First World War. However, what is striking are the continuities between the two disciplines: history largely accepted the catechistic form of instruction evident in classical pedagogy. Instruction was by set texts, especially selected extracts collected from various "authorities" in history. These texts also involved compilations of primary sources and secondary syntheses. The object of study as well as the method was the same as classics: both disciplines studied societies with fixed and laudable values, in the case of history Britain and the empire. Historical authorities were consulted in the same way as classical authors, to reveal processes by which stable development and enduring qualities of mind had evolved over time.[100] Political and constitutional history dominated and remained central until well after the Second World War.[101] By the inter-war years the connection with public service was marked, Oxford historians making up what have been called "the moral haberdashers of

[99] T. J. H. Bishop, *Winchester and the Public School Elite: A Statistical Analysis* (Faber and Faber, 1967), p. 27; C. G. Stevens, *Winchester Notions: The Dialect of Winchester College*, ed. Christopher Stray (Athlone Press, 1998).

[100] Reba Soffer, "Modern History" in Brock and Curthoys, *The History of the University of Oxford*. See also Peter R. H. Slee, *Learning and a Liberal Education: The Study of Modern History in the Universities of Oxford, Cambridge, and Manchester, 1800–1914* (Manchester University Presss, 1986).

[101] James Vernon, "Narrating the Constitution: The Discourse of 'the Real' and the Fantasies of Nineteenth-Century Constitutional History" in James Vernon (ed.), *Re-reading the Constitution: New Narratives in the Political History of England's Long 19th Century* (Cambridge University Press, 1996).

Fig. 6.1 The Eureka machine: a clockwork randomising automatic device for producing Latin hexameter lines

the governing elite",[102] practising a discipline the last thought of which was to question the established order. Certain individuals rejected this – Tawney, Namier and Laski, for example – but they had to leave Oxford.

[102] Soffer, "Modern History", p. 393.

This was the situation at one end of the public-school career. At the other end of the school career entry to the public school through the increasingly numerous preparatory schools also encouraged "cramming", the prelude and companion to "grinding".[103] Indeed such schools were often known as "crammers", as were the institutions preparing entrants to the civil service exam. Located in London, and doubly expensive as the crammed had to board in London as well as pay for the school, these became an essential part of many civil service careers.[104] Cramming and grinding were in large measure a product of the examination, of course.

As we have seen, so-called high bureaucratic "Administrative Capacity" denoted a particular sort of mind, a particular kind of "intelligence" as it would later come to be known. This "effortless superiority, imbued with a cultivated scepticism" was perhaps the major style of mind cultivated by elite education and rooted in the high bureaucracy; certainly at its highest levels, for example Eton, although there was much emulation of this style all the way down the hierarchy. As we have seen, Thomas Balogh, adviser to the 1964 Wilson government, described this in its late manifestations as a "tolerant scepticism obtained by ... a formal kind of education, which developed powers of dialectical argument only".[105] More friendly witnesses were of much the same mind. Chapman described the Oxbridge tutorial as involving the ferreting out of information, and the persistent examination of alternative viewpoints so that concise and informed general accounts would be possible. It was not what you knew that mattered but the manner of knowing it, form over content, dialectic over speculation and originality, and supposed "rigour" over creativity – above all the safe and not the radical.

Therefore civil servants did not necessarily make the best intellectuals, and were decidedly not men of ideas. On the contrary, the "absolute nonentity" of the top civil servant was his highest merit, his very freedom from ideas.[106] What Balogh and Chapman identified was rooted in places like the schoolrooms of Shrewsbury in the 1870s. It was the examination that did most to translate what were in effect the educational class prejudices of the well-off into something that could be evaluated as "intelligence" and publicly promulgated and justified as "merit". Things tend to

[103] David Leinster-McKay, *The Rise of the English Prep School* (The Falmer Press, 1984).
[104] R. A. Chapman, *Leadership in the British Civil Service* (Croom Helm, 1984); also *Ethics in the British Civil Service* (Routledge, 1988).
[105] Thomas Balogh, "The Apotheosis of the Dilettante in the Establishment of Mandarins" in Hugh Thomas (ed.), *Crisis in the Civil Service* (Anthony Blond, 1968), and R. A. Chapman, *Leadership in the British Civil Service*.
[106] Chapman, *The Higher Civil Service in Britain* (Constable, 1970), p. 190.

change slowly in Britain: from the 1870s to the 1960s, and thence to the 2010s, the equation of merit with this formal and safe style of "intelligence" is evident, this forming what amounts to an ideology of merit, which is policed by the academics as much as anyone else, especially the Oxbridge version. Only the social groups that have benefited have changed; those who have continued to lose out are much the same.

The examination itself was about discovering and measuring a subject who could be "objectively" tested. The corollary of the measurability of intelligence came to be that it was regarded as innate. However, as Richard Sennett and many others have argued, ability is not innocent of experience, for example the experience of an expensive education and having the parents to pay for it. It is not only this, however, nor the elevation of form over content, for the sort of "meritocratic" intelligence that was born in the nineteenth century has privileged only certain sorts of ability, in particular mathematical and verbal activity. It was and is these that constitute the object of testing, whereas visual and auditory ability were relinquished. As Sennett says, this is "not to deny that ability exists or that there are differences between people. Rather, in the search to consummate the project of finding a natural aristocracy the mental life of human beings has assumed a surface and narrowed form. Social reference, sensate reasoning, and emotional understanding have been excluded from that search, just as have belief and truth."[107] This "surface and narrowed form" of human ability is everywhere apparent in the life of the British and the educational institutions that have nurtured it. The exclusion of "belief and truth" is there in the British civil servant's allergy to ideas, and it is there in the disengaged, dialectical and ultimately dessicated caste of mind behind it. From the corporealisation of the natural aristocrat as the high civil servant, to the contempt historically shown towards the intellectual and cultural resources of the children of the powerless, this pernicious pedagogy of merit is deeply rooted in British culture.

As for the history of the examination itself there are various milestones on the way to the idea of the innateness of "intelligence". A good number of these were linked to Oxford and Cambridge, although in other continental regimes, pre-eminently eighteenth-century Prussia, it was the state that played the pioneering role. The Cambridge mathematical Tripos of 1747 has been described as the "leading edge" of the examination system, and the Oxford Examination Statute of 1800 was another

---

[107] Richard Sennett, *The Culture of the New Capitalism* (Yale University Press, 2006), pp. 120–1.

such milestone. The civil service examination itself was of fundamental significance for the development of the public examination system in general.[108] Educational examinations were and are aimed particularly at the young, and therefore at forming character early on. Examinations were viewed as doing this in a number of ways. They were early on valued as *competitive*, and thus inherently moral when contrasted with patronage and its supposed corruption and place-seeking. The examination also encouraged perseverance and self-discipline. For men like Thomas Arnold and Jowett the examination's purpose was as much about its form as its content, and in the Northcote-Trevelyan Report the examination was explicitly linked to the moral value of work.[109]

Civil service reform also created a clear divide between "mechanical" and "intellectual" labour, one fostered by contemporary "public moralists" and their sanctification of intellectual labour, in particular John Stuart Mill.[110] Lowe's Civil Service Order of 1870 introduced the examination and with it the intellectual–mechanical distinction across the whole service. With the expansion of the civil service to a quarter of a million by 1911 the organisation of the state was increasingly based on the model of the machine. This was made explicit in Haldane's *Report on the Machinery of Government* of 1918.[111] The sanctification of intellectual work was one means of negotiating solutions to the contemporary clash of the rival governmental rationales of patronage and merit; the code of "honourable secrecy" was another, as has been seen. In so far as the civil service examination borrowed from the curriculum of the Ancient Universities, which it did heavily, the content of the examination actively contributed to the achievement of ethical detachment. For, like the ethic of work and service this content had a highly sanctified character itself, most of all in classics.

The examination of course functioned as a governmental technique in ways which extended beyond the civil service. It produced outcomes that were seemingly *transparent* because they were based on measuring "merit". Merit itself was seen as a brake on the arbitrary excesses of government, so that it was also understood as creating greater *accountability*. However, it also created greater *efficiency* through the principle of accountability: one could count and therefore calculate government, making efficiency possible, and preventing thereby government's unnecessary proliferation. For Gladstone merit would introduce Treasury control into the home civil

---

[108] John Roach, *Public Examinations in England 1850–1900* (Cambridge University Press, 2008).
[109] Asa Briggs's essay on Thomas Arnold in Briggs, *Victorian People*.
[110] See Collini, *Public Moralists*.
[111] Jonathan Agar, *The Government Machine* (MIT Press, 2002).

service, so enshrining accountability as an institutional reality.[112] Merit, accountability and efficiency thus created a neutral space of government ostensibly outside political control. Their importance in liberal regimes is obvious.

The civil service examination itself was of course not only aimed at the Administrative Class but at lower levels too, even if before 1870 these examinations were still fairly rudimentary.[113] The Civil Service Commission saw its task as raising ambition and emulation in society at large by its examination initiatives. Indeed, the whole idea of the public examination was that it would *create* the very public it was supposedly examining, for its putative openness was not only aimed at those taking part but at those witnessing the phenomenon itself. Very much like the assembling of the expert's "witness" in seventeenth-century science, the "scientific" instrument now became the examination not the air pump, so that a form of mass witnessing was created whereby the public so produced complemented the scientific characteristics of the instrument involved.[114] In terms of the history of the public examination, the Commission began to conduct entrance examinations for the Army in 1870, when the abolition of commission purchase dealt a heavy blow to the old patronage system.[115] To the list of direct governmental initiatives in the area of national education should therefore be added the Royal Commission on Military Education of 1860.

The Civil Service Commission explicitly saw its task as relating higher level entry to higher level education nationally. The ideal for a first-class clerkship in the civil service was the elite public school and Oxford man. In turn, the universities themselves were major actors in making sure Oxbridge staffed the higher reaches of the civil service, going as far in the case of Jowett's Balliol as developing a probationary period at Oxford as a prerequisite for entrance to the Indian Civil Service. Jowett was deeply committed to the success of his younger charges, especially exam success, also to their achievement of public honours.[116] Sir John Seeley after him, founder of the Cambridge modern history school and a major architect of university reform, was equally interested in the university as a tool for preparing men for public service, particularly through reform of the college system and the institution of the college tutor. Like Benjamin Jowett he was also interested in university extension education. The 1886 Ridley Commission on the civil service, concerned to create a more

---

[112] Osborne, "Bureaucracy as a Vocation".   [113] Roach, *Public Examinations*, Chs. 7–9.
[114] See above, pp. 123–4.   [115] Roach, *Public Examinations*, Ch. 9.
[116] Ibid., Ch. 11, esp. p. 258.

unified civil service by means of the examination, decided that civil service exams should be directly organised along Oxford and Cambridge lines so as to further strengthen the civil service/Oxbridge connection. However the new world of the examination and merit was rooted in the reformed public school, and it is to this I now turn.

7 "The fathers govern the nation": the public school and the Oxbridge college

The fathers govern the nation; the mothers govern the fathers; but the boys govern the mothers, and I govern the boys.

Dr Richard Barnaby, Headmaster of Westminster School, 1639–1695[1]

The engineering of governorship – of mastership over oneself and others worked upon the raw material of the human body. It did so in systematic and innovative ways: in terms of the *curriculum* – of grammar and the ancient languages and cultures – something of this has already been seen, the body as well as the spirit being the object of the exercise. In the first section of this chapter, on "making mastery", the creation of what I call docile and active bodies will be considered systematically as we move from the public school and College curriculums alone to the daily life and built, material forms of the schools and the two great universities. This will help show in the case of the schools how what were already, historically, marketised institutions, and in practice surprisingly inchoate ones organisationally, were given coherence and direction, both at the level of the school and at the level of the whole public school governmental project and the "system" it enabled.

It was the school and College form of the "house" that more than anything else gave cohesion to the disparate experience of school life. It was not the only thing of course, and the systematic organisation of space and time that was seen in the schools from roughly the mid-nineteenth century also served to give them unity and comparability. Both of these elements continue our theme of the making of "centres" as well as of systems, for just as the file was at the centre of administration, and the cheap, stamped and enveloped letter at the centre of the postal system, so the classification and ordering of behaviour, above all in the form of the house, were at the centre of the inculcation of governance. In the second section of this chapter therefore I shall explore the hold of the regime of the house on the institution itself

---

[1] Cited in M. L. Charlesworth, *J. B. Oldham of Oldham's Hall* (privately published, 1986), p. 24.

and on the formation of the boy, for it is in the relationship to the house and home, the most powerful and intimate settings of human life, that we will discern the extraordinary hold of the public school and the College on the mind of the British ruling classes, and on British society more widely. The *domus* was far more than a symbol alone. The spatial patterns of the house were repeated and reinforced at every step of the formation of the governing classes: the government office, the gentleman's club as a home away from home, and the school "house". The most significant of these houses was the last one, the one that in relation to the first house, the initial "home", provides us with the clearest understanding of how mastery was made. Finally, in this chapter, by way of approaching the conclusion of the book on the relationship between the past and the present of the British state, I shall from time to time stray from my "period" in the direction of the late twentieth century, having already trespassed into the eighteenth in search of the long view.

I   Making mastery

Firstly, the "public" schools. The nature of the public school has been widely misunderstood because most public-school history has been produced by insiders, by men (almost invariably men) who themselves attended and sometimes taught at public schools. Even when these men are professional historians, such is the hold of the schools on the British higher education system that these historians are also quite likely to be insiders in this way. Whilst this has certain benefits – insiders have inside knowledge – the public-school literature has in large measure bought into the myths of the public schools themselves, myths that have also wormed their way into the national psyche. The schools have taken on a certain cult-like character in their own and in the national imagination. They have mistakenly been viewed as coherent, stable and centralised organisational forms, each form, "The School", being assumed to embody a distinct ethos and tradition, a unified will expressed over centuries in some cases. The consequence of this is that their real institutional nature has been lost sight of.

Contrary to myth, the schools were and in important respects remain rather dispersed, disunited institutions with strong centripetal tendencies. The school house expressed an essential ambiguity, for if it gave the school its beating heart, especially after the 1880s when the house was successfully enlisted in the fashioning of school unity, it was also an institution of centripetal force. The heart of the house beat both with and at variance to the pulse of the school. So tradition, ethos and unity were the products of conscious and elaborate technological and material engineering and not the end-product of centuries of "tradition". We have already seen how the new disciplinary self-government after the 1860s was concerned with shaping the inwardness of the boy through the means of premeditated regimes of discipline and surveillance. Freedom was in short "organised", to continue another of our overarching themes. In some respects this had a decidedly liberal character, the disciplined freedom of *self*-government replacing the old quasi-anarchy. Arnold echoed widespread sentiment in believing that boy self-government reflected the long tradition of British liberty. However, the "organised freedom" of boy self-government and the exaltation of British freedom were as much characteristic of conservatives as liberals (whether with a capital "C" or not). In fact, many of the schools had strong, not to say rabid, Tory proclivities. Nonetheless, parents of the most varied political persuasions sent their children to these schools regardless, just as they sent them regardless of knowing they would be unhappy and mistreated. So, to emphasise the point again, we had better call this "organised freedom" rather than "liberal", though at bottom the world view of the schools as of the British governing classes was broadly liberal. And, as the other side of liberal governance was authority, hierarchy and subordination were the kin of freedom. As I have said, the public school and the public schoolboy were miniature universes of the state.

The "invented tradition" of "The School", and the schools, is now fairly well known,[2] the schools being part of a systematic and far-ranging attempt to create institutions that would serve the needs of a rapidly expanding world power.[3] However, what this "tradition" means for the history of the state and how it actually worked is not appreciated. Disciplinary boy self-government was, as we have seen, only one of a number of weapons in the new armoury of the schools, among them also not only the enhanced role of the house system but also that of the systems of prefects and of pastoral care and tutorship. These were all designed to enhance a new sort of corporate identity for each school, the intended effect being to make each school unique, so that being *from* a particular school came to matter in a new way. At the same time all schools were to be basically the same, subscribing to the same Clarendon model.

The literature on the schools has also in large part failed to acknowledge the overriding fact that the schools were first and foremost market

---

[2] Eric Hobsbawm and Terence Ranger (eds.), *The Invention of Tradition* (Cambridge University Press, 1992); John Raymond Honey, *Tom Brown's Universe: The Development of the Victorian Public School* (Millington, 1977), Ch. 8 on Clifton College as a good example of the *ex nihilo* public school, with its made-to-measure school song, school dress, etc.

[3] Richard Symons, *Oxford and Empire: The Last Lost Cause?* (Oxford University Press, 1991).

institutions, selling a commodity, namely education. Although they had "charitable" status, and in some cases were created by the Crown, they operated in a highly competitive environment the imperatives of which were always economic. They vied with each other in a marketplace, one which was about money and prestige. If the profit motive did not formally rule it dominated. Masters and fellows were in education to make a living, and they had a keen appreciation of the place of profit in their own advancement in life. They handled a real economic and social resource, a good in the basic sense. Without this good – education – life chances were, and are, gravely limited. This works in at least two ways. Without education one cannot manipulate the numerical and verbal symbols and logics involved in the more complex tasks of getting on in life. And without education of a well-regarded kind one is deficient in what has been called social capital, for education is more than instrumental alone. It buys social skills and social contacts. Therefore, far from being somehow inherently "collective" institutions the schools were marketised, individualised and atomised in ways that have not been recognised. In many respects they were and are characteristically liberal institutions, so that there was no contradiction between the supposedly traditional public school and British modernity; quite the opposite in fact, just as in Britain as a whole established elites were the agents of "modernising" economic and political change.

Before moving on to the making of mastery proper it is therefore most important to unearth something of this largely unacknowledged private, atomised and market character of the schools. How was this manifest? Despite reform this aspect of the schools did not change much from the old days to the new. Firstly I will look at the old days. Rugby School correspondence from the 1790s enables us to eavesdrop on the shoptalk of the masters in the days before reform. Thomas James, Rugby's then headmaster, instructed his self-described "son" Samuel Butler, whom he had taught at Rugby (he writes of Shrewsbury, where Butler ended up as a famous headmaster):

I am of the opinion that your Fortune might very profitably be made in that city. There is a school there having from £1,300 to £1,500 a year, of which the Head Master has not above £100 a year, but he has allowances for Assistants, an excellent house and School built in a superior style ... The school was once the Eton or the Westminster of Wales & all of Shropshire ... Now the present Master does nothing.[4]

---

[4] Letter from James at Upton-on-Severn to Butler at St John's, Cambridge, 23 January 1797. See also 2 March 1797, 17 October 1797, 24 October 1800, from W. H. D. Rouse, *A History of Rugby School* (London, 1898).

The Shrewsbury gentry were searching for a new headmaster and James suggests that Butler learn the particulars of the school from histories of the county: "you would play a game in which you would be sure to be a wonderful winner ... the world would greatly patronise you, & you would be sure of accumulating a great fortune ... Let a man be ever so great at the university, yet when once he has left it, & has been melted down into the great mass of the world, he loses a very considerable share indeed of that consequence and attention ...". He went on, "I heartily wish you well, & therefore I wish you not to marry until you have either got hold of the old woman's estate you write about, or until you have cast anchor upon some safe shore."

Before the Clarendon Commission it was widely recognised that in all schools, Eton included, masters and fellows regularly milked the revenues, headmasters profiteering especially freely.[5] After reform, in the 1860s and 70s, at Eton as elsewhere parents frequently hired a "coach" to supplement school teaching, someone who might not come from the school at all. However, most of the remuneration of the schoolteachers, including the head, came directly from parents to teachers themselves in the shape of various fees, formal and informal (including "leaving presents" at Eton). The relationship was therefore a monetary one, and as such individualised and atomised. The lowly assistant masters in the Lower School at Eton were however paid by the Head, and got only £30 per annum. This was supplemented by what private tutoring they could get among the Eton pupils (in their own private "Pupil Room").[6] In this the schools simply reproduced the division of much industrial capitalism at the time, namely subcontracting. There was then very little if anything of a centralised school bureaucratic machinery. In the 1860s the College was said to be in administrative chaos, something which was said to have gone on for centuries. At Eton headmaster de Warre established a central school office in the 1880s (before then the headmaster and his butler did the books!).[7] However, nothing like a "modern" central administration existed for some time and the old heterogeneity lingered strongly.

This was apparent above all with houses and housemasters. These men were in effect hotelkeepers, concerned to run their house so as to make money, which they very frequently did in considerable quantities. They dealt directly with the economic affairs of the house: not until 1945 in

---

[5] Tim Card, *Eton Established: A History from 1440 to 1860* (John Murray, 2001), Chs. 14–16.
[6] Ibid., Ch. 15.
[7] L. Byrne and E. Churchill, *Changing Eton: A Survey of Conditions based on the History of Eton since the Royal Commission of 1862–64* (Jonathan Cape, 1937).

Eton were the boys' bills dealt with by the school itself, not the house-master. The housemaster, at Eton and elsewhere, traditionally made up his own list of boys for the house, the headmaster having no power of veto. If moving on from one house to another it was often the case that the housemaster would take his boys with him. Housemasters financed, built and sometimes designed their own houses. Headmasters themselves, as at Eton, privately financed the building of teaching facilities. The Rev. Stephen Hornby of Eton built six classrooms and a lecture theatre at his own expense; headmaster Hawtrey two decades later the science schools.[8] Money-making and pedagogic innovation were neatly combined. In the 1860s the lowly assistant masters were getting in on the boarding racket too, competing with the housemasters to board boys as a supplement to their poor salary. Housemasters at Eton and elsewhere lived in consider-able pomp.[9] The eventual development of central feeding, not seen at Shrewsbury until as late as the 1960s, did something to curb this institu-tional anarchy, houses coming more under the control and administration of a central school authority.[10] However, as we shall see, the house still ruled and the new prominence of headmasters after Clarendon was in practice curtailed by the power of housemasters.

Just after the First World War, and long after the reform process began, things at Eton had changed little. The Eton master C. R. L. Fletcher complained in 1919 to Rhodes James, the Provost, about the naked profit-seeking of all levels among the masters.[11] He also deplored how the College charged exorbitant rents to the housemasters, just as they in turn battened on their charges (it was only just before the First World War that the College began to build houses and rent them out itself).[12] He excoriated the "extravagance" of Eton and "our horrid desire for more money", almost everyone being involved, with the honourable exception of young masters and those too poor to meet the swollen expenditures of the superrich of their day. The College supplied appalling accommoda-tion to its young masters, who were sometimes forced to live outside the town. Housemasters fed their charges extravagantly to make a reputation, and starved them at other times when economy demanded it. All that was asked of parents by those in charge of admissions was "are they rich

---

[8] Tim Card, *Eton Renewed: A History from 1860 to the Present Day* (John Murray, 1994). See also papers of Hornby in the Eton College Archives (ECA).

[9] P. S. H. Lawrence, *An Eton Camera, 1920–1959* (Michael Russell, 1980), p. 67.

[10] As also at Harrow, for example; P. M. H. Bryant, *Harrow* (1936), Ch. V.

[11] Eton College Archives (ECA), P6/4/Misc – Fletcher to Provost.

[12] Sir Arthur Campbell Aingier, *Memories of Eton 60 Years Ago* (London, 1917), Chs. II–IV, on life in a dame's house, a tutor's house and in college; Ernest Gambier Parry, *Life in an Eton House: With Some Notes on the Evans Family* (London, 1907).

enough?", there being little or no care in admissions policy. The school had got far too big as a result. Institutional arrangements further fed the situation: the legally established link between some schools and Colleges, in this case Eton and King's College Cambridge, resulted in King's being a "closed shop" for Eton teachers. The King's link, even after "reform", was widely seen as choking off all innovation, though it was partly improved in 1857.[13] In Henry Salt's time at Eton, as a master in the 1860s and 70s, there was also a thriving black market among the boys selling their expertise in the Composition classes.[14]

All this was reflected in school administration. In public-school archives, rather than finding detailed reports on the boys, clearly it is in the "private" correspondence of masters to parents that a lot of school business was done, again an extraordinarily decentralised and laissez faire way of doing things. At Eton these "private" reports on behaviour and ability were regular, if brief, and seem to have been a part of the masters' own correspondence rather than being kept in the central school archive. At least as important as these letters and reports were the more informal connections set up with the boy and the boy's family, which lasted long after he attended school and were sometimes lifelong (several generations of the same family would frequently have gone to the same school and even shared teachers).[15] One notable housemaster, J. B. Oldham at Shrewsbury, was said to have written 3,000 letters a year throughout his long life, most of them extremely lengthy, to present and past scholars and their parents.[16] We shall meet Oldham again later in this chapter and have cause to mention his almost half-century long correspondence with one "old boy", who from beginning to end he addressed as "Dear Puss". Oldham built, financed, designed and hugely profited from his creation of "Oldham's Hall" between 1911 and 1932, when he was forced to retreat if not retire after a scandal about his relationship with another of the "Dear Puss" kind. Oldham Hall existed in this correspondence as well as in its stones and mortar. Once again, writing can be seen to be at the centre of governance. As with the enormous and complicated letter collections of the politicians, which were the filaments of the webs out of which high politics was woven, it was the "private correspondence" of the

---

[13] Card, *Eton Renewed*, p. 15.

[14] Henry Salt, *Memories of Bygone Eton* (London, 1928), Ch. 3.; also on Verse Manufactory.

[15] Eton College Archives, EA, ED 42/1, pp. 1–14, 20, 22, 44, 45 for some of this reporting correspondence; it appears only circuitously and partly by chance that such private correspondence with parents ended up in the archives. For a typical report see ED/22/45/29/July 1885, letter to Mrs Anderson. Reports seem to have come from housemasters and subject tutors. See also ED/22/4/4/3.

[16] Charlesworth, *J. B. Oldham of Oldham's Hall*, p. 49.

governors that was the technological means for creating the various "centres" of communication without which the state would not have functioned.

Turning now to the mechanics of making mastery, what has been almost entirely left out of the public-school literature is serious theoretical reflection on the spatial and temporal reorganisation of the daily routine of the school. It is here that we are able to turn with great advantage to the work, of all people, of Michel Foucault.[17] As an institution the English public school was more Foucauldian than Foucault. It was in fact a good deal more Foucauldian than the contemporaneous public school proper, the school for the worker and the poor, the sort of school Foucault had in mind in his brilliant writing on this subject. To be a Foucauldian school took money, and state investment in popular education came only *after* the public school, which with its vast private resources had independently pioneered much of the educational innovation that slowly went into mass schooling. Foucault was not aware of this ironical state of affairs, just as he was not sufficiently aware of how the making of what he called "docile bodies" concerned the bodies of the well-to-do as well as those of the poor.

Nor did he recognise that in order to be one who governed others it was also necessary to be an active as well as a docile body. This the poor were not taught, but the rich were. He was especially interested in the spatial dimensions of disciplinary institutions, and it is valuable to follow him as he outlines the epistemological geography by means of which institutions were made more system-like. He starts by outlining the elements of what he calls "enclosure" and "partitioning", so that places and individuals are aligned with one another; this was a tactic of what he calls "anti-concentration", involving the knowledge of presences and absences, where and how individuals might be located, supervised and calculated.[18] School routine was made up precisely of this strict partitioning of space and time. The daily routine of the public school has been described for the 1870s[19] (after this time it became even more regimented).[20] It is apparent that what Foucault called the "exhaustive use" of time was much in evidence, the value of time now having to be maximised in a newly rigorous fashion. All this of course echoes the earlier discussion of the role of the Post Office in ordering time and space. Routine in the 1870s

---

[17] Michel Foucault, *Discipline and Punish* (Penguin, 1979).   [18] Ibid., pp. 141–9.
[19] David Holloway, "A Day in the Growth of Brown Minor" in *The World of the Public School* (Weidenfeld & Nicolson, 1977) ("Introduction" by George Macdonald Fraser).
[20] Thomas Bamford, *Rise of the Public Schools: A Study of Boys' Public Boarding Schools in England and Wales from 1837 to the Present Day* (Nelson, 1967), p. 74 on the highly regulated regime of the end of the century.

went as follows: boys typically rose at 7 am followed by chapel at 7.30 and then the first lesson of the day, before house breakfast at 8.30 or 9. Chapel and meals would be taken together, at which occasions the manifold hierarchies of school life would be rigorously observed, in the sense both of rituals strictly followed and the enforcement of a visual regime of "hierarchical observation", hierarchies being maintained by a greater degree of physical observation than previously.[21]

The teaching would take place until midday, followed by two hours of games until dinner at 2. Games and sports themselves became systematic from around this time, new orderings of time and space organising what had earlier been disordered, anarchic and often extremely violent activities. This helped to shape the whole future nature not only of British but of world sport, as in the codification of the rules of association football (or soccer). Schools were now able to compete with each other whereas previously each had its own esoteric sporting traditions and rules, although these continued in many cases. There might be no afternoon lessons on Tuesday, Thursday and Saturday, on other days for two to three hours, so great was the devotion to sport and the making of the masculine body. Sometimes there was teaching on Sunday, a day which frequently included three religious services and two sermons! A certain amount of free time in the afternoon and early evening was however followed by "prep" for the following day between 7:30 and 9 pm. A meal would be had at 9, followed by prayers at 9.30, sometimes for the assembled school, sometimes for the house, and then lights out at 10 for juniors and 10.30 for seniors. This interest in time routines was exemplified in the increasingly salient written *table*. The new *timetable* exemplified the "exhaustive use" of time, as opposed to the older timetable which aimed at the eradication of idleness. The new timetable therefore extracted maximum utility from time, just as in the new time regimes of contemporary industry.

Foucault also wrote of the organisation of what he terms "geneses", new unfolding of time. Disciplinary methods increasingly revealed temporality as linear, the moments of this time being integrated by means of a stable, terminal point. This he calls "evolutive time". But there is also "social time", the discovery of evolution in terms of "progress".[22] The two great discoveries of the eighteenth century (only applied fully in the nineteenth) – the progress of societies and the geneses of individuals – were thus put together in new techniques of power. At the centre of this

---

[21] Royston Lambert, *The Hothouse Society: An Exploration of Boarding-School Life through the Boys' and Girls' own Writing* (Weidenfeld & Nicolson, 1968), pp. 96–105.

[22] Foucault, *Discipline and Punish*, pp. 156–62.

seriation of time one finds "exercise", graduated tasks that are repetitive and different, but always graduated so that growth and observation are assured. This was so in terms of the body as well as the mind. The exercise of both was now linked to discipline via this seriation of time. The body was worked upon through graduated playground or gymnasium exercises, for example. This eventually became apparent at the lowest educational levels, in the British elementary schools of the late nineteenth century.

The timetable did the same for space as for time, every time being accompanied by a distinct space that filled it just as time itself had to be "filled". This disciplinisation of space took form in the physical nature of institutions, in part in terms of the principle of "hierarchical observation", most famously in the reformed prison, but also in terms of the school, particularly the system of hierarchical observation employed in English public schools, namely the monitorial system of prefects and "fags". Linked to observational practices were corrective ones, the judicial model of punishment as force and example giving way to punishment as correction, exercise and training. Punishment became cold and indifferent, as Foucault puts it, not savage and vindictive, though it certainly retained much of these qualities. Its regime was now ever present, not sporadic and explosive as of old. As a result, punishment and reward could themselves be measured and balanced for each individual, graded to his or her own example. In this way, the *normal* and *abnormal* were established, so enabling the location and specification of the individual against this disciplinary grid. Observation and correction were thus aimed not at expiation and repression but at a normalisation and individuation that "refers individual action to a whole that is at once a field of comparison, a space of differentiation, and the principle of a rule to be followed".[23]

Spatial governance involved the alignment of places and individuals. In this "disciplinary power" Foucault talks about the spatial elements as interchangeable but they are not so much about territory as rank, the place one occupies in a classification, as in the order of exam classification and as in the classroom. The examination as a subject has dimensions extra to those already considered,[24] for it involved not only the event itself but the "examining process" in society as a whole, so that pedagogy was in fact only part of a general process, seen for example in medicine, which from the late eighteenth century took its terms of reference not from the textual traditions of different authorities but from the "domain of objects perpetually examined". The hospital as well as the educational institution

---

[23] Ibid., p. 182. See also for popular developments the excellent John Donald, *Sentimental Education: Schooling, Popular Culture and the Regulation of Liberty* (Verso, 1992), Ch. 1.
[24] See above, pp. 259–62.

began to be a place of perpetual and continual examination, the examination becoming central to the elaboration of new sorts of information, which now flowed two ways – to the examined and to the examiner – so that examinations produced what were becoming "sciences" as well as producing "individuals".[25]

The file, the report and from the late nineteenth century the photograph,[26] functioned side by side with the examination in this respect. The outcome was a documentary system that made possible comparison and classification, as a result producing the individual, no longer the species, as a case, one involving as Foucault puts it "the everyday individuality of everybody".[27] The individual in the examination could be "marked" and ranked in a table as a consequence of this.[28] The examination "mark" may in this respect be understood precisely in the sense that Bruno Latour deploys the idea of the "immutable mobile", as the trace that makes governance possible.[29] It was a trace that the Clarendon Commission put near the centre of its thinking about the future governance of elite schooling, its general recommendations including promotion in school by results, achieved by a scale of marks, results that should not only be listed but publicly promulgated in the form of specifications of orders of merit. The spatial expression of this was the phenomenon of *classes*, the space that expressed this the classroom and the ordered layout of the classed schoolroom itself, individuals being put in particular places and rankings.[30]

As well as the classroom there was the minute classification and ordering of how space was actively occupied (sitting, standing, holding oneself, ways of occupying school space in general). By the 1870s in popular education, some time after the public school, the single schoolroom began to be replaced by a school hall surrounded by individual classrooms. The phenomenon of the corridor, linking different classrooms, and borrowed from Prussia, also made an early public-school appearance.[31] The necessity to operate in ancient buildings at first tended to hold

---

[25] Foucault, *Discipline and Punish*, pp. 184–5.

[26] Patrick Joyce, *The Rule of Freedom: Liberalism and the Modern City* (Verso, 2003), pp. 202–4.

[27] Foucault, *Discipline and Punish*, p. 191.

[28] See Keith Hoskins, "History, Power and Knowledge: the Genealogy of the Urban Schoolteacher" in Stephen J. Ball (ed.), *Foucault and Education: Disciplines and Knowledge* (Routledge, 1990).

[29] See the discussion above, p. 152.

[30] Howard Staunton, *The Great Public Schools of England* (London, 1865), p. lii.

[31] Malcolm Seabourne and Roy Lowe, *The English School: Its Architecture and Design*, vol. II, *1870–1970* (Routledge & Kegan Paul, 1977), Ch. 3. See also Frank Smith, *The History of English Elementary Education 1760–1902* (University of Liverpool Press, 1931), pp. 215–6.

the development of the classroom back in the older institutions. In the new purpose-built public schools of the second half of the nineteenth century, and the new buildings of the old schools, the classroom was designed-in from the beginning, and eventually specialist teaching facilities were added, gyms and laboratories especially. Some of the old, Clarendon schools relocated from the insalubrious and ancient environments of central London to the country, or at least into the suburbs.

The age-old practice of teaching all in one room seems to have been abandoned first at Rugby.[32] In Eton in the late eighteenth century there were only six "forms" or classes, but by the 1860s eleven in the upper school alone, though there was still a considerable age range in any one form or division.[33] There was also the increasingly careful delineation of functional spaces within the school as a *residential* institution, as with the segregated and "cellular" form of study and sleeping arrangements in the schools, one individual to a sleeping space, whether in a dormitory or, for older boys, a separate room.[34] Certainly there was no longer more than one boy to a bed. One individual to a study place might however only mean a "cubicle" in a larger study room or dormitory.[35] Nonetheless by the 1860s and 70s boys at the old public schools had at least a modified sort of privacy.[36] One can speak here, following Foucault, of a certain individuation of space, cellular divisions in which individual subjectivity was nurtured. However, the accent should be on a modified privacy, the individual here as in so many other respects being subordinated to the collective, so that the route to the individual self-government of boys was paradoxically through the collective.

Early-twentieth-century Winchester is a case in point. At Winchester it was the prefects who had studies, not the rest of the boys, who lived what private life they could in "toys", rows of one-man benches along the walls of the study hall, each with its own writing shelf, bookcase and wooden partition.[37] At Winchester before the First World War the "toy" might have afforded "a delightful sense of comfort and privacy",[38] but this was

[32] Seabourne and Lowe, *The English School*, vol. 1, pp. 242–3.
[33] Ibid., and see Ch. 11 (2) on new schools. Frederick How, *Six Great Headmasters* (London 1905), Ch. 2. W. Whyte, "Building a Public School Community", *History of Education*, 30:6 (2003), Pt. II.
[34] Tom Crook, "Power, Privacy and Pleasure: Liberalism and the Modern Cubicle", *Cultural Studies*, 21:4–5 (July/September 2007).
[35] Clarendon Report, *Parl. Papers, 1864, XX*, Public School Commission, First Report of Her Majesty's Commissioners, Section 16, Bedrooms.
[36] Holloway, "A Day in the Growth of Brown Minor".
[37] T. J. H. Bishop, *Winchester and the Public School Elite: A Statistical Analysis* (Faber & Faber, 1967), Ch. 1.
[38] A. L. Irvine, *Sixty Years at School* (PIG Wells, 1958).

more in the nature of a kind of refuge in the storm of public school life. The "toy", or as it was also known at Winchester the "horsebox", was simply a desk with a partition behind and before, with the cupboard and bookshelves at the side. In the mind of the pupil who enjoyed this sense of privacy, the "toy" was still hardly even a cubicle, for as a former pupil put it, "We had not even the privacy of cubicles". The "cubicle" or study had its own dangers for the school authorities. Such dangers were particularly the preserve of the new breed of "experts" on school life that emerged from about the 1880s onwards. Usually public-school masters themselves, they evolved "scientific" accounts of school spaces and how these should be divided and measured – for instance in relation to the virtues of the dormitory as against the private sleeping room. Not surprisingly, the latter was seen as more conducive to the "secret act" (masturbation), and the former to the advantages of that "ventilation" so beloved of contemporaries.[39] The contemporary "science" of health and hygiene attached itself to the schools as to everything else in Victorian Britain. The notable and influential headmaster of Uppingham School, Edward Thring, was representative in giving a clear expression to what he called the "theory" of school building and its types.[40] He was very aware of how architecture shaped behaviour. As the schools increasingly competed with one another they vied to display their awareness of this new science of school spaces, one perceived to be represented par excellence by the "Prussian model" of the classroom with a connecting corridor.

A science of examinations was rather slow to emerge. Henry Latham helped to lay its foundations in his *On the Action of Examinations* of 1877, usually regarded as the beginning of a more scientific and analytical approach, the work also being a pioneering psychology of examinations. Experimental psychology itself developed somewhat later alongside the emergence of statistical methods, establishing what by 1900 became known as "educational science", with its own methods, journals and university "experts". Like a free-trade economist Latham argued for the value of competition in terms of the stimulation it would give the market for education.[41] For Latham as for so many others the examination was a preparation for the struggle of life. As much as the actual subject itself it was about "the power of enduring hardness", of mastering the hard and distasteful task.[42]

---

[39] Clement Dukes, *Health at School* (London, 1887), Ch. VI on "The Master's Boarding-House". Dukes was a master at Rugby and supposedly "the leading expert on school hygiene". See also Whyte, "Building a Public School Community".

[40] H. D. Rawnsley, *Edward Thring, Teacher and Poet* (London, 1889).

[41] John Roach, *Public Examinations in England 1850–1900* (Cambridge University Press, 2008), p. 273.

[42] Ibid., p. 275.

The power of "enduring hardness" was not only central to the examination but to the whole of elite education. Mathematics and classics were peculiarly well fitted to the operation of competition, because they enabled the *measurement* of merit to be made. Their very nature made the "mark" feasible. This was because of their highly formalistic and mechanical nature, as we have seen.[43] Classics no less than mathematics offered what a Winchester headmaster at the end of the old regime, a hundred years later than Clarendon, called an "objective canon of perfection".[44]

Religion and the school chapel were also key sites of order. The school chapel was as organised as the rest of school life. At Eton in the 1860s each boy had his own assigned place in chapel. Edward Thring took a direct hand in the design of the school chapel, just as of the school as a whole. He believed that Uppingham was successful because "God gave us a spirit of wisdom to attend to fringes, and blue, and purple, and scarlet ribbons and Pompeian red". According to Thring, "Whatever men say or think, the Almighty intelligence is, after all, the supreme and final arbiter of schools."[45] This aesthetic found expression in the boys' studies as well as, and above all, in the school chapel.[46] At Radley William Sewell had what he claimed was a "metaphysical" sense of school architecture: everything at Radley, "from the organisation of the school to the choice of carpets", was informed by the Athanasian Creed.[47] The chapel rose greatly in prominence in the design of the schools: the "lofty", "imposing" and "ancient" Perpendicular Gothic Collegiate Style predominated and became the growing consensus of what a public school should look like.[48] Badly designed schools came to be thought of as meaning poor education for boys. From the 1870s the newly built girls' schools of the time slavishly followed the model of the boys' schools.

The site of prayer, collective memory and ritual gathering, the chapel was thought of by many as the crowning building of the school. Men like Sewell and Thring brought the authority of the supreme and final arbiter to bear in the chapel sermon and address. Sermons and addresses in all the leading schools constantly affirmed the dangers of sin, the virtues of self-control and the proper use of freedom; also the value of practical

---

[43] See above, pp. 242–62.

[44] John Thorn, *The Road to Winchester* (Weidenfeld & Nicolson, 1989), Ch. 12.. He was of the view that the traditional school subjects had produced a highly intellectualist teaching which had produced an "emotionally arid" product, extraordinarily well adapted to the examination.

[45] Edward Thring, *Addresses* (London, 1887), p. 75.

[46] George R. Parkin, *Edward Thring: Headmaster of Uppingham School, Life Diary and Letters* (London, 1898), p. 121.

[47] Whyte, "Building a Public School Community", p. 618.   [48] Ibid., p. 620.

religion.[49] Thackeray at Eton advocated a simple and clear cathecisation of the boys, which was to be "faithful and painful" and not "inventive and captious".[50] The aim was to include the run-of-the-mill student for he too was to be a leader of men. As Thring put it: "I speak most of all to the common sailors amongst you, as you may be called; the stupid, the backward, the undistinguished many ... Rise up then, you crowd of common life, the great hearted, and the world is yours. The lives of all in the ship may be given to the weakest among you ... you can lead if you choose, if the common sailors choose."[51] Such men, unconcerned about calling their charges stupid and backward, of course subscribed to strict hierarchies of ability. One of Thackeray's sermons at Eton was entitled "The Value of Inequality": "God's world (let us remember) is established and ordered on the basis not of equality, but of inequality. It must, therefore, be right that they exist." Invoking Social Darwinian thought, he went on to observe that "it is out of inequality that all progress comes".[52]

Thus was the English schoolboy sent out to rule the world. Also to a considerable extent the American schoolboy, for there is nothing as striking as how similar the less well-known example of the enormously influential elite US boarding school was, and is, to the English public school.[53] The British model was copied down to the smallest detail, as it was to a lesser degree in US university buildings. The American school regime differed only because it was less prepared than its English cousin to flaunt its wealth and privilege openly, as with the public parading of the besuited boys of Eton. On the other hand, the political technologies of the school and college were less in evidence in Scotland than in England, though as with Fettes College (attended by former Prime Minister Tony Blair) this tradition was certainly present. At university level Scotland had relatively

[49] George Butler, *Sermons Preached in Cheltenham College Chapel* (Cambridge and London, 1862); *Sermons and Lectures Delivered in Eton College Chapel, In the Years 1848–9*, unpublished, printed in Eton by E. P. Williams, 1849; Francis St John Thackeray, *Sermons Preached in Eton College Chapel, 1870–1897* (London, 1897); G. Moberly, *Sermons, Preached at Winchester College: Second Series with a Preface on "Fagging"* (London, 1848); Rev. Charles Wordsworth, *Christian Boyhood at a Public School: A Collection of Sermons and Lectures delivered at Winchester College*: vol. i, *Duties and Ordinances* (London, 1846).

[50] Thackeray, *Sermons*, Sermon XV, "The Value of Inequality", 28 February 1897, p. xxvii.

[51] Rev. Edward Thring, *Four Sermons Preached in Uppingham School Chapel ... Sundays after Trinity, 1881* (unpublished, printed in Uppingham by John Hawthorne, 1881), "The School", p. 19.

[52] Thackeray, *Sermons*, Sermon XV, "The Value of Inequality", 28 February 1897, p. xxvii; and see Whyte, "Building a Public School Community", pp. 209, 210.

[53] Peter W. Cookson Junior and Carolyn Hodges Pursell, *Preparing for Power: America's Elite Boarding Schools* (Basic Books, 1985).

small universities with few individual colleges. It was also more open to continental influences than the English case, and like continental students Scottish ones were more likely to live in the town and not the university itself.[54] Altogether a more civilised model.

There were many other aspects of the making of disciplined bodies. Food for example was part of the discipline daily routine engendered, for in what was usually its unvarying awfulness and predictability it was aimed at extinguishing personal choice. Erving Goffman describes food as one among many elements of the "mortified self", a self involved in the breaking down of that potentially recalcitrant self brought into the "total institution" from the outside world.[55] His total institution in writing was the asylum, but he cites George Orwell's marvellous account of the physical ordeals of his own public school, Eton, and it is instructive to jump forward from the 1870s to the days of Orwell for a moment to record his words:[56]

It is not easy for me to think of my schooldays without seeming to breathe in a whiff of something cold and evil-smelling – a sort of compound of sweaty socks, dirty towels, faecal smells blowing along the corridors, forks with old food between the prongs, neck-of-mutton stew, and the banging doors of the lavatories and the echoing chamberpot in the dormitories.

The cult of games also contributed greatly to the uniformity of the boy's appearance and the regularity of his behaviour. A great deal has been written on the subject of the cult of games, and athleticism in public schools, a cult growing enormously in the late nineteenth century, though rooted in the mid-nineteenth century emergence of muscular Christianity, that characteristically English combination of evangelicalism and liberal learning.[57] The obvious relevance of pedagogic athleticism to the themes of this chapter is apparent, the disciplining of the body in the form of the creation not only of *docile* but also of *active* bodies. The purpose of organised games and sport generally was stated explicitly, indeed ad nauseam, to be the creation of leadership, the making of an active subject. In order to govern others it was necessary therefore to be an

[54] Paul Venable Turner, "Introduction" in *Campus: An American Planning Tradition* (MIT Press, 1984).

[55] Erving Goffman, *Asylums* (London, 1961) , pp. 14–28.

[56] George Orwell, "Such, Such were the Joys", *Partisan Review*, XIX (September–October 1952).

[57] J. A. Mangan, *Athleticism in the Victorian and Edwardian Public School: The Emergence and Consolidation of Educational Ideology* (Cambridge University Press, 1981); David Newsome, *Godliness and Good Learning: Four Studies on a Victorian Ideal* (John Murray, 1961).

active as well as a docile body – there was an intimate relationship between the two.

To be an active governor one first needed to enter the valley of submission and be made docile. Here the relationship between the home and the school begins to come more fully into our picture. The ties that bound the boy to his home were brutally and sharply broken. One historian of the public schools has illuminatingly described the school as involving a process of separation strikingly akin to the anthropological elements of rites of passage.[58] As in some African societies, and following Van Gennep's classic model, there is first the process of separation, especially separation from women, which is complete and harsh. Then there is the process of transition, before the final process of incorporation. The operation of transition involved the many ritual humiliations of public school life, not least "fagging" for older boys (in effect acting as their servants). As well as being a device of hierarchical observation, fagging was an initiation process, experienced first by the younger boy, and then by the same boy as he grew older and acquired his own fag.[59] One learned to be both servant and master, for the whole rationale of the school as represented in the fagging system was the extinction of disorganised freedom prior to the building up of the organised form in the shape of self-dependence.

Submission and self-abasement were therefore a necessary prelude to the creation of self-reliant independence, and inflicting harm and pain on others just as it had been inflicted on you. Masochism preceded sadism in this awful world. It is with this subject, hidden from at least public discussion until recent times, that one has to invoke writing of more modern vintage of which there is little better than that of the Old Etonian Nick Fraser. In his account of the Eton of fairly recent times Eton boys actively enjoyed receiving and giving physical punishment, which was endured without much sense of shame, justice or responsibility, except for the ultimate responsibility to Eton that is.[60] Physical beating was in fact authorised until fairly recently and was historically endemic in almost all public schools:[61] everyone beat and was beaten, for almost any reason. The great reforming headmasters of the mid-nineteenth century were to a man great floggers, and in the prep schools, which after the 1860s fed the public schools, the emphasis was also very much on toughening up the boys.[62] If the old system of punishment by force and example

---

[58] Honey, *Tom Brown's Universe*, pp. 216 ff.   [59] Ibid., p. 216.
[60] Nick Fraser, *The Importance of Being Eton: Inside the World's Most Powerful School* (Short Books, 2006), p. 85.
[61] John D'Ewes Evelyn Firth, *Winchester* (London, 1936), Ch. 7 on beating in the 1860s.
[62] David Leinster-McKay, *The Rise of the English Prep School* (The Falmer Press, 1984).

was transformed, the old ritual character of punishment continued. At Eton, for example, flogging was surrounded by rituals which might variously involve school assemblies to witness the event, particular traditions of holding the boy down (by his fellow pupils), the manner of the beating itself, and then the return of the boy to school life as if nothing had happened – he would be in trouble the next day if he showed weakness as a result of the beating.[63] Prefectorial power could include permission to inflict corporal punishment: the "solemn ritual" of a prefectorial beating in a hushed schoolhouse has been described in some detail for recent times, solemnity being achieved not by public assembly but by the boys being systematically confined to their studies during the beating itself.[64]

These rituals of course scaled the heights of British political power. This is a description of the kind of experiences former Prime Minister Tony Blair would have been familiar with at his public school in Edinburgh, Fettes College:

I remember Tony was beaten at the age of 17–18, it was for insolence or something quite ludicrous. Beatings were a regular part of school life for all of us. There were various types: there was a thing called a "school beating", which would be in the main library and every school prefect would have a run at you with a cane and by tradition you were allowed a day in the sanatorium afterwards. That would be about 12 people (beating you). And then there was a "house beating", which was a lesser thing where you would be called upstairs and beaten by all the prefects in the house. It was just part of the world there. The legacy of being beaten at Fettes in those days? First of all if you had survived it, you had survived a very trying and troubling time. I'm not sure in those days it did you much good at making you a rounded person able to relate to others in society. I suppose the thing was that you had to try and ensure that it didn't irreparably damage you.[65]

Irreparable damage at the public school involved the "hardening" process, and in the imperial world, and the post-imperial one, this hardening made it all the easier to inflict irreparable damage on others. Prior to the First World War the public schools had gone through a remarkable phase of militarisation, formal officer training being integrated into public school life as never before (see the cover illustration of this book). One cannot underestimate the importance of violence to the public school regime therefore. This violence was aimed both at breaking and damaging the beaten boy but always with the aim of building him up again by making him in turn the beater. The historian of Harrow School describes the beating of one of the big boys, a "bully", by a purportedly weak prefect. In

[63] Bamford, *Rise of the Public Schools* on Eton, and see also Fraser, *The Importance of Being Eton*, pp. 85ff.
[64] Lambert, *The Hothouse Society*, p. 186.
[65] Mark Ellen, "'He could Talk his Way out of Things'", *Observer*, 27 April 2003.

the prefect's later memory this beating was clearly the essential, transformative experience of his life, giving him strength and what he called "self-reliance". The moment of truth came for him when he saw the bully whimpering and begging him to stop, for this was the moment when transformation occurred. As the prefect put it: "this was the greatest crisis of my life. I had found myself and my self-reliance. I finished his full 10 strokes, of course."[66] Transformation, something obviously deeply related to sadomasochism, was of course also the teacher's experience in beating. Edward Thring reported in 1864 on how it was one of the greatest days in the history of his school when at great length and with much pleasure he publicly flogged a large group of boys who had been caught running away from school. A mass purgation of the school was thereby achieved.[67] Not without reason was beating known as *le vice anglais*.

The prefect system was systematically used as a training in character for the older boys, not least by Arnold at Rugby, though the system predated him. In the sixth form, this achieved its most sophisticated elaboration. For the "Sixth" was about real power, for there the prefects, and even more so house captains and heads of school, actively shared power with adults,[68] including the power to inflict beatings. Of course, there was in all this a power within power, in the sense of the "unofficial" subculture of the boys, prefects as well as the others. This might serve as a source of resistance and opposition within schools, but the public schools were very successful in aligning unofficial and official school cultures, such an alignment being in important measure the yardstick of a successful school.[69] Public school culture could involve the "incorporation" of dissent, the "bolshie" or the "intellectual" being licensed as one "caste" among others in the school.[70] The resolute rebels of Lindsay Anderson's film *If* always have the cards stacked against them. However, the sufficiently resolute might trump authority by aping it, more radical dissenters putting on the garb of the official public school culture the better to undermine its authority, as in the case of the so-called "Cambridge spies", men who were however bred-in-the-bone public-school men, for whom a certain sort of public-school Englishness was perhaps the ultimate loyalty. More generally, the combination in Britain of left politics with support and often veneration for the manifestly elite

---

[66] Christopher Tyerman, *A History of Harrow School 1324–1991* (Oxford University Press, 2000), p. 337.
[67] John Thorne, *The Road to Winchester* (Weidenfeld & Nicolson, 1989), p. 97.
[68] Lambert, *The Hothouse Society*, Ch. 6.   [69] Ibid., Ch. 8, esp. pp. 225–6.
[70] Ibid., p. 245.

public-school and Oxbridge college, is particularly telling evidence of the hold of this very peculiar education on the British imagination.

Subordination and abasement became manifest in eventual power and domination for the older boys, but it was also present in distinction too. The sixth form might often be taught by the headmaster, and headmasters frequently put a premium on individual ability, so that something like a cult of boyhood genius was sometimes apparent. This is especially the case with Eton, where a (strictly licensed) "eccentricity, coupled with a sense of intellectual dash and humour", was particularly applauded.[71] Scholarship boys, for example members of the Colleges at Eton and Winchester, composed another of these superior groups, superiority involving trusting the boy to be a "man", although at Winchester all boys were in school parlance called "men" anyway. It is here, with such elite groups, that the new familiarity of teacher and taught came into its own, the development of personal interest in particular boys taking form for example in the "private reading" at Eton after Hawtrey's time. This encouraged the emergence of groups and coteries, inner circles of favourites.[72] Gladstone was a product of Hawtrey, and Eton was his inspiration "to learn and to do" in life. At Arnold's Rugby this favouritism was also the case, such circles doing much to shape public school history, as we have seen.[73]

Making active bodies also involved imbuing the boy with a sense of the divinity of his right to tell, indeed order, others what to do. In doing this the importance of *where* the boy was to *who* he was had first to be engineered. This was done by developing the notion of a distinct and unrepeatable identity to the school, a uniqueness that the pupil could partake of in the form of the ethos of the school. Of course not all schools could be Eton or Winchester, but this did not stop them attempting to aspire, and in practice the attempt at uniqueness was often represented in the dismal picture of the minor public school's attempt to emulate its betters.[74] What the schools shared in common was however equally important as what distinguished one from another. Indeed, the truth is that difference was a factor of sameness: the *system* of the schools as a whole depended, and depends, on this cultivation of difference within an overall basic uniformity.

[71] Bamford, *Rise of the Public School*, p. 70.
[72] How, *Six Great Headmasters*, on Hawtrey.   [73] See above, pp. 243–8.
[74] Recognition of this has recently helped produce in the UK the phenomenon of a website devoted to such schools, very aptly titled www.crappublicschools.org. On the site the virtual public school St Swinesend is the epitome of the "crap public school".

In considering the *quiddity* of the schools there was firstly the boy's sense that it was above all important to be *from* a particular school. This was a matter, secondly and quite precisely, of *being* itself, of the daily forming and reforming of the boys' bodies and minds by the inculcation of the myths of school tradition. Being *from* a school has recently been given brilliant expression by Nick Fraser in his *The Importance of Being Eton*. Nonetheless, although his is an account of Eton in relatively recent times, from what is known of the College it would seem to hold substantially for former times too. "Being Eton" involved being a certain kind of person: one was carefully measured and controlled, one knew what needed to be known, and did what needed to be done, practising the art of compromise and avoiding scenes and public disagreements. One was able to hold tight while appearing to let go. The College liked to think that its products did not conform to any particular "type", and that it encouraged nonconformity and originality. Not conforming, one got on everywhere and with everyone.[75] However, this was a "nonconformity" that was the product of a most rigid kind of conformity, conformity down to the minutest of details, spiritual as well as secular, involving total submission to the ethic of the school, and not any real, awkward version of nonconformity.

Eton was not just connected to the centres of English/British power, it *is* and always has been itself such a centre, as it was in origin a Royal foundation, designed to serve the religious and secular needs of political elites from the very beginning (together with its King's College, Cambridge partner) (see Figure 7.1). It was therefore part of the very origins of centralised power and the centralised state, part of the state machinery in fact, as was the analogous institution of All Souls College in Oxford, the founder of which, Bishop Chichele, described the aim of his college as being the production of a learned clerical "militia" to serve Church and State.[76] A geography of British power expresses this old connection to the state: Windsor Castle and Eton College sit close by one another on opposite sides of a bend in the river Thames, together making up a hugely impressive visual image of British history and British power. In turn, Etonians have always liked to think of themselves as representing a particular type of national identity, though this is Englishness rather than Britishness.

In fact, conformity took a dreadful toll on Etonians, and Fraser refers to the "near autism" of the Eton product, the dreadful price of conformism in terms of the results of self-absorption, and the fear of not being up to the

---

[75] Fraser, *The Importance of Being Eton*, p. 65.
[76] All Souls College website: www.all-souls.ox.ac.uk/content/Statutes.

Fig. 7.1 Eton College and environs, aerial picture, *c.* 1930s?

College mark. A lifetime of uncontested authority produced the "dark side" of Eton, the side which created people whose ultimate loyalty was not to family, friends, the Oxbridge college, nor to God. Not even to the state and the nation, but to the School. If made into expert governors such people were in the end not really made for the world at all, only for the company of other Etonians, and other public schoolboys at a pinch. Old Etonians are in later life seen by Fraser to be uncomfortable in the company of women, and Fraser remarks a tendency to marry the sisters of friends, who had also been to Eton or at least similar schools.[77] Boy-to-boy sex was "normal" at Eton, and was not the same as homosexuality, but it contributed to the feeling of many that they could only be loved by men and were not loved or capable of being loved by women. One understands better the loyalties of the "Cambridge spies" to their own kind and their own code.

"Near autism" is an excellent term, for with it we are in the realm of the somatic, of *being* an Eton body. Fraser helps us understand the work that went into making this body: the ascetic dimension was involved, as in

[77] Fraser, *The Importance of Being Eton*, p. 58.

putting up with and even liking corporal punishment.[78] As well as the ascetic there was the better known athletic dimension, but also the little regarded aesthetic one. For just as in living in England one lived in an old country, at Eton one lived in the exquisite physical manifestation of that antiquity, among "the stones of Eton". Memory itself linked one always to the College, for in memory one was always there, always young and "happy". Property linked one to Eton too, and to England: the kind of people who went to Eton, then and since, are the people who actually own this ancient England.[79] Winchester College was another such school. It too encouraged a cult of the unique. Anthony Sampson, in his 1960s *Anatomy of Britain*, singled out Winchester and Balliol College, Oxford as more cult than college.[80] Winchester's reputation as *the* authentic public school and a unique community was closely linked to the antiquity of the institution, an antiquity represented like Eton in "the stones of Winchester". However, other aspects of bodily functioning were involved in making the public school militia. Language was especially important, only now spoken as opposed to written language. One historian of the College, T. J. H. Bishop, notes how up to 1950 the school maintained a "parochial culture" of its institutions.[81] He understands three factors as maintaining this traditionalism, namely the body of school lore and etiquette known as "Notions", collective living, and the monastic character of this living, the latter expressing the deliberate estrangement from the outside world that characterised the schools.

In essence, "Notions" said "we are Winchester". "Notions" gave rise to an extraordinary dictionary, recently republished.[82] It is worth dwelling for a moment on this phenomenon. A. L. Irvine's account of his entry to the school prior to the First World War is illuminating: on entering "Seventh Chamber" he encountered a "pater", a "second year man" who taught him his "Notions", before he became in the course of the following fortnight a "junior".[83] Or so was the theory, for he failed his first exam, and was as a consequence "crappled", while his "pater" was "spanked". He took a second test a week later and passed. In the course of time neither of his "sons" let him down (his second son became the

---

[78] Ibid., pp. 71–2.

[79] We like to think of other nations, for example Italy, especially the Italy of Berlusconi, as exemplifying the politics of the proprietor, but the term "proprietorial" belongs also to the British case.

[80] Anthony Sampson, *Anatomy of Britain Today* (Hodder & Stoughton, 1965), p. 227.

[81] T. J. H. Bishop, *Winchester and the Public School Elite*, p. 27.

[82] C. G. Stevens, *Winchester Notions: The Dialect of Winchester College*, ed. Christopher Stray (Athlone Press, 1998). John S. Farmer, *The Public School Word-Book: A Contribution . . . Our Great Public Schools* (London, 1900).

[83] A. L. Irvine, *Sixty Years at School*, Ch. 11.

Viceroy of India). Loyalty thus became memory work, akin to classics teaching, as has been seen.[84] Language was important in other ways too. After the railways and the geographical spread of the schools the conditions existed in which a "public school accent" would emerge.[85] This had developed so far that by the mid-twentieth century it was equated with Received Pronunciation and Standard BBC English, and was perhaps the socially dominant form of spoken English. According to one phonetic expert, it was only possible to acquire a public school accent *proper* before the age of fifteen years.[86] By around 1900 therefore a "new aristocracy" of the public school had emerged, an increasingly visible national elite coming into prominence at a time when old elites were being refashioned. This refashioning was evident in the decline of rural society and the beginnings of the retreat of urban and industrial England before the renewed hegemony of London and the south east. This was reflected in the capitulation of radical, bourgeois England, if not Britain, to the public school and the Conservative Party. The "old-boy" network, so often remarked but nonetheless so significant in British history, had come fully into being.[87] A human "system" had been put in place therefore, human connectivity expanding alongside and in harness with the system connectivity of communication and economic infrastructure, of the administration of the state, and of the new party-political apparatus.

II   The *domus*

The root of the school was the house. The marketised and institutionally dispersed entity that was the public school was given coherence by the house, both at the level of the school and at the level of the public school governmental project and the "system" it enabled. It is correct to use the term "system" in this context, for what we seem to see cohering in the half-century before the First World War is something as tightly woven as we have identified a system to be. The parallels with the transition in large-scale technological systems from the network to the system are close. For what we see happening at this time is the emergence of a system of human connections that paralleled the system of connections pioneered in communication and its technologies, including rail, road and postal communication. The vast expansion of the postal system, and the extraordinary rapidity of its operation, was an essential part of what enabled the public school (and Oxbridge college) systems to function, allowing Shrewsbury's J. B. Oldham to circulate his 3,000 letters a year.

---

[84] See above, pp. 253–62.   [85] Honey, *Tom Brown's Universe*, p. 223.
[86] Bishop, *Winchester*, pp. 16–17.   [87] Honey, *Tom Brown's Universe*, pp. 229–37.

The parallel with the India Office and with other departments of state is also evident when we recall the built form of the India Office and the relationship of the government office to the houses and homes of the well-to-do. The actual places of power in British society, the key sites of governmental London, saw the dominant patterns of class relations in Britain replayed in the theatre of the state, particularly the master servant relationship. In the India Office this took the idealised form of the aristocratic-cum-high-bourgeois "town house", hierarchical and male-dominated. The household structure of the old Post Office of about 1800 and that of the new individual offices such as the Oxford Post Office that were considered earlier reinforce the point of the centrality of the house to the built forms of the state. The *domus* thus served as a material template for the governing powers, in its actual physical mani-festations acting as a sort of machine for the reproduction of the status quo of power.

This echoed the entire public and private life of the governing classes, as I have indicated (the Houses of Parliament; the London club; the various houses of God; and no doubt the brothel too, the house of the devil). In this context the account of the formation of the modern governor in the last chapter is relevant: this involved the twin ideas of independence and authority and the ownership of the property that sanctioned that inde-pendence. There was no more potent symbol of such independence than the property owner's domicile, his house. This extended down through the social order as well: politically, the male head of household was the defining category in political debate and in the actual electoral organisa-tion of the country. Power in British society was therefore almost com-pletely masculinised. It is here also that we may recollect how the common good for the governors of the liberal state was not conceived of as a condition of equality and democracy. Rather, it was imagined in terms of an orderly, hierarchical state.[88] It was the job of the liberal governor, a propertied, educated and civilised man, to administer government for a public good that most of the public could not know and had to be taught. We should also recall how the high official in Britain wielded power in the belief that the "general temper of his mind is created by, and therefore adapted to, the invincible facts of life and government in a great and closely organised community".[89] He embodied the state, in all his British common knowledge, as a perfectly typical "ordinary sensible Briton" who was a product of the educated classes, which is to say a product of the public schools and Oxbridge.

---

[88] See above, pp. 233–9.   [89] See above, p. 222.

Because power was masculine the man of power was therefore a kind of father, the father as head of household being the pinnacle of power. This father was in watch over the state, a state that was the embodiment of the long history and traditions of the nation, as he conceived them. The nation was the "home" but the state was the house that gave the home its true meaning, an embodiment of it in persons, a materialisation of it in non-human things, and its metaphysical principle in the things of the spirit. Thus because the father ruled the house we can not only think of the governor as the father of the state but even more the state as the father of the governor, and of everyone in the nation state too. The state was a father. Our father the state exemplified completely the nature of power in British society, and the class relations which this nature gave rise to.

It is in this context that we can begin to understand the enormous power of "the tiny universe" of the school house and the college, the template for our father's house, the state in miniature. It was in the school house and the college as house that the most crucial lessons in the young person's life were learned, for it was there that the scripts of house, home and family were played out in the most dramatic fashion. There were different kinds of "house" depending on the degree to which the school was geographically and functionally centralised. The new purpose-built schools of the late nineteenth century, including those which had moved out of a teeming London, took this more spatially centralised form, different from old schools like Eton and Shrewsbury, in which the house had the most significance. However, centralisation occurred more after than during the years up to 1920 and the house was of great importance in all cases. The house was either a discrete built entity, or a clearly distinct section of a building, offering communal eating, sleeping, learning and praying. It was presided over by a housemaster and servants, and perhaps the house-master's wife.

The school houses seem to have become increasingly masculinised after the mid-nineteenth century. For instance at Eton some houses had previously been run by "dames", women who rented the house. In these discipline seems to have been more lax than later, in male-only settings.[90] The name "dame" in fact stuck to Eton housemasters themselves for some time although the old institution of women-run houses faded after mid-century. However, though there was a determined attempt to make the house-cum-universe a male preserve, apart from the school/house matron and the master's wife there were often female servants. The conduct of these servants was strictly regulated and they lived in separate quarters, for

---

[90] Parry, *Life in an Eton House.*

parents sometimes sent their children away in part to be free of what was perceived to be harmful influence of domestic servants at home. It was felt servants could be better controlled in the regimented world of the school. This they were, but isolation from women was never complete. The house and the housemaster thus became surrogates for the home, and it was in fact about this time that the legal doctrine that the authority of the schools stood in the place of that of the parents developed. Before the 1850s the legal category of *in loco parentis* had only legal meaning for wards of court. From this time, in line with the expansion of the schools, it came to have much wider common law usage.

The connections between house, home and the university college were as firm as in the case of the school. As recent work has shown, Oxbridge and University of London student life and student accommodation in the late nineteenth century was modelled upon that of the "orderly Christian household". Daily routine strongly echoed the routine of upper-class versions of this household, namely rituals of rising, of being looked after by servants, of collective meals (formal and informal); the routine of daily chapel and study, sport, and so on. Although this work shows how gender roles were experimented with in these pedagogic settings, the strongly masculinised nature of the intrinsic hierarchies involved was marked.[91] Public schools and Oxbridge colleges still use the terms house and *domus* to describe their identities: Christ Church College, Oxford is known as "the House", and the newsletter of Balliol College is titled *Floreat Domus*, invoking – and economically exploiting – a permanent youth.

The public-school house ethos involved the active and self-conscious inculcation of leadership and self-discipline through subordination to the house, which in turn at least in theory was seen as a microcosm of the school. The house represented a hierarchy within the hierarchy of the school, the lesser one reinforcing the greater.[92] However, as will already be evident, the house was in practice largely a law, and a world, unto itself. How can we understand the enormous hold of the regime of the house, and so understand the mind of the British ruling classes? The public schools have been compared to the monarchical court, the monastery and the prison. They were undoubtedly all three. The form of the monastery was and is all-apparent in the school (and the university), in their set routines and physical architecture. However it was the house, the English manor house, more than the monastery, that provided the basis for the

---

[91] Jane Hamlett, "'Nicely Feminine, yet Learned': Student Rooms at Royal Holloway and the Oxford and Cambridge Colleges in the Late Nineteenth Century", *Womens History Review*, 15:1 (March 2006).

[92] Lambert, *The Hothouse Society*, Ch. 5, "'This Tiny Universe' The House".

principles of school/college management and the template of the architectural form.[93]

The component parts of the college and public school represented reworked forms of the manor house (and to some degree the monastery): the gatehouse, the master's lodge, the masters'/fellows' and students' chambers and studies, the combination or common room for the teachers, the treasury or the muniments room, together with the sites of collective life in the shape of the hall, the library, the chapel, the garden and the enclosed quadrangle. All of these composed a material set of behaviour repertoires which were of great effect. For instance the passage of the master through the college was engineered so that he would have easy access to all its parts, sheltered from the elements, and able if he so desired to come and go with discretion. Built forms were supplemented by detailed written regulations covering the allocation of internal spaces, how one should move through them and how one should behave.[94] Aesthetic design was part of this too, for education of the eye was apparent in the antiquity and beauty of college and school forms. Design aimed at developing the mind was evident in the layout of gardens, quadrangles and chapels as sites of contemplation. Collective life and individual subjectivities were so formed.

However, if one seeks the material and emotional bedrock of the institutions of elite education it is to the house that one needs to turn. I shall deal first with the school and then with the Oxbridge college. As we have seen, the ties that bound the boy to his home were deliberately broken preparatory to learning submission, itself preparatory to learning dominion. The transition from the domestic house to the school house was critical in the creation of the public-school product. The routine of the school involved the deliberate estrangement of the outside world, and in particular the world of home. In this routine home life was characterised as feminine and "domestic" and women were seen as incapable of putting the interests of those they loved below those of any outside body.[95] The masculinity of the boy was therefore involved in the fabrication of a persona in which professional detachment, career ambition, public service and indeed the active pursuit of public office were crucial elements. The school became associated with public life therefore, from which the home was rigidly separated, a process of separation based on this systematic

---

[93] Robert Willis and John Willis Clark, *The Architectural History of the University of Cambridge*, 3 vols. (first published in 1886, Cambridge University Press, 1988), vol. III, Pt. 3 Ch. 2 on the component parts of the college.

[94] Whyte, "Building a Public School Community", pp. 247–66; Turner, *Campus: An American Planning Tradition*, pp. 247–66.

[95] Bishop, *Winchester*, p. 28.

"othering" of domestic life. By contrast, at public school boys were prematurely referred to as men, as "Mr"; by the end of the nineteenth century the use of Christian names among the boys themselves seems to have ended.[96] This deliberate estrangement of the outside world was reflected in the careful control of those who entered and left the school; also the control of what pupils did outside school, which was overseen by elaborate rules and by prefectorial supervision.[97] Again, this is the world of the total institution so memorably described by Erving Goffman.

However, shorn of the crucial realm of the first home and its domestic affections, as has been seen the school house retained many of the attributes and architectural forms of the upper-class household. The separations and losses, and the compensations and reinventions, that went on formed the mentality of the schoolboy. From what we know of the domestic background of the upper-class household the sense of separation and even trauma may have been considerable.[98] It is clear that Victorian domestic life was the seat of considerable family affection and intimacy, in which the father was involved. This reflected the change from the eighteenth century, when home and work, private and public, had not been so separate. From age three to seven years the mother had charge of the boy's education in this new regime of the domestic affections. There is some evidence however that children destined for boarding school were at least partly prepared at home by an early introduction to the "hardening" process, at sometimes as young as seven or eight years.[99] Also, the higher up the social scale the more masculine and authoritarian family authority structures seem to have been.[100] The hardening process was perhaps more evident later on after the end of patronage, when the examination and preparation for it in the schools became more than previously a financial *investment* by the family in its future, an investment in education as a set of mental competencies that would be invaluable in the financial returns life would bring, but also an investment in the equally rewarding

---

[96] Honey, *Tom Brown's Universe*, pp. 222–3.

[97] Lambert, *The Hothouse Society*, Ch. 7, "The Outside World".

[98] Lucy Delap et al. (eds.), *The Politics of Domestic Authority in Britain since 1800* (Palgrave Macmillan, 2009); Eleanor Gordon and Gwyneth Nair, *Public Lives: Women, Family and Society in Victorian Britain* (Yale University Press, 2003); Trev Lynn Broughton and Helen Rogers (eds.), *Gender and Fatherhood in the Nineteenth Century* (Palgrave Macmillan, 2007); Judith Flanders, *The Victorian House: Domestic Life from Childbirth to Deathbed* (Harper Collins, 2003); Nick Duffel, *The Making of Them: British Attitudes to Children and the Boarding School System* (Lone Arrow Press, 2000); Vyven Brendon, *Prep School Children: A Class Apart over Two Centuries* (Continuum, 2009).

[99] Christina Heward, *Making a Man of Him: Parents and their Sons' Education at an English Public School 1929–50* (Routledge, 1988).

[100] Flanders, *The Victorian House*, Ch. 2.

status and contacts that education in the right school would foster. Again, elite education was part of the workings of the liberal market. Whether prepared in advance or not the transition to boarding school was momentous.

Obviously, the relationship with the home environment varied, but overall the shift to the public school and to the second house must have been immensely difficult psychologically. If the child had been boarding at a preparatory school there might be a third shift in location though there the house model may not have applied, and as we have seen these schools were totally focused upon and obsessed with the public school proper, for this was the experience of house and home that mattered most. Age of entry to the public school itself varied greatly, anything from as young as seven to thirteen. At this distance in time to get inside what was going on is difficult, but we can proceed further in understanding by taking first the direction of present-day psychological accounts of the boarding school experience, which clearly have a bearing on experience in the past.[101] What seems to have happened in the erasure of the home was the erasure of the personhood of the child, his silencing by adults, so that he became self-censoring, internally controlled to a remarkable degree as part of his survival strategy. Outcomes varied of course, but loyalty to the school became a substitute for loyalty to home, although loyalty to the school was only one expression of the tendency towards loyalty to collective institutions in general – the regiment, the firm, the government department, above all the state itself, as well as the school. The intense conservatism of British institutional life, its failure to change, is clearly rooted in this caste of mind and its educational nurture.

A somewhat different route from the psychological one needs to be taken if the depths of the experiences at play in the making of the British governor are to be understood. This route lies in the phenomenology of places and spaces, above all the phenomenology of the house. Here the work of that great philosopher of the spaces of our lives, Gaston Bachelard, enables us to move further.[102] In his *Poetics of Space* he writes of how "in its countless aveoli space contains time. That is what space is for." His subject of study is how memories are housed, quite literally housed, within the rooms of the house, and in its many other spaces too. This involves "the systematic psychological study of the sites of our

---

[101] The following account is based on Duffel, *The Making of Them*. Duffel, a psychologist, is also the founder of the self-help group Surviving Boarding School. There was a BBC television documentary in the *Forty Minutes* series with the same name as the book, the film being made by Colin Luke.

[102] Gaston Bachelard, *The Poetics of Space* (Beacon Press edn, 1994).

intimate lives".[103] As he writes, "All really inhabited space bears the essence of the notion of home". The house in particular "is one of the greatest powers of integration for the thoughts, memories and dreams of mankind ... Its councils of continuity are unceasing. Without it man would be a dispersed being. It maintains him through the storm of heavens and through those of life ... It is body and soul. It is the human being's first world." Before he is "cast into the world ... man is laid in the cradle of the house ... Life begins well, it begins enclosed, protected, all warm in the bosom of the house." In this understanding we make our homes as we go through life, but the house goes with us always as it is through this form that we most fully know what home is. The first house above all, but also the subsequent ones as we go through life. These successive houses reverberate one with another, the new shaping the old and the old the new. Following Bachelard we can see how for the public schoolboy, so early exposed to the transition from one house and home to another, and then to another in the university college, the house was of such defining importance, its successive forms and the relationships between these forms serving to both make and prevent him being a "dispersed being".

Memory and identity, loss and security were all inseparable from the spaces of place in the form of the house and home. We speak of something being *in*habited, and what matters here is the sense of existence being within what Bachelard calls "the original shell ... one's first shell, where one's whole being is had". This sets up the reverberations that work their way through later houses and homes, echoing down through all of life. The original shell "protects, and encloses". Only "something closed must retain our memories", so that this image of the home "moves us at an unimaginable depth". Memory and the organic body are intertwined, including the times of the body, as the body goes through life and ages.[104] We are reminded of the words of Pierre Bourdieu: "What is learned by the body is not something that one has, but something that one is."[105] As Bachelard says, "The house ... is a group of organic habits. After twenty years, in spite of all the other anonymous stairways, we would recapture the reflexes of the "first stairway", we would not stumble on that rather high step ... The feel of the tiniest latch has remained in our hands." This is so most of all for the first house, but all the subsequent ones are a product of the first, for it is there that memory starts, is anchored, and from which it is amplified through life's course. But

---

[103] Ibid., p. 8.
[104] Ibid., pp. 4–7 for these quoted extracts, and p. 33, citing Villiers de l'Isle-Adam.
[105] See above, pp. 35–6, 106.

which is the first house, the true home? Of course, it is the family one, the one experienced in early childhood. However, if it is the case that the public school systematically set out to destroy the influence of the first home with the second, the school house, then if it did its job as well as it aimed to perhaps it became the original house, the one from which memory started and was amplified through life, that which prevented one being a "dispersed being".

In the sense pursued by Bachelard we never really leave our houses, especially the "first" one. The literature on the schools gives frequent expression to the public schoolboy as living a life of "permanent adolescence". We are reminded of the "near autism" of Eton schoolboys that we have already encountered, how the Old Etonian never really left school. But the Old Etonian we have seen to perhaps owe the ultimate loyalty to the school and not to anything else, the state included. If this was the case for Eton it would have applied elsewhere, but perhaps with less vehemence. Therefore, our father may have been Eton, The School and the House, not the state, for many of these governing men. However, for all practical purposes, in the business of government and the operations of power in British society, our father the state was the father that mattered, God the Father one might say. Worship of school, house and college were at bottom about the worship of power and in the end the state won out, for as the ultimate expression of power if one was really serious about its use it was best to worship there rather than in the school and college. Better there to play what old Etonians liked to call the "great game" of power.

The harsh absolutism of the schools involved lifelong consequences therefore, as the old loyalties of the original home were ruthlessly expunged. Cyril Connolly, writing in the inter-war years about what he termed a "Theory of Permanent Adolescence", understood the domination of post-school life by the public-school experience.[106] Thomas Arnold wished to rush children out of boyhood, to turn boys into men. By the late nineteenth century something approaching a cult of boyhood had in fact emerged in the public schools. This was however still umbilically connected to the cultivation of manliness, particularly in the new cultivation of military prowess. Boys would be boys again, but now not nature's or God's wild children of the eighteenth century but the premature men who as the British officer class were slaughtered en masse in the killing fields of the Great War.[107] Writing more sympathetically than Connolly on the inter-war public school of his own experience, Evelyn

[106] Cyril Connolly, cited in Parker, ibid., p. 92.
[107] Peter Parker, *The Old Lie: The Great War and the Public School Ethos* (Constable, 1987), pp. 92 ff.

Fig. 7.2 Photograph of
J. B. Oldham

Waugh noted how the strength of the whole public-school system was
drawn from men who found refreshment in the company of youth and
were content to spend a lifetime in a kind of second youth, preserving the
continuity of their first one.[108]

School houses themselves varied of course. Detailed accounts of school
houses are somewhat rare, but one is available for J. B. Oldham's
Shrewsbury School house mentioned earlier, "Oldham's Hall" (the convention at Shrewsbury being that houses were called halls). This was
entirely his creation, indeed his property (see Figures 7.2 and 7.3).
Altogether he spent sixty years associated with Shrewsbury, a period
including his own boyhood education. He was raised in a rectory and
afterwards went to a preparatory school run by his clerical uncle. This
clerical background was fairly typical of pre-First World War public-
school teachers. His development was almost entirely among men, his
father stern and distant, his mother warm and close. His father was a pupil

[108] Evelyn Waugh, cited in J. A. Mangan, *Athleticism in the Victorian and Edwardian Public
School*, p. 114.

Fig. 7.3 Oldham's Hall, Shrewsbury School

of Temple at Rugby. Like so many of his comfortably well-set-up peers he could trace ancestry back to various notables in British history, including one of Nelson's admirals and Hugh Oldham, the founder of Exeter College, Oxford. The world of the British governing class was not only small, but one of blood.

His pedagogical view was that only by remaining a bachelor could he give proper attention to "his" boys, believing that Britain's greatness was due to the devotion of celibate men to young ones.[109] Oldham was in effect a celibate father. By being such he could be the centre of the boys' world, and it is true that during term time Oldham never spent a night away from the house, and if a boy was sick in the holidays he also remained. Being a celibate father he could spend money on his charges, reducing fees, helping them get to university and so on. He was, as an acquaintance put it, in the circumstances perhaps a little unfortunately, on "all fours with the boys", his supposedly disengaged position meaning that he could talk in an impersonal way to boys about sex.[110] It is here as in other respects true that, however well the public school succeeded in expunging the first home, at least its feminine domestic affections, it

---

[109] Charlesworth, *J. B. Oldham of Oldham's Hall*, p. 30; "Reminiscences by James Basil Oldham, 1882–1962", typescript in Shrewsbury School library, together with the hand-written MS.
[110] Oldham, "Reminiscences", ibid.

always had to draw on the emotional and symbolic force of the original. The teacher had to be a father, a celibate one or not. However, to be a father was also to be a "friend".

Not however a mother, although if the housemaster was married this possibility was present, though strictly supervised for fear of mollycoddling. Before the First World War married housemasters were in the minority, although younger, more outgoing and lively masters than Oldham could offer more direct emotional support than this strangely distant yet passionate man did. Such young teachers were the talk of Shrewsbury before 1914, after which war decimated their ranks.[111] Oldham – Basil as he was known – was, very interestingly, a sort of transitional figure, harking back in his celibacy to earlier days but entirely representative of the new, or relatively new, pastoral closeness of teachers and boys. This pastoral role meant intimate involvement in the boy's life as both a father and a friend, yet this intimacy was in his case peculiarly guarded. Basil hardly ever opened the door that led from his quarters to the house at large, leaving the management of the house to the servants (sequestered at the back of the house), but above all to his monitors and his carefully chosen head of house. These, and sick, miserable or otherwise vulnerable boys he allowed to enter the "private side", where he called them by their first names, surnames only being used in the house. Within his quarters boys were invited to dine, and indeed taught how to "dine" properly. In the style of the Oxbridge College they would then read him their essays over port and coffee.

Oldham took his charges on "reading parties" and on holiday, something married housemasters did as well. The closeness of this involvement meant an eventual "breakdown" and the "disgrace" of a man who, in the words of his biographer, "lived beyond his emotional means". His letters show an extraordinarily fretful, self-critical man, highly sensitive to the mood and behaviour of his boys, the homoerotic passion ever present and, almost, ever repressed. In the fashion of the time the inevitable scandal, when it came, was hushed up with the connivance of the parents and school authorities, and Basil continued pretty much unhindered in his long association with the school, although not now as a housemaster.[112] Oldham's Hall was organised on the pattern of the upper-class household, the household of the master in his highly salubrious living quarters and the household of the boys and the servants in the "house" proper. The house

[111] C. A. Alington, *Two Men: A Memoir* (Oxford University Press, 1919).
[112] Letters and papers of J. B. Oldham deposited by A. E. Gunther, 1976. The letters of Oldham to Gunther, his "Puss", run from 1910 to 1956. M. L. Charlesworth, *J. B. Oldham of Oldham's Hall*, Ch. 12 "Crisis".

after leaving was almost as important as during youth, Basil's letters, to many pupils other than his beloved "Puss" alone, keeping its memory continually alive, supported annually by the house dinner for returnees. He literally kept open house for old boys, as when he designed the house he made sure that at least half a dozen rooms were available for old-boy visitors and their parents, who he also assiduously cultivated in his letters.

Turning to the house in relation to the Oxbridge college, I have noted how at Oxford and Cambridge the search for a generalised, less subject-specific and more academic form of knowledge was moralised and given a new kind of authority by the pastoral role of the "don" and the reinvention of the college. The Oxbridge appropriation of the reforming public-school emphasis on master–boy closeness has in fact been seen as one of the most important achievements of the Victorian generation of dons.[113] The "private hour" at the public school was echoed by the "tutorial" of the Oxbridge college. From the 1860s at Oxford and Cambridge the refashioning of the college and the tutor system went hand in hand.[114] This involved the creation of properly constituted governing bodies, purified by open elections to fellowships. After Jowett became Master of Balliol in 1866 college members were allowed to retain their fellowships subsequent to marriage.[115] In 1882 celibacy restrictions on fellowships were finally removed in the university as a whole. Earlier, in 1871, the religious tests were repealed. In turn, now interested in a "career", the don set out to make a living out of cultivating this new sort of pastoral authority, the tutorial experience becoming a central part of college life.[116]

However, as with the whole edifice of a reinvented liberal education, all this went hand in hand with a markedly authoritarian form of discipline. Schools and colleges were prisons as well as monasteries, houses and courts. It was from the 1860s that college discipline became more marked. The use of fines, "gatings", and of disciplinary proctors and their "bulldog" underlings patrolling the streets, were only some of the means used to enforce an increasingly draconian discipline (this was very much like the public schools and their abolition of early-nineteenth-century boy *carnivalia*). Material interventions were also made, in the form of walls built and ditches dug around colleges. Tutors now lived in, or very near

[113] M. C. Curthoys, "The College in the New Era" in M. S. Brock and M. C. Curthoys (eds.), *The History of Oxford*, vol. VI, *Nineteenth-Century Oxford*, Pt. 1 (Oxford University Press, 1991), p. 133; J. D. R. Connell, *Eton: How it Works* (Faber and Faber, 1967), Ch. 4.
[114] For Cambridge see C. N. L. Brooke, *A History of the University of Cambridge*, vol. IV, *1870–1900* (Cambridge University Press, 1995).
[115] John Prest, "Balliol for Example" in Brock and Curthoys (eds.), *The History of Oxford*.
[116] Sheldon Rothblatt, *The Revolution of the Dons: Cambridge and Society in Victorian England* (Cambridge University Press, 1981), Ch. 7.

the college, in college houses. The regime of the college took on much of the principle of "exhaustive use" seen in the public schools: chapel and lectures were made compulsory, dinners were to be eaten in hall, and in terms of pedagogic method the increasing refinement of the university examination enabled it to control students by means of the necessity of the hard work of preparation. Exhaustive use, seen also in new residence requirements at the college and university, was therefore paralleled by the new earnestness, which also reflected developments at public school. All the changes were evident in nineteenth-century Cambridge; and at Oxford, with its higher degree of college autonomy, were indeed even more marked.

Enshrining the new seriousness, discipline, and internalised authority, was the new idea of the college as a community. The college was to be a new sort of household and home. With the development of the college system went a large amount of administrative work on the part of the fellows and tutors, the institution becoming increasingly complex. The college developed as an object of institutional loyalty, the life of the mind, the career life, the social life of the student, and the life of the college as a unity, becoming increasingly one thing. The college now came to absorb all or most of the undergraduates' time, unlike previously. It became more an undergraduate institution than before, less one of the fellows.[117] "College" came to mean the body of undergraduates and teachers, as opposed to the governing body. At the same time, the student body was itself increasingly homogenous, being almost completely drawn from the public schools. "College" became not only a distinct cultural institution, but a distinct economic one as well: before the 1860s and 70s outside sources had supplied college economic needs (including much of food and provisioning), but after this time the college became increasingly self-sufficient. Cultural autarky developed in terms of the JCRs (Junior Common Rooms) of the 1850s and 60s, which developed out of debating societies.

Like in the public school, the new athleticism, reflected in the cult of games, meant that sport became a vital element inculcating loyalty to the college.[118] At the centre of a distinct life world, the college further reproduced the aesthetic and the ascetic as well as the athletic changes evident in the schools. The aesthetic and the ascetic were deeply interfused. Both fed a certain seduction – the attractions of college itself, the beauty of its

---

[117] M. C. Curthoys, "The College in the New Era" in Brock and Curthoys (eds.), *The History of Oxford*.

[118] Mangan, *Athleticism in the Victorian and Edwardian Public School*, Ch. 6. Leslie Stephen, *Sketches from Cambridge by a Don* (London, 1865).

built forms, and the allure of the life of the tutor. If in practice usually anything but ascetic (there were servants to do the hard work and feasts to be eaten), self-indulgence nonetheless sat quite happily with the attitudinising of neo-monastic asceticism. This is evident in those who invented this new life world: the mystique of the don owed a great deal to Mark Pattison as well as Leslie Stephen.[119] As we have seen Pattison had a central role in the contemporary sanctification of learning, and for him in turn the new concept of the don owed much to the example of Thomas Arnold. For Pattison the college was self-consciously a work of neo-monastic reconstitution, in which the aesthetic and ascetic were one.

As Rothblatt has noted, this reinvented college life involved in turn the evocation of ancient tradition and the mystique of ivy-covered walls.[120] These years saw the onset of the notion of Oxbridge as "the dreaming spires", a sort of pedagogic nirvana. Leslie Stephen was well aware of how powerfully the mystique and seductiveness of the college also worked upon the sensibilities of students' parents. In describing the meeting of the college tutor and the parent in his *Sketches of Cambridge* of 1865 Stephen noted the subjection of the parent to the new college aesthetic. He describes the hushed admiration of parents and students, as the dead college Masters looked down upon them in "placid contempt" from the walls of the college hall, and the awe that the glories of the chapel windows inspired. The furniture of the college suggested studious medieval leisure. The antiquity and beauty of the surroundings created what was called an air of "historical purpose and serenity", requiring of the student a sense of humility and self-denial.[121] The ancient college buildings exerted their unerring powers, but the tutor was as much subject to these as anyone else, for as Stephen said, "the surroundings fit the accomplished tutor as naturally as a tortoise is fitted by its shell".[122] In looking at the powers of Oxbridge it is necessary then not to lose sight of how the other face of monkish devotion was, and still is, material wellbeing and bodily pleasure. How much of all this has changed is a subject of the next chapter.

The pinnacle of the old Oxbridge seems to have been reached in the inter-war years however, for instance at Oxford, which Brian Harrison describes in fascinating detail.[123] Also in rather indulgent detail it must be

---

[119] Stephen, ibid.

[120] Sheldon Rothblatt, *Tradition and Change in English Liberal Education: An Essay in History and Culture* (Faber and Faber, 1976).

[121] Rothblatt, *The Revolution of the Dons*, p. 236.   [122] Quoted in ibid., p. 236.

[123] Brian Harrison, "College Life 1918–1939" in Brian Harrison (ed.), *The History of the University of Oxford*, vol. VIII, *The 20th Century* (Oxford University Press, 1994); V. H. H. Green, *Oxford Common Room: A Study of Lincoln College's Mark Pattison* (Edward Arnold, 1957).

said, for it is plain that the historian Harrison is entranced by this world. His description comes from one of the many volumes of an edition of the history of Oxford University in which almost all the contributors are drawn from that institution, in one way or another, something itself worthy of note as one more expression of the power of the house, namely the house history.[124] The power of the *domus* was especially marked for unmarried dons at Oxford in the inter-war years, and married ones were readily drawn back from the conjugal to the college house. Oxford was rather slow to adjust to the married life of dons, college officers in the 1930s who were married not questioning their duty to leave home at 10 pm during term time to sleep in college.[125] One way of handling the relationship between home and college was for the wife to sink herself in college affairs, something which often happened and which was a distinct echo of how at Harrow before the Second World War all new wives were expected to wear their wedding dress when first entertained on "the Hill", as if they were marrying the school itself.[126]

The Senior Common Room of the college was a home within a home, a club within a club. In Harrison's account of inter-war college life at Oxford one finds many echoes of the seductions of permanent adolescence. As he describes it, the Senior Common Room was a collegiate theatre that put on "nightly performances of the stylised and much prized art of conversation". Rules seem to have proscribed the topics of religion, politics and women, and anything too earnest or deep was excluded. This was the venue in which arrested development could masquerade as wit and intellectual brilliance. The rich and powerful were part of the masquerade too, being regular visitors at SCR "High Table" occasions. These and other similar collective college occasions were also intimately related to the operations of memory, especially of student memory. Harrison describes how for those "up" at Oxford in the 1920s,

there was much about Oxford to delight the ear as well as the eye, and their recollections often dwell upon sounds – the trumpet which summoned Queen's men to dinner, the bells announcing mealtimes and chapel services, Latin graces precisely recalled across half a century. Add to these memories of the roaring fires in one's room on returning from football, Mr Cross's "unforgettable" anchovy toast at Jesus, and above all the smallness of the college's architectural scale, the beauty of its buildings, the closeness of its relationships.[127]

---

[124] Stefan Collini, *English Pasts: Studies in Culture and History* (Oxford University Press, 1999) for a Cambridge don's acerbic view of this Oxford enterprise.
[125] Harrison, "College Life 1918–1939", pp. 85–6.
[126] Christopher Tyerman, *A History of Harrow School 1324–1991* (Oxford University Press, 2000), p. 475.
[127] Harrison, "College Life 1918–1939", pp. 85–6, 103.

Such memories gave Oxford men a taste for club-like structures wherever they went in later life. Through A. D. Lindsay and G. D. H. Cole, the collegiate ideal even contributed to the political theorist's repertoire of state utopias, the house and the college directly fathering the state, also in Lindsay's case another university, Keele, founded by Lindsay, Master of Balliol, in its original form in 1949. The egregiously privileged life of Oxford, so much "othered" from the world around it, was not something rejected as inappropriate to an egalitarian and democratic society, but as compatible with it, and in some cases a model for it. The Oxford of this inter-war time, for all the development of research from the late nineteenth century, continued in large measure to see education as more than solely academic. Education was still understood as holistic, engaging the whole person, and especially cultivating "leadership and organisation". Colleges were still small, and always closely related to national elites (an undergraduate might expect with some certainty to be invited to tea with the powerful). This was a time before a specific student culture emerged, at least a culture defining itself by excluding the dons. The tutors attended student functions, the dedicated "college man" keeping in touch with students when they had "gone down", often on a lifelong basis, as with the Shrewsbury master Basil Oldham and his "Puss". At a time when employment appointments were made by personal contact, employers regularly consulted tutors about applicants.

The Junior Common Room represented an all-male, ritualised, and indeed almost Masonic exclusiveness, one based on the pervasive public-school background. This exclusiveness could be distinctly racist, especially anti-semitic.[128] Between the wars estrangement from the world was perhaps even more marked, with the morning roll-call and evening closing hours rigidly enforced. College paternalism extended beyond college walls to the proportion of students who lived outside college, in the case of Oxford mostly near the college in the town's central streets. Social intercourse with Oxford town was severely limited, and the corporate life of the college was intensified in all manner of ways, particularly in terms of an inter-collegiate rivalry which took on even more than previously the house loyalties of public school. College life was also developed in terms of the cultivation of the alumni, so that the *domus* of the old college, like the old school, stretched through time as well as space: in Oxford opinion "The colleges were second families and second homes to their sons". Memory was systematised into lifelong bonds by the college's increasingly sophisticated cultivation of its old members as a financial as well as a

---

[128] Ibid., pp. 95–7.

political and cultural resource. And what a resource these old boys were! Of the one hundred and sixty-eight British Cabinet ministers between 1905 and 1940, fifty-three were educated at Oxford, of which fourteen came from Balliol and nine from Christ Church.[129]

Not much seems to have changed by 1960. This is the Master of Balliol in that year:

Every true Oxford man would agree that the essence of Oxford is college life. To have one's own rooms, on one's own staircase, making one's friendships with undergraduates and dons, to have meals together, to drop into one's own JCR, read in one's College Library, worship in one's College chapel, play on one's own field or row from one's own boathouse – all these, taken together, make up the experience men come to Oxford to get and always treasure. It is on this intimacy of daily life that Oxford education is based. From this it derives its unique value. The college is more than a hostel; it is more than just a private society of teachers and pupils; it is a household, a very large one, of course, but a household all the same. There is nothing quite like it and its Cambridge counterpart in the whole world.[130]

It is to the continuities and discontinuities between the world I have been describing and our own that I turn in the final chapter, but the subject of the state and the *domus* cannot be left before considering some other sorts of state house, particularly the prison one.

Postscript: another kind of state house

Figure 7.4 is a picture of Galway Gaol, newly built in 1809 to the design of Gloucester County Gaol in England. It is the other face of the state, the face of violence and coercion, in this case the house of "correction", although the external and a good deal of the internal character of this kind of house also mirrored the built forms of the "welfare" that was extended to the people of Britain and Ireland, the forms of workhouses, hospitals and asylums for the "insane". In practice, these too were also concerned with "correction" in their different ways, their regimes also being regimented. This other face of the state was talked about earlier in terms of the transition from the old order of violence to the new one of normalisation and reform. Galway Gaol pointed to the past and future in this respect, in that conditions in the prison in the early 1880s were for half the prisoners cramped, dungeon-like and punitive, and for the others rationally cellular and reformatory. The prison yard was set up on panopticon principles, with the various "labour sheds" being visible from a central point. However Mountjoy Gaol in Kilmainham, Dublin was

---

[129] Ibid., p. 106.
[130] Cited in Keith Thomas, "College Life 1945–1970" in Harrison (ed.), *The History of the University of Oxford.*

Fig. 7.4 Galway Gaol

the true sign of things to come, heralding the precocious emergence of the "convict system" in Ireland:[131] opened in 1864 its east wing, modelled on Pentonville Prison in London, is an extraordinary example of the new prison architecture.

However, if the old order of violence was left behind, the state now relied on the violence of order, in the sense not only that order had to be backed by violence, but that violence, if now in the legally sanctioned form of institutional coercion, still entered into the mundane routines of the state. Prisoners in these new kinds of institutions, like public schoolboys in their houses, were minutely monitored for their conduct and application to work, marks being allotted for behaviour, everything being set down in little ruled squares with the figures trotted up at the end of the long weeks, months and years.[132] Their fates depended on these marks. Also, like

---

[131] See above, pp. 44–5.

[132] Jarlath Waldron, *Maamtrasna: The Murders and the Mystery* (Edmund Burke, 1992), p. 306. See also for the extraordinarily monitorial regime of Irish prison, at once coercive and rational, "Fifth Report of the General Prisons Board, Ireland, 1882–83; with Appendices", *Parl. Papers*, 1883, C.3757.

public school, the new type of person that it was the aim of this routinised coercion to design should learn "self reliance" in the process.[133] The physical form of the house similarly reflected the household. Even in the new prisons the staff often lived on the premises, and in the Galway case the space between the cookhouse, itself immediately below the execution chamber, and the condemned cells was filled with the living quarters for unmarried warders, the basement housing the living quarters of "the keeper" and his family.

In the yard of this prison in December 1882 three men were executed by hanging for the horrendous murder of five of a Joyce family in the vicinity of Maamtrasna, county Mayo, in the August of that year, the executed men being Myles Joyce, Pat Joyce and Pat Casey. One of them, Myles Joyce, was almost certainly innocent and the others very possibly so; similarly a number of others who were sentenced to penal servitude for life. Almost all the men involved in what came to be called the "Maamtrasna murders" did not speak English, including Myles Joyce. Myles was represented by a defence lawyer who knew no Irish. The court interpreters used were either unwilling or unable to convey the impassioned stories of the accused, who were convicted on the basis of the evidence of paid informers. The jury was composed of ten Protestants and two Roman Catholics. This is how an appalled James Joyce described the fate of his namesake (all Joyces originate from this area around Maamtrasna, but the family of James Joyce had emigrated to Cork long before these events):

The magistrate, "Ask him if he was in the vicinity at the time". The old man began speaking once again, protesting, shouting, almost beside himself with the distress of not understanding or making himself understood, weeping with rage and terror. And the interpreter once again replied drily: "He says no, your worship" . . . The figure of this bewildered old man, left over from a culture which is not ours . . . is a symbol of the Irish nation at the bar of public opinion.[134]

This James Joyce was not wrong about, but Myles Joyce was also a symbol of the reality of British justice in Ireland and of the organised violence of the state generally, a justice that was cruel and unrelenting in its desire to achieve convictions at all costs, unashamedly using the law to terrorise the population. This indeed was a case of the violence of order. It has had many subsequent echoes in British, Irish and imperial history down the years. Myles Joyce's death was an awful one: protesting his innocence to

---

[133] Patrick Carroll-Burke, *Colonial Discipline: The Making of the Irish Convict System* (Four Courts Press, 2000), pp. 158–9.
[134] James Joyce, "Ireland at the Bar" (1907) in Kevin Barry (ed.), *James Joyce: Occasional, Critical and Political Writing* (Oxford University Press, 2008), pp. 145–6.

the end, his terrified movements in his last moments dislodged the noose from around his neck and he was strangled to death after two minutes of the utmost agony. The violence of the state was duly registered and recorded in complete bureaucratic detail; ten different sorts of document were needed in order for the inquest jury to identify the bodies of the executed. The file and the form were as indispensible here as everywhere else.[135]

The murders seem to have been in part a family feud, but seemingly in greater part revenge against what was perceived to be a family of "informers", those held responsible for the recent executions of the men who had assassinated the land agent of Sir Arthur Guinness (Lord Ardilaun), and his son. The area in which this happened was the Joyce Country (*Dúiche Sheoighe* in Irish), just to the north of Connemara, and covering the western parts of counties Mayo and Galway, a place we have already encountered in terms of the history of communication.[136] My father was born in the valley immediately to the south of Maamtrasna, and shared the same townland as the widow of one of the three men hanged, to which she returned after his execution, subsequently, like so many in the area, emigrating to America. In these years the ancient Irish-language culture of the west of Ireland, which had suffered so much in the years of the Famine, was increasingly subject to the "civilisation" of post offices, prisons, schools and the English language. However, it still represented a true "other" of the British state and its civilisation. As James Joyce put it, this was "a culture which is not ours", not indeed the culture of his own part-anglicised Irishness, never mind the culture of English civilisation. Myles Joyce's was a culture the difference of which is starkly indicated in the figure of his grieving wife, "keening" outside Galway Gaol for nine days after his execution.[137]

To outsiders this culture represented something alien and barbaric, at other times droll and romantic, especially to the uncomprehending English and Anglo-Irish landowners that dominated its economy to the end of the century. The people of this place are gentle, hospitable and humourous, but the hard and beautiful land that they lived by was at this time a violent one. Lord Mountmorres, a local landowner, had been assassinated in the immediate area only a little while before Ardilaun's agent. It was rumoured he acted as a "spy" for that other great house of the

---

[135] For the circumstances of the death see Waldron, *Maamtrasna*, Ch. 9.
[136] See above, pp. 70–1.
[137] Keening is a form of vocal lament associated with mourning, traditional in Ireland, Scotland, African and other cultures. The word comes from the Irish/Scots Gaelic term *caoineadh*, to cry.

state in Ireland, Dublin Castle, the hated centre of quasi-colonial British governance in Ireland. The immediate area was also the original home of the "boycott", directed against a land agent of that name (the military and Orangemen had to be drafted in to harvest the crops of targeted landlords). It was also a centre of "Ribbonmen Fenianism", committed to physical force unlike the contemporaneous and hugely popular Land League. Those involved in the crime were reputed to be members of "the Herd's League" branch of the Ribbonmen.

The assassination was accompanied by the age-old repertoire of supposedly "primitive" peasant rebellion, namely the destruction or sabotage of crops, livestock and premises, accompanied by violence against the police, the military and collaborators. Violent or peaceful, all forms of agitation in the tumultuous "Land Wars" of the region were concerned to reform the iniquitous landlord system which had inflamed these people to violence.

William Gladstone was of course responsible for reforming the old landlord system, but he was no different from the great majority of the political and administrative class of the British state at the time in standing foursquare in defence of the law and against Myles Joyce.[138] Gladstone was an Old Etonian, bred in vastly different kinds of houses from Joyce. The Anglo-Irish landowning class, absentee and resident, were also products of the English public schools, heirs and agents of an English civilisation engendered in the *domus* of the school and the college. Thus the cradle of the British state engendered the grave of Myles Joyce.

---

[138] A local parish priest of the area has produced a remarkable narrative of the murders, which includes an account of how the case became a cause célèbre at the time; Waldron, *Maamtrasna*. See also Mindy Ina Silverboard, "Ireland, the Newspaper Press and Liberal Governmentality: The Formulation of Expertise on the 'Irish Question', 1880–9" (University of Manchester Ph.D. thesis, 2003).

8   Conclusion: legacies of the liberal Leviathan

How much has the British state changed in the course of the twentieth century and up to the present? In certain and fundamental respects little. The more things change the more they remain the same continues to be an adage particularly appropriate to Britain. In other respects however change has been considerable: that renowned anatomist of Britain Anthony Sampson, when comparing his first "anatomy" of Britain in 1965 with his most recent one of 2004, writes that "Revisiting some of the seats of power after 40 years, I felt like Rip van Winkle waking up after a revolution."[1] There have been key changes therefore, as will be seen, for instance the displacement of the old hierarchies of gender, though as always change was qualified here too. How one views change depends on the perspective one chooses of course. Mine is a long-term one and so the largely neoliberal state Sampson was anatomising in 2004 cannot but look like a case of the chickens of the liberal state coming home to roost. Nonetheless, as I shall argue later, the degree and type of change in the very recent past suggests that the degree of rupture between the past and the present of the liberal state is becoming ever more marked.

The view from the 1960s was different: the world of the Master of Balliol in 1960, glimpsed at the end of the last chapter, really does not seem all that different from the world of Oxbridge sixty or eighty years before. And, up to the present, the old elite educational system continues to produce the British governing classes. Two instances dramatically illustrate this, one from the 1980s and one from the new century. Firstly, in 1982 Sampson records how the two leading public schools of Winchester and Eton at that time supplied the top two managers at the BBC, all five chairmen of the banks, the editor of *The Times*, and the head of the home *and* the foreign

---

[1] Anthony Sampson, *Who Runs This Place? The Anatomy of Britain in the 21st Century* (John Murray, 2004), p. 343, and see the chapter from which this title is drawn, Ch. 25, "Who Runs This Place?"; see also Anthony Sampson, *Anatomy of Britain Today* (Hodder & Stoughton, 1965).

civil services.[2] Secondly, of Britain's new coalition government of 2010 *The Independent* newspaper concluded, "If Britain looked like its government, about 4 million adults would have gone to Eton."[3] One in ten of the coalition government ministers went to one school, Eton; the Prime Minister was an Old Etonian; and the Chiefs of Staff of the Prime Minister and Chancellor of the Exchequer were old Etonians, one of them a former head boy. Outside Parliament one of the foremost pretenders to the throne of the Conservative Party leadership, the Mayor of London Boris Johnson, publicly flaunted the "importance of being Eton" with a degree of success that would have amazed 1960s Britain. Twenty per cent of government ministers in 2010 attended the leading public schools, and two-thirds were privately educated (93 per cent of the national population were state educated). The preponderance of Oxford and Cambridge was overwhelming. Families still mattered too: five of the government ministers had MP fathers, two more had married daughters of Cabinet ministers and three could trace connections to past prime ministers. The shopkeeper revolution of the Thatcher years seemed to have come to naught.[4] Likewise the much-vaunted reign of successive grammar-school Prime Ministers, Conservative and Labour.

The roots of what I record for 1982 and 2010 are, as we have seen, deeply embedded in the history of the British state. The technologies and personnel of elite pedagogy have always been to the fore in shaping the British governing classes, and the British state has historically drawn great strength from the resulting cultural unity, a strength expressed in the extraordinary resilience of key institutions, both within and outside the state. The capacity of these to successfully reinvent themselves is one of the chief reasons why it has been so difficult to challenge and reshape the institutions of the British state, and thereby reshape British society. To make such a challenge one might begin by attending to what the state actually is rather than what interested parties take it to be. This latter I have tried to do in the following ways.

I have argued for the credibility of thinking about the state as a matter of embodied practice and in terms therefore of people's daily habituation to it, so that it has very often operated below the level of their conscious awareness. It is also the outcome of the material processes and powers that flow through it and give it shape and direction. The state is in fact so near to being what can be termed "a way of life" as to make most political rhetoric seem even more spurious than is commonly felt to be the case.

---

[2] Anthony Sampson, *The Changing Anatomy of Britain* (Hodder & Stoughton, 1981), p. 127.

[3] "A Government of Straight, White, Privately Educated Men", *Independent*, 7 August 2010.

[4] Geoffrey Wheatcroft, *The Strange Death of Tory England* (Penguin, 2005).

Contrary to it being either merely a neutral administrative apparatus or a malign monster – somehow "out there" – it is on the contrary already "in here", in us. It is an integral part of contemporary being, without which the most common of tasks would be impossible. Despite neoliberal attempts to "roll" it back this is the irrevocable outcome whose origins I have traced. These attempts seem self-defeating, though no less dangerous and misguided because of this. Even a "small state" has in present circumstances to be in actual fact always a big one, as Margaret Thatcher found out, when despite her best efforts the state sector continued to grow. And setting up the small state of neoliberal aspirations in the present only leads to the big state of another sort, that of coercion, security and regulation, when that is it does not create so many social and economic problems that the big state has to be called back in to save the day.

The state has therefore become "naturalised", part of our "common sense" and common knowledge, so that the exploration of the constitution of this sense and knowledge has been a principle subject of the book. Thinking about it in this way returns attention to my original question, "what is the state?" The answer to this question was approached in terms of how order has been brought to what in practice was and is a diverse set of political interventions and institutions. The production of order involved a new salience for systems. In turn it involved the creation of order within systems by means of the creation of what I termed "centres"; and finally, related to the other two aspects, it involved the mobilisation of the will to govern. The technopolitical, which is to say political "technique" in both human and non-human forms, has been my interest. This sense of living within "systems" has become ever more marked since the techno-state's beginnings. The divine, the natural, the moral and, increasingly from the late nineteenth century, the social, all offered models of order and system. These have been followed in recent times by a reinstatement of the model of the market, now divested of its earlier moral overtones.

Because the state, at least in its highly developed Western forms, is grounded in us, the "us" of state personnel as well as the "us" who are the subjects of the state, certain important political consequences have followed. What these are depends upon how this process of grounding or embedding has been carried out. In the liberal state it was carried forward in such a way as to lead to the obfuscation of the fact that the state is not a "thing" that stands outside us, an assumption that of course still guides political practice today, on the left, right and in the centre. The assumption that it was, and is, such and thus something separate from society, we have seen to be central to the state in its liberal form and crucial for the operation of the organisation of freedom. This was apparent in the study of the Post Office especially, where what I called the learning of the state involved the message that the state and a liberal economy, society and polity were different things.

However, this liberal learning of the state is rather paradoxical, for if the state is in us then the most logical political lesson is that state and society are one and that this being so the state should be positively embraced, because in embracing it one is but realising and recognising oneself. This lesson has been a slow one to be learned in British history. Nonetheless, the partial and usually qualified victory of the liberal lesson needs to be recognised, and this I have pointed out in various places. Again, the Post Office is a relevant case, where the idea of "the nation working for itself" enunciated by Frank Scudamore reflected this ambivalence.[5] This idea was of a piece with more communal understandings of the state that have always been a presence in British history, especially in the mid-to-late twentieth century, when a sense of collective ownership of the state developed in which the gap between state and society lessened, so that more socialised versions of the state emerged. However, in Britain over the long term the liberal lesson has dominated, mostly because the state has remained in the hands of those who wished it to dominate, and mutual or collective ideas of the state have been muffled or silenced by the force of liberal understandings, including ones of a more social caste.

The state, as I have suggested, is one aspect of a broader history of "connectivity", and my purpose has not been, even if it were possible in one book, to chart the many other connections, systems and networks that exist outside the state and interact with it. Therefore, I have not offered a detailed account of where, by what means and by whom the boundaries of the state have been drawn, although I have shown many instances of outside forces acting on the state and helping to draw these boundaries. For instance the role of extra-state educational institutions in the formation of state educational institutions, and most of all the formation of the knowledge of how to govern the state. As well as this I have considered business and social interests and networks in the account of the Post Office, where the postal network was seen to interact with many other networks and systems before it too became a system. There the question of "translation" and "mediation" was seen to be critical, and therefore also mediators – human *actors* and non-human *actants* – that had the capacity not merely to transfer across domains but to translate between them. This work of translation, the work of the state in another sense, is where the privileged capacity of the state to organise social power is situated, and this organisation involved integration with the social in different ways

---

[5] See above, p. 84.

according to the environment it operated in, as we have seen particularly clearly in the cases of postal communication in Ireland and India, and where and how these differed from the mainland.

However this very capacity to coordinate and translate between the networks and systems, and interests and groups, which are outside itself, points to how it is the state itself that needs to be at the centre of the picture. In coordinating other elements beyond itself, in enlisting and redefining them, it is the role of the state in drawing boundaries that seems to have been of singular importance. The same goes for the salience of the state in all the many other tasks, beyond purely this one, that are necessary for the organisation of political power out of the ingredients of the social. These other tasks we have seen to involve a fundamental human activity, namely communication in the form of writing; also a fundamentally human place, the house. This salience of the state, albeit understood in a different way from conventional accounts, I have argued for throughout. This is to give the state a particular historical importance of course. Furthermore, this importance is deepened when we remember how, in emphasising the materiality of things and bodies, as with writing and houses, we arrive at the conclusion that the state is *actually* and not only metaphorically naturalised, literally so, because it is part of nature, human and non-human.

The people who did the most critical work of translation were chiefly the high bureaucrats and politicians; also the "experts" of different sorts, particularly the academic version of the expert. The British state was in important measure the outcome of the interactions of these figures, as we have seen. However, this is only part of the picture. For in the matter of the actual architects of the state I have emphasised how the state was "co-produced", and was therefore the outcome of the labour of many obscure men and women. We may recall here in their different government departments men like Frank Scudamore, George Chetwynd, Forbes Watson, Nathaniel Wordsell, Clements Markham, Charles Danvers, and the lowly Locke at the Home Office, with his "uncanny nose for papers". As well as these there were the low-level clerks with their on-the-job initiative and input into the workings of the state. Indeed, the operations of the state often involved curbing and disciplining this initiative. This sense of connection to the state would have been individualist but also collectivist, something evident today in the National Health Service. "Common knowledge" was not only drawn from common places but was often held in common by men and women of the "common" classes. Even if the power of these people was limited, they were active agents in the creation of the state.

Thus the cultural forms that are expressed in the state and the technological forms in which it is materially embedded give it an extraordinary resilience, whether in its liberal or non-liberal forms, and to some degree whether it is strong or weak, for it should be remembered that the cultural and material forms of weak states are often as deeply embedded as those in strong ones. For example, Berlusconi may have gone from the Italian scene, at least for now, but not the "weak" Italian state, which remains the hardy child of a history in which family has mattered more than civil society. Without understanding all this historical, material and social rootedness of the state it will be difficult to reform the state in the ways which are now urgently required. Urgently, because now the stark choice (at least in Britain and Europe) seems to be between the market, the unbridled corporation and the state.[6] However much, on right and left, the state since the third quarter of the twentieth century has disappointed expectations, it appears to be our main hope if the chaos of the markets and the excessive power of the corporations are to be avoided. It is necessary for the citizens to claim ownership of a state that is already in truth theirs but has for too long been taken from them. Which brings us to the question of the legacies of the liberal Leviathan in the twentieth century and to how more recent times in Britain compare with the picture I have drawn up to the 1920s or so.

In terms of what I called the communications state, there seems to have been little difference, until relatively recent times, from the great Victorian and Edwardian versions of the Post Office I have explored. Real change only happened in the 1970s. The graph presented earlier, for the total number of post offices in the UK, is a nice illustration of this, 1880 to 1970 marking the triumph of the system.[7] This is how a historian of the Royal Mail describes the 1950s in comparison with the 1890s, and the description effectively conveys the continuities in British society as well:

A postman, counter clerk or sorter from the 1890s, magically transported to the middle of the 1950s, could have turned up for work almost anywhere in the country and found himself in utterly familiar surroundings in the sorting halls, men in much the same uniforms were preparing the mails with similar, and in some cases actually the very same, office fittings. There was recognisably the same graded, acronym-laden hierarchy in place ... Mailbags were tied, and open coal fires were set, just as they had been for generations, often in the very same buildings, and the discipline and quasi-military atmosphere were as pervasive as ever – all the more so since 1945.[8]

Low and slow technology indeed, and all along in the book I have argued for the salience of this technological register. However, by the 1950s

[6] Colin Crouch, *The Strange Non-Death of Neoliberalism* (Polity Press, 2011).
[7] See above, p. 136 and Duncan Campbell-Smith, *Masters of the Post: The Authorised History of the Royal Mail* (Allen Lane/Penguin, 2011), pp. 168, 167.
[8] Ibid., pp. 390–1.

technology had accelerated and elevated itself in many areas of government. The era of what I earlier called technological government proper, which succeeded the communications state, was becoming evident everywhere. The effect of two world wars has been to greatly accelerate the consolidation of the technological state, particularly in the guise of what has been called the "warfare state", war spilling over into peacetime in the shape of the influence of military technology on economic development and the political power of the industrial interests responsible for this technology.[9] We earlier saw other, more recent examples of technological government in the shape of the technological standardisation evident in the operations of the European Union.[10] This was integrated with the "information revolution" that really took off in the 1990s. Within the Post Office itself the era of mechanisation gave way after the Second World War to that of automation, eventually leading to the current electronic system of postcode recognition, the new postal codes themselves now being absolutely central to the social, political and commercial operations of British life, but also to those of the "data state" as it has been called. This particular variety of the information state, now so completely indebted to the Internet, had its origins in the communications form of the nineteenth-century state.

Since the attack on the World Trade Center in 2001 the always close relationship between the "data state" and the security function of the state has deepened further. The operations of this sort of technology, bizarrely enough, are however about governing the future, in terms of "risk", as much as governing the present. The systematic governance of what has not happened reminds us of the irrationality inextricable from the rationality of the state. This development has brought in its train armies of "experts" and their attendant industries, all with their own vested interests, and all overlapping and often competing with one another. Far from the state being in charge of the resulting situation, it sometimes seems apparent that there is no one in charge.[11] At the "centre" of the state, at least from this perspective, there frequently appears to be nothing very much at all, a disturbing state of affairs indeed.

Communications in the new technological key, the electronic one, therefore became relevant to the state in entirely new forms in the twentieth century as technology enabled new directions, one of the most important of which was the broadcasting of radio and television. Here we can see how the

---

[9] David Edgerton, *Warfare State: Britain 1920–1970* (Cambridge University Press, 2007).

[10] On technological government see above, p. 43.

[11] Nikolas Rose, "Freedom in an Age of Insecurity", paper to the LSE "Understanding Freedom" seminar series, April–July 2009. See also the numerous papers in the ESRC seminar series "Government and Freedom", 2008–10, organised by Tony Bennett, Francis Dodsworth, Nikolas Rose and myself, at www.archive.cresc.ac.uk/projects/government.

form of the state that accompanied this new phase of communication differed from the nineteenth-century version. This difference was in step with the transition from around 1900 to a more state-friendly "social liberalism", away from the more individualist earlier versions. What is particularly interesting about the Post Office is that it straddled both versions of the state, and because of this was in fact probably the single most important force giving birth to the new. Whereas the "free press" was quintessentially nineteenth century in sympathy (which of course has not prevented it from being profoundly influential in the twenty-first century), the idea of "public service" broadcasting continued the old state interest in communications but also represented the new relationship between the state and communications reflected in social liberalism.

As Stuart Hall has pointed out, the idea of the BBC after its formation in 1922, initially out of the Post Office, was that as a public corporation it would quite literally incorporate all the various interests of the nation, and with a single voice supposedly represent the differing tastes, values, regions and nations that made up the "United Kingdom".[12] Until the 1950s and the arrival of commercial television "public service" was very decidedly about serving a nation that was embodied in the empire and the institutions of the state, particularly monarchy and political unionism. Between 1922 and 1956 the BBC has been understood as perhaps the central site at which a sense of British national identity was created.[13] The special position of the BBC was that it was a state monopoly, yet outside state control. As such, rather like the earlier characterisation of the telegraph as a quintessentially liberal system because it was free and without a centre, the BBC was, and still is, a decidedly liberal institution, one now in the mould of twentieth-century social or public-service liberalism. This manifestation of the state was however for some considerable time to remain a decidedly paternalistic one. For the "voice" of the BBC that purported to represent the people, the state and the nation, at least until the 1950s and 60s, was the upper-middle-class voice of the well-to-do south east of England telling the great majority of people what was good for them. Commercial television from the 1950s threatened this old public-service vision, and the old class voice was replaced by the babble of populist voices that have ensued. However, the BBC's "cultural streaming" of radio after 1945, representing the different heights of intellectual "brow", did presage what was to come.

---

[12] Stuart Hall, "Popular Culture and the State" in Tony Bennett and Colin Mercer (eds.), *Popular Culture and Social Relations* (Open University Press, 1986).
[13] Thomas Hajkowski, *The BBC and National Identity in Britain, 1922–1953* (Manchester University Press, 2010).

The liberal vision of the BBC inhered in the idea of a public service that in one voice could with a sense of balance, moderation and tolerance steer a middle line that would somehow represent all different groups, tastes and views, yet reflect back to them a version of the "British public" that was inclusive and unanimous, despite all the differences. Like the civil servants we encountered earlier,[14] this sort of middle-ground "neutrality" was a product of political engineering, now as then reflecting the views of British "educated opinion". Nonetheless, looking at the broadcasting systems of other states one can only give thanks for much of this educated opinion, and once again it is evident that the emphasis on Public Duty inherited from the old governing order of the nineteenth century produced things of enduring value, even though it was accompanied by all sorts of class prejudice and paternalism, and an ever-present devotion to power. The best of the civil service, the best of Oxford's efforts for public education for example,[15] the best of the legal profession and the best of the political classes who have not completely surrendered to politics as a profession, are other parts of this legacy, one as we shall see now almost entirely hollowed out from within.

Nonetheless, aware of all this, the BBC still needs to be recognised for what it was and still is, however populist it has become, namely a completely characteristic creation and reflection of the liberal state. It is as Lord Reith put it "a public service, not only in performance but in constitution – but certainly not as a department of state".[16] This delicate positioning involved being in the state and drawing its authority from it as a state monopoly, but yet not being of the state as a government department because it was a public corporation. However it had been given its constitution by the state, which could change or revoke it at any time. As a state monopoly it was charged by the state with representing the (multi-) nation state. It was forever precariously balanced between dependence and independence because it shared the perennial problem of the liberal state itself, which was supposed to embody the nation and yet stand above as its supposedly neutral regulator. In Britain, given the great importance of television historically from the 1960s, whether state monopoly or commercial but regulated, the state as a way of life became apparent in a new way, as it did with the massive expansion of the National Health Service from about the same time. To an unprecedented degree

---

[14] See above, pp. 216–28.
[15] Harry Judge (ed.), *The University and Public Education: The Contribution of Oxford* (Routledge, 2007), especially Vernon Bogdanor, "Oxford and the Mandarin Culture: The Past that is Gone".
[16] Cited in Stuart Hall, "Popular Culture and the State", p. 42.

the leisure and the health of the citizen became the concern of the state as the most intimate sectors of family, personal and private life were penetrated by it, the BBC and the NHS becoming in the process symbols of British national identity.

The two world wars that followed 1914 considerably accelerated the powers of the technostate-cum-warfare state. They also served to bring back some of the power of the technical expert. After 1900, in part as a consequence of the Boer War, increasing fears about "national efficiency" meant that a new and more active role was once again given to the scientist in government, especially between 1920 and 1970.[17] The demands of winning the First World War involved an unparalleled intervention in the running of the economy and in the operations of social life, but the very fact that Britain – in comparison to other European states and other bureaucracies still a limited state – was so effectively able to mobilise itself for war is eloquent testimony to the strength and efficiency of the pre-war liberal state, which was not a state dominated by technical experts. And generally in British history, at least until fairly recently, the ultimate subservience of the specialist to the generalist in governmental administration was apparent.

However the already great effectiveness of the "limited" pre-1914 state is testimony to, if not the militarisation of values in British society, then certainly the inculcation of mental and corporeal discipline of all sorts, and one frequently based on the militarisation of the body as in the sorting halls of the 1950s Post Office. This operated throughout the institutions of central and local government to some extent, and extended outside to those academies of governance, the public schools. As we have seen, this militarisation of supposedly civilian realms of conduct took a marked form in Ireland, and of course in the empire as a whole. State legitimacy in wartime enabled the state to do some remarkably illiberal things, effectively, as in the Second World War, militarising almost all of society. However, as has been suggested, this illiberalism was rooted in the forms of order liberalism inculcated.[18] Therefore, the emphasis traditionally given to the two world wars in hastening the development of the state is somewhat misplaced, for the state was rooted in liberal order far more than war.

War in turn further legitimised the state, bringing it even more into the centre of people's lives, and so enmeshing them more deeply in techno-political systems which in turn served further to secure the naturalisation of the state. One of the most important factors legitimising the increased

---

[17] Edgerton, *Warfare State, passim.*   [18] See above, pp. 5–8.

role of the state was conscription in the armed services, and one of the most important general outcomes of war was the idea that "planning" (understood in many different ways) was from now on a fully legitimate part of governmental enterprise. Yet at the same time, as is widely recognised, after the end of war there was a return to business as usual, although more after the First than the Second World War. The "total war" of 1939–45 hastened the development of the welfare state, though its origins really lay in Victorian and Edwardian liberal social engineering. After 1945 the decisive shift had taken place towards the recognition of state intervention and planning as now the norm, not the exception, and towards the idea that something called "society" could now be moulded by political will. However, in line with the rhythm of British history, the militarisation of society in wartime did not lead to the increased political role of the military thereafter (unlike with the inter-war German army), although the army's role in empire before 1914 had led to a new degree of political ambition before the first war.[19] This was blunted afterwards, and the non-militarisation of the governing British elites continued to be the case.

However, as we have seen, the origins of the state as a way of life lay much earlier in time than the period of the two world wars. This is why the still-prevailing view that the British state was a weak and limited one quite far into the twentieth century is so misleading. It is a view expressed in the well-known adage of A. J. P. Taylor, which is still repeated as an article of faith by British historians, namely that "Until 1914, a sensible, law-abiding Englishman could pass through life and hardly notice the existence of the state beyond the post-office and the policeman."[20] If you were a well-off middle-class Englishman like Taylor, that is. If you were working class, poor, Irish, or one of the "criminal classes" matters were otherwise, for these were the social elements most exposed to what by 1914 was the long-developed and sophisticated security apparatus of the state. Of course what Taylor was most unaware of was the whole enormous remit of the technostate and infrastructural power behind such figures as the policeman and the postman.

The initiatives that Taylor overlooked included a range of reforms which meant that the citizen's entire life course began to become tied into the operations of the state, intimate and personal life inexorably becoming its concern. The state therefore took shape in an entirely new version of the

---

[19] Hew Strachan, *The Politics of the British Army* (Oxford University Press, 1997); Ian Beckett (ed.), *The Oxford History of the British Army* (Oxford University Press, 1994).

[20] A. J. P. Taylor, *English History, 1914–1945* (Oxford University Press, 1965), p. 1. This view is cited as axiomatic at the very beginning of the recent collection of essays on the British state, in n. 1, p. 1 of the "Introduction" to S. J. D. Green and R. C. Whiting (eds.), *The Boundaries of the State in Modern Britain* (Cambridge University Press, 1996).

system, the life-course system, becoming ever present as one went through life, "cradle to grave" as later descriptions of the welfare state put it. Education became free and compulsory by 1891. Taking education and childhood first, elementary education was at that time up to the age of ten, and shortly after the Great War this was extended to fourteen. As we have seen, long before this time the rigidly applied content of elementary education enforced, or attempted to enforce, an enormous and deadening uniformity upon the children of the majority.[21] The government of childhood was extended into the family as a whole with the Children's Act of 1908. Work life as well as childhood and family was involved, for labour and social legislation before the Great War extended from the payment of national insurance and unemployment benefit to that of "old-age pensions", so that old age as well as childhood was embraced. Housing and town planning Parliamentary Acts in 1908 and 1915 opened the way to still further new dimensions of state involvement.[22] In line with these changes, government departments themselves, as in the case of the Education Department, began to develop a clear sense of their unity and purpose from the 1880s and 90s.

Many figures other than the postman and policeman were by 1900 already long-familiar members of the cast of the state, and these included sanitary, factory and health inspectors, the poor-law official, the local councillor and the central-government bureaucrat. The growing army of local-government inspectors were not a negligible political force, developing a strong sense of *esprit de corps* which could be mobilised in criticism of the politicians and the central state.[23] In the same way local government was anything but a negligible force, quite the opposite, as consideration of the city as a major arena for the rule of freedom has made plain. However, the local and the central state here played essentially the same tune, the "municipal socialism" emerging in the 1890s being in the key of managerialist social engineering rather than any real socialism. A strong central state held on to the essentials of power.

The same could be said for the nations within the United Kingdom. This was clear in the case of Scotland. Its MPs at Westminster had for far back into the nineteenth century formed what was in effect a Scottish

---

[21] See above, pp. 80–1.

[22] See the chapters on the British state by Jose Harris, "Society and the State in Twentieth-Century Britain" and Pat Thane, "Government and Society in England and Wales, 1750–1914" in F. M. L. Thompson (ed.), *The Cambridge Social History of Great Britain* (Cambridge University Press, 1990), vol. III.

[23] Tom Crook, "Sanitary Inspection and the Public Sphere in Late Victorian and Edwardian Britain: A Case Study in Liberal Governance", *Social History*, 32:4 (2007), and Christopher Hamlin, *Social History*, forthcoming.

sub-Parliament, which with the connivance of London settled a lot of local Scottish business, along with the connivance of Scottish town councils and supervisory boards.[24] What this meant was that while political assimilation was dominant at the level of central and parliamentary government, Scottish control was retained at the level of the city, the burgh and the locality. This meant that national identity could be retained in a bastardised form, one very beneficial to property. This was the pattern for Britain outside Ireland, the local state representing the disposition of social forces at work within the regions and localities, chiefly those of the urban and rural well-to-do. This disposition was however accommodated by the central state.[25] What this amounted to was essentially a trade-off of central for local power. However, this trade-off meant that the central power remained pretty much untouched. For the individual nations the trade-off was also one-way, a bourgeois nationalism remaining parochial and self-serving. That is, until recently, for the rise of a new kind of Scottish and Welsh nationalism threatens to challenge the territorial integrity of the UK.

The new kind of government that emerged before 1920 operated with the governmental model of "the social" in mind, "society" and the social from the late nineteenth century themselves taking on the qualities of an ordered system, just as before this the economy had done. Instead of the old "natural order" religion and political economy models that had underpinned the state previously, different currents of thought emerged which put a positive valuation on the state and upon community as preconditions for individual self-realisation. German Idealist thought, socialism and New Liberalism represented only some of the new ways of rethinking the state at the time. This rethinking revolved around the realisation that the state must work through the characteristics of society in a much more direct way than hitherto, constituting loyalties, obligations and rights which were more collective than previously. The idea of the "social" came to be characteristic of the entire period in the history of the British state up to the 1970s. Notions of a distinct social sphere, separate from the economic and political ones, had emerged much earlier of course,[26] and these had in part been based upon the idea that the characteristics of this social were evident in the biological sphere, in the vital characteristics of "populations", so that subsequent ideas of the social were often understood in organic, biological terms.

---

[24] T. M. Devine, *The Scottish Nation 1700–2007* (Penguin Books, 2000), p. 288.

[25] Ibid., pp. 287–9.

[26] Patrick Joyce (ed.), *The Social in Question: New Bearings in History and the Social Sciences* (Routledge, 2002).

Thus from around the turn of the twentieth century the idea of a social realm as autonomous developed alongside older understandings. The social question now became a sociological question, as it has indeed in good measure remained until the present, the social sciences since the early twentieth century progressively strengthening their influence on government, markedly so in recent decades in the case of the social science of economics. As Jose Harris has shown, the state from the late nineteenth century became ever more knowledgeable about society.[27] Society, like the economy, was understood to work according to its own laws and to have its own systemic properties; and to be divorced from moral questions, although in practice political interventions were invariably designed to change moral behaviour.[28] One major result of this questioning of the state, and of new conceptions of society as a system, was the extensive "social" legislation we have been considering, widely seen as the foundation of the twentieth-century "welfare state". In 1911 the National Insurance Act in particular represented a new departure whereby government was prosecuted in accordance with the supposed social characteristics of the governed (age, family circumstances, gender, labour), serving in turn to consolidate this social view of the world.

Individual rights, and the rights of families, were in this new dispensation secured not by individual economic action alone but by state action. The provision of pensions and benefits was now secured as a matter of "social" rights, so that individual rights were connected to a web of obligations, rights and solidarities extending across the individual's life, across the lives of all individuals in a population, and between individuals across generations. In short, as a *system* of social relations. However, all of this effort and much of what was to follow in the post-1945 welfare state was liberal in character, even if of the social variant of liberalism. The 1911 Act was consciously designed to provide a framework within which workers were to practice the long-familiar virtue of self-help. If the new political compact of welfare involved the idea of social responsibility, this was essentially the path to realising individual responsibility. What was fundamental to both organic and inorganic individualism, as the "social" and "pre-social" variants of liberalism have been termed, was indeed the individualism.

---

[27] Harris, "Society and the State in Twentieth-Century Britain", p. 78; also "Political Thought and the State" in Green and Whiting (eds.), *The Boundaries of the State*, and Part II of this volume, "The Economy". See Ben Jackson, *Equality and the British Left* (Manchester University Press, 2007), for the later contributions of sociology and economics.

[28] For a fuller account of the twentieth-century state–society relationship see Patrick Joyce, *Encyclopaedia Britannica* entry for the "History of Britain 1815 to the Present", entered 2008.

It has to be remembered, particularly by those who wish to recall a golden age of social democracy in post-1945 Britain, that the social was necessarily a way of governing people, governance through "the social". Simply, there is no credible political rationality available that does not at some stage need to confront the problem of how large numbers of people in highly complex societies are to be governed. Coherent social-democratic alternatives to social liberalism in Britain, never highly developed, have historically been unable to balance governance in the name of the social as the common good (fraternity), with equality, and with forms of practical statecraft which combine participatory, or at least highly reformed representative democracy, and serious thought about how large populations are to be governed.[29] This failing of the left is a general one, and indeed in developing his ideas about governmentality Foucault was attempting to inject some realism into the French left of his day, which he recognised operated without a coherent political rationality, unlike liberalism.

Politically in the twentieth century, in terms now of what I called the state of men, the fundamental structures of the nineteenth-century liberal state have remained substantially in place up to the present (feminism and the undoubted decline of the old form of patriarchal masculism notwithstanding). The historian Ross McKibbin has given expression to this continuity in party-political terms, noting how the prolongation of the established institutions and elites was reinforced rather than lessened after 1920, for as he argues the effect of the decline of political Liberalism after 1914 weakened the robustness of British political culture.[30] Popular Liberalism, in the form of Scottish, Welsh and Irish radicalism, had to some extent stood outside the hierarchies of the Anglo-centric British state. Even before this, as was indicated earlier, radicalism and popular Liberalism after Chartism involved a critique of what contemporaries capitalised as "privilege", not war against the system as a whole, neither the capitalist system nor the political system.[31] This has also been apparent in terms of the presence in British history of collective identities that can properly be called populist, being characterised by an emphasis not so much on class difference as on social inclusiveness and common interests,

[29] Tony Judt's recent book, while a wonderful analysis and description of the illness that blights the land, is notably brief about what can be done about it: *Ill Fares the Land: A Treatise on Our Present Discontents* (Penguin, 2010).

[30] Ross McKibbin, *Parties and People: England 1914–1951* (Oxford University Press, 2009), Ch. 5, and his *Classes and Cultures: England 1918–1951* (Oxford University Press, 2009).

[31] See above, p. 110.

for instance the people as opposed to the ruling class, or the producers versus the idlers.[32]

What was so often at issue in these attitudes was then privilege, not hierarchy. As the writings of Jon Lawrence have shown, the politics of the Labour Party made common cause with these identities, certainly when the Party was most successful.[33] This sort of outlook on the world continued very strongly into the recent past, as the work of Mike Savage shows.[34] In this it is striking how much correspondence there was with past attitudes: in his reworking of the post-1945 survey literature Savage discerns a sense of class identity, but this was widely occupationally dispersed beyond manual labour, and concerned the common feeling of all those who do not set themselves apart, socially and culturally. As earlier, the emphasis is on being true to oneself, being authentic, and, particularly important, being "ordinary". In general, many in the working classes have historically had a fairly conflictual sense of politics and some-times of class, largely in the form of Richard Hoggart's "Us and Them", but by and large they accepted the social order.[35] So, what has historically been uppermost has been a series of populist understandings of the social order, understandings which could be politically conservative, radical or Labourist.[36] Or not party political at all, as in the present consumer-populist dispensation of neoliberal, British mass culture.

Labour, unlike British radicalism before it, took a much more positive view of the British state, so that historically the Labour Party and its leadership simply did not feel the need for wholesale institutional reform. The old working-class leadership was in awe of British traditions, espe-cially the glories of "the British constitution". On the other hand the new post-Second World War middle-class party leadership, the so-called "revisionists", were intent on fighting what they regarded as inefficiency and securing "modernisation". The Labour Party was a mirror of the widespread popular acceptance of the prevailing structures of social and political authority, serving only to magnify these. Of authority it should be noted, not necessarily of structures of inequality, Labour having a highly

---

[32] Patrick Joyce, *Visions of the People: Industrial England and the Question of Class* (Cambridge University Press, 1991), and (ed.), *Class: A Reader* (Oxford University Press, 1995).

[33] John Lawrence, "Paternalism, Class and the British Path to Modernity" in Simon Gunn and James Vernon (eds.), *The Peculiarities of Liberal Modernity in Britain* (University of California Press, 2011).

[34] Mike Savage, *Identities and Social Change in Britain since 1940: The Politics of Method* (Oxford University Press, 2010); Mike Savage, Tony Bennett et al. (eds.), *Culture, Class, Distinction* (Routledge/CRESC, 2009).

[35] Richard Hoggart, *The Uses of Literacy* (Chatto & Windus, 1967).

[36] Patrick Joyce, *Visions of the People*, and *Democratic Subjects: The Self and the Social in Nineteenth-Century England* (Cambridge University Press, 1993).

developed tradition of egalitarianism, some traditions of fraternity, but almost no tradition of understanding and confronting power.[37] The belief that a democratic state could be created by redistributing wealth but not real social and political authority is still a feature of all the major parties, right and left.[38] Labour has always drawn back from attacking the fundamental institutions of the British state, those of representative democracy, the private educational system and Oxbridge, and bureaucracy, in large measure because it actively subscribed to them. The public schools, for example, remained untouched, secure against the threat of abolition once the class-based Education Act of 1944 made it clear that their position was safe.[39] Later on, at the time of the introduction of "comprehensive", ostensibly more egalitarian, secondary education the self-professed egalitarian Anthony Crosland did not touch the public schools nor prevent direct-grant schools becoming public ones.[40]

As Ross McKibbin argues, the 1940s in Britain failed to produce a functioning social democracy. Perry Anderson puts this view in broader and essentially accurate perspective,[41] writing of Britain's rulers:

From the second half of the nineteenth century onwards they did not, and with reason, on the whole regard the working class either as tremendously dangerous or particularly helpless. When Labourism materialised as its principal political expression in the twentieth century, they by and large greeted it, with no less reason, as essentially safe and potentially helpful ... So, educational reforms never created a common school system, the most fundamental of all sources of cultural division. The health system led private practice to flourish at the expense of public service ... historically, in the hybrid arrangements that resulted: bureaucratic conceptions proposing, market considerations disposing – liberals and conservatives met Labour halfway.

"Halfway" is perhaps generous to Labour.

The idea of a "golden age" of social democracy is then, as I have suggested, illusory, although because Labour did not achieve it the aspiration to go beyond the prevailing social liberalism towards something that would challenge underlying liberal tenets was present amongst intellectuals, voters and party workers. However it was not well served by Labour. In Europe the idea of a social democratic golden age has limited purchase too, although its centre-left parties quite rightly looked to the British welfare state with admiration after 1945. Inter-war social turmoil in Europe was followed by the cataclysm of a second world war, and the result after 1945

---

[37] Jackson, *Equality and the British Left*.   [38] McKibbin, *Parties and People*, Ch. 6.
[39] Ibid., pp. 198–200.   [40] Ibid., p. 201 on Crosland.
[41] Perry Anderson, *Spectrum: From Right to Left in the World of Ideas* (Verso, 2005), pp. 54–5. See also from the other end of the political spectrum Maurice Cowling, *The Impact of Labour 1920–1924* (Cambridge University Press, 1971), pp. 10, 11.

was a top-down version of democracy, whether Christian, liberal or social, and whether in the form of nation states or the EU. Continuing what was already a strong post-1918 tradition of state invention, consequent upon the breakup of traditional power blocs, there was little that was more than democratic in name after 1945 in social democracies engineered by bureaucrats and judges who, guided by a widespread fear of popular sovereignty, often did not favour elected institutions, never mind partic-ipatory democracy.[42] Needless to say however, the different models of social-democratic welfarism in Europe were and are vastly more morally attractive, and far less politically and economically injurious, than the neoli-beral state that has in varying measure succeeded them.[43]

If the mythology of a golden age of social democracy is found wanting, even more wanting is the historical political narrative of the centre, libera-lism's own self-image. In understanding freedom as a mode of governance, in considering the political technologies that organise freedom and in looking at the historical connection between liberalism and power, I have indicated the realities underlying the pretensions of the narrative of the liberal state, pretensions that still greatly inform the common sense of the British, or at least the English. As for the political narratives of the right, these, in so far as they do not share the failings of the liberal narrative, which they very largely do, are equally wanting. These deal in a story of aborted modernity, odd enough for a Conservative party that is philo-sophically conservative but not at all odd for one that is philosophically liberal. Thatcherism in particular took this story on board from the histo-rians who had manufactured it. In these accounts Britain is seen as an old country in a benign but also in a pernicious sense, the latter as exemplifying in its ossified social and economic structures the absence of a true moder-nity that has yet to be achieved, and which can be ushered in by the right. However, as I have repeatedly argued in the book, the modernity of Britain is apparent very early in its history and has been assured by the very liberalism the right sometimes criticises but in fact itself espouses. It is equally plain that this liberalism has not only cohabited with "traditional" social hierarchies but that the relationship between the two was comple-mentary, not contradictory.

The underlying liberalism of the British state can be seen to be reflected in the actual forms of the welfare state that it helped fashion. After the 1939–45 war the conversion to public ownership was reflected not in democratic but in bureaucratic models of organisation. The Second

---

[42] See Jan-Werner Muller's revealing argument in his *Contesting Democracy: Political Ideas in Twentieth-Century Europe* (Yale University Press, 2011).

[43] For the different models see Judt, *Ill Fares the Land*, pp. 73–6.

World War had served only to strengthen Labour's belief in the existing values of the British state, and the welfare state, for all its great achievements (above all perhaps the non-insurational public-service health system), generally reflected these values. Its principles of organisation were fundamentally liberal in character, owing more to nineteenth-century models of civic behaviour than anything else. William Beveridge, the chief liberal architect of the social-welfare state, echoed the past and predicted the future in deriding the "Santa Claus state", believing in the application of a narrow version of self-help in the cause of creating a successful liberal, market economy.[44] This vision was never effectively challenged and the ethos of market liberalism has remained tenacious. By the late 1950s Britain was spending less on social services than all its major industrial rivals and many of its minor ones.[45] The 1944 Education Act was felt to be sufficient, and education was to be left to the "experts", with the result that the idea of "innate intelligence" developed rapidly and so the pernicious doctrine of "meritocracy". By the 1950s "equality" had fallen into disrepute, another victim of the Cold War.[46]

What has actually eventuated in the twentieth century has been a prolongation of much of the old liberal order, followed by its partial challenge, which was then succeeded by the introduction of a neoliberal hybrid in many ways more incoherent than the old order or its challenger. Overall there has been a greater plurality of elites and a greater diversity of the sources of wealth after the decline of landed society, so that the model of the higher reaches of British society that is now most cited is one of the series of elite circles interlocking more haphazardly than before. The term "upper class" continued however to have purchase into the 1960s, reflecting the remarkable prolongation of the old governing classes.[47] The class composition of the higher civil service itself very slowly became somewhat more lower-middle class, with the development of new state-service cadres and the consolidation of greater "meritocracy". Chapman's account of leadership in the British civil service, published in 1984,[48] still nonetheless dwells on the preponderance of the Clarendon public schools

[44] Jim Fyrth (ed.), *Labour's Promised Land? Culture and Society in Labour Britain 1945–51* (Lawrence & Wishart, 1995).

[45] Ibid., p. 128.

[46] Steve Iliffe, "An Historic Compromise: Labour and the Foundation of the National Health Service" in ibid.

[47] Frank Mort, *Capital Affairs: The Making of the Permissive Society* (Yale University Press, 2010), Ch. 3; Brian Harrison, *Finding a Role: The United Kingdom, 1970–1990* (Oxford University Press, 2010) and *Seeking a Role: The United Kingdom, 1951–1970* (Oxford University Press, 2009), Ch. 4; McKibbin, *Classes and Cultures*, Ch. 1.

[48] A. Chapman, *The Higher Civil Service in Britain* (Constable, 1970), pp. 17–23, and *Leadership in the British Civil Service* (Croom Helm, 1984).

and Oxbridge, civil servants continuing to have a consciously elaborated training in character and leadership. In the 1980s the gentleman's club life of the Whitehall "village" was still almost as strong as a half-century before.[49] Between 1918 and 1970 the majority of Permanent Secretaries had fathers drawn from the clergy (especially), the armed services and the public service itself, just like the late-nineteenth-century Indian and Home Civil Services.[50] Writing in 1970 of the 1956 intake of high civil servants Chapman remarked the continuing significance of a prior service background.[51] The state service class had changed little by then, meritocracy notwithstanding. In the present, thankfully it must be said for citizens of the market state, the nineteenth-century service ethic seems to continue in the bureaucracy, if in feebler form, despite the inroads made by Wilsonian efficiency, Thatcherite managerialism and New Labour "outsourcing", although whether it will survive Coalition privatisation is unclear.[52]

Economical governance, in the form of the "fiscal constitution", which we have seen to be a major instrument through which the bureaucracy of the state of freedom operated, itself survived the new challenges of the early twentieth century and prospered. The determination that this "constitution" should be kept inviolate from outside manipulation, "knaveproof" as it was put, was central to government far into the twentieth century.[53] The Treasury itself remained fundamentally Gladstonian long into the new century, conceiving of its role as "the national housekeeper and not the national breadwinner". It did not conceive of the way the economy worked as a particular problem, the role of the Treasury and the Bank of England being, as Peter Clarke puts it, "servicing a self-acting system". This all depended on keeping economics out of politics, and although the premises of this were challenged over the free-trade issue at the turn of the twentieth century,[54] Victorian economics continued to be central to the British state until the emergence of the influence of Keynes in the 1940s and 50s, though the inter-war economic situation did something to bring the old system into question. After the Second World War economists moved into

---

[49] On the earlier period H. E. Dale, *The Higher Civil Service of Great Britain* (Oxford University Press, 1941), Ch. 2 on daily life, esp. p. 30; also Ch. 4.

[50] Anthony Kirk-Green, *Britain's Imperial Administrators 1858–1966* (Macmillan, 2000), on the Indian Civil Service.

[51] Peter Barberis, *The Elite of the Elite: Permanent Secretaries in the British Civil Service* (Ashgate, 1996), and *The Civil Service in an Era of Change* (Dartmouth, 1997).

[52] R. A. W. Rhodes, *Everyday Life in British Government* (Oxford University Press, 2011).

[53] Peter Clarke, "The Treasury's Analytical Model of the British Economy between the Wars" in Mary Furner and Barry Supple, *The State and Economic Knowledge: The American and British Experiences* (Cambridge University Press, 1990).

[54] Frank Trentmann, *Free Trade Nation: Commerce, Consumption, and Civil Society in Modern Britain* (Oxford University Press, 2009).

government, and economics into politics. As with earlier moves towards a more "corporatist" economy between the wars, the attempt to present a neutral state was apparent in the party consensus over economic and labour policy, this "Butskellite" accommodation, the "welfare state" with its economic hat on, unravelling with the arrival of neoliberalism.[55]

Again, the roots of this social and economic consensus and of a state perceived to be neutral go deep. For it has been recognised by historians that the mark of the relatively secure relationship between liberal state and society that had evolved in Britain by the late nineteenth century was that other comparable nations in Europe had failed to negotiate quite the same co-operative relationship between state and society seen there.[56] In Britain this depended on a strong not a weak state. Recognition of this serves to once again question – as with the eighteenth-century state – the stereotyped understanding of distinctions between Britain and Europe.[57] Namely, a Europe of a strong state and weak civil society, and a Britain with a weak state and strong civil society. It needs to be remembered that many state powers – to enter private dwellings, to minutely regulate public spaces, for instance – were established in Europe only half a century after they were apparent in Britain, especially in the urban governance of freedom in Britain.[58] A similar time lag was evident in the imposition of income tax, something that brought with it a vast expansion in the powers of the state and of its knowledge apparatus. Taxation like this relied heavily on trusting the state, and the state trusting the citizen. Even the vast powers of the French post-Revolutionary state did not have the administrative firepower to carry off an income tax, and was anyway, like its citizens, too deeply wedded to privacy.[59]

It is however in the area of elite education that the most revealing continuities are to be found. There we get a stronger sense of elite coherence amidst very recent twentieth- and twenty-first-century change. In many respects Oxbridge since the 1960s has seen not the eclipse but the further evolution of the institution of the college, so that it can be said to serve now not the old governing class and the old class system, but the new

---

[55] Martin Daunton, *Just Taxes: The Politics of Taxation in Britain, 1799–1914* (Cambridge University Press, 2002).
[56] Martin Daunton, *Trusting Leviathan: The Politics of Taxation in Britain, 1914–1979* (Cambridge University Press, 2001), p. 183.
[57] See above, p. 238.   [58] See above, pp. 188–9.
[59] Peter Baldwin, "The Victorian State in Comparative Perspective" in Peter Mandler (ed.), *Liberty and Authority in Victorian Britain* (Oxford University Press, 2006). See also Peter Baldwin, *The Narcissism of Minor Differences: How America and Europe are Alike* (Oxford University Press, 2009), and the convincing review by Michael Mann which indicates they are a lot less unlike than Baldwin thinks: "Family Resemblances", *New Left Review*, 63 (May–June 2010).

governing class, in the form of governance through meritocracy. The old pastoral power has however lived on, if in a colder climate than in the inter-war years. Nonetheless, even before 1920 the greater academic emphasis in elite education was resulting in the identification of an Oxbridge back-ground as the cultural capital of perceived talent and merit, middle-class entrants coming to conceive of themselves as representing a sort of "middle way" between aristocracy and the business interests.[60] This cultural capital was still very much based on extra-academic attributes. For instance, in the 1940s if entrants to the Administrative Class of the civil service were drawn more from the poorer sections of the upper-middle class than previously, for these men who lacked the confidence and social graces of the Old Etonian, Oxbridge was a "social revelation", an introduction to a new world of power, connections and influence, and not only intellect.[61]

This was true after the 1940s also, although with the combination of entrance and scholarship examinations introduced in 1962 the old "commoner" entry and status were eclipsed by a wholly meritocratic entrance scheme (one of course still based on the manifest inequalities of the British education system, above all in the shape of the public schools, which accommodated themselves to the new meritocracy very rapidly and successfully). The Anderson Report of 1962 led to Local Education Authorities now paying fees and subsistence for those gaining entry to British universities, and although grants were means tested this meant the end of the old reliance on scholarships for poor grammar school boys.[62] However, the proportion of the nation's children going to university in 1966 was still very small.[63] It had climbed dramatically to 30 per cent by the mid-1990s, most however from better-off backgrounds still, though with the current introduction of university fees this high figure is falling and is set to fall further. Before 1939 the proportion was minute, 1.5 per cent in 1919, 1.7 per cent in 1939, less than in any other comparable European state it should be noted.

---

[60] Paul R. Deslandes, *Oxbridge Men: British Masculinity and the Undergraduate Experience, 1850–1920* (Indiana University Press, 2005). Robert Anderson, *British Universities Past and Present* (Continuum, 2006).

[61] Dale, *The Higher Civil Service*, Ch. 4.

[62] McKibbin, *Classes and Cultures*, Ch. 6. I was an early recipient of the LEA grant in 1965, having moved on from secondary modern school to work, before going to university at Keele and Balliol College, Oxford. Both of these institutions are important parts of the story I have told in this book, and both are linked by the operations of the educational elite, Keele University being the brainchild of the Master of Balliol A. D. Lindsay. See my "More Secondary than Postmodern", *Rethinking History*, 5:3 (December 2001).

[63] See Table 8, "Destination of leavers from different types of school in 1966" (England and Wales)", *The Public Schools Commission: First Report*, vol. I, *Report* (HMSO, 1968), p. 38.

There was a departure from the old nineteenth-century emphasis on character, and the old symbiosis between public school and Oxbridge was to some degree weakened; certainly the old parity of life experience and social condition between Oxbridge and pre-Oxbridge times was altered, so that the old centrality of the power of the *domus* was greatly weakened, at least in its existing and long-maintained form. This weakening was further reinforced by the Family Reform Act of 1969 which meant that students were no longer *in loco parentis* in the public school and college, being legally made adult at the age of eighteen. Sexually mixed colleges from the 1970s also greatly reinforced this change, as did the parallel decline of the old servant and master relationship that had marked the college staff–student relationship in the past. The house of the state had been fairly thoroughly renovated therefore, if not altogether rebuilt. In British society generally liberalising legislation, feminism and the dramatic emergence of women out of the home and into the workforce profoundly changed the old gender balance, and therefore the whole paternalist relationship between the family and the state that had underpinned representative democracy as well as the cultivation of the arts of government amongst the elite. The emergence of more postgraduate-centred institutions from the 1970s also played its part in diluting the older pedagogic ordering of power. Nonetheless, the sense that the "real" Oxbridge experience is an undergraduate and not a postgraduate one is still strong.

The new academicism meant that the "tutorial" itself became more businesslike and less pastoral, as the old "reading" of the subject gave way to its "teaching".[64] However, a considerable degree of continuity is evident also, above all in respect to the formalism of the new academicism, which in many respects can be said to reproduce the formalism of older pedagogic methods which we have seen to be so important. This formalism was evident in the continuing power of the examination, and thus in the formalism and narrowness of what could be learned and taught, at school and at university. Chapman's work on the civil service in 1970 dwelt on how the Oxford tutorial was still very much about the ferreting out of information, the persistent examination of alternative viewpoints, so that concise and informed general accounts would be possible. It was not what one knew but how one processed knowledge that mattered most, so that the tutorial, certainly so in respect of the kind of civil servants it produced, was not about the reproduction of the best intellectuals, of men of ideas, but in one rather unkind formulation that of the "absolute nonentity" of the top civil servant,

---

[64] Keith Thomas, "College Life, 1945–1970" in Brian Harrison (ed.), *The History of the University of Oxford*, vol. VIII, *The 20th Century* (Oxford University Press, 1994), p. 196, and "Science and the Colleges", *Oxford Magazine*, No. 184 (Michaelmas Term, 2000).

his (and slowly her) greatest merit being his (or her) very freedom from ideas.[65] The Oxford tutorial itself – the college system being always stronger there than in Cambridge – was in fact still highly suited to the high civil service: in 1988 Oxford had forty-six successes in the final selection for the civil service, its nearest rival Cambridge fourteen. In terms of Foreign Office entry, Oxford had ten out of twenty-three in that year.[66]

However, what is still striking is the continuing force of college life despite all this.[67] Increased numbers in the 1960s led to increased college building, and the numbers of undergraduates living outside college went down from 1970. The physical restoration of Oxford in the 1960s meant a new presence for the old university, and with it a reinvention of the college. The development of mixed residential institutions also meant that social life was resituated around the college. If the numbers of independent/public school entrants declined at certain times, the old school–college links recovered their usual robust health eventually, until today, with a very small proportion of the school population, the independent schools still produce roughly half of Oxbridge entrants. This state of affairs does not seem to trouble these institutions unduly, their efforts to secure social equality of admission being neutralised by their slavish devotion to unimaginative ideas of what "intelligence" is and to educational "merit" as measured by the examination.[68] As Stefan Collini, a Cambridge academic, has put the matter:

Cambridge still functions as, among other things, a long coming-out party for some of the more examination-adept among the children of the professional and upper middle classes of, predominantly, South East England (including London). All this is a reminder of how it has also maintained its intimate links with the governing elite. One of the things which will seem to historians of a hundred years hence most in need of explaining is how it was that (through the 1980s) the state continued to subsidise the existence of colleges, a few of which are seriously rich in their own right.

As the more sympathetic Keith Thomas of Oxford put it, in the end "the collegiate ideal thus emerged from the tumult of the 1960s and early 1970s

---

[65] Chapman, *The Higher Civil Service*, pp. 194–5.
[66] Michael Brock, "The University since 1970" in M. S. Brock and M. C. Curthoys (eds.), *The History of Oxford*, vol. VI, *Nineteenth-Century Oxford* (Oxford University Press, 1991), Pt. I, p. 771.
[67] On this see ibid.; also A. H. Halsey, "The Franks Commission" in Harrison (ed.), *The History of the University of Oxford*, vol. VIII, pp. 726–31, 769–72; also Brian Harrison, "College Life 1918–1939" in the same volume.
[68] For a revealing 1960s definition of "merit", by the Chancellor of Oxford, namely the line steered between Eton and Manchester Grammar School, cloister and commerce, see Joseph A. Soares, *The Decline of Privilege: The Modernisation of Oxford University* (Stanford University Press, 1999), p. 443.

into undiminished vitality". In its modified state, "the Oxford college would continue to flourish and provide its members with a living and working environment superior to that yet devised by any other academic institution".[69]

The reinvention of Oxbridge was accompanied by that of the public schools. Now responsive to the demands of educational success, and sensitive to the requirements and aspirations of the newly wealthy from the 1960s,[70] *noblesse oblige* was replaced by teaching pupils how to help themselves, the schools being seminaries for the inculcation of modern freedom in the era of emerging neoliberalism.[71]

The Labour government of Harold Wilson said a lot but did nothing. The headmaster of Winchester, John Thorn, put it thus: "Wilson, Crossman, Crosland, Jay, Healey had highly trained minds and believed in the iron rules of good grammar, in the importance of intellectually tough sixth forms. They had no wish to see such things slip away in the name of social equality and fairness."[72] Quite so, these men were true children of the nineteenth-century public school, themselves products of the grammar grind and the playing field, the possessors of the sort of athletic mind these very athletic institutions produced. Intellectual gymnastics and not ideas, calculation not inspiration, this for them and many other political leaders before and since, was the kind of intellectual merit that should count in government and in society. The spin machine of the public schools came into operation from the 1970s. Victory to the public-school system was by then becoming apparent in the manifest failings of the comprehensive, state system.[73] From this time the public schools, which rebranded themselves as "independent" schools, have never looked back, as the composition of the current Coalition government indicates. The schools still serve as the institutional and pedagogic anchor of the new sorts of governing elites of the "market state" which emerged from the 1980s, as the old "social state" fell apart.

From this time the model of the market as a self-regulating system was itself reinvented with new force, although neoliberalism in the long historical perspective was simply a continuation of the state of freedom by other

---

[69] Thomas, "College Life, 1945–1970", p. 215; and Stefan Collini, "Company Histories: Cambridge University PLC and Social Anthropology Ltd" in *English Pasts: Essays in History and Culture* (Oxford University Press, 1999), pp. 278–9.

[70] Christopher Tyerman, *A History of Harrow School 1324–1991* (Oxford University Press, 2000).

[71] Ibid., pp. 546–64.

[72] John Thorn, *The Road to Winchester* (Weidenfeld & Nicolson, 1989), p. 97. See also Geoff Dench (ed.), *The Rise and Rise of Meritocracy* (Blackwell, 2006).

[73] Thorn, ibid.

means. Social life itself was marketised so as to be amenable to governmental interventions. In a multitude of ways the citizen's life was thrown
open to the idea that the capacity for self-realisation could only be truly
obtained through individual activity. Institutions like the National Health
Service were reformed as a series of internal markets. These markets were
to be governed by what has been called "the new public management",
which originating in the USA found its true home in Britain, despite the
real advances of the social state. The market state involved a focus upon
accountability, with explicit standards and measures of performance.
The ethical change involved a transition from the idea of public service
to one of private management.

Parallel to this "culture of accountability" was the emergence of an
"audit society" in which formal, and professionally sanctioned, monitoring systems replaced the trust that earlier versions of relationship
between state and society had invested in professional specialists of all
sorts. The professions themselves, for instance university teaching, were
opened up to this sort of audit, which was all the more onerous because,
directed from above, it was carried out by the professionals themselves, so
preserving the fiction of professional freedom. The social state gave way
to a state that was now regarded as "enabling", permitting the citizen,
the school, the firm, the locality, and so on, to freely choose. This politics
of choice was common across the political board, though in the New
Labour vision there was a more active concern to create ethical subjects
who would exchange rights for obligations in a new realisation of marketised communities. In turn this emphasis on ethicised "community" has
been plagiarised by the Conservatives under David Cameron in the form
of the so-called "big society".

This new relation of state and society has involved the devolution of
rule to the citizen himself and herself, something reflected in the host of
self-help activities to be found in Britain from the 1990s, from the new
concern with alternative health therapies to the management of schools.
Reflecting this situation, in which the state made the citizen a consumer or
a "client", was the increasingly important role of the consumption of goods
in constructing "lifestyles" through which individual choice would supposedly realise self-expression and self-fulfilment. The old power of the pen
and of the house, so much the themes of my account of the state, had not
so much disappeared in this new dispensation as been reinvented, or at
least resituated. They are still at the centre of state concerns in the present,
and have just as much resonance as in previous times, although now in
dramatically altered forms. The house, as a spatial centre where the drama
of governance is played out, now takes the form of the ordinary domestic
habitation. There a new kind of hyper-privatised self has developed.

This haven of the domicile, the "house" in a new register, but still a primary locus of security, dreaming and identity, was the prime site in which lifestyle satisfaction could be achieved. It was also the place from which the new world of risk and boundless consumer possibility outside could be managed from the security of inside.

The new sort of liberal self emerging was thrown open to the governance of the free market as much as the governance of the state of freedom. The instrument that navigated the world outside was in fact simply a new version of the pen, and the new emblem of the contemporary communications state in its advanced technological form, namely the electronic keypad. This was in effect where the new power of writing lay. As we have seen the management of information systems, and the government of the Internet, came to the fore in Britain as in almost every other state. In Britain the surveillance state took an extraordinarily highly developed form, from the multiplication of CCTV to the much more disturbing ramifications of what I called earlier the "data state" and the governance of the future. A brave new political world emerged in which the hyper-privatised self was joined to entirely new kinds of electronic community, the virtual communities of the Internet of course, and in Britain especially the community of television, in the revealing new form of "reality TV". In this new realisation of the privatised liberal individual – this new object of organised freedom – was born in a reciprocal and complementary process the collective identities he and she inhabited. These, as I have suggested, were fundamentally populist in character.

In the light of these changes, the state had become re-formed in a new way, one however which seems still in considerable measure in line with the long historical trajectory of the state of freedom. This devolution of power to the individual self meant the central state lost power in some directions, particularly to the armies of non-state "experts" that emerged in private health, finance, lifestyle management and the other parts of the self-help industry. However there was limited chance of a "rule of experts" usurping the state, and the new technologies of the self these experts deployed were still highly orchestrated by the state, which initiated some forms of expertise and appropriated others. Despite these dramatic changes the continuities with the Victorian and Edwardian state settlement are strongly apparent in the argument I have so far presented. A late Victorian would not have felt totally out of place in Britain up to the 1970s, and in some respects perhaps even in the late 1980s. Obviously it would be mistaken to underestimate the degree of change over the long-term, and the new forms and meanings given to old social and political processes and institutions in the long history of the liberal state and of organised freedom. Nonetheless, the degree of continuity is everywhere striking.

However, the degree of separation from this past since the early 1990s is, as I earlier suggested, also striking. The neoliberal, more hybrid, state succeeded earlier forms of the state of freedom, which had themselves absorbed and neutralised the partial challenge to liberalism by social democracy after 1945. This new version of the liberal state appears however to be far less coherent and socially anchored than the old forms. The causes of this lie in the instabilities created by the information revolution of the 1990s, the economic crises of the succeeding decade, and the economic and political globalisation which directly threaten the long-established power of the nation state. For Britain existence within the European Union posed similar problems to globalisation.

On the one hand, however, in navigating these instabilities Britain typically enough appeared to be going forward to the past, not as historians would advise back to the future. Increased inequalities of all sorts have proliferated since the 1980s, chillingly recalling an old history.[74] The state became more and more centralised, so that nothing much appeared to have changed there either, and the educational system seemed well on the way back to Victorian times, with versions of payment by results at one end of the age spectrum, and the end of the great tradition of public university education at the other. The financial City of London however perhaps best represents what was going on, for it symbolises the incoherence and instability of the new dispensation and the high degree of rupture from the past. It became in effect an offshore financial centre in which its most important institutions were not British at all. London itself became a global city, to all intents and purposes detached from the rest of the country. Globally networked, the educational institutions that serviced the city became globally networked too. The London School of Economics and the London Business School led the way and the power of Oxbridge lessened, although with the effective end of public education Oxbridge was also on the way to this globalised condition if it was to financially prosper. The leading public schools also became globalised institutions, for their astronomically high school fees tended to force out many but by no means all British parents. The public-school brand went global, Harrow for instance opening a branch of the shop in China. In sum, the British state was being globalised from without and de-Anglicised from within, with the emergence of more vibrant nationalisms than previously.

---

[74] Pat Thane (ed.), *Unequal Britain: Inequalities in Britain since 1945* (Continuum, 2010); also Henrik Jensen (ed.), *The Welfare State: Past, Present and Future* (Edizioni Plus, Universita di Pisa, 2002).

The speed and completeness of the decline of the old class and status order is striking, and along with it the decline of the predominance of the old Duty ethic. Anthony Sampson has pointed to the emergence of a new Establishment, in effect one that came to power by denigrating and undermining the old one, a populist anti-Establishment Establishment in effect.[75] However, this Establishment appears to be far less coherent than the old forms of the governing classes. Its centre of gravity has shifted more than previously to advertising, public relations and (especially) the media. However there are all sorts of links to what is still probably central, assuming there is any more a centre, namely the business-political complex, as we should rightly call it, expressed as this is in the power of the business political lobby and the great corporation. The consumer populism that drove the economy in the boom years represented the full alliance in action, based on credit, shopping and the manipulation of dreams as it was. The economy was of course eventually driven over the edge, although the chief credit for this has to go to the unregulated City-based financial interests. For all the rhetoric of choice a new and dangerous kind of cultural uniformity had emerged, which was partly the result and partly the cause of the profound disaffection with politics and the political classes that, socially high and low, has with increasing force marked Britain in the last few years. This loss of faith in the political classes and politics, effectively the end, temporary or not, of the belief in the neutrality of the state that was established in Victorian times, both reflected and compounded the instability of the political situation in general, and the incoherence of the new elites.

Instability and incoherence were represented most dramatically by the new reign of money, not Duty as in previous times. Therefore, if we look for the principle of "connectivity" of the very recent state of freedom then it is here, in money, that we find an important element of it. As Anthony Sampson put it, "It was in the nature of Britain's democracy that there was no single dominating centre, and much of the power depended on the fixers and go-betweens who would connect one circle with another."[76] The new fixers and go-betweens operate with the material technologies of money, and in a situation where trust is enormously low and risk is enormously high money is a weak and unreliable, as well as morally empty, source of connection, not only for the new elites but also for the body politic. As Sampson recognises, the "centre" of the state in Britain today appears increasingly to be an empty place. This situation is compounded by the emergence of a dedicated political class, made up of politicians and

---

[75] Sampson, *Who Runs This Place?*, pp. 347–8.   [76] Ibid., p. 349.

policy advisers whose only reality is politics itself. The old ethical style of life of the politician has moved on from the long-lived legacy of the late Victorian politics of public duty, also from the party politics that followed it, and which was so much influenced by what went before. In this kind of politics everything had not yet been sacrificed to the central executive, and to the *Lebensführung* of the politician as now a fully professional one.[77]

Unable to accommodate change, to achieve stability, and least of all unable to achieve equality, as society has become more diverse and plural the state and its institutions have remained rigid and are increasingly alienated from the public. It is not the case that social democracy has failed, for in Britain it can be said never to have been properly tried, that is with political and historical clear-sighted determination. The belief that a democratic state could be created by redistributing wealth but not social and political authority still characterises British politics, and for this to change the governed have to take on the work of governance themselves. It is truly time for those who are in reality the state's practitioners to become its guardians. Our "doxic submission" is not assured,[78] however much the state of freedom has sought to make us, the children of freedom, the willing subjects of our own subordination.[79]

---

[77] Harrison, *Finding a Role*, pp. 448–52.   [78] See above, p. 36.

[79] In a projected third volume on the relationship of freedom and power in Britain, titled *The Children of Freedom*, I aim to consider the years since 1945 in more detail than is possible here.

Select bibliography

ARCHIVAL SOURCES

POST OFFICE

POST 1: Post Office: Treasury Correspondence 1686–1977

POST 10: Post Office: Records on the Conveyance of Mails by Road, Inland Services 1786–1990

POST 11: Post Office: Records on Conveyance of Mail by Railways 1827–1975

POST 12: Post Office: Contracts and Voyage Records on the Conveyance of Inland Mails by Sea 1748–1965

POST 14: Post Office: Inland Mails Organisation and Circulation Records 1757–1982

POST 17: Post Office: Inland Mail: Organisation, Circulation and Sorting 1797–1988

POST 18: Post Office: Travelling Post Offices 1832–1992

POST 19: Post Office: Postal Business Statistics 1839–1990

POST 21: Post Office: Maps 1757–1991

POST 22: Post Office: Counter Operations and Services *c*. 1910–2001

POST 23: Post Office: Inland Mail Services: Letter Post 1636–1989

POST 24: Post Office: Newspaper Post 1791–1996

POST 25: Post Office: Inland Mail Services: Parcel Post 1824–1985

POST 30: Post Office: Registered Files, Military Papers

POST 40: Post Office: Postmaster General's Reports: Documents 1791–1841

POST 58: Post Office: Staff Nomination and Appointments 1737–1972

POST 59: Post Office: Staff: Establishment Books 1791–1983

POST 61: Post Office: the Uniforms and Discipline 1765–*c*. 1995

POST 62: Post Office: Staff: Welfare 1855–1999

POST 63: Post Office: Staff: Training 1869–1990

POST 64: Post Office: Staff: Medical Provision and Sick Leave 1892–1985

POST 65: Post Office: Staff Association 1866–1995

POST 68: Post Office: Rules and Instructions 1729–2003

POST 72: Post Office: Headquarters Administration and Policy 1786–1972

POST 73: Post Office: Regional Administration and Operations 1860–1959

POST 75: Post Office: Savings Bank, Insurance and Investment Services 1828–1975

POST 76: Post Office: Engineering 1882–1984

POST 82: Post Office: Telegraphs, Post Office (Inland) 1837–1939

POST 83: Post Office: Telegraphs, Post Office (Overseas) 1849–1934

POST 92: Post Office: Post Office Publications 1855 to Present

POST 97: Post Office: Private Office Papers: Lord Walsingham, Joint Postmaster General 1787–92

POST 98: Post Office: Private Papers: Sir Francis Freeling, Secretary 1793–1829

POST 100: Post Office: Private Papers: Rowland Hill 1836–79

POST 107: Post Office: Notices to the Public and Instructions 1768–1937

POST 111: Post Office: Newspaper Cuttings 1685 to Present

POST 120: Post Office: Investigations Department 1836–1993

PUBLIC SCHOOLS

Eton College Archives

ECR 60/4 Appointment of Provosts

ECR 60/5 Appointment of Fellows

ECR 60/6 Provosts and Fellows

P series – Provost's papers

P1: Rev. Joseph Goodall (1760–1840)

P3: Edward Craven Hawtrey, Provost 1853–62

P4: John James Hornby (1826–1909), Provost 1884–1909

P5: Edmond Warre (1837–1920), Provost 1909–18

P6: Montague Rhodes James (1862–1936), Provost 1918–36

ED Series 1–218: Masters' and parents' letters, journals, reports, diaries, miscellaneous

Eton Calendar

Eton College Chronicle

Arthur Benson Scrapbook

Rugby School Archives

Miscellaneous printed items, including sermons

Shrewsbury School Library Collection

"Reminiscences by James Basil Oldham, 1882–1962", typescript, together with the handwritten manuscript

Letters and papers of J. B. Oldham deposited by A. E. Gunther, 1976

INDIA OFFICE

EUR.F.102, 111: India Office Memoranda

L/AG/29: Accountant General's Records, 1601–1974, Correspondence of the Department, 1807–1959

L/AG/30: Accountant General's Records, 1601–1974, Home Establishment Records, *c.* 1800–1959

L/P&J/6: Public and Judicial Department Records, Departmental Papers: Annual Files, 1880–1930

L/P&S/3: Political and Secret Department Records, Home Correspondence, 1807–1911

L/PO: Private Office papers, *c.* 1858–1948

L.PWD/6: Public Works Department Records, 1839–1931, Departmental Papers: Public Works, Annual Files, 1880–1926

L/R/4: Record Department Records, 1859–1959, Internal Department Papers, 1876–1951

L/R/7: Record Department Records, 1859–1959, Departmental Papers, Annual Files, 1913–48

V/27: Official Publications, *c.* 1760–1957, Monographs, 1774–1950

X: Map Collections, 1700–1960

Z/F/4: Registers and Indexes, *c.* 1700–1950, Registers of Board's Collections, 1794–1858

OFFICIAL PAPERS

PARLIAMENTARY PAPERS

Parliamentary Papers, 1838, Minutes of Evidence Taken before the Select Committee on Postage

Journal of the House of Commons, 1838, VIII

Parliamentary Papers 1856 (368), XIV

Parliamentary Papers 1857, session 2 (152)

Parliamentary Papers, 1864, XX, Public School Commission, First Report of Her Majesty's Commissioners (Clarendon Report)

Parliamentary Papers, 1877 (312) XV, Select Committee on Public Offices

Parliamentary Papers, 1883 (C.3757), Fifth Report of the General Prisons Board, Ireland, 1882–83; with Appendices

Parliamentary Papers, 1912, Royal Commission on Public Records, India Office Evidence

The Public Schools Commission, First Report, vol. I, *Report* (HMSO, 1968)

WEBSITES

www.all-souls.ox.ac.uk/content/Statutes

www.bbc.co.uk/comedy/yesminister

www.crappublicschools.org

www.dp-dhl.com.en.about_us.history

www.earlyofficemuseum.com

www.headington.org.uk

www.history.ac.uk/reviews/review/790

www.inventorsabout.com

www.nationalarchives.gov.uk
www.officemuseum.com
www.postalheritage.org
www.somersethouse.org.uk/history
www.unask.com/website/handwriting

REFERENCE WORKS CITED. PLACE OF
PUBLICATION, NOT PUBLISHER DETAILS,
GIVEN FOR WORKS BEFORE 1950

Abbot, Evelyn, *The Life and Letters of Benjamin Jowett, M.A.* (London, 1897), 3 vols.
Agar, Jonathan, *The Government Machine: A Revolutionary History of the Computer* (MIT Press, 2003).
Aingier, Sir Arthur Campbell, *Memories of Eton 60 Years Ago* (London, 1917).
Alder, Ken, *Engineering the Revolution: Arms and Enlightenment in France, 1763–1815* (Princeton University Press, 1997).
  "Making Things the Same: Representation, Tolerance and the End of the Ancien Regime in France", *Social Studies of Science*, 28:4 (1998).
Aldford, Robert D., "Paradigms of Relations between State and Society", reprinted in John A Hall (ed.), *The State: Critical Concepts* (Routledge, 1994), 2 vols., vol. I.
Alington, C. A., *Two Men: A Memoir* (Oxford University Press, 1919).
Allen, B. M., *Sir Robert Morant* (London, 1935).
Allen, Michael and Hecht, Gabrielle (eds.), *Technologies of Power* (MIT Press, 2001).
Allen, Natalie, *Through the Letter-Box* (N. Allen, 1988).
Anderson, Perry, *Arguments within English Marxism* (NLB and Verso, 1980).
  Spectrum: From Right to Left in the World of Ideas (Verso, 2005).
Anderson, Robert, *British Universities Past and Present* (Continuum, 2006).
Annan, Noel, *The Dons: Mentors, Eccentrics, Geniuses* (Harper Collins, 1999).
  "The Intellectual Aristocracy" in J. H. Plumb (ed.), *Studies in Social History: A Tribute to G. M. Trevelyan* (Longmans Green, 1955).
Anon., *The Administration of the Post Office, from the Introduction of Mr. Rowland Hill's Plan of Penny Postage Up to the Present Time ...* (Edinburgh, 1844; Col. H. W. Hill (ed.), London, 1949).
  How to Write: A Pocket Manual of Composition and Letter Writing (Glasgow, 1883).
[William Dockwra], *A Penny Well Bestowed, Or a Brief Account of the New Design contrived for the great increase of Trade, and Ease of Correspondence, to the great Advantage of the Inhabitants of all sorts, by Conveying of LETTERS or PACQUETS under a Pound Weight, to and from all parts within the Cities of London and Westminster; and the Out Parishes within the Weekly Bills of Mortality, For One Penny* (London, 1680).
Archer, R., *Secondary Education in the Nineteenth Century* (London, 1921).
Ascham, R., *The Scholemaster* [1570] in Ascham, R., *English Works*, ed. W. A. Wright (Cambridge University Press, 1970), reprint of the 1904 edition.

Asendorf, Christoph, *Batteries of Life: On the Story of Things and their Perception in Modernity* (California University Press, 1993).

Ashworth, W. J., "England and the Machinery of Reason 1782 to 1830" in Iwan Rhys Momus (ed.), *Bodies/Machines* (Berg, 2002).

"Memory, Efficiency and Symbolic Analysis: Charles Babbage, John Herschel and the Industrial Mind", *Isis* (1996).

"System of Terror: Samuel Bentham, Accountability and Dockyard Reform during the Napoleonic Wars", *Social History* 23:1 (January 1998).

Aspinall, A., *Politics and the Press, c. 1780–1850* (London, 1949).

Bachelard, Gaston, *The Poetics of Space* (Beacon Press edn, 1994).

Baer, Laura, *Lines of the Nation: Indian Railway Workers, Bureaucracy and the Intimate Historical Self* (Columbia University Press, 2007).

Baldwin, Peter, *The Narcissism of Minor Differences: How America and Europe are Alike* (Oxford University Press, 2009).

"The Victorian State in Comparative Perspective" in Peter Mandler (ed.), *Liberty and Authority in Victorian Britain* (Oxford University Press, 2006).

Balogh, Thomas, "The Apotheosis of the Dilletante in the Establishment of Mandarins" in Hugh Thomas (ed.), *Crisis in the Civil Service* (Anthony Blond, 1968).

Bamford, T. W., "Thomas Arnold and the Victorian Idea of the Public School" in Brian Simon and Ian Bradley (eds.), *The Victorian Public School: The Development of the Educational Institution* (Gill & Macmillan, 1975).

Rise of the Public Schools: A Study of Boys' Public Boarding Schools in England and Wales from 1837 to the Present Day (Nelson, 1967).

Banton, Mandy, *Administering the Empire, 1801–1968 – A Guide to the Records of the Colonial Office* (University of London, Institute of Historical Research, 2008).

Barberis, Peter, *The Civil Service in an Era of Change* (Dartmouth, 1997).

The Elite of the Elite: Permanent Secretaries in the British Civil Service (Ashgate, 1996).

Barry, Andrew, *Political Machines: Governing a Technological Society* (Continuum Press, 2001).

Barthes, Roland, *Writing Degree Zero: Elements of Semiology* (Hill & Wang, 1977).

Bates, L. M., *Somerset House: Four Hundred Years of History* (Muller, 1967).

Bayly, Christopher, *The Birth of the Modern Age, 1780–1914* (Blackwell, 2005).

Empire and Information: Intelligence Gathering and Social Communication in India, 1780–1870 (Cambridge University Press, 1996).

Becker, Peter and von Krosigk, Rüdiger (eds.), *Figures of Authority: Contributions towards a Cultural History of Governance from the Seventeenth to the Twentieth Century* (PIE, Peter Lang, 2008).

and Clark, Willliam (eds.), *Little Tools of Knowledge: Historical Essays on Academic and Bureaucratic Practices* (University of Michigan Press, 2001).

"Objective Distance and Intimate Knowledge: On the Structure of Criminalistic Observation and Description" in Becker and Clark (eds.), *Little Tools of Knowledge.*

Beckett, Ian (ed.), *The Oxford History of the British Army* (Oxford University Press, 1994).

Bennett, Edward, *The Romance of the Post Office* (London, 1919).

Bennett, Tony, "Habit, Instinct, Survival; Repetition, History, Biopower" in Simon Gunn and James Vernon (eds.), *The Peculiarities of Liberal Modernity in Britain* (California University Press, 2011).

and Dodsworth, Francis, Rose, Nikolas and Joyce, Patrick, organisers of the "Government and Freedom" seminar, ESRC seminar series 2008–10, at www.archive.cresc.ac.uk/projects/government.

and Savage, Mike et al., *Culture, Class, Distinction* (Routledge, 2009).

Bentley, Michael, "'Boundaries' in Theoretical Language about the British State" in S. J. G. Green and R. C. Whiting (eds.), *The Boundaries of the State in Modern Britain* (Cambridge University Press, 1996).

Bernal, Martin, *Black Athena: The Afroasiatic Roots of Classical Civilization,* vol. I, *The Fabrication of Ancient Greece 1785–1985* (Vintage, 1991).

Biagini, Eugenio, *Liberty, Retrenchment and Reform: Popular Liberalism in the Age of Gladstone, 1860–1880* (Cambridge University Press, 1992).

"Neo-Roman Liberalism: 'Republican' Values and British Liberalism, circa 1860–1875", *History of European Ideas,* 29 (2003).

Biernacki, Richard, *The Fabrication of Labour: Germany and Britain, 1640–1914* (California University Press, 1995).

"Method and Metaphor after the New Cultural History" in Victoria E. Bonnell, and Lynn Hunt (eds.), *Beyond the Cultural Turn: New Directions in the Study of Society and Culture* (University of California Press, 1999).

Bishop, T. J. H., *Winchester and the Public School Elite: A Statistical Analysis* (Faber and Faber, 1967).

Bizup, Joseph, *Manufacturing Culture: Vindications of Early Victorian Industry* (University of Virginia Press, 2003).

Blackbourn, David, *The Conquest of Nature: Water, Landscape and the Making of Modern Germany* (Jonathan Cape, 2006).

Blakeley, Brian L., *The Colonial Office, 1868–1892* (Duke University Press, 1972).

Blunt, Edward, *The ICS: The Indian Civil Service* (London, 1937).

Bödeker, Hans Erich, "On the Origins of the 'Statistical Gaze': Modes of Perception, Forms of Knowledge, and Ways of Writing in the Early Social Sciences" in Peter Becker and William Clark (eds.), *Little Tools of Knowledge.*

Bogdanor, Vernon, "Oxford and the Mandarin Culture: The Past that is Gone" in Harry Judge (ed.), *The University and Public Education: The Contribution of Oxford* (Routledge, 2007).

Bourdieu, Pierre, *Distinction: A Social Critique of the Judgement of Taste* (Routledge & Kegan Paul, 1984).

Practical Reason: On the Theory of Action (Stanford University Press, 1998).

"Rethinking the State: On the Genesis and Structure of the Bureaucratic Field", *Sociological Theory,* 12:1 (March 1994).

The State Nobility. Elite Schools in the Field of Power (Polity Press, 1996).

Bourne, J. M., *Patronage and Society in Nineteenth-Century England* (Edward Arnold, 1986).

Bowen, H. V., *The Business of Empire: The East India Company and Imperial Britain, 1756–1833* (Cambridge University Press, 2005).

Bramston, John, *The Colonial Office from Within* (London, 1901).

Branco, Rui, "Fieldwork, Map Making and State Formation: A Study in the History of Science and Administration" in Peter Becker and Rüdiger von Krosigk (eds.), *Figures of Authority: Contributions towards a Cultural History of Governance from the Seventeenth to the Twentieth Century* (PIE Peter Lang, 2008).

Bremner, H. M., "Nation and Empire in the Government Architecture of Mid-Victorian London: The Foreign and India Office Reconsidered", *Historical Journal*, 48:3 (2005).

Brewer, John, *The Sinews of Power: War, Money and the English State 1688–1783* (Unwin Hyman, 1989).

Bridges, Sir Edward, "Administration: What is it? And can it be Learned?" in A. Dunshire (ed.), *The Making of an Administrator* (Manchester University Press, 1956).

Portrait of a Profession: The Civil Service Tradition (Cambridge University Press, 1950).

Briggs, Asa, *Victorian People: A Reassessment of Persons and Themes 1851–1867* (Penguin, 1965).

Victorian Things (Sutton edn, 2003).

Brock, M. S., "The University since 1970" in M. S. Brock and M. C. Curthoys (eds.), *The History of Oxford*, vol. VI, *Nineteenth-Century Oxford* (Oxford University Press, 1991).

Brooke, C. N. L., *A History of the University of Cambridge*, vol. IV, *1870–1900* (Cambridge University Press, 1995).

Broughton, Trev Lynn, and Rogers, Helen (eds.), *Gender and Fatherhood in the Nineteenth Century* (Palgrave Macmillan, 2007).

Browning, R., *Political and Constitutional Ideas of the Court Whigs* (Louisiana University Press, 1982).

Bruford, W. H., *The German Tradition of Self-Cultivation: "Bildung" from Humboldt to Thomas Mann* (Cambridge University Press, 2010).

Bryant, P. M. H., *Harrow* (London, 1936).

Buckham, George, *The Universal Penman* (London, 1741).

Burchell, Graham, "Peculiar Interests: Civil Society and Governing 'The System of Natural Liberty'" in Graham Burchell *et al.* (eds.), *The Foucault Effect* (Harvester, 1991).

Burdon Haldane, Richard, *Richard Burdon Haldane: An Autobiography* (London, 1929).

Burgess, Henry, *A Plan for Obtaining a More Speedy Postage Communication Between London and the Distant Parts of the Kingdom* (London: Printed for the Author, 1819).

Burrow, J. W., *Whigs and Liberals: Continuity and Change in English Political Thought* (Oxford University Press, 1988).

Burtt, S., *Virtue Transformed: Political Argument in England, 1688–1740* (Cambridge University Press, 1992).

Busbridge, E. M., *Collins Letter Writing and Etiquette* (London, 1908).

Butler, George, *Sermons and Lectures Delivered in Eton College Chapel, in the Years 1848–9*, unpublished, printed in Eton by E. P. Williams, 1849.

Sermons Preached in Cheltenham College Chapel (Cambridge and London, 1862).

Byrne, L., and Churchill, E., *Changing Eton: A Survey of Conditions based on the History of Eton since the Royal Commission of 1862–64* (London, 1937).

Callon, Michel (ed.), *The Laws of the Markets* (Blackwell, 1998).

Calvert, C. A, *History of the Manchester Post Office, 1625–1900* (J. E. Lee, 1967).

Campbell-Smith, Duncan, *Masters of the Post: The Authorised History of the Royal Mail* (Allen Lane/Penguin, 2011).

Cantwell, John G., *The Public Record Office 1838–1958* (HMSO, 1991).

Caplan, Jane and Torpey, John, *Documenting Individual Identity: The Development of State Practices in the Modern World* (Princeton University Press, 2001).

Card, Tim, *Eton Established: A History from 1440 to 1860* (John Murray, 2001).
Eton Renewed: A History from 1860 to the Present Day (John Murray, 1994).

Carralho, David, *Forty Centuries of Ink* (London, 1904).

Carroll, Patrick, *Colonial Discipline: The Making of the Irish Convict System* (Four Courts Press, 2000).
Science, Culture, and Modern State Formation (University of California Press, 2008).

Carter, Philip, "Polite 'Persons': Character, Biography and the Gentleman", *Transactions of the Royal Historical Society*, 12 (2002).

Castells, Manuel, *The Rise of Network Society* (Blackwell, 2000).
Ceylon Civil Service Manual, Being a Compilation of Government Minutes, Circulars, Etc, with an Appendix Containing a Summary of Colonial Regulations, a List of Legislative Enactments in Force, and a Glossary of Ceylon Terms. Corrected up to 30th of November 1865 (London, 1865).

Chakrabarty, Dipesh, *Provincialising Europe: Postcolonial Thought and European Difference* (Princeton University Press, 2007).

Chandler Jr., A. D., *Strategy and Structure: Chapters in Industrial Enterprise* (MIT Press, 1962).
The Visible Hand: The Managerial Revolution in American Business (Harvard University Press, 1977).

Chandos, John, *Boys Together: English Public Schools, 1800–1864* (Oxford University Press, 1985).

Chapman, R. A., *Ethics in the British Civil Service* (Routledge, 1988).
The Higher Civil Service in Britain (Constable, 1970).
Leadership in the British Civil Service (Croom Helm, 1984).
and J. R. Greenaway, *The Dynamics of Administrative Reform* (Croom Helm, 1980).

Charlesworth, Michael, *J. B. Oldham of Oldham's Hall* (privately published, 1986).

Chartier, Roger *et al.* (eds.), *Correspondence: Models of Letter-Writing from the Middle Ages to the Nineteenth Century* (Polity, 1997).

Chester, Norman, *The English Administrative System* (Oxford University Press, 1981).
Civil Service Calendar, 1886, Containing the Official Regulations of Her Majesty's Civil Service Commissioners (London, 1886).

Clanchy, Michael, "Does Writing Construct the State?", *Journal of Historical Sociology*, 15:1 (March 2002).
From Memory to Written Record: England 1066–1307 (Blackwell Wiley, 1992).

Clarke, M. L., *Classical Education in Britain 1500–1900* (Cambridge Univrsity Press, 1959).

Clarke, Peter, "The Treasury's Analytical Model of the British Economy between the Wars" in Mary Furner and Barry Supple, *The State and Economic Knowledge: The American and British Experiences* (Cambridge University Press, 1990).

Clinton, Alan, *Post Office Workers: A Trade Union and Social History* (George Allen & Unwin, 1984).

Collini, Stefan, "Company Histories: Cambridge University PLC and Social Anthropology Ltd" in Stefan Collini, *English Pasts: Essays in History and Culture*.

English Pasts: Essays in History and Culture (Oxford University Press, 1999).

English Pasts: Studies in Culture and History (Oxford University Press, 1999).

Collins, Randall, *Weberian Sociological Theory* (Cambridge University Press, 1986).

Colls, Robert, *The Identity of England* (Oxford University Press, 2002).

Colvin, H. M. et al., *The History of the King's Works*, vol. VI, 1782–1851 (HMSO, 1973).

Connell, J. D. R., *Eton: How it Works* (Faber and Faber, 1967).

Cooke, C. J., *Irish Postal History: Sixteenth Century to 1935* (London, 1935).

Cooke Taylor, W., *Notes of a Tour in the Manufacturing Districts of Lancashire* (1841; Frank Cass reprint, 1968).

Cookson Junior, Peter W., and Pursell, Carolyn, *Preparing for Power: America's Elite Boarding Schools* (Basic Books, 1985).

Cooper, Frederick, *Colonialism in Question: Theory, Knowledge, History* (University of California Press, 2002).

Corrigan, Philip and Sayer, Derek, *The Great Arch: English State Formation as Cultural Revolution* (Basil Blackwell, 1985).

Coulmas, Florian, *The Writing Systems of the World* (Blackwell, 1989).

Cowburn, Philip (ed.), *A Salopian Anthology: Some Impressions of Shrewsbury Life during Four Centuries* (Macmillan, 1964).

Cowling, Maurice, *The Impact of Labour 1920–1924* (Cambridge University Press, 1971).

Cromwell, Valerie, *Revolution or Evolution: British Government in the Nineteenth Century* (Longman, 1977).

Crook, Tom, "Power, Privacy and Pleasure: Liberalism and the Modern Cubicle", *Cultural Studies*, 21:4–5 (July/September 2007).

"Sanitary Inspection and the Public Sphere in Late Victorian and Edwardian Britain: A Case Study in Liberal Governance", *Social History*, 32:4 (2007).

and O'Hara, Glen (eds.), *Statistics and the Public Sphere in Britain, c. 1800–2000* (Routledge, 2011).

Crouch, Colin, *The Strange Non-Death of Neoliberalism* (Polity Press, 2011).

Curthoys, M. C., "The College in the New Era" in M. S. Brock and M. C. Curthoys (eds.), *The History of Oxford*, vol. VI, *Nineteenth-Century Oxford*, Pt 1 (Oxford University Press, 1991).

Dale, H. E., *The Higher Civil Service of Great Britain* (Oxford University Press, 1941).

Daston, Lorraine, "Scientific Objectivity: With and Without Words" in
    Peter Becker and William Clark (eds.), *Little Tools of Knowledge*.
    and Gallison, Peter, *Objectivity* (Zone Books, 2007).
Daunton, M. J., *Just Taxes: The Politics of Taxation in Britain, 1799–1914*
    (Cambridge University Press, 2002).
    Progress and Poverty: An Economic and Social History of Britain 1700–1850
    (Oxford University Press, 1995).
    Royal Mail: The Post Office since 1840 (Athlone Press, 1985).
    Trusting Leviathan: The Politics of Taxation in Britain, 1914–1979 (Cambridge
    University Press, 2001).
Davidoff, Leonore, *The Best Circles* (Ebury Press, 1986).
Davis, Mike, *Late Victorian Holocausts: El Niño Famines and the Making of the Third
    World* (Verso, 2002).
Davis, Tom and Brown, Frances, "The Acquisition of Handwriting in the
    UK" (Department of English, University of Birmingham paper on
    writing styles, dated 1994, available at www.unask.com/website/handwriting).
Dean, Mitchell, *Governmentality* (Sage, 1999).
Delap, Lucy et al. (eds.), *The Politics of Domestic Authority in Britain since 1800*
    (Palgrave Macmillan, 2009).
Dench Geoff (ed.), *The Rise and Rise of Meritocracy* (Blackwell, 2006)
Deslandes, Paul R., *Oxbridge Men: British Masculinity and the Undergraduate
    Experience, 1850–1920* (Indiana University Press, 2005).
Devine, T. M., *The Scottish Nation 1700–2007* (Penguin Books, 2000).
Dewey, Clive, *Anglo-Indian Attitudes: The Mind of the Indian Civil Service*
    (Hambledon, 1993).
Dodsworth, Francis, "'Civic' Police and the Condition of Liberty: The
    Rationality of Governance in Eighteenth-Century England", *Social History*,
    29:2 (2004).
    "Masculinity as Governance: Police, Public Service and the Embodiment of
    Authority, c. 1700–1850" in M. L. McCormack (ed.), *Public Men: Political
    Masculinities in Britain, 1700–2000* (Palgrave, 2007).
    "*Virtus* on Whitehall: The Politics of Palladianism in William Kent's Treasury
    Building, 1733–62, *Journal of Historical Sociology* 18:4 (2005).
Donald, John, *Sentimental Education: Schooling, Popular Culture and the Regulation
    of Liberty* (Verso, 1992).
Duffel, Nick, *The Making of Them: British Attitudes to Children and the Boarding
    School System* (Lone Arrow Press, 2000).
Duffy, Francis, "Office building and Organisational Change: On the Sun
    Insurance Office in London, 1849" in A. D. King (ed.), *Buildings and
    Society: Essays on the Social Development of the Built Environment*
    (Routledge & Kegan Paul, 1980).
Du Gay, Paul, "Max Weber and the Moral Economy of Office", *Journal of Cultural
    Economy*, 1:2 (July 2008).
Dukes, Clement, *Health at School* (London, 1887).
Eastwood, David, "'Amplifying the Province of the Legislature': The Flow of
    Information and the English State in the Early-Nineteenth Century",
    Historical Research, 62 (1989).

Edgerton, David, *Warfare State: Britain, 1920–1970* (Cambridge University Press, 2006).

Edney, Matthew E., *Mapping an Empire: The Geographical Construction of British India, 1765–1843* (Chicago University Press, 1999).

Edwards, Paul N., "Infrastructure and Modernity: Force, Time, and Social Organisation in the History of Socio-Technical Systems" in Thomas J. Misa, Philip Brey and Andrew Feenberg (eds.), *Modernity and Technology* (MIT Press, 2003).

Ellen, Mark, "'He could Talk his Way out of Things'", *The Observer*, 27 April 2003.

Ellis, K., *The Post Office in the Eighteenth Century: A Study in Administrative History* (Oxford University Press, 1958).

Encyclopaedia Britannica, 1885 (vol. xix).

Eyler, John, *Victorian Social Medicine: The Ideas and Methods of William Farr* (Johns Hopkins University Press, 1979).

Faber, Geoffrey, *Jowett: A Portrait with Background* (Faber and Faber, 1957).

Farmer, John S., *The Public School Word-Book: A Contribution . . . Our Great Public Schools* (London, 1900).

Faubion, James D. (ed.), *Michel Foucault: The Essential Work*, vol. III, *Power* (Allen Lane/Penguin, 2001).

Feldman, Ilana, *Governing Gaza: Bureaucracy, Authority and the Work of Rule, 1917–1967* (Duke University Press, 2008).

Ferguson, James, *The Anti-Politics Machine: "Development", Depoliticisation, and Bureaucratic Power in Lesotho* (University of Minnesota Press, 1994).

Ferrugia, Jean Y., *The Letter Box* (Centaur Press, 1969).

Firebrace, Sir Aylmer, *Fire Service Memories* (Andrew Melrose, n.d.).

Firth, John D'Ewes Evelyn, *Winchester* (London, 1936).

Fischer, Steven Roger, *The History of Reading* (Reaktion Books, 2005).

   The History of Writing (Reaktion Books, 2005).

Flanders, Judith, *The Victorian House: Domestic Life from Childbirth to Deathbed* (Harper Collins, 2003).

Foucault, Michel, *Discipline and Punish: The Birth of the Prison* (Penguin, 1991).

   "Governmentality" in James D. Faubion (ed.), *Power* (Allen Lane/Penguin, 2001).

   "Lecture Two, 14 January 1976" in Mauro Bertani et al. (eds.), *Society must be Defended: Lectures at the Collège de France, 1975–76* (Penguin, 2003).

Fraser, Nick, *The Importance of Being Eton: Inside the World's Most Powerful School* (Short Books, 2006).

Frisby, David, *Simmel and Since: Essays on Georg Simmel's Social Theory* (Routledge, 1992).

Fry, G. K., *Statesman in Disguise: The Changing Role of the Administrative Class of the British Home Civil Service 1853–1966* (Macmillan, 1969).

Fyrth, Jim, *Labour's Promised Land? Culture and Society in Labour Britain 1945–51* (Lawrence & Wishart, 1995).

Gardiner, J., *A Generall Survey of the Post Office, with Severall Useful Remarques to The particulars of it Most humbly presented To his Royal Highness James Duke of Yorke* (London, 1677).

Gaur, Albertine, *A History of Calligraphy* (British Library, 1994).

Geoffrey, Thomas, *The Moral Philosophy of T. H. Green* (Oxford University Press, 1987).

Georges, Jean, *Writing: The Story of the Alphabet* (Thames & Hudson, 1992).

Ginsborg, Paul, *Italy and its Discontents: Family, Civil Society, State, 1980–2001* (Penguin, 2001).

Gladden, E. N., *The Civil Services of the United Kingdom 1855–1970* (Frank Cass, 1967).

Goffman, Erving, *Asylums* (Penguin, 1961).

Goody, Jack, *The Logic of Writing and the Origin of Society* (Cambridge University Press, 1986).

Gordon, Eleanor, and Nair, Gwyneth, *Public Lives: Women, Family and Society in Victorian Britain* (Yale University Press, 2003).

Goswami, Manu, *Producing India: From Colonial Economy to National Space* (University of Chicago Press, 2004).

Green, V. H. H., *Oxford Common Room: A Study of Lincoln College's Mark Pattison* (Edward Arnold, 1957).

Gregory, Derek, "The Friction of Distance", *Journal of Historical Geography*, 13:2 (April 1987).

Griffiths, A. R. G., *The Irish Board of Works 1871–1878* (Garland, 1987).

Guldi, E. Joanna, *Roads to Power: Britain Invents the Infrastructure State* (Harvard University Press, 2012).

Gunn, Simon and Vernon, James (eds.), *The Peculiarities of Liberal Modernity in Imperial Britain* (University of California Press, 2011).

Habermas, Jurgen, *The Structural Transformation of the Public Sphere: An Enquiry into a Category of Bourgeois Society* (Polity, 1992).

Hadley, Elaine, *Living Liberalism: Practical Citizenship in Mid-Victorian Britain* (University of Chicago Press, 2010).

Haines, Robin F., *Charles Trevelyan and the Great Irish Famine* (Four Courts Press, 2004).

Hajkowski, Thomas, *The BBC and National Identity in Britain, 1922–1953* (Manchester University Press, 2010).

Hall, Stuart, "Popular Culture and the State" in Tony Bennett and Colin Mercer (eds.), *Popular Culture and Social Relations* (Open University Press, 1986).

Halsey, A. H., "The Franks Commission" in Brian Harrison (ed.), *The History of the University of Oxford*, vol. VIII, *The 20th Century* (Oxford University Press, 1994).

Hamlett, Jane, "Nicely Feminine, yet Learned": Student Rooms at Royal Holloway and the Oxford and Cambridge Colleges in the Late Nineteenth Century, *Women's History Review*, 15:1 (March 2006).

Hamlin, Christopher, *Public Health and Social Justice in the Age of Chadwick: Britain 1800–1854* (Cambridge University Press, 1998).

Social History, forthcoming.

Handbook of Civil Service: A Complete Guide, Etc to the Various Departments of the Public Service (London, 1861).

Hannah, Leslie, *The Rise of the Corporate Economy* (Methuen, 1983).

'Visible and Invisible Hands in Great Britain' in A. D. Chandler and H. Daerns (eds.), *Managerial Hierarchies: Comparative Perspectives on the Rise of the Modern Industrial Enterprise* (Harvard University Press, 1980).

Hanson, L., *Government and the Press, 1695–1763* (Oxford, 1936).

Hardt, Michael and Negri, Antonio, *Commonwealth* (Harvard University Press, 2009).

Harling, Philip, *The Waning of "Old Corruption": The Politics of Economical Reform in Britain 1759–1846* (Oxford University Press, 1996).

and Mandler, Peter, "From 'Fiscal Military' to Laissez-Faire State: Britain 1760–1850", *Journal of British Studies*, 4 (1993).

Harries-Jenkins, Gwynn, *The Army in Victorian Society* (Routledge, 1977).

Harris, Jose, "Economic Knowledge and British Social Policy" in Mary O. Furner and Barry Supple, *The State and Economic Knowledge: The American and British Experiences* (Cambridge University Press, 1990).

"Political Thought about the State in Britain" in S. J. G. Green and R. C. Whiting (eds.), *The Boundaries of the State in Modern Britain* (Cambridge University Press, 1996).

"Society and the State in Twentieth-Century Britain" in F. M. L. Thompson (ed.), *The Cambridge Social History of Great Britain* (Cambridge University Press, 1990).

Harris, Roy, *The Origins of Writing* (Duckworth, 1986).

Harrison, Brian, "College Life 1918–1939" in Brian Harrison (ed.), *The History of the University of Oxford*, vol. VIII, *The 20th Century* (Oxford University Press, 1994).

Finding a Role: The United Kingdom, 1970–1990 (Oxford University Press, 2010).

Seeking a Role: The United Kingdom, 1951–1970 (Oxford University Press, 2009).

Harvey, Penelope and Knox, Hannah, "Abstraction, Materiality and the 'Science of the Concrete' in Engineering Practice" in Patrick Joyce and Tony Bennett (eds.), *Material Powers*.

Hawkins, Chris, *A History of the Signature* (Createspace, 2011).

Hawthorne, Nathaniel, *The Scarlet Letter* (Boston, 1850).

Hay, Colin et al., *The State: Theories and Issues* (Palgrave, 2006).

Headrick, Daniel R., *Power over Peoples: Technology, Environments, and Western Imperialism, 1400 to the Present* (Princeton University Press, 2010).

The Tentacles of Progress: Technology Transfer in the Age of Imperialism, 1850–1940 (Oxford University Press, 1988).

Hecht, Gabrielle, *The Radiance of France: Nuclear Power and National Identity* (MIT Press, 1998).

Hellmuth, Eckhart and Brewer, John (eds.), *Rethinking Leviathan: The Eighteenth Century in Britain and Germany* (Oxford University Press, 1999).

Henkin, David M., *The Postal Age: The Emergence of Modern Communications in Nineteenth-Century America* (University of Chicago Press, 2006).

Heward, Christina, *Making a Man of Him: Parents and their Sons' Education at an English Public School 1929–50* (Routledge, 1988).

Hicks, Dan and Beaudry, Mary C. (eds.), *The Oxford Handbook of Material Culture Studies* (Oxford University Press, 2011).

Hill, Rowland, *Post Office Reform: Its Importance and Practicability*, 2nd edn (London, 1837).

History of the Human Sciences, Special Issue, "Who Speaks? The Voice in the Human Sciences", 10:3 (August 1997).

Hobsbawm, Eric and Ranger, Terence (eds.), *The Invention of Tradition* (Cambridge University Press, 1992).

Hoggart, Richard, *The Uses of Literacy* (Chatto & Windus, 1967).

Holloway, David, "A Day in the Growth of Brown Minor" in *The World of the Public School* (Weidenfeld & Nicolson, 1977).

Honey, John Raymond, *Tom Brown's Universe: The Development of the Victorian Public School* (Millington, 1977).

Horne, H. O., *A History of Savings Banks* (Oxford, 1947).

Hoskin, Keith, "History, power and knowledge: the genealogy of the urban schoolteacher" in Stephen J. Ball (ed.), *Foucault and Education: Disciplines and Knowledge* (Routledge, 1990).

How, Frederick, *Six Great Headmasters* (London, 1905).

How, James, *Epistolatory Spaces: English Letter Writing from the Foundation of the Post Office to Richardson's Clarissa* (Ashgate, 2003).

Hughes, Thomas, *Networks of Power: Electrification in Western Society, 1880–1930* (Johns Hopkins University Press, 1983).

  et al., (eds.), *The Social Construction of Technological Systems: New Directions in the Sociology and History of Technology* (MIT Press, 1987).

Hugill, Peter J., *Global Communications since 1844: Geopolitics and Technology* (Johns Hopkins University Press, 1999).

Hungarian Radio and Television Museum, Budapest Post Office, 2000, exhibition guides.

Iliffe, Steve, "An Historic Compromise: Labour and the Foundation of the National Health Service" in Fyrth, Jim (ed.), *Labour's Promised Land? Culture and Society in Labour Britain 1945–51* (Lawrence & Wishart, 1995).

Independent, The, "A Government of Straight, White, Privately Educated Men", 7 August 2010.

India List Civil and Military, The (London, 1882).

Indian Postal Guide, The (London, 1858, 1861).

Innes, Joanna, *Inferior Politics: Social Problems and Social Policies in Eighteenth-Century Britain* (Oxford University Press, 2009).

Irvine, A. L., *Sixty Years at School* (PIG Wells, 1958).

Jackson, Ben, *Equality and the British Left* (Manchester University Press, 2007).

Jackson, Donald, *The Story of Writing* (The Calligraphy Centre, 1981).

Jefferies, Sir Charles, *The Colonial Office* (Allen & Unwin, 1995).

Jenkyns, Richard, *The Victorians and Ancient Greece* (Basil Blackwell, 1984).

Jensen, Henrik (ed.), *The Welfare State: Past, Present and Future* (Edizioni Plus, Universita di Pisa, 2002).

Jessop, Bob, *State Theory: Putting the Capitalist State in its Place* (Polity Press, 1990).

John, Richard E., *Network Nation: Inventing American Telecommunications* (Harvard University Press, 2010).

  Spreading the News: The American Postal System from Franklin to Morse (Harvard University Press, 1995).

Johnson, Peter, *Mail by Rail: The Travelling Post Office* (Ian Allen, 1995).

Jones, Raymond, *The Nineteenth-Century Foreign Office: An Administrative History* (LSE monographs; Weidenfeld & Nicolson, 1971).

Jones, Stuart, *Intellect and Character in Victorian England: Mark Pattison and the Invention of the Don* (Cambridge University Press, 2007).

"The Scholar as Saint: Mark Pattison on Intellectual Culture" *(draft research paper*, 2007).

Journal of Historical Sociology, "Symposium on the State", March 2002.

Jowett, Benjamin, *The Politics of Aristotle* (Oxford, 1885), 2 vols.

Joyce, James, "Ireland at the Bar" (1907), in Kevin Barry (ed.), *James Joyce: Occasional, Critical and Political Writing* (Oxford University Press, 2008).

Joyce, Patrick, *Democratic Subjects: The Self and the Social in Nineteenth-Century England* (Cambridge University Press, 1993).

Encyclopaedia Britannica entry for the "History of Britain 1815 to the Present", 2008 revision.

"More Secondary than Postmodern", *Rethinking History*, 5:3 (December 2001).

"Power, the State and the Political", *British Journal of Sociology*, Centenary Number Special Issue, 2010.

"The Return of History: Postmodernism and the Politics of Academic History in Britain", *Past and Present*, 158 (February 1998).

The Rule of Freedom: Liberalism and the Modern City (Verso, 2003).

Visions of the People: Industrial England and the Question of Class, 1840–1914 (Cambridge University Press, 1991).

"What is the Social in Social History?", *Past and Present*, 206 (February 2010).

"Work", *The Cambridge Social History of Great Britain, 1750–1950*, vol. II (Cambridge University Press, 1990).

Work, Society and Politics: The Culture of the Factory in Later Victorian England (Harvester, 1980).

and Bennett Tony (eds.), *Material Powers: History, Cultural Studies and the Material Turn* (Routledge, 2010).

and Dodsworth, Francis (eds.), "Liberalisms, Government, Culture", Special Issue of *Cultural Studies*, 21:4–5 (July–September 2007).

(ed.), *Class: A Reader* (Oxford University Press, 1995).

(ed.), *The Social in Question: New Bearings in History and the Social Sciences* (Routledge, 2002).

Judt, Tony, *Ill Fares the Land: A Treatise on Our Present Discontents* (Penguin, 2010).

J. W. K., "The House that Jack Built", *Cornhill Magazine*, II (July–December 1860).

"Of the House that Scott Built", *Cornhill Magazine*, XVI (July–December 1867).

Kafka, Ben, "Hunting the Plumed Mammal: The History of 'Bureaucracy' in France, 1750–1850" in Peter Becker and Rüdiger von Krosigk (eds.), *Figures of Authority*.

Kaminsky, Arnold P., *The India Office, 1880–1910* (Mansell Publishing, 1986).

Kantorowicz, Ernst, *The King's Two Bodies: A Study in Mediaeval Political Theology* (Princeton University Press, 1957).

Kaye, Sir John William, *The Administration of the East India Company: A Story of Indian Progress* (London, 1853).

Keane, John, in James Tully (ed.), *Meaning and Context: Quentin Skinner and His Critics* (Cambridge University Press, 1988).

Kharkhordin, Oleg, "What is the State? The Russian Concept of *Gosudarstvo* in the European Context", *History and Theory*, 40 (May 2001).

Kieve, David L., *The Electric Telegraph: A Social and Economic History* (David and Charles, 1973).

Kinealy, Christine, *This Great Calamity: The Irish Famine 1845–52* (Gill & Macmillan, 1994).

King, C. A., *Historical Summaries of Post Office Services* (London, 1906).

Kirk-Green, Anthony, *Britain's Imperial Administrators 1858–1966* (Macmillan, 2000).

Klein, Lawrence E., "Politeness and the Interpretation of the British Eighteenth Century", *The Historical Journal*, 45:4 (2002).

Kula, Witold, *Measures and Men* (Princeton University Press, 1986).

Kuper, Adam, *Incest and Influence: The Private Life of Bourgeois England* (Harvard University Press, 2009).

Lambert, Royston, *The Hothouse Society: An Exploration of Boarding-School Life through the Boys' and Girls' own Writing* (Weidenfeld & Nicolson, 1968).

Langford, Paul, *Englishness Identified: Manners and Character 1650–1850* (Oxford University Press, 2000).

   Public Life and the Propertied Englishman, 1689–1798 (Oxford University Press, 1991).

Latour, Bruno, *Pandora's Hope: Essays on the Reality of Science Studies* (Harvard University Press, 1999).

   Reassembling the Social: An Introduction to Actor-Network-Theory (Oxford University Press, 2005).

   Science in Action: How to Follow Scientists and Engineers through Society (Harvard University Press, 1987).

Laven, David, *Venice and Venetia under the Hapsburgs, 1815–1835* (Oxford University Press, 2002).

Law, John, *After Method* (Routledge, 2004).

   Organising Modernity: Social Order and Social Theory (Blackwell, 1994).

   "Technology and Heterogeneous Engineering: The Case of the Portuguese Expansion" in Wiebe Bijker, Thomas Hughes and Trevor Pinch (eds.), *The Social Construction of Technological Systems* (MIT Press, 1987).

Lawrence, Jonathan, "Paternalism, Class and the British Path to Modernity" in Simon Gunn and James Vernon (eds.), *The Peculiarities of Liberal Modernity in Britain* (University of California Press, 2011).

Lawrence, P. S. H., *An Eton Camera, 1920–1959* (Michael Russell, 1980).

Lee, C., "The Service Industries" in R. Floud and D. McLoskey (eds.), *The Economic History of Britain since 1700*, 2nd edn, vol. II, *1860–1939* (Cambridge University Press, 1994).

Lehmberg, S. E., *Sir Thomas Elyot: Tudor Humanist* (University of Texas Press, 1960).

Leinster-McKay, David, *The Rise of the English Prep School* (The Falmer Press, 1984).

Lewins, William, *Her Majesty's Mails: An Historical and Descriptive Account of the British Post Office. Together with an Appendix* (London, 1864).

Lowder, J. W. A., *A Postal History of London, 1635–1960*. Lowe, Donald M. *History of Bourgeois Perception* (Harvester, 1982).

Luhmann, Niklas, *Social Systems* (Stanford University Press, 1995).

Lyons, Martyn, *Readers and Society in Nineteenth-Century France: Workers, Women, Peasants* (Palgrave Macmillan, 2001).

Machlachan, Patricia L., *The People's Post Office: The History and Politics of the Japanese Postal System, 1871–2010* (Harvard University Press, 2011).

Machray, Robert, "The India Office", *India Magazine* (October 1900).

Malchow, H. L., *Gentlemen Capitalists: The Social and Political World of the Victorian Businessman* (Macmillan, 1991).

Mangan, J. A., *Athleticism in the Victorian and Edwardian Public School: The Emergence and Consolidation of Educational Ideology* (Cambridge University Press, 1981).

Mann, Michael, "Family Resemblances", *New Left Review*, 63 (May–June 2010).

Manual of the Rules and Regulations Applicable to Members of the Indian Civil Service (Calcutta, 1887).

Manufacturer and Builder, March 1875.

Marinetto, Michael, *Social Theory, The State and Modern Society: The State in Contemporary Social Thought* (Open University Press, 2007).

Markham, Sir Clements, *A Memoir on the Indian Surveys* (London, 1871).

Marriott, J. W., *The Secret of Good Letter Writing* (London, c. 1943).

Martin, Henri-Jean, *The History and Power of Writing* (Chicago University Press, 1994).

Marx, Karl, *Capital: A Critique of Political Economy*, vol. i (Penguin Books edn, 1976).

Marx, Leo, "Technology: The Emergence of a Hazardous Concept", *Technology and Culture*, 51 (July 2010).

Mayr, Otto, *Authority, Liberty and Autonomous Machinery in Early Modern Europe* (Johns Hopkins University Press, 1986).

McCarthy, Justin, *A History of Our Own Times* (1880), vol. i.

McCormack, M. L., *The Independent Man: Citizenship and Gender Politics in Georgian England* (Manchester University Press, 2005).

McCulloch, Gary, *Philosophers and Kings: Education for Leadership* in Modern England (Cambridge University Press, 1991).

McDonagh, Oliver, *Early Victorian Government 1830–1870* (Weidenfeld & Nicolson, 1977).

McKibbin, Ross, *Classes and Cultures: England 1918–1951* (Oxford University Press, 2000).

   Parties and People: England 1914–1951 (Oxford University Press, 2009).

McLeod, Roy, "Introduction" in Roy McLeod (ed.), *Government and Expertise: Specialists, Administrators and Professionals, 1860–1919* (Cambridge University Press, 1998).

McNeely, Ian F., *The Emancipation of Writing: German Civil Society in the Making, 1790s–1820s* (University of California Press, 2003).

Messick, Brinkeley, *The Calligraphic State: Textual Domination and History in a Muslim Society* (University of California Press, 1993).

Migdal, Joel, *State in Society: Studying How States and Societies Transform and Constitute One Another* (Cambridge University Press, 2001).

Mill, John Stuart, "Evidence before the Select Committee of the House of Lords on India affairs" in John M. Robson et al. (eds.), *The Collected Works of John Stuart Mill*, vol. XXX, *Writings on India* (University of Toronto Press, 1990).

Miller, P. N., *Defining the Common Good: Empire, Religion and Philosophy in Eighteenth-Century Britain* (Cambridge University Press, 1994).

Miller, Peter and Rose, Nikolas, "Political Power beyond the State: Problematics of Government", *British Journal of Sociology*, 42:2 (June 1992).

Misa, Thomas J., *Leonardo to the Internet: Technology and Culture from the Renaissance to the Internet* (Johns Hopkins University Press, 2011).

Brey, Philip and Feenberg, Andrew (eds.), *Modernity and Technology* (MIT Press, 2003).

Mitchell, Timothy, *Carbon Democracy: Political Power in the Age of Oil* (Verso, 2011).

Colonising Egypt (University of California Press, 1992).

"The Limits of the State: Beyond Statist Approaches and their Critics", *American Political Science Review*, 85:1 (March 1991).

The Rule of Experts: Egypt, Techo-Politics and Modernity (University of California Press, 2002).

Moberly, G., *Sermons, Preached at Winchester College: Second Series with a Preface on "Fagging"* (London, 1848).

Moir, Martin, *A General Guide to the India Office Records* (The British Library, 1988).

Money, John, *Experience and Identity: Birmingham and the West Midlands 1760 1800* (Manchester University Press, 1977).

Moon, Antonia, "Destroying Records, Keeping Records: Some Practices of the East India Company and of the India office", British Library unpublished research paper.

Mort, Frank, *Capital Affairs: The Making of the Permissive Society* (Yale University Press, 2010).

Morus, Iwan Rhys, *Frankenstein's Children: Electricity, Exhibition and Experiment in Early Nineteenth-Century London* (Princeton University Press, 1998).

"The Nervous System of Britain" in Morus, I. R. (ed.), *Bodies/Machines* (Berg, 2002).

review of Michael Faraday, *Experimental Researches in Electricity*, in *British Journal for the History of Science*, 34:4 (December 2001).

Muir, D. N., *Postal Reform and the Penny Black: A New Appreciation* (National Postal Museum, 1990).

Mukerjea, Devabrata, *The Post Office* (Calcutta, 1919).

Mukerji, Chandra, *Impossible Engineering: Technology and Territoriality on the Canal du Midi* (Princeton University Press, 2009).

"Jurisdiction, Inscription, and State Formation: Administrative Modernism and Knowledge Regimes", *Theory and Society* (February 2011).

Territorial Ambitions and the Gardens of Versailles (Cambridge University Press, 1997).

"The Unintended State" in Patrick Joyce and Tony Bennett (eds.), *Material Powers*.

Muller, Jan-Werner, *Contesting Democracy: Political Ideas in Twentieth-Century Europe* (Yale University Press, 2011).

Nettl, J. P., "The State as a Conceptual Variable" in John A. Hall (ed.), *The State: Critical Concepts* (Routledge, 1994), vol. I.

Newsome, David, *Godliness and Good Learning: Four Studies on a Victorian Ideal* (John Murray, 1961).

Nezos, Renna, *Graphology: The Interpretation of Handwriting* (Rider, 1986).

O'Connor, James, "Aspects of Galway Postal History 1638–1984", *Journal of the Galway Archaeological Society*, 44 (1992).

Ogborn, Miles, *Indian Ink: Script and Print in the Making of the East India Company* (Chicago University Press, 2007).

O'Malley, L. S. S., *The Indian Civil Service 1601–1930* (London, 1931).

Orwell, George, "Such, Such were the Joys", *Partisan Review*, XIX (September–October 1952).

Osborne, Thomas, "Bureaucracy as a Vocation: Governmentality and Administration in Nineteenth-Century Britain", *Journal of Historical Sociology*, 7:3 (1994).

Barry, Andrew and Rose, Nikolas (eds.), *Foucault and Political Reason: Liberalism, Neoliberalism and Rationalities of Government* (UCL Press, 1996).

Otis, Laura, *Networking: Communicating with Bodies and Machines in the Nineteenth Century* (University of Michigan Press, 2001).

Otter, Christopher, "Making Liberal Objects: British Techno-Social Relations, 1860–1900" in Patrick Joyce and Tony Bennett (eds.), *Material Powers*.

"Making Liberalism Durable: Vision and Civility in the Late Victorian City", *Social History*, 27:1 (January 2002).

The Victorian Eye: A Political History of Light and Vision in Britain, 1800–1910 (Chicago University Press, 2008).

Parker, Peter, *The Old Lie: The Great War and the Public School Ethos* (Constable, 1987).

Parkin, George R., *Edward Thring, Headmaster of Uppingham School: Life Diary and Letters* (London, 1898).

Parris, Henry, *Constitutional Bureaucracy: The Development of British Central Administration since the Eighteenth Century* (Allen & Unwin, 1969).

Parry, Ernest Gambier, *Life in an Eton House: With some Notes on the Evans Family* (London, 1907).

Parry, Jonathan, *The Rise and Fall of Liberal Government in Victorian Britain* (Cambridge University Press, 1993).

Pearson, Christopher, *The Modern State* (Routledge, 1996).

Pellew, Jill, *The Home Office 1848–1914: From Clerks to Bureaucrats* (Heinemann Educational, 1982).

Perry, C. R., *The Victorian Post Office: The Growth of a Bureaucracy* (Royal Historical Society, 1992).

Petroski, Henry, *The Invention of Useful Things* (Vintage, 1994).

The Pencil: A History of Design and Circumstance (Alfred A. Knopf, 2000).

Pevsner, Nikolaus, *A History of Building Types* (Thames & Hudson, 1976).

Pickering, Andrew, *The Mangle of Practice: Time, Agency and Science* (Chicago University Press, 1995).

Plant, Robert, "T. H. Green: Citizenship, Education and Law" in Harry Judge (ed.), *The University and Public Education: The Contribution of Oxford* (Routledge, 2007).

Pocock, J. G. A., *The Machiavellian Moment: Florentine Political Thought and the Atlantic Republican Tradition* (Princeton University Press, 1975).

Virtue, Commerce, and History: Essays in Political Thought and History, Chiefly in the Eighteenth Century (Cambridge University Press, 1985).

Ponot, René, *De Plomb, d'encre & de lumiere: essai sur la typographie & la communication écrite* (Imprimerie Nationale, 1982).

Poovey, Mary, *Genres of the Credit Economy: Mediating Value in Eighteenth- and Nineteenth-Century Britain* (Chicago University Press, 2008).

A History of the Modern Fact: Problems of Knowledge in the Sciences of Wealth and Society (Chicago University Press, 1998).

Making a Social Body: British Cultural Formation 1830–1864 (Chicago University Press, 1995).

Port, M. H., *Imperial London: Civil Government Building in London 1850–1915* (Yale University Press, 1995).

POST 100/1, *Rowland Hill's Private Journal*, vol. I, 1839–41.

Postai es Tavkozlesi Museumi Alapitvany Evkonyve, 2001 (Budapest, 2002).

Potter, David C., *India's Political Administration* (Oxford University Press, 1986).

Prenderville, Gary, "Correspondence, Power and the State: An Historical Geography of the Irish Postal Service, 1784–1831" (University of Dublin Ph.D., 2006).

Prest, John, "Balliol for Example" in M. S. Brock and M. C. Curthoys (eds.), *The History of Oxford*.

Raadschelders, Joseph C. N., *Handbook of Administrative History* (Transaction Publishers, 1998).

Rawnsley, H. D., *Edward Thring, Teacher and Poet* (London, 1889).

Reynolds, M., *A History of the Irish Post Office* (MacDonnell & Whyte Ltd, 1983).

Rhodes, R. A. W., *Everyday Life in British Government* (Oxford University Press, 2011).

Roach, John, *Public Examinations in England 1850–1900* (Cambridge University Press, 2008).

Robinson, Howard, *The British Post Office: A History* (Princeton University Press, 1948).

Robinson, Martin, *Old Letter Boxes* (Shire, 1987).

Robson, John M. et al. (eds.), *The Collected Works of John Stuart Mill*, vol. xxx, *Writings on India* (University of Toronto Press, 1990).

Roeder C., *Beginnings of the Manchester Post Office* (Manchester, 1905).

Rose, Nikolas, "Advanced Liberalism" in Nikolas Rose, *Powers of Freedom: Reframing Political Thought* (Cambridge University Press, 1999).

"Freedom in an Age of Insecurity", paper to the LSE "Understanding Freedom" seminar series, April–July 2009.

Governing the Soul: The Shaping of the Modern Self (Routledge, 1989).

The Politics of Life Itself: Biomedicine, Power and Subjectivity in the Twenty-First Century (Princeton University Press, 2007).

Rosenheim, James M., *The Emergence of a Ruling Order: English Landed Society 1650–1750* (Longman, 1998).

Roseveare, Henry, *The Treasury 1660–1970: The Foundations of Control* (George Allen & Unwin, 1973).

Roth, Joseph, *The Radetzky March* (Granta, 2003).

Rothblatt, Sheldon, "The Limbs of Osiris: Liberal Education in the English-Speaking World" in Sheldon Rothblatt (ed.), *Tradition and Change in English Liberal Education: An Essay in History and Culture* (Faber and Faber, 1976).

    The Revolution of the Dons: Cambridge and Society in Victorian England (Cambridge University Press, 1981).

    and Wittock, Bjorn (eds.), *The European and American University since 1800: Historical and Sociological Essays* (Cambridge University Press, 1993).

Rouse, W. H. D., *A History of Rugby School* (London, 1898).

Sainsbury, George, *A Letter Book: Selections with an Introduction on the History and Art of Letter Writing* (London, 1922).

Salt, Henry, *Memories of Bygone Eton* (London, 1928).

Sampson, Anthony, *Anatomy of Britain Today* (Hodder & Stoughton, 1965).

    The Changing Anatomy of Britain (Hodder & Stoughton, 1981).

    Who Runs this Place? The Anatomy of Britain in the 21st Century (John Murray, 2004).

Savage, Mike, *Identities and Social Change in Britain since 1940: The Politics of Method* (Oxford University Press, 2010).

    et al. (eds.), *Culture, Class, Distinction* (Routledge/CRESC, 2009).

Schaffner, Martin, "The Figure of the Questions versus the Prose of the Answers: Lord Devon's Inquiry in Skibbereen, 10 September 1844" in Peter Becker and William Clark (eds.), *Little Tools of Knowledge*.

Schellenberg, T. R., *Modern Archives: Principles and Techniques* (Chicago University Press, 1956).

Schivelbusch, Wolfgang, *The Railway Journey: The Industrialisation of Time and Space in the 19th Century* (Berg, 1986).

Schneer, Jonathan, *London 1900: The Imperial Metropolis* (Yale University Press, 1999).

Scott, James, *Seeing Like a State: How Certain Schemes to Improve the Human Condition have Failed* (Yale University Press, 1998).

Seabourne, Malcolm and Lowe, Roy, *The English School: Its Architecture and Design*, vol. II, *1870–1970* (Routledge & Kegan Paul, 1977).

Sengoopta, Chandak, *Imprint of the Raj: How Fingerprinting was Born in Colonial India* (Macmillan, 2003).

Sennett, Richard, *The Culture of the New Capitalism* (Yale University Press, 2006).

Shagan, Ethan, *The Rule of Moderation: Violence, Religion and the Politics of Restraint in Early Modern England* (Cambridge University Press, 2011).

Shapin, Steven, *A Social History of Truth: Civility and Science in Seventeenth-Century England* (Chicago University Press, 1994).

    and Schaffer, Simon, *Leviathan and the Air-Pump: Hobbes, Boyle, and the Experimental Life* (Princeton University Press, 1985).

Sharma, Aradhana and Gupta, Akhil (eds.), *The Anthropology of the State: A Reader* (Blackwell, 2006), "Introduction: Rethinking the State in an Age of Globalisation", for an excellent overview.

Shusterman, Richard (ed.), *Bourdieu: A Critical Reader* (Blackwell, 1999).

Siegert, Bernhard, *Relays: Literature as an Epoque of the Postal System* (Stanford University Press, 1999).

Silberman, Bernard, *Cages of Reason: The Rise of the Rational State in France, Japan, the United States, and Great Britain* (University of Chicago Press, 1993).

Silverboard, Mindy Ina, "Ireland, the Newspaper Press and Liberal Governmentality: The Formulation of Expertise on the 'Irish Question', 1880–9" (University of Manchester Ph.D. thesis, 2003).

Simmel, Georg, 'The Metropolis and Mental Life' in K. M. Woolf (ed.), *The Sociology of Georg Simmel* (New York, 1950).

Singh, Nihar Nandan, *British Historiography on British Rule in India: The Life and Writings of Sir John William Kaye, 1814–1876* (Janaka Prakashan: Patna, 1986).

Skinner, Quentin (ed.), *Families and States in Western Europe* (Cambridge University Press, 2011).

"The State" in T. Ball et al. (eds.), *Political Innovation and Conceptual Change* (Cambridge University Press, 1989).

Skocpol, Theda, *States and Social Revolutions: A Comparative Analysis of France, Russia, and China* (Cambridge University Press, 1979).

Slee, Peter R. H., *Learning and a Liberal Education: The Study of Modern History in the Universities of Oxford, Cambridge, and Manchester, 1800–1914* (Manchester University Press, 1986).

Smith, Adam, *An Inquiry into . . . the Wealth of Nations*, ed. Campbell, Skinner and Long (Liberty Fund, 1981), IV.

Smith, C. Suameraz, "Rule by Record".

Smith, Frank, *The History of English Elementary Education 1760–1902* (University of Liverpool Press, 1931).

Smith, R. S., "Ruling-by-Record and Ruling-by-Reports: Complementary Aspects of the British Imperial Rule of Law", *Contributions to Indian Sociology*, 19:1 (1985).

Sneyd-Kynnersley, Edmund, *H. M. I.: Some Passages in the Life of One of H. M. Inspectors of Schools* (London, 1908).

Soares, Joseph A., *The Decline of Privilege: The Modernisation of Oxford University* (Stanford University Press, 1999).

Soffer, Reba, "Modern History" in M. G. Brock and M. C. Curthoys (eds.), *The History of the University of Oxford*.

Spangenberg, Bradford, *British Bureaucracy in India: Status, Policy, and the ICS in the Late Nineteenth Century* (Manohar Book Service, 1976).

Staples, Nathanial, *Observations on the Indian Post Office and Suggestions for its Improvement* (London, 1850).

Staunton, Howard, *The Great Public Schools of England* (London, 1865).

Steiner, Zara, *The Foreign Office and Foreign Policy, 1898–1914* (Cambridge University Press, 1970).

Steinmetz, George, *State/Culture: State Formation after the Cultural Turn* (Cornell University Press, 1999).

Stephen, Leslie, *Sketches from Cambridge by a Don* (London, 1865).

Stevens, C. G., *Winchester Notions: The Dialect of Winchester College*, ed. Christopher Stray (Athlone Press, 1998).

Stoler, Ann Laura, *Along the Archival Grain: Epistemic Anxieties and Colonial Common Sense* (Princeton University Press, 2010).

Carnal Knowledge and Imperial Power: Race and the Intimate in Colonial Rule (University of California Press, 2002).

et al., *Tensions of Empire: Colonial Cultures in a Bourgeois World* (University of California Press, 1997).

Strachan, Huw, *The Politics of the British Army* (Oxford University Press, 1997).

Stray, Christopher, *Classics Transformed: Schools, Universities, and Society in England, 1830–1960* (Oxford University Press, 1998).

Grinders and Grammars: A Victorian Controversy (The Textbook Colloquiam, 1995).

"Paradigms of Social Order: The Politics of Latin Grammar in 19th-Century England", *Bulletin of the Henry Sweet Society*, 13 (1989).

Symonds, R., *Oxford and Empire: The Last Lost Cause?* (Oxford University Press, 1992).

Szakoltzai, Arpad, *Max Weber and Michel Foucault: Parallel Life-Works* (Routledge, 1998).

Taussig, Michael, *The Magic of the State* (Routledge, 1997).

Taylor, A. J. P., *English History, 1914–1945* (Oxford University Press, 1965).

Taylor, David, *The New Police in Nineteenth-Century England: Crime, Conflict and Control* (Manchester University Press, 1997).

Taylor, Henry, *The Statesman: An Ironical Treatise on the Art of Succeeding* (Cambridge, 1927), with an introductory essay by Harold J. Laski.

Tenner, Edward, *Our Own Devices: How Technology Remakes Humanity* (Alfred A. Knopf, 2003).

Why Things Bite Back: Technology and the Revenge of Effect (Fourth Estate, 1996).

Thackeray, St John Francis, *Sermons Preached in Eton College Chapel, 1870–1897* (London, 1897).

Thane, Pat, "Government and Society in England and Wales, 1750–1914" in F. M. L. Thompson (ed.), *The Cambridge Social History of Great Britain* (Cambridge University Press, 1990), vol. III.

(ed.), *Unequal Britain: Inequalities in Britain since 1945* (Continuum, 2010).

Theakston, Kevin, *Leadership in Whitehall* (Macmillan, 1999).

Thomas, Hugh (ed.), *Crisis in the Civil Service* (Anthony Blond, 1968), Ch. 1.

Thomas, Keith, "College Life, 1945–1970" in Brian Harrison (ed.), *The History of the University of Oxford*.

"Science and the Colleges", *Oxford Magazine*, 184, Michaelmas Term, 2000.

Thompson, E. P., "Eighteenth-Century English Society: Class Struggle without Class", *Social History*, 3:2 (May 1978).

"The Peculiarities of the English" in *The Poverty of Theory and Other Essays (Merlin Press*, 1978).

Thompson, R. S., *Classics or Charity? The Dilemma of the Eighteenth-Century Grammar School* (Manchester University Press, 1971).

Thomson, K. Graham, (ed.), *The Pan Book of Letter Writing* (Pan, 1961).

Thorn, John, *The Road to Winchester* (Weidenfeld & Nicolson, 1989).

Thring, Rev. Edward, *Addresses* (London, 1887).

Four Sermons Preached in Uppingham School Chapel . . . Sundays after Trinity, 1881 (unpublished, printed in Uppingham by John Hawthorne, 1881).

Todd, T., *William Dockwra and the Rest of the Undertakers: The Story of the London Penny Post, 1680–82* (Cousland & Sons, 1952).

Tombs, R. C., *The King's Post: Being a Volume of Historical facts relating to the Posts, Mail Coaches, Coach Roads, and Railway Mail Services of and connected with the Ancient City of Bristol from 1580 to the present time* (Bristol, 1905).

Tooze, Adam, *Statistics and the German State, 1900–1945* (Cambridge University Press, 1991).

Trentmann, Frank, *Free Trade Nation: Commerce, Consumption, and Civil Society in Modern Britain* (Oxford University Press, 2009).

"Materiality in the Future of History: Things, Practices and Politics", *Journal of British Studies*, 48 (April 2009).

and Daunton, Martin, "Worlds of Political Economy: Knowledge, Practices and Contestation" in Frank Trentmann and Martin Daunton, *Worlds of Political Economy: Knowledge and Power in the 19th and 20th Centuries* (Hargrave, 2004).

Tribe, Keith, "Political Economy and the Science of Economics in Victorian Britain" in Martin Daunton (ed.), *The Organisation of Knowledge in Victorian Britain* (Oxford University Press, 2005).

Trollope, Anthony, *An Autobiography* (Edinburgh, 1883), 2 vols.

Turner, Paul Venable, *Campus: An American Planning Tradition* (MIT Press, 1984).

Tyerman, Christopher, *A History of Harrow School 1324–1991* (Oxford University Press, 2000).

University of Bielefeld Collaborative Research Centre (SFB 584), papers from *The Political as Communicative Space in History*, December 2010.

Ure, Andrew, *The Philosophy of Manufactures* (London, 1841).

Valverde, Mariana, *Diseases of the Will: Alcohol and the Dilemmas of Freedom* (Cambridge University Press, 1998).

Law's Dream of Common Knowledge: The Cultural Lives of Law (Princeton University Press, 2003).

Van der Vleuten, Erik and Kaijser, Arne, *Networking Europe: Transnational Infrastructure and the Shaping of Europe, 1850–2000* (Science History Publications, 2006).

Vernon, James, *Hunger: A Modern History* (Harvard University Press, 2007).

"Narrating the Constitution: The Discourse of 'the Real' and the Fantasies of Nineteenth-Century Constitutional History" in James Vernon (ed.) *Re-reading the Constitution: New Narratives in the Political History of England's Long 19th Century* (Cambridge University Press, 1996).

Politics and the People: A Study in English Political Communication, 1815–1867 (Cambridge University Press, 1993).

Vincent, David, *The Culture of Secrecy: Britain, 1832–1998* (Oxford University Press, 1999).

Literacy and Popular Culture: England 1750–1914 (Cambridge University Press, 1993).

Vincent, John, *The Formation of the British Liberal Party, 1857–1868* (Harvester Press, 1966).

The Governing Passion: Cabinet Government and Party Politics in Britain 1885–86 (Harvester Press 1974).

(ed.), *The Crawford Papers: The Journals of David Lindsay 27th Earl of Crawford and 10th Earl of Balcarres 1871–1940 during the Years 1892 to 1940* (Manchester University Press, 1984).

Virk, D. S., *Indian Postal History 1873–1923* (Indian Postal Association, 1991).

Vyve, Brendon, *Prep School Children: A Class Apart over Two Centuries* (Continuum, 2009).

Waldron, Jarlath, *Maamtrasna: The Murders and the Mystery* (Edmund Burke, 1992).

Walsh, W. H., "The Zenith of Greats" in M. G. Brock and M. C. Curthoys (eds.), *The History of the University of Oxford*, vol. ii.

Warwick, Andrew, *Masters of Theory: Cambridge and the Rise of Mathematical Physics* (University of Chicago Press, 2003).

Wasson, Ellis Archer, *Born to Rule: British Political Elites* (Sutton Publishing Ltd, 2000).

Watson, E., *The Royal Mail to Ireland: Or an Account of the Origin and Development of the Post Between London and Ireland through Holyhead, and the Use of the Line of Communication by Travellers* (London, 1917).

Watson, John Forbes, *Report on the Illustration of the Archaic Architecture of India, &c.* (India Musuem, 1869).

Report on Indian Wheat (HMSO, 1879).

Weinberg, Ian, *The English Public Schools: The Sociology of Elite Education* (Atherton Press, 1962).

Whalley, Joyce, *The Pen's Excellence* (Taplinger, 1982).

The Student's Guide to Western Calligraphy: An Illustrated Survey (Shambhala, 1984).

Writing Implements and Accessories from the Roman Stylus to the Typewriter (David and Charles, 1975).

Wheatcroft, Geoffrey, *The Strange Death of Tory England* (Penguin, 2005).

White, Ralph, "The Anatomy of a Victorian Debate: An Essay in the History of Liberal Education", *British Journal of Educational Studies*, 34:1 (1986), 38–65.

Whyman, Susan, "Letter Writing and Literacy in the North of England 1700–1800", Manchester University research paper, May 2008.

The Pen and the People: English Letter Writers, 1660–1800 (Oxford University Press, 2010).

Sociability and Power in Late Stuart England: The Cultural Worlds of the Verneys (Oxford University Press, 1999).

Whyte, W., "Building a Public School Community", *History of Education*, 30:6 (2003), Pt II.

Willey, Basil, *Nineteenth Century Studies: Coleridge to Matthew Arnold* (Chatto & Windus, 1949).

Willis, Robert and Willis Clark, John, *The Architectural History of the University of Cambridge*, 3 vols. (first published in 1886, Cambridge University Press, 1988), vol. iii.

Wilson, H. S., *The Travelling Post Offices of Great Britain and Ireland: Their History and Postmarks* (The Railway Philatelic Group, 1996).

Wilson, Jon, *The Domination of Strangers: Modern Governance in Eastern India, 1780–1835* (Palgrave Macmillan, 2007).

Wiseck, Dwayne R. and Pike, Robert M., *Communications and Empire: Media, Markets and Globalization 1860–1930* (Duke University Press, 2007).

Wood, Sir Alexander Renton, *The History of the Colonial Office* (London, 1889).

Wordsworth, Rev. Charles, *Christian Boyhood at a Public School: A Collection of Sermons and Lectures delivered at Winchester College*, vol. I, *Duties and Ordinances* (London, 1846).

Wright, Maurice, "Treasury Control 1854–1914" in Gillian Sutherland (ed.), *Studies in the Growth of Nineteenth-Century Government* (Routledge & Kegan Paul, 1977).

Treasury Control of the Civil Service 1854–1874 (Oxford University Press, 1969).

Yates, Edmund, *Edmund Yates: His Recollections and Experiences* (London, 1884).

Zweig, Stefan, *Beware of Pity* (Pushkin Press, 2008).

The Post Office Girl (Pushkin Press, 2008).

Index